# Perspectives on Deterrence

# Perspectives on Deterrence

EDITED BY

Paul C. Stern
Robert Axelrod
Robert Jervis
Roy Radner

*Committee on Contributions of Behavioral and
Social Science to the Prevention of Nuclear War*

*Commission on Behavioral and Social Sciences
and Education*

*National Research Council*

OXFORD UNIVERSITY PRESS
New York   Oxford
1989

355.0217
P466

Oxford University Press

Oxford  New York  Toronto
Delhi  Bombay  Calcutta  Madras  Karachi
Petaling Jaya  Singapore  Hong Kong  Tokyo
Nairobi  Dar es Salaam  Cape Town
Melbourne  Auckland

and associated companies in
Berlin  Ibadan

Copyright © 1989 by Oxford University Press, Inc.

Published by Oxford University Press, Inc.,
200 Madison Avenue, New York, New York 10016

Oxford is a registered trademark of Oxford University Press

All rights reserved. No part of this publication may be reproduced,
stored in a retrieval system, or transmitted, in any form or by any means,
electronic, mechanical, photocopying, recording, or otherwise,
without prior permission of Oxford University Press.

Library of Congress Cataloging-in-Publication Data
Perspectives on deterrence / [edited by] Paul C. Stern . . . [et al.] ;
  Committee on Contributions of Behavioral and Social Science to the
  Prevention of Nuclear War ; Commission on Behavioral and Social
  Sciences and Education.
    p.  cm.
  Based on papers from a two day workshop, held Nov. 1986.
  Bibliography: p.
  Includes index.
  ISBN 0-19-505763-5.
  ISBN 0-19-505764-3 (pbk.).
  1. Deterrence (Strategy)—Congresses.  2. Nuclear warfare—
Congresses.  I. Stern, Paul C., 1944–  .  II. National Research
Council (U.S.). Committee on Contributions of Behavioral and Social
Science to the Prevention of Nuclear War.  III. National Research
Council (U.S.). Commission on Behavioral and Social Sciences and
Education.
U162.6.P46 1989
355'.0217—dc19                    88-19606  CIP

9 8 7 6 5 4 3 2 1

Printed in the United States of America
on acid-free paper

# Foreword

In 1985 the National Research Council established the Committee on Contributions of Behavioral and Social Science to the Prevention of Nuclear War and gave it the responsibility to identify, evaluate, and communicate to appropriate audiences knowledge about behavior and society that may have value to practitioners concerned with preventing nuclear war. The topic of deterrence interested the committee from the outset because of its central role in strategies for preventing nuclear conflict, its interdisciplinary nature, and its intellectual roots in behavioral science. To analyze deterrence, one must work at several levels of analysis: international relations, national politics, organizational behavior, and individual and small-group decision making. The concept of deterrence is essentially psychological, in that it presumes the actions of a state (a potential initiator of a challenge to an international status quo) to be influenced by its perceptions of an adversary's response to such a challenge. Deterrent policies are in part aimed at impression management, at manipulating the would-be initiator's perceptions and thus forestalling challenges to one's national interests.

Although deterrence is a cornerstone of defense planning for both of the superpowers, there are many unevaluated claims about how, when, why, and whether deterrence works. The committee was concerned to find and assess the evidence relevant to those claims.

Nuclear deterrence raises uniquely difficult issues. Nuclear war has not occurred, but many factors in addition to deterrence may have contributed to that outcome. Considering the lack of direct evidence, the committee decided to go beyond the usual strict focus on arms control and look more broadly at deterrence in the hope that a fresh approach might be enlightening. It conducted a two-day research workshop in November 1986 at which two dozen scholars met to explore the reasons deterrent strategies may succeed or fail. Although the ultimate concern was deterrence between nuclear powers, the substantive focus alternated between nuclear deterrence and other situations that have certain formal similarities to it. The participants examined historical evidence about nonnuclear military deterrence as well as evidence from formal models and from empirical studies of conflict in economic, social, and interpersonal domains.

Prior to the workshop, its organizers, committee members Robert Axelrod, Robert Jervis, Roy Radner, and study director Paul C. Stern, requested brief sets of notes from six of the participants. Each set was to summarize a particular body of literature and to serve as a basis for discussion. The modest hope was that the discussions would yield ideas for future research by the scholars and the committee. But instead of six short summaries, the organizers received six formal papers. At the workshop, several of the discussants added points that were also worth recording. It became clear that without waiting for future research, enough material was available to convert the first drafts of the papers and some of the discussants' comments into a thought-provoking volume.

This book is the result. The editors have added an introduction to the participants' contributions that presents the intellectual framework for the workshop and a conclusion that identifies some common threads in the contributions.

The entire work of organizing and conducting the conference, and the subsequent development of this volume, have been in the able hands of the editors and staff member Jo Husbands. The chapters have been carefully reviewed by members of the committee and a number of others. The views expressed in the chapters are those of the authors.

We are indebted to the Carnegie Corporation of New York, the John D. and Catherine T. MacArthur Foundation, and the National Research Council Fund for their support of the committee and to the Harry Frank Guggenheim Foundation and the National Science Foundation for their support of Robert Axelrod's work on this project.

We wish also to acknowledge the important role of the Commission on Behavioral and Social Sciences and Education of the National Research Council, which was responsible for organizing this committee. Special thanks are due David A. Goslin, former executive director of the Commission, for his unswerving support of the committee's efforts from its inception through the planning stages of this volume, and to Committee member Alexander George, whose help in developing the concept for the 1986

# Foreword

workshop and editorial suggestions to the volume's contributors and editors were vital to this project.

> William K. Estes and Herbert A. Simon, *Cochairs,*
> *Committee on Contributions of Behavioral and*
> *Social Science to the Prevention of Nuclear War*

*Notice:* The project that is the subject of this book was approved by the Governing Board of the National Research Council, whose members are drawn from the councils of the National Academy of Sciences, the National Academy of Engineering, and the Institute of Medicine. The members of the committee responsible for the book were chosen for their special competences and with regard for appropriate balance.

This book has been reviewed by a group other than the authors according to procedures approved by a Report Review Committee consisting of members of the National Academy of Sciences, the National Academy of Engineering, and the Institute of Medicine.

The National Academy of Sciences is a private, nonprofit, self-perpetuating society of distinguished scholars engaged in scientific and engineering research, dedicated to the furtherance of science and technology and to their use for the general welfare. Upon the authority of the charter granted to it by the Congress in 1863, the Academy has a mandate that requires it to advise the federal government on scientific and technical matters.

The National Academy of Engineering was established in 1964, under the charter of the National Academy of Sciences, as a parallel organization of outstanding engineers. It is autonomous in its administration and in the selection of its members, sharing with the National Academy of Sciences the responsibility for advising the federal government. The National Academy of Engineering also sponsors engineering programs aimed at meeting national needs, encourages education and research, and recognizes the superior achievements of engineers.

The Institute of Medicine was established in 1970 by the National Academy of Sciences to secure the services of eminent members of appropriate professions in the examination of policy matters pertaining to the health of the public. The Institute acts under the responsibility given to the National Academy of Sciences by its congressional charter to be an adviser to the federal government and, upon its own initiative, to identify issues of medical care, research, and education.

The National Research Council was organized by the National Academy of

Sciences in 1916 to associate the broad community of science and technology with the Academy's purposes of furthering knowledge and advising the federal government. Functioning in accordance with general policies determined by the Academy, the Council has become the principal operating agency of both the National Academy of Sciences and the National Academy of Engineering in providing services to the government, the public, and the scientific and engineering communities. The Council is administered jointly by both Academies and the Institute of Medicine.

# Committee on Contributions of Behavioral and Social Science to the Prevention of Nuclear War

**William K. Estes,** *Cochair*, Department of Psychology, Harvard University
**Herbert A. Simon,** *Cochair*, Department of Psychology, Carnegie-Mellon University
**Kenneth J. Arrow,** Department of Economics, Stanford University
**Robert M. Axelrod,** Institute of Public Policy Studies, University of Michigan
**Seweryn Bialer,** Research Institute on International Change, Columbia University
**Barry M. Blechman,** Defense Forecasts, Inc., Washington, D.C.
**George W. Breslauer,** Department of Political Science, University of California, Berkeley
**Timothy J. Colton,** Center for Russian and East European Studies, University of Toronto
**Philip E. Converse,** Institute for Social Research, University of Michigan
**Clifford J. Geertz,** The Institute for Advanced Study, Princeton University
**Alexander L. George,** Department of Political Science, Stanford University
**Robert Jervis,** Institute for War and Peace Studies, Columbia University
**Catherine McArdle Kelleher,** School of Public Affairs, University of Maryland, College Park
**Harold H. Kelley,** Department of Psychology, University of California, Los Angeles
**Roy Radner,** Mathematical Sciences Research Center, AT&T Bell Laboratories
**Jack P. Ruina,** Center for International Studies, Massachusetts Institute of Technology

**Philip E. Tetlock,** Department of Psychology, University of California, Berkeley
**Charles Tilly,** Center for Studies in Social Change, New School for Social Research
**Charles H. Townes,** Department of Physics, University of California, Berkeley
**Amos Tversky,** Department of Psychology, Stanford University

**Paul C. Stern,** Study Director
**Jo L. Husbands,** Senior Research Associate
**David A. Goslin,** Executive Director, Commission on Behavioral and Social Sciences and Education
**Elizabeth C. Addison,** Senior Program Assistant
**Beverly R. Blakey,** Administrative Secretary

# Workshop Participants

**Robert Axelrod,**\* Institute of Public Policy Studies, University of Michigan
**Richard Betts,** Brookings Institution
**John A. C. Conybeare,** Department of Political Science, University of Iowa
**Daniel Druckman,** Commission on Behavioral and Social Sciences and Education, National Research Council
**William K. Estes,**\* Department of Psychology, Harvard University
**Michael G. Fry,** Department of History, University of Southern California
**John Lewis Gaddis,** Department of History, Ohio University
**Jack A. Goldstone,** Department of Sociology, Northwestern University
**David A. Goslin,** Commission on Behavioral and Social Sciences and Education, National Research Council
**Jo L. Husbands,** Commission on Behavioral and Social Sciences and Education, National Research Council
**Robert Jervis,**\* Institute for War and Peace Studies, Columbia University
**Harold H. Kelley,**\* Department of Psychology, University of California, Los Angeles
**Richard Ned Lebow,** Peace Studies Program, Cornell University
**Jack S. Levy,** Department of Political Science, University of Minnesota
**Barry O'Neill,** Department of Industrial Engineering, Northwestern University
**Charles Plott,** Division of Humanities and Social Sciences, California Institute of Technology
**Dean G. Pruitt,** Department of Psychology, State University of New York, Buffalo

**George H. Quester,** Department of Government and Politics, University of Maryland
**Roy Radner,*** Mathematical Sciences Research Center, AT&T Bell Laboratories
**Paul W. Schroeder,** Department of History, University of Illinois
**Martin Shubik,** Cowles Foundation for Research in Economics, Yale University
**Herbert A. Simon,*** Department of Psychology, Carnegie-Mellon University
**Paul C. Stern,** Commission on Behavioral and Social Sciences and Education, National Research Council
**Philip E. Tetlock,*** Department of Psychology, University of California, Berkeley
**Charles Tilly,*** Center for Studies of Social Change, New School for Social Research
**Peter Wallensteen,** Department of Peace and Conflict Research, Uppsala University
**Robert Wilson,** Stanford Business School, Stanford University
**David B. Yoffie,** Harvard Business School, Harvard University

*Member of the Committee on Contributions of Behavioral and Social Science to the Prevention of Nuclear War

# Contents

**1** Deterrence in the Nuclear Age: The Search for Evidence  3
*Paul C. Stern, Robert Axelrod, Robert Jervis, and Roy Radner*

**2** Deterrence: A Political and Psychological Critique  25
*Richard Ned Lebow*

**3** Some Thoughts on "Deterrence Failures"  52
*George H. Quester*

**4** Failed Bargain Crises, Deterrence, and the International System  66
*Paul W. Schroeder*

**5** Historians and Deterrence  84
*Michael G. Fry*

**6** Quantitative Studies of Deterrence Success and Failure  98
*Jack S. Levy*

**7** Game Theory and the Study of the Deterrence of War  134
*Barry O'Neill*

**8** Deterrence in Oligopolistic Competition  157
*Robert Wilson*

**9** The Use of Deterrent Threats in International Trade
Conflicts 191
*John A. C. Conybeare*

**10** The Empirical Study of Trade Deterrence 211
*David B. Yoffie*

**11** Deterrence in Rebellions and Revolutions 222
*Jack A. Goldstone*

**12** The "Aggressive Male" Syndrome: Its Possible Relevance for
International Conflict 251
*Harold H. Kelley and Greg Schmidt*

**13** Aggressive Behavior in Interpersonal and International
Relations 287
*Dean G. Pruitt*

**14** Conclusions 294
*Paul C. Stern, Robert Axelrod, Robert Jervis, and Roy Radner*

Contributors 327

Index 331

# Perspectives on Deterrence

# 1
# Deterrence in the Nuclear Age: The Search for Evidence

## PAUL C. STERN, ROBERT AXELROD, ROBERT JERVIS, and ROY RADNER

Throughout history nations have advanced their ambitions by conducting or threatening military operations against others; the likely objects, in turn, have tried to deter such operations by building defenses or retaliatory power. In the nuclear era, the concept of deterrence by threat of retaliation is the foundation of the security policies of the superpowers. It is therefore critical to examine the efficacy of retaliatory threats. The purpose of this volume is to address the central practical question about deterrence: Under what conditions do deterrent threats succeed or fail in international crises?

Careful observers recognize that the advent of nuclear arsenals has qualitatively altered the ancient dynamic of threat and response in three ways. First, retaliation is more important in the present era because even the most powerful state cannot protect itself against devastation by a nuclear power that has sufficient weaponry and motivation. Second, the barbarity of all-out nuclear war undercuts the threat to use nuclear weapons and raises great uncertainty about nonnuclear threats as well when the nuclear powers are involved. Third, although the capacity for nuclear retaliation makes many threats less credible, it simultaneously increases the price both sides will pay if there is a major war. The result is that deterrence may hold even if a nuclear response to any particular military adventure is highly unlikely. Nuclear powers are restrained from major confrontations because of knowledge that such conflicts may lead to nuclear war despite the desire of both sides to avoid that outcome.

The United States and the Soviet Union want to avoid situations in which one side or the other might become so seriously threatened as to lose restraint, or, because of the pressure of a crisis, fatally misjudge its opponent and bring about inadvertent nuclear war. But how can they best keep the adversary from taking fatal missteps, and how can they recognize those errors before making them themselves?

The above description capsulizes the situation of deterrence facing the superpowers now and in the foreseeable future. No arms reduction plan that is likely to be adopted or strategic defense technology now expected would alter the basic facts of deterrence in the nuclear age. The confrontation between nuclear arsenals shapes the entire range of the superpowers' foreign policies. It obviously shapes nuclear deterrent strategies: threats to use nuclear weapons in the event of direct attack on a superpower's homeland (what some call basic nuclear deterrence) or on its allies or other vital national interests (extended nuclear deterrence). But nuclear deterrence is not the only deterrence that is crucial in the present era. Nuclear arsenals cast a shadow over the whole range of superpower competition because any military challenge by one superpower to the other's interests has the potential to lead, either directly or indirectly, to a nuclear response. The fact of deterrence in the nuclear age requires that the leaders of the superpowers, when they engage in global competition, consider that nuclear war might begin not only with a direct and planned attack, but by inadvertence and escalation. The possibility of inadvertent nuclear war raises the stakes much higher than before for policies that threaten the use of force to deter less-than-strategic challenges to a superpower's interests.

There seem to be only two solid bases for thinking and policymaking regarding deterrence in the nuclear age: lessons from history and relevant theory. But both approaches are beset with difficult problems. One lesson of history is that lessons of history are often misapplied, and moreover, inferences from history involve radical extrapolations because of the discontinuity between the prenuclear and nuclear ages. With regard to theory, the problems are twofold. One is the questionable accuracy of classical theories of deterrence in accounting for the past behavior of states in international crises. In the nonnuclear context, the conception of a straightforward relationship in which stronger and clearer deterrent threats yield fewer challenges to one's interests has been subject to important criticism (for a recent summary, see Jervis, Lebow, and Stein, 1985). The other problem lies in asserting that a proposition that is questionable in the prenuclear context is reliable in the nuclear context, in the absence of evidence from nuclear confrontations.

Despite these difficulties, the importance of understanding deterrence relationships in the nuclear age calls for strenuous efforts to exploit all available approaches. In that spirit, the purpose of the workshop that led to this volume was to review and analyze the subject of deterrence with special attention to evidence about deterrence in nonnuclear situations and knowledge and experience from a broad range of domains that might yield some of the needed understanding. Our intention was not to seek simple prescriptions for policy, but rather to review the kinds of empirical evidence and theoretical analysis that might contribute to informed judgments.

Our strategy has been to spread a wide net. We bring together the work of experts in various fields where knowledge is potentially relevant to the range of deterrence situations involving nuclear powers. Our hope is to identify convergences and contradictions across fields that may illuminate issues of deterrence or suggest fruitful directions for research. We hope by this strategy to capture some new insights into the deterrence process and particularly into the communication and decision processes and the international contexts that may predispose deterrent threats to result sometimes in restraint and sometimes in escalation. Although we realize that the relevance of each field of knowledge we consider is indirect at best, the possibility remains that, as in many scientific fields, collation of strands of indirect evidence may yield new insights.

This chapter begins with a brief characterization of what may be called "classical deterrence theory" and a set of critiques of that approach, based largely on empirical studies of international crises. We then set forth a strategy for selecting and examining lines of evidence that might shed light on the underlying questions about the effectiveness of deterrent threats that are the crux of debate in the field. Twelve subsequent chapters explore particular lines of evidence, and the concluding chapter identifies some hypotheses and research directions that emerge from the work presented here.

## Classical Deterrence Theory and Its Critics

Political leaders have employed deterrent strategies for many centuries but have seldom, if ever, attempted to explicate them in systematic theoretical terms. What may be called "classical deterrence theory" was developed deductively and in abstract form in the 1950s and 1960s and rested upon a set of behavioral assumptions, the most important of which was that states could be treated as unitary rational actors (e.g., Brodie, 1959; Kahn, 1964; Schelling, 1960, 1966; Snyder, 1961). Although this abstract deterrence theory was accompanied by detailed and often sophisticated analyses of national strategy, its essence is captured by the following central propositions:[1]

1. Wars are often caused by states that actively seek to expand their influence, whether out of imperialistic motives or out of what their leaders see as legitimate dissatisfactions with the status quo (expansion).

2. These states act as a function of opportunity, that is, when the expected net benefits of mounting a challenge to the status quo exceed the expected costs of overcoming other states' defenses (opportunity).[2] Defenders of a status quo situation must therefore raise the costs of challenging it to an unacceptable level. The following three propositions indicate ways of doing this:

   2a. Deterrence is stronger when a state has the capability to impose great costs on a potential attacker (capability).
   2b. Deterrence is stronger when a state is committed to respond to an attack by imposing such costs (commitment).
   2c. Deterrence is more effective when a state's commitments are clearly communicated (communication).

   These three propositions imply the expectation that clear communication of the intent and ability to impose great costs will make a threat credible in the mind of the would-be challenger. Thus, classical deterrence theory implies an additional assumption:

3. Potential attackers are reasonably adept at assessing the defender's capabilities, understanding its commitments, and correctly interpreting its communicated intentions (perceptiveness).

Practitioners of deterrence in the United States, accepting that these propositions apply to the state's adversaries and particularly to the Soviet Union, believe that if the state possesses the capability to punish a challenger severely and makes clear its intention to do so, the adversary will refrain. They have developed a wide range of response options in implementation of the general doctrine of "flexible response," which replaced "massive retaliation," designed hopefully to deter and/or meet different levels of threat to any status quo situation with a sufficient, credible, and appropriately graduated punishment. All these policies, though drawing on an abstract theory of strategic interaction, rely at bottom on a set of behavioral assumptions about would-be challengers, a theory of how nation-states in conflict actually use and respond to military threats. Because some of the policies involve the possibility of nuclear warfare, the theory of deterrence is a most important behavioral theory: Never before has so much been staked on such a theory and the ability of practitioners to implement it.

A number of researchers over the past decades have questioned the validity and policy applicability of these general deterrence propositions on the basis of historical analysis of past international crises (e.g., George and Smoke, 1974; Snyder and Diesing, 1977; Jervis, 1979; Lebow, 1981; Jervis, Lebow, and Stein, 1985). Their criticisms center on the assumption that states involved in deterrence relationships (i.e., challengers and defenders) can be regarded as unitary rational actors. Their studies, which draw on historical analyses of international military conflict, provide evidence that in the following ways, the propositions of classical deterrence theory require significant qualification or refinement if they are to be applied to modern states in conflict.

## Opportunity and Perceived Necessity

Several studies suggest that states sometimes challenge the status quo even when the likely net benefit of a challenge in terms of a state's international interests is less than the net benefit of refraining from the challenge. For instance, Richard Ned Lebow concludes from his studies that "policymakers who risk or actually start wars pay more attention to their own strategic and domestic political interests than they do to the interests and military capabilities of their adversaries" (Lebow, 1985a:216). The critics argue, in essence, that challenges depend more on a calculus of internal necessity than of foreign opportunity or necessity (Lebow, 1981; Jervis, Lebow, and Stein, 1985; see also Chapter 2, this volume). An important policy implication of this view is that policies aimed at preventing a challenge by strengthening deterrents can sometimes be misdirected.[3]

## Capability and Commitment

"Conflict-spiral" theorists argue that an increased capability of attack or a strengthened or reiterated deterrent threat can under certain circumstances contribute to a failure of deterrence. The concept of "security dilemma" in international relations reminds us that when a state takes strong action to protect itself against a perceived threat, that action is itself often perceived as a threat because it is interpreted as an increased capability or commitment to attack. The object of the deterrent threat can respond by strengthening its own capabilities or even by taking initiatives or actions that the initial deterrent threat was intended to prevent (Jervis, 1976; Osgood, 1962; White, 1970). Some historical cases seem to follow this pattern (e.g., North, 1967; Snyder, 1985), which has a plausible psychological dynamic.

## Communication and Perceptiveness

In several historical instances, statements of intention to retaliate that were credible as judged by third parties seem to have been misinterpreted by the nation to which they were being communicated (George and Smoke, 1974; Snyder and Diesing, 1977; Lebow, 1981; Jervis, Lebow, and Stein, 1985).

National leaders during crises seem to have ignored or severely discounted information that was available to them and that was relevant to their estimation of the outcomes of actions they were contemplating. Although there is debate over the accuracy of this judgment in particular historical instances (Orme, 1987; Lebow, 1987b), the evidence is strong enough and consistent enough with well-documented psychological and organizational processes (e.g., George, 1980; Janis and Mann, 1977; Jervis, 1976) to warrant more careful attention.

Recent studies have raised additional questions about the general applicability of classical deterrence theory and its underlying assumptions to policymaking in the nuclear age. For instance, it can be quite difficult to perceive whether or not another state is seeking to expand its influence and therefore to know whether the remaining deterrence propositions are applicable (Jervis, 1979). If deterrence policies are instituted in the absence of an adversary's intent to expand, conflict may increase because the adversary perceives the policies as threats. Also, studies of crisis stability have called attention to the possibility that the high stakes, short decision times, and decisional complexities characteristic of modern international crises and exacerbated in nuclear crises may severely limit the ability of national leaders to make the rational choices deterrence practitioners expect of themselves and their adversaries (Bracken, 1983; Blair, 1985; Jervis, 1989; Lebow, 1987a; Holsti, 1989).

In sum, the behavioral critics of deterrence have very different expectations about the behavior of national leaders in international crises from those suggested by classical deterrence theory and implicit in typical deterrence policies. Classical theory and many deterrence analysts assume that national leaders generally follow the norm of "rational choice," especially in the nuclear age, because it is in their national interest to do so. The critics emphasize the well-known limits to rationality caused by cognitive limitations, emotional processes, bureaucratic politics, and domestic political imperatives, and assert that in many critical instances pure rationality breaks down despite the national interest. There are many differences between the two approaches, but much of the difference flows from conflicting assumptions about information processing, decision making, and behavior in crisis. Such assumptions are empirically testable, at least in principle.

## Sources of Evidence

This volume pursues an empirical approach to deterrence by examining it as one might any other behavioral phenomenon: by searching for evidence that

## Deterrence in the Nuclear Age: The Search for Evidence

can shed light on the validity of relevant theoretical propositions. Our goal is not to arrive at a global assessment of the validity of classical deterrence theory. What is most relevant for decision makers is not the abstract deductive theory but propositions about international competition that can be embodied in strategies that may or may not be appropriate in a given situation. Hence, we believe it is more productive to look for conditional statements about when deterrent strategies are likely to be effective than to attempt a global assessment of a formal theory. In other words, deterrence is best regarded as context-dependent. We presume that threats and deterrents will work in some instances and not in others; although some of the variation is random, some is systematic. We focus, therefore, on the conditions under which a strong and highly credible threat of punishment produces restraint in an adversary, and the conditions under which such a threat is likely to be ineffective or counterproductive. This approach is not new: The Appendix to this chapter lists a score of empirical hypotheses about deterrence gleaned from a limited review of the literature.

We recognize that policies to prevent challenges to the status quo include not only deterrent threats but rewards or inducements used either alone or in conjunction with threats. That is, deterrence theory is best regarded as a subset of an "influence theory" (George and Smoke, 1974) whose details are yet to be worked out. As many observers have noted, a mixture of threats and inducements may be more effective for influencing an adversary than a strategy relying only on threats (Axelrod, 1984; George, Hall, and Simons, 1971; Snyder and Diesing, 1977). However, because threats are central to the debate about deterrence, they are the primary focus here; we treat inducements conceptually as factors that can influence the effectiveness of threats.

Our main purpose in studying deterrent threats is to advance understanding of the conditions under which they are likely to succeed or fail in the U.S.–Soviet context. Our central concern is with preventing nuclear war. But as we have already noted, this concern is not limited to basic and extended nuclear deterrence; our concern also extends to lower levels of direct or indirect challenges that might escalate into a military clash between U.S. and Soviet forces and possibly to the use of nuclear weapons.

Evidence is very limited regarding the various kinds of deterrence practiced by the superpowers in the nuclear age. For instance, there have as yet been no failures of basic or extended nuclear deterrence. That fact is consistent with deterrence theory in that it may imply that the superpowers' deterrent forces and the shared fear of possibly uncontrollable escalation have always been sufficiently strong and credible to prevent the superpowers from making direct attacks on each other's homeland or other vital interests— although not so effective as to prevent all serious challenges to each other's interests. But the historical record is also consistent with positions that reject some of the assumptions of classical deterrence theory. An absence of war can be due not only to respect for the adversary's deterrent force but to a failure to notice a weakness of resolve on the adversary's part, or a choice not to seize upon the opportunity to exploit such a weakness for whatever reasons—for example, for fear that to do so might entail serious domestic costs. Alternatively, peace may have been maintained as much in spite of as because of deterrence. It is possible that neither side required a great deal of deterring and that nuclear threats have unnecessarily increased the level of international conflict. The absence of nuclear conflict may also owe much to good fortune—that at the most critical times, each side has correctly assessed the opponent's vital interests and judged it as committed to defending them. With new leaders or changing conditions, critical assessments of this kind may be less accurate, and faith in the efficacy of deterrent strategy in a particular situation may prove to have been tragically unfounded. Given the high stakes, such possibilities should not go unexplored, even though the evidence from the history of nuclear deterrence is so severely limited.

Evidence about lesser conflicts between the United States and the Soviet Union is also limited, both in extent and in usefulness. Information is sorely lacking about Soviet decision making, and even in the United States much of the relevant information is unavailable, at least for an extended period after the events. Moreover, in most of these conflict situations, the fear of all-out war and the role of nuclear weapons were both slight. Even with respect to the Cuban Missile Crisis, during which the two superpowers came closest to the brink of war, scholars and policymakers disagree as to the role of fear of nuclear war and of U.S. nuclear superiority in influencing the outcome. Lesser superpower crises such as those in Angola and the Horn of Africa may be important for understanding deterrence, but their implications are uncertain because none of these crises between the United States and the Soviet Union led to, or even seriously threatened the possibility of, any kind of shooting war between them.

It therefore seems important to seek other sources of insight about how and when deterrence works. It is risky to rely on formal theoretical models, because they are only as good as their simplifying assumptions, and it is never clear without evidence which assumptions are realistic and which are not. Moreover, the leap from theory to strategy requires judgments about the nature of the situation that cannot be guided by theory alone. Thus, the need for evidence is inescapable, but the vast majority of available evidence is only indirect.

One must be cautious in evaluating indirect evidence. Because the possibility of nuclear confrontation has altered the calculus of security decisions in what may well be decisive ways, one cannot confidently extrapolate across situations. In what ways, then, can indirect evidence be useful?

We address this question first by suggesting several dimensions that, taken together, characterize competition between the two superpowers:

1. *High stakes*—for leaders, their positions, their lives, the future of their societies, and possibly all human culture are potentially at stake;
2. *Complex, pluralistic political systems*—the actors are not unitary, and internal conflicts and politics can affect and even determine decisions;
3. *Cultural difference*—the actors are the state leaderships of nations that do not share a common language, history, or culture;
4. *Rough equality of power*—each side has the capability to prevent the other from achieving any goals it decides are too threatening to its interests;
5. *Absence of a superordinate authority* capable of imposing a resolution of disagreements or conflicting interests;
6. *Importance of punishment*—an important element of deterrence in the nuclear era is the ability to threaten harm to the adversary if it challenges important interests as distinguished from defending oneself, that is, the familiar distinction between punishment and defense as bases for deterrence; and
7. *Partially converging goals*—both superpowers prefer a system of nuclear deterrence to a failure of deterrence that results in war that is, or threatens to escalate to, nuclear war.[4]

We propose that these dimensions are useful for assessing the relevance to superpower conflict of indirect evidence from other situations of conflict and threat. The more of these characteristics a situation shares with the superpower conflict, the more likely it is that knowledge about it is relevant to deterrence between the superpowers. Moreover, the differences along these dimensions between a particular conflict situation and the superpower conflict can suggest particular questions to raise about the applicability of knowledge about that situation.

Many types of threats and responses may be studied in an effort to understand deterrence between nuclear powers. The situation that bears closest resemblance is that of deterrence between *non*nuclear powers, but even its relevance for superpower deterrence can be questioned. Conclusions about specific instances of nonnuclear deterrence depend heavily on interpretation of the historical evidence (Orme, 1987; Lebow, 1987b), and drawing conclusions about nuclear states depends on generalizing and then extrapolating to quite a different situation (see Chapters 3 and 4, this volume). Even minor conflicts between nuclear states, such as occur in parts of the world neither superpower considers vital to its interests, are qualitatively different from any situations faced by nonnuclear powers because of the possibility of escalation to nuclear war. In the past, states that believed they had meaningful military superiority could threaten or begin to escalate, because their military advantage could provide a foundation for coercing the other side and because they could expect a meaningful military victory in the event of all-out war. But now, states are restrained by the possibility of nuclear punishment: The strategic U.S.–Soviet reality is one in which all-out war would be the worst possible outcome for both sides. Of course, coercion is still possible, but not on the same basis as in the past. This difference introduces uncertainty into any inference from nonnuclear conflicts to even minor conflicts between nuclear states. Generalization must also be tempered by the recognition that the United States and the Soviet Union individually and as a pair of powers are different in important ways from the parties to past international conflicts.

Even greater care is needed in drawing lessons from the study of conflicts of the kind examined in later chapters that are not international or that are not military, because such conflicts usually differ from nuclear power conflicts along more than one of the dimensions above and involve very different choices. Table 1.1 summarizes the extent of similarity between conflict involving nuclear states and other conflict situations that can involve deterrencelike processes. Even though the differences are of major significance, as the table shows, these other types of experience suggest some hypotheses for further assessment. Each line of indirect evidence suggests some insights into the ways nuclear states use and respond to threats, and several different lines of evidence, each offering a different perspective, may offer, if cautiously assessed, deeper insight than any one alone. Careful interpretation of several lines of evidence may reveal some consistent relationships or it may, through divergences in the evidence, suggest the kinds of conditions that make the difference between deterrence failures and successes. By analyzing the differences between nuclear power deterrence situations and other conflicts that share with it some distinguishing features, we may be able to generate improved hypotheses about deterrence successes and failures or at least improve understanding of why different lines of evidence suggest different conclusions.

## Assessment of Indirect Evidence

From the many areas of research with potential relevance to deterrence between nuclear powers, we have selected six. Our selection was guided

**Table 1.1.** Degree of Similarity Between Various Types of Conflict and Nuclear States' Conflict.

| | High Stakes | Complex Political Systems | Cultural Difference | Equality of Power | Absence of Superordinate Authority | Importance of Punishment | Partially Converging Goals |
|---|---|---|---|---|---|---|---|
| Nonnuclear military deterrence | moderate | strong | strong | moderate | moderate | slight | strong |
| Trade wars | slight | strong | moderate | moderate | moderate | variable | moderate |
| Oligopoly competition | slight | moderate | nil | moderate | slight | moderate | slight |
| Revolution | strong | moderate | variable | nil | moderate | slight | slight |
| Interpersonal | slight | nil | nil | strong | nil | moderate | moderate |

by considerations of similarity on at least some of the dimensions noted above and by the judgment that knowledge was available that could be summarized for our purpose. The next five chapters focus on deterrence involving nonnuclear states. As already noted, some of those studies have called into question the applicability of central assumptions of classical deterrence theory to international conflict situations. In Chapter 2, Richard Ned Lebow summarizes some of those studies and some propositions they suggest about when deterrence succeeds or fails. George Quester in Chapter 3 warns of pitfalls in drawing inferences about the nuclear context from historical evidence. He argues that the thinking of U.S. and Soviet leaders is probably not as faulty or irrational as it may seem from available documents and suggests that the prospect of nuclear war motivates more caution on the part of national leaders than they show when the consequences of error are less severe.

Chapters 4, 5, and 6 discuss some of the broader issues in the use of historical evidence to study deterrence. Paul Schroeder adds a dimension to the analysis of historical cases in Chapter 4 by noting how the effect of threat in two-state confrontations depends on recent agreements between the states and on the international "system" or "regime" within which they are made. In Chapter 5, Michael Fry argues that more historical research on deterrence could be fruitful, but notes disciplinary reasons why historians rarely undertake such research. He also identifies four structural changes in the world system since the advent of nuclear weapons that must be considered in evaluating historical evidence about deterrence. Jack Levy in Chapter 6 reviews quantitative studies of the use of international threats. A quantitative approach, in principle, can avoid some of the problems of interpretation that face the case approach by aggregating cases and dealing statistically with random variation due to oddities in particular situations or inconsistencies in interpretation. The chapter reports on the few regularities and the many unanswered questions in the literature on the effect of threats on the incidence and outcomes of wars.

In Chapter 7, Barry O'Neill examines the literature on formal game theoretic models of deterrence. From the early days of deterrence theory, such models have played an important role in thinking about deterrence processes. O'Neill distinguishes several purposes of game theoretic models and notes some new developments in this field, including attempts to formalize concepts such as crisis stability, credibility, expectation, and resolve, which figure prominently in recent analyses of a nonformal kind but were not incorporated explicitly in earlier formal models.

Chapters 8 through 13 examine four kinds of conflicts that differ from confrontations between the nuclear superpowers in that they are not both international and military: oligopolistic competition, trade wars, conflicts between states and insurgent movements, and interpersonal conflict. In oligopolistic competition, large bureaucratic economic organizations struggle to control access to raw materials or markets, with some possibility that one competitor will be annihilated. These conflicts are like war in the nuclear age in that large organizations are involved, outside sources often cannot impose a resolution, and there is a significant potential for using strategies of retaliation. They are unlike war in the stakes and the lack of important cultural differences. Robert Wilson, in Chapter 8, reviews the theory of oligopolistic competition for its implications about the use of threats.

Trade wars pit states against each other in what generally remains nonviolent economic competition. States threaten retaliation to deter what they consider unfair competition with their industries. Trade wars are like warfare in the nuclear age to the extent that no international authority can impose a settlement, that complex bureaucratic organizations are the main actors, and that cultural differences play an important role. In some instances, the possibility of retaliation is a significant factor. The stakes are much lower, however, and the existence of an overwhelming common interest in a peaceful settlement is often not acknowledged. In Chapter 9, John Conybeare reviews the economic theory of trade wars as it applies to the use of threats and notes the degree to which historical trade wars conform to the theory. David Yoffie in Chapter 10 focuses on the empirical study of trade wars and the bargaining efforts through which states try to avoid them. Yoffie's preliminary examination of two U.S.–Japan trade conflicts suggests four factors that may mediate the effectiveness of threat in international trade competition: domestic politics, particularly the presence of a domestic consensus for strong action; the specificity of relationship between the threat and the action to be deterred; the existence of international norms for retaliation; and the level of centralization in decision making.

Struggles between state authorities and internal revolutionaries are like international military conflict in their potential for bloodshed, including the deaths of the leaders. However, because the insurgents are usually very different organizationally from a national state, they may respond differently to threats; moreover, the ability to use force is usually distributed very unequally between the sides, so that at least for the regime in power, defensive strategies tend to predominate over retaliatory ones. Jack Goldstone examines the literature on revolutions and insurgencies in Chapter 11, summarizing what that literature has to say about when and how states can make the most effective use of threats to suppress revolution. He finds that the effectiveness of states' deterrents to revolution depends on their use of measured responses to their opponents, their willingness to adhere to established norms of legitimate action, and on the stake of potential revolutionaries in the status quo. Goldstone also notes that strength sufficient to deter outright attacks on the state may not deter its opponents from seeking other gains, particularly through influencing potential allies.

Finally, we have included two chapters on interpersonal conflict. Although such conflicts are quite unlike conflicts between nuclear powers on most of the dimensions we have identified, they may nevertheless be instructive for two reasons. Interpersonal conflicts are the root experiences through which national leaders and others learn to think about conflict, so may therefore affect how they perceive and respond to threats and the conditions under which they are inclined to use threats or carry them out. In addition, interpersonal conflict is frequently used as a metaphor for international conflict, for example, when national leaders wish to generate public support for a war effort; through public opinion, metaphors from interpersonal conflict may constrain the responses national leaders can make during international conflicts. In Chapter 12, Harold Kelley and Greg Schmidt identify a set of conditions under which individuals tend to set aside their propensity to seek their own benefit rationally in favor of a desire to punish an adversary without much regard to personal cost. Dean Pruitt, in Chapter 13, elaborates on the ways frustration and related emotional reactions may influence international conflicts. His chapter also summarizes findings from the study of small-group mixed-motive situations in terms of their implications for national leaders seeking to pursue a firm-but-fair strategy in international competition.

The volume as a whole offers a variety of perspectives on deterrence, each of which highlights a different set of variables as important determinants of the effectiveness of threats. The juxtaposition of various approaches and lines of evidence does more than add to the list of potentially interesting variables; it also suggests some interesting and relatively unexplored paths to the understanding of deterrence. We describe these in some detail in the concluding chapter.

Several contributors, for instance, suggest ways that the concept of legitimacy can be made useful for the study of deterrence, mainly by a focus on national leaders' judgments about the legitimacy of their own and their adversaries' actions. One hypothesis of several that flow from this line of thinking is that actions that are judged illegitimate are likely to be viewed as stemming from malevolent intent. If this hypothesis is true, practitioners of deterrence need to think not only about how a challenge or threat may change an adversary's cost–benefit calculus, but also about how the adversary will judge the legitimacy of that action. If a would-be challenger regards its claim for change in the status quo as legitimate, the challenger may regard efforts to deter change as malevolent. Similarly, if a defender of a status quo situation perceives a claim for change to have some legitimacy, it is likely to perceive a challenge as limited; whereas, if the claim is seen as without legitimacy, it is likely to be perceived as a sign of malevolent intent and an indication of additional challenges to come.

The psychological papers in this volume (Chapters 12 and 13) provide some data to support and specify a commonly stated belief that the uses of and responses to threat are systematically affected not only by thoughtful choice and the cognitive limitations on it, but sometimes also by predictable emotional reactions. The papers identify a particular action–reaction dynamic as leading to the breakdown of rational decision process and note that this dynamic is most likely to be triggered in a deteriorated relationship or when one of the adversaries has suffered recent frustrations. This hypothesis specifies situations that may increase the probability of nuclear war through inadvertence, and it is testable. It can be readily examined by comparing national leaderships' choice processes and decisions in domestic and international contexts that vary in terms of whether one or both actors has suffered recent foreign policy frustrations or sees the bilateral relationship as deteriorated.

The papers in this volume suggest research directions for the formal analysis of deterrence as well as for empirical studies. They suggest ways that the simplifying assumptions of early deterrence models might be fruitfully relaxed to employ more behaviorally defensible assumptions about the bounds of rationality, the formation of expectations about the adversary, and the nature of private information. Models based on such assumptions seem likely to produce more illuminating analyses than are now available.

The editors have found it enlightening to examine deterrence from the various perspectives represented by the contributions to this volume. We hope and believe others will find the exercise similarly useful.

## Appendix: Some Empirical Propositions About Deterrent Threats

Advocates of deterrent strategies argue that the most effective way to prevent challenges from states that may be contemplating them is with threats of force backed by the capability to make good the threats. But some critics of deterrence believe that in some situations such threats of force exacerbate conflict because they are perceived as aggressive rather than defensive acts. Other critics believe that threats are often irrelevant because the object of the threat is responsive mainly to domestic pressures and so does not pay close attention to external threats in making its decisions.

The central empirical problem in evaluating deterrent policies is to identify the conditions under which deterrent threats "work," that is, serve to prevent challenges to the interests of the party issuing the threats. In addressing that problem, classical deterrence theory focuses on the actions of the side making the threats, whereas some critics of abstract deterrence theory emphasize the actions and perceptions on the side receiving the threat and have explicitly distinguished "initiation theory" from "commitment theory" and "response theory" (George and Smoke, 1974). As both parties to a deterrence interaction are obviously important, the two perspectives taken together suggest a broad range of propositions or hypotheses that may account for variation in the success of policies based on deterrent threats.

Following is a list of propositions developed at the outset of our study from an brief scanning of works that take an empirical rather than an abstract approach to the problem of deterrence (esp. George and Smoke, 1974; Jervis, 1976; and Jervis, Lebow, and Stein, 1985). The list, which highlights the variables most often named in this literature as significant, was prepared to help participants in the workshop examine the indirect evidence from various deterrencelike phenomena for insights that might illuminate the study of deterrence. A list such as this, although useful heuristically, necessarily oversimplifies deterrence situations in three important ways. First, the propositions are in *ceteris paribus* form and do not account for interactions of the variables named in different propositions. Second, the propositions do not stress the dynamics of interaction between the deterrer and the object of its threats. Third, the list does not strongly emphasize that deterrent threats are particular: They deter some of the object's possible challenges but not others. The last two simplifications are especially significant because the literature is emphatic about the importance of strategy in deterrence. Deterrent threats and responses to them are usually understood as interventions in a relationship that involves conflict or competition in which the relative positions of the parties can change over time as a result of those interventions and in which both parties have options for achieving their goals by acting outside the arena that is the focus of any particular deterrent threat. Because of these important differences between a list of simple propositions and the dynamic complexity of deterrence situations, we did not seek insights for policy by evaluating the propositions individually, and we did not ask the workshop participants to do so. We treated the propositions as heuristic devices, recognizing that many of the deterrencelike relationships the participants would discuss differed from a list of static propositions in the same way that deterrence relationships differ from the propositions below.

## Propositions Focusing on the Side Using Deterrent Threats

1. *Capability*. Threats work better when they are accompanied by the military capability to defend successfully the interests one threatens to defend or, through retaliation, to impose great costs on a potential attacker.

    1a. Threats work when the side making them holds the military advantage.

    1b. Threats *fail* when the side making them holds the military advantage, because under these conditions threats are more likely to be seen as aggressive acts and to be met with force.

2. *Interest*. Threats work better when the vital interests of the side making them are "strongly engaged by what is at stake in the area or country in question" (George and Smoke, 1974:560).

3. *Commitment*. Threats work better when the side making them has committed itself to the defense of its interests, for example, with declared policies, contingency plans, and so forth, or to imposing great costs through retaliation.

4. *Communication*. Threats work better when the commitment of the state making them is clearly communicated through appropriate declarations and actions.

5. *Reputation for defense*. Threats work better when the side making them has defended its interests in similar situations in the past.

6. *Reputation for recklessness*. Threats work better when the side making them has built a reputation for being risk-seeking or for placing low value on the lives and property of its citizens.

## Propositions Focusing on the Side Receiving Deterrent Threats

7. *Costs of accepting the status quo*. Threats work better when the side receiving them sees the costs of accepting the status quo as relatively low, for example, when

- —its central values are not involved;
- —the issue involves no principles that apply to important other cases;
- —retreat is possible without breaking important commitments;
- —the side making the threat is believed to have limited goals;
- —the side receiving the threat does not believe concessions will lead to further demands;
- —the threat is seen as deriving from a desire for security;
- —the threat is seen as not violating "common standards of proper relations between juridically equal actors" (Jervis, 1976:101); and
- —the side making the threat refrains from humiliating the other, inflicting gratuitous punishment, or making illegitimate demands.

8. *Risk aversion.* Threats work better when the side receiving them is risk averse (e.g., places "high subjective value on preserving the lives and property of its citizens") (Jervis, 1976:100).

9. *Inattention.* Threats are likely to *fail* when the side receiving them does not notice they have been made or does not perceive that they are significant (e.g., when the signals are lost in the noise of diplomatic communication).

10. *Perceived need to challenge.* Threats are likely to *fail* when leaders of the side receiving them see no alternative to making a challenge. They may see a challenge as the only way to address internal problems or achieve foreign objectives, or they may judge that their situation vis-à-vis the other will only worsen as time passes unless they challenge now.

11. *Wishful thinking.* Threats are likely to *fail* when the side receiving them misinterprets available evidence and thus underestimates the other side's likelihood or ability to make good the threats. This may happen because judgment is clouded by a perceived need to challenge (see Proposition 10), because the side receiving the threat cannot believe the other side sees it as aggressive, or because it believes it is so strong that the other would be foolhardy to carry out the threat.

12. *Controlled pressure* or *strategic response.* Threats are likely to *fail* when the side receiving them believes that despite the existence of a credible threat, it can design an option for challenging the status quo for which the side making the threat lacks an effective response.

13. *Fait accompli.* Threats are likely to *fail* when the side receiving them believes that with a quick strike it can change the status quo before the side making the threat can react with an effective response.

14. *Limited probe.* Threats are likely to *fail* when the side receiving them believes it can "design around" the defender's commitment or can use limited, low-risk probes to make the defender clarify or abandon

commitments that had been broadly and vaguely defined. [Propositions 12–14 are derived from George and Smoke, 1974.]

## Proposition Focusing on the Conflict Situation

15. *Chicken game.* Threats work better in situations that resemble the game of "Chicken" but not the game of "Prisoners' Dilemma."[5]

## Propositions About Reassurance

Some writers about deterrence argue that nations can sometimes prevent challenges to their vital interests and make their deterrents more effective by use of nonthreatening influence techniques, often called *reassurances.* Although the literature does not yet seem to provide a clear definition of reassurance or clear distinctions between reassurance, conciliation, concession, appeasement, and other partly synonymous terms, it is possible to infer from the literature some very tentative propositions about when reassurances or conciliatory acts may work—that is, about when they may decrease the probability of challenges.

16. *Concessions.* There are conflicting suppositions about what happens when one side grants the demand or desire of a would-be challenger. Presumably, the alternative propositions hold under different sets of conditions.

    16a. *Appeasement.* Concessions encourage further demands when
    — "a retreat takes a state past a salient point";
    — "the adversaries do not have a common conception of fair play and reciprocation";
    — "the concession is made in a way that indicates that the state would sacrifice a great deal in order to avoid a war"; and
    — "the state retreats even though the costs of doing so are very high" (Jervis, 1976:101).

    16b. *Olive branch.* Concessions made in the absence of pressure from the other side can help break the arms-hostility cycle.

17. *Diplomatic alternative.* Reassurance to the other side that there is some chance of attaining its foreign objectives by diplomatic means rather than by resort to force or the threat of force decreases the chance it will challenge one's interests militarily.

18. *Solving domestic problems.* Initiatives that offer the other side assistance in addressing pressing internal problems that are contributing to

pressure on its leaders to initiate a challenge will decrease the chance it will challenge one's interests.
19. *Restraining arms races.* Reassurance that a militarily stronger side making a deterrent threat is favorably inclined to keep the relative strengths of the two sides from becoming more imbalanced in its favor will decrease the likelihood of a challenge.
20. *Decoupling.* Threats work better when accompanied by reassurance that restraint by the other side on the issue at stake will not be taken as signaling willingness to make concessions on other issues.
21. *Face-work.* Threats work better when accompanied by reassurance that concessions will not be followed by public humiliation, additional punishment, or further demands that would cause the other side to lose face.

## NOTES

1. These propositions are modified from a list developed by George and Smoke (1974:59–60).

2. A more refined formulation of this proposition allows that states may initiate challenges out of perceived necessity as well as opportunity. As scholars have pointed out since the 1960s, often citing the Japanese decision to attack the United States in 1941 (Russett, 1963, 1967), states sometimes challenge the status quo despite the expectation that costs will outweigh gains, if the expected cost of not attacking is even greater. Thus, the rationality assumption of classical deterrence theory is consistent with the idea of a state attacking despite the expectation of a net loss, if alternative policies would yield a greater net loss.

3. Responsiveness to domestic pressures is not at all inconsistent with the assumption of pure rationality that underpins classical deterrence theory. But the policy implications are much different depending on whether an analyst emphasizes a would-be challenger's domestic or international costs and benefits. A focus on international gains and losses points defenders to policies that strengthen their deterrents, whereas an emphasis on domestic gains and losses suggests other policies, sometimes generically labeled "reassurance" (Lebow, 1985b), that aim to avoid actions that would increase the pressures on a would-be challenger to test one's commitments.

4. Other distinguishing characteristics might be added to this list, such as that with nuclear arsenals punishments can be irreversible and momentous decisions must sometimes be made under extreme time pressure. Generally, these characteristics set the superpower competition apart from other conflict situations, none of which has them in such an extreme degree. We thank an anonymous reviewer for calling our attention to this point.

5. Oye (1986:8) describes "Chicken" as follows: "Two drivers race down the

center of a road from opposite directions. If one swerves and the other does not, then the first will suffer the stigma of being known as a chicken (CD) [CD signifies the payoff to one who "*c*ooperates" when the other "*d*efects"] while the second will enjoy being known as a hero (DC). If neither swerves, both will suffer grievously in the ensuing collision (DD). If both swerve, damage to the reputation of each will be limited (CC). Each driver's preference ordering is DC > CC > CD > DD."

"Prisoners' Dilemma" is described by Oye (1986:7) as follows: "Two prisoners are suspected of a major crime. The authorities possess evidence to secure conviction on only a minor charge. If neither prisoner squeals, both will draw a light sentence on the minor charge (CC). If one prisoner squeals and the other stonewalls, the rat will go free (DC) and the sucker will draw a very heavy sentence (CD). If both squeal, both will draw a moderate sentence (DD). Each prisoner's preference ordering is DC > CC > DD > CD."

The strategic difference between the two games is most evident to a player who expects the opponent to defect. In "Chicken," that expectation gives a player an incentive to cooperate, whereas the same expectation in "Prisoners' Dilemma" creates an incentive to defect. For additional analyses of applications of game theory to international relations, see Oye (1986) and sources cited therein.

## REFERENCES

Axelrod, R., 1984. *The Evolution of Cooperation.* New York: Basic.
Blair, B., 1985. *Strategic Command and Control.* Washington: Brookings.
Bracken, P., 1983. *The Command and Control of Nuclear Forces.* New Haven, Conn.: Yale University Press.
Brodie, B., 1959. *Strategy in the Missile Age.* Princeton, N.J.: Princeton University Press.
George, A., 1980. *Presidential Decisionmaking in Foreign Policy: The Effective Use of Information and Advice.* Boulder, Colo.: Westview.
George, A., Hall, D., and Simons, W., 1971. *The Limits of Coercive Diplomacy.* Boston: Little, Brown.
George, A., and Smoke, R., 1974. *Deterrence in American Foreign Policy: Theory and Practice.* New York: Columbia University Press.
Holsti, O., 1989. Crisis decision-making. In P. E. Tetlock, J. L. Husbands, R. Jervis, P. C. Stern, and C. Tilly, eds., *Behavior, Society, and Nuclear War,* Vol. 1. New York: Oxford University Press.
Janis, I., and Mann, L., 1977. *Decision-Making: A Psychological Analysis of Conflict, Choice, and Commitment.* New York: Free Press.
Jervis, R., 1976. *Perception and Misperception in International Politics.* Princeton, N.J.: Princeton University Press.
——— 1979. Deterrence theory revisited. *World Politics* 31:289–324.

―――― 1989. Psychological aspects of crisis stability. In R. Jervis, *The Implications of the Nuclear Revolution*. Ithaca, N.Y.: Cornell University Press.

Jervis, R., Lebow, R. N., and Stein, J. G., 1985. *Psychology and Deterrence*. Baltimore: Johns Hopkins University Press.

Kahn, H., 1964. *Thinking About the Unthinkable*. New York: Avon.

Lebow, R. N., 1981. *Between Peace and War: The Nature of International Crisis*. Baltimore: Johns Hopkins University Press.

―――― 1985a. Conclusions. In R. Jervis, R. N. Lebow, and J. G. Stein, eds., *Psychology and Deterrence*. Baltimore: Johns Hopkins University Press, pp. 203–32.

―――― 1985b. The deterrence deadlock: Is there a way out? In R. Jervis, R. N. Lebow, and J. G. Stein, eds., *Psychology and Deterrence*. Baltimore: Johns Hopkins University Press, pp. 180–202.

―――― 1987a. *Nuclear Crisis Management: A Dangerous Illusion*. Ithaca, N.Y.: Cornell University Press.

―――― 1987b. Deterrence failure revisited. *International Security* 12(1):197–213.

North, R. C., 1967. Perception and action in the 1914 crisis. *Journal of International Affairs* 21(1):103–12.

Orme, J., 1987. Deterrence failures: A second look. *International Security* 11:96–124.

Osgood, C. E., 1962. *An Alternative to War or Surrender*. Urbana, Ill.: University of Illinois Press.

Oye, K. A., 1986. Explaining cooperation under anarchy: Hypotheses and strategies. In K. A. Oye, ed., *Cooperation Under Anarchy*. Princeton, N.J.: Princeton University Press.

Russett, B. M., 1963. The calculus of deterrence. *Journal of Conflict Resolution* 7:97–109.

―――― 1967. Pearl Harbor: Deterrence theory and decision theory. *Journal of Peace Research* 4:89–105.

Schelling, T. C., 1960. *The Strategy of Conflict*. New York: Oxford University Press.

―――― 1966. *Arms and Influence*. New Haven, Conn.: Yale University Press.

Snyder, G. H., 1961. *Deterrence and Defense*. Princeton, N.J.: Princeton University Press.

Snyder, G. H., and Diesing, P., 1977. *Conflict Among Nations: Bargaining, Decision Making, and System Structure in International Crises*. Princeton, N.J.: Princeton University Press.

Snyder, J. L., 1985. Perceptions of the security dilemma in 1914. In R. Jervis, R. N. Lebow, and J. G. Stein, eds., *Psychology and Deterrence*. Baltimore: Johns Hopkins University Press, pp. 153–79.

White, R. K., 1970. *Nobody Wanted War: Misperception in Vietnam and Other Wars*. Rev. ed. New York: Doubleday/Anchor.

# 2

# Deterrence: A Political and Psychological Critique

## RICHARD NED LEBOW

Postwar American security policy was built on a foundation of deterrence. In the early Cold War period, American leaders relied on nuclear deterrence to discourage Soviet or Chinese attacks against American allies in Western Europe and the Far East. When these countries developed the means to launch intercontinental nuclear attacks of their own, the United States counted on deterrence to prevent an attack against itself. Over the years, successive American administrations have also attempted to use deterrence to moderate the policies of Third World states with which the United States or its allies have come into conflict. Partisans of deterrence assert that it has kept the peace between the superpowers and has been useful in managing lesser conflicts. This chapter disputes both claims.[1]

When discussing deterrence it is important to distinguish between the theory of deterrence and the strategy of deterrence. The former pertains to the logical postulates of deterrence and the assumptions on which they are based. Put succinctly, deterrence is an attempt to influence another actor's assessment of its interests. It seeks to prevent an undesired behavior by convincing the party who may be contemplating it that the cost will exceed any possible gain. Deterrence presupposes that decisions are made in response to some kind of rational cost–benefit calculus, that this calculus can be successfully manipulated from the outside, and that the best way to do this is to increase the cost side of the ledger. Different scholars have developed their own variants of deterrence theory. All of them, however, are based on these assumptions.

Deterrence strategy is concerned with applying the theory of deterrence to real world conflicts. It has given rise to its own body of theory about how this is best accomplished. The first wave of this theory, almost entirely deductive in nature, was developed in the 1950s and 1960s by such scholars as Bernard Brodie (1959), William Kaufmann (1954), and Thomas Schelling (1966). Most of these works stressed the importance of imparting credibility to commitments and explored various mechanisms leaders could exploit toward this end. The literature of this period is often referred to as classical deterrence theory (Jervis, 1979).

Classical deterrence spawned a number of critiques. For our purposes the most interesting were those that attempted to evaluate deterrence strategy in light of empirical evidence from historical cases. The work of Milburn (1959), Russett (1967), Snyder and Diesing (1977), and George and Smoke (1974) is representative of this wave of theorizing. These scholars sought to refine the strategy of deterrence in order to make it more useful to statesmen. Milburn, Russett, and George and Smoke argued that deterrence might be made more efficacious if threats of punishment were accompanied by promises of reward for acceptable behavior. George and Smoke and Snyder and Diesing sought to divorce deterrence from its Cold War context and root it in a less politically specific theory of initiation.

Empirical analyses of deterrence had implications for the postulates of deterrence theory. On the basis of their case studies, George and Smoke (1974) argued for a broader formulation of rational choice. They hoped that this would enable the theory to incorporate domestic political concerns and other factors affecting foreign policy behavior that deterrence theory had not previously taken into account.

This essay incorporates and expands upon elements of previous critiques to develop a more far-reaching critique of deterrence. The scholars I have cited argue that deterrence sometimes fails because it is implemented poorly or applied in circumstances in which it is inappropriate. Their criticisms, and those of George Quester in Chapter 3, are directed primarily at the strategy of deterrence. I argue that deterrence is by its very nature a seriously flawed strategy *and* theory of conflict management. I do not believe that attempts to improve and reformulate the theory will produce a better fit between its expectations and observable behavior across cases.

The critique of deterrence that Janice Gross Stein and I have developed (Lebow and Stein, 1987a) has three interlocking components: the political, psychological, and practical. Each exposes a different set of problems with the theory and strategy of deterrence. In practice, these problems are often linked; political and practical factors interact with psychological processes to multiply the obstacles to successful prediction of state behavior and successful conflict management.

The political component examines the motivations behind foreign policy challenges. Deterrence is unabashedly a theory of "opportunity." It asserts that adversaries seek opportunities to make gains and pounce when they find them. Case studies of actual conflicts point to an alternative explanation for resorts to force, which we term a theory of "need." The evidence indicates that strategic vulnerabilities and domestic political needs often constitute incentives to use force. When leaders become desperate, they may resort to force even when the military balance is unfavorable and there are no grounds for doubting adversarial resolve. Deterrence may be an inappropriate and even dangerous strategy in these circumstances. For if leaders are driven less by the prospect of gain than they are by the fear of loss, deterrent policies can provoke the very behavior they are designed to forestall by intensifying the pressures on the challenger to act.

The psychological component is also related to the motivation behind deterrence challenges. To the extent that policymakers believe in the necessity of challenging commitments of their adversaries, they become predisposed to see their objectives as attainable. When this happens, motivated errors can be pronounced and identifiable. They can take the form of distorted threat assessments and insensitivity to warnings that the policies to which our leaders are committed are likely to end in disaster. Policymakers can convince themselves, despite evidence to the contrary, that they can challenge an important adversarial commitment without provoking war. Because they know the extent to which they are powerless to back down, they expect their adversaries to accommodate them by doing so. Policymakers may also seek comfort in the illusion that their country will emerge victorious at little cost to itself if the crisis gets out of hand and leads to war. Deterrence can thus be defeated by wishful thinking.

The practical component of the critique describes some of the most important obstacles to implementing deterrence. These derive from the distorting effects of cognitive biases and heuristics, political and cultural barriers to empathy, and the differing cognitive contexts the deterrer and would-be challengers are apt to use to frame and interpret signals. Problems of this kind are not unique to deterrence; they are embedded in the very structure of international relations. They nevertheless constitute particularly severe impediments to deterrence because of the deterrer's need to understand the world as it appears to the leaders of a would-be challenger in order to manipulate effectively their cost–benefit calculus. Failure to do this in the right way can result in deterrent policies that actually succeed in making the proscribed behavior more attractive to a challenger.

The first two components of this critique challenge core assumptions of deterrence theory. The third component is directed at the strategy of deterrence. But it also has implications for deterrence theory. If the strategy of deterrence is so often unsuccessful because of all of the practical difficulties associated with its implementation, then the theory of deterrence must be judged a poor guide to action.

In assessing deterrence theory it is imperative to distinguish between the motives and opportunity to carry out a military challenge. Classical deterrence theory takes as a given a high level of hostility on the part of the adversary and assumes that a challenge will be made if the opportunity exists. In the absence of opportunity, no challenge will occur even though hostility remains high. Because it sees aggression as opportunity driven, deterrence theory prescribes defensible, credible commitments as the best way to prevent military challenges.

Our case material points to the importance of motive; hostility cannot be treated as a constant. In practice, it waxes and wanes as a function of specific foreign and domestic circumstances. There are, moreover, few states or leaders who are driven by pure hostility toward their adversaries. Hitler is the exception, not the rule. This is not to deny the existence of opportunity-based challenges. Postwar examples include India's invasion of Pakistan in 1971, Iraq's invasion of Iran in 1980, and Israel's invasion of Lebanon in 1982.

In most adversarial relationships, leaders resort to military challenges only in extraordinary circumstances. Our cases suggest that this is most likely to occur when leaders confront acute political and strategic vulnerabilities. In these circumstances, military challenges may be carried out even when there is no apparent opportunity to do so. Leaders may convince themselves, quite without objective reason, that such opportunity exists. When leaders do not feel impelled by political and strategic needs, they are unlikely to carry out challenges even when they perceive the opportunity to do so.

The matrices in Tables 2.1 and 2.2 summarize some of the most important differences between the classical theory of deterrence and our findings about military challenges. These differences are explained by the political and psychological components of our critique of deterrence. The third component of that critique, the practical difficulties of implementing deterrence, pertains primarily to deterrence as a strategy. However, to the extent that it indicates the

**Table 2.1.** Deterrence Matrix.

|  | *Opportunity (in the form of an adversary's vulnerable commitment)* | |
|---|---|---|
|  | No | Yes |
| *Motive* (hostility assumed constant) | No challenge | Challenge |

**Table 2.2.** Lebow–Stein Matrix.

|  |  | Opportunity (in the form of an adversary's vulnerable commitment) | |
|---|---|---|---|
| *Motive* (needs in the form of strategic and domestic value) | Low need | No challenge | No challenge |
|  | High need | Possible to likely | Very likely |

pervasive presence of serious obstacles in the way of applying deterrence, it suggests that deterrence theory is not a good guide for formulating strategy.

In the real world, there can be no truly dichotomous distinction between opportunity and need as motives for military challenges. Many, if not most challenges, contain elements of both motives. In the case of Iran–Iraq, many analysts (Heller, 1984; Tripp, 1986) argue that Iraq attacked because of a complex mixture of motives. It saw the opportunity to take advantage of Iran's internal disarray—clearly a motive of opportunity—but also acted out of fear that the Ayatollah Ruhollah Khomeini would attempt to export Iran's revolution in order to overthrow Iraq's regime. Most of the cases we examined were nevertheless skewed toward one or the other of the extremes. For purposes of analysis we have classified these cases accordingly.

## Data and Method

Most of the evidence on which this analysis is based comes from historical case studies Janice Stein and I have published in *Between Peace and War* (Lebow, 1981), *Psychology and Deterrence* (Jervis, Lebow, and Stein, 1985) and various articles. Both books analyzed deterrence encounters from the perspective of both sides; they examined the calculations, expectations and actions of the challenger as well as those of the would-be deterrer. As the key to understanding deterrence successes and failures lies in the nature of the interactions between the adversaries, case studies of this kind shed more light on these phenomena than analyses of the deliberations and policies of only one of the involved parties.

Most of these cases are deterrence failures. Janice Stein and I have chosen to work with failures because they are more readily identifiable, thereby facilitating the construction of a valid universe of cases. Deterrence successes can result in inaction. Failures, by contrast, lead to serious crises and often to wars. Events of this kind are not only highly visible but almost always prompt memoirs, official inquiries, and other investigations that provide the data essential for scholarly analyses. Deterrence failures are also more·revealing than deterrence successes of the complexities of international relations. Understanding why deterrence fails may lead to insights into the nature of conflict as well as to a more general understanding of the circumstances in which deterrence is likely to succeed or fail and the reasons why this is so. Nevertheless, restricting analysis to deterrence failures imposes costs. Explanations of the causes of failure can only be tentative, because some of the factors that appear to account for failure may also be at work when deterrence succeeds. Hypotheses derived from a controlled comparison of cases of deterrence failure will ultimately have to be validated against identified instances of deterrence success.

What is a deterrence failure? The goal of deterrence is to dissuade another actor from carrying out a proscribed behavior. In the context of international relations, the most important objective of deterrence is prevention of a use of force. To do this, the theory stipulates that the deterrer must carefully define the unacceptable behavior, make a reasonable attempt to communicate a commitment to punish transgressors (or deny them their objectives), possess the means to do this, and demonstrate the resolve to carry through on its threat (Kaufmann, 1954; Kissinger, 1960; Brodie, 1959; Kaplan, 1958; Milburn, 1959; Quester, 1966; Schelling, 1966:374).[2] When these conditions are met and the behavior still occurs, we can speak of a deterrence failure.[3]

Researchers can and do disagree among themselves about the extent to which any or all of these conditions were met in a specific instance. These disagreements usually concern the credibility of the threat, something deterrence theorists consider to be the quintessential condition of the strategy's success. Unfortunately, it is also the most difficult to assess. This can be a serious problem, as it hinders a determination of whether a deterrence failure was due to the inadequacy of the strategy or merely to the failure of the country in question to implement it adequately. Deterrence supporters invariably argue the latter when critics make the case for the former (Orme, 1987; Lebow, 1987b).

The ongoing debate about the efficacy of deterrence is fueled by the inherent subjectivity of all interpretations of historical events. One way to cope with this problem is to use a sample large enough to minimize the significance of disagreements about individual cases. My arguments are therefore based on 10 examples of deterrence failure.[4] These cases are interesting not only because they document a pattern of deterrence failure, but because they illustrate diverse reasons why failures occur. Evidence from conflicts in which leaders used other kinds of strategies of conflict management will also be introduced where it is relevant.

There is a further difficulty that arises from presenting arguments based on case studies. In contrast to experimental or survey research, it is impossible to summarize data of this kind in a succinct manner. Nor would such a summary establish the validity of the findings even if it can be demonstrated that the nature of the data base and the data analysis conformed to accepted research practice. As I have already observed, the reader must be convinced of the correctness of our interpretation of individual cases. Consequently, it is important to convey something of the flavor of the cases and the basis for our interpretation of the evidence. For this reason I have chosen to incorporate as much case material as space permits. Readers who are interested in the data are referred to *Psychology and Deterrence*, *Between Peace and War*, and the several journal articles cited for a fuller exposition of the cases.

## Political Failings

Deterrence theory assumes that utility, defined in terms of the political and material well-being of leaders and their states, can readily be measured. But political and national interests are subjective concepts. They are perceived different by different leaders, making it extremely difficult for outsiders to determine, let alone measure. It is even more difficult, if not impossible, to weigh the relative importance of emotional, intangible, unquantifiable concerns that history reveals to be at least as important for most peoples, Americans included, as narrow calculations of political interest. Why, for example, did the South challenge the North, which was clearly superior in military power and potential? Why did the Confederacy continue the struggle at tremendous human and economic cost long after leaders and soldiers alike recognized it to be a lost cause? Other examples can be cited where a people wittingly began or continued a struggle against great or even impossible odds in the face of prior and even convincing efforts by the superior military power to portray the certain and disastrous consequences of a military challenge or continued resistance. From the Jewish revolts against the Romans to the Irish Easter Rising and the resistance of the beleaguered Finns in 1940, history records countless stories of peoples who began or continued costly struggles with little or no expectation of success. Honor, anger, or national self-respect proved more compelling motives for action than pragmatic calculations of material loss and gain were reasons for acquiesence or passivity.

Both the theory and strategy of deterrence mistake the symptoms of aggressive behavior for its causes. Specifically, it ignores the political and strategic vulnerabilities that can interact with cognitive and motivational processes to compel leaders to choose force.

In a previous study, I analyzed a class of acute international crisis, brinkmanship, whose defining characteristic was the challenger's expectation that its adversary would back away from its commitment in preference to war (Lebow, 1981). I found that, much more often than not, brinkmanship challenges were initiated without good evidence that the adversary lacked either the capability or resolve to defend its commitment; on the conrary, in most instances the evidence available at the time pointed to the opposite conclusion. The commitments in question appeared to meet the four necessary conditions of deterrence: they were clearly defined, repeatedly publicized, and defensible, and the defending states gave every indication of their resolve to use force in defense of them. Not surprisingly, most of these challenges resulted in setbacks for the initiators, who were themselves compelled to back down or go to war.

Faulty judgment by challengers could most often be attributed to their perceived need to carry out a brinkmanship challenge in response to pressing foreign and domestic threats. The policymakers involved believed that these threats could be overcome only by means of successful challenge of an adversary's commitment. Brinkmanship was conceived of as a necessary and forceful response to danger, as a means of protecting national strategic or domestic political interests before time ran out. Whether or not their assessment of international and domestic constraints was correct is a separate question for research. What is relevant is that leaders perceived acute domestic pressure, international danger, or both.

The extent to which policymakers contemplating challenges of their adversaries are inner-directed and inwardly focused is also a central theme of Janice Gross Stein's two contributions to *Psychology and Deterrence* (1985a, 1985b). In her analysis of the five occasions between 1969 and 1973 when Egyptian leaders seriously contemplated the use of force against Israel, Stein argues that decision making in all of these instances departed significantly from the core postulates of deterrence theory. All five decisions revealed a consistent and almost exclusive concentration by Egyptian leaders on their own purposes, political needs, and constraints. They spoke in almost apocalyptic terms of Egypt's need to liberate the Sinai before the superpower detente progressed to the stage where Egyptian military action became impossible. They alluded again and again to the escalating domestic crisis that could be arrested only if the humiliation of 1967 were erased by a successful military campaign. By contrast, Israel's interests, and the imperatives for action that could be expected to flow from these interests, were not at all salient for Egyptian leaders. They thought instead of the growing domestic and international constraints and of the intolerable costs of inaction.

In 1969, in the War of Attrition, the Egyptian failure to consider the

## Deterrence: A Political and Psychological Critique

relative interests of both sides resulted in a serious error. Egyptian leaders did not miscalculate Israel's credibility but rather the scope of Israel's military response. They attached a very low probability to the possibility that Israel would extend the war and carry out deep penetration bombing attacks against Egypt and escalate its war objective to the overthrow of Nasser. This was a miscalculation of major proportions given the magnitude of the punishment Israel in fact inflicted upon Egypt.

Egypt's inability to understand that Israel's leaders believed that defense of the Sinai was important not only for the strategic depth and warning time it provided but also as an indicator of resolve was merely one cause of its miscalculation in 1969. Egyptian leaders overestimated their own capacity to lay down favorable ground rules for a war of attrition and underestimated that of Israel. They also developed a strategy to fight the war, to culminate in a crossing of the canal, that was predicated on a fatal inconsistency: the belief that Egypt could inflict numerous casualties on Israel in the course of a war of attrition, but that Israel would refrain from escalating that conflict in order to reduce its casualties.

These faulty assessments and strategic contradictions are best explained as a motivated response to the strategic dilemma faced by Egyptian planners in 1969. Egypt could neither accept the status quo nor sustain the kind of military effort that would have been necessary to recapture the Sinai. Instead, Egypt embarked upon a poorly conceived limited military action. The wishful thinking and biased estimates were a form of bolstering; this was the way Egyptian leaders convinced themselves that their strategy would succeed. Israel's deterrent failed, not because of any lack of capability or resolve, but because Egypt's calculations were so flawed that they defeated deterrence.

Egyptian decision making in 1969 provides an example of what may be the most frequent cause of serious miscalculation in international crisis: the inability of leaders to find a satisfactory way to reconcile two competing kinds of threats. Our cases indicated that the psychological stress that arises from this decisional dilemma is usually resolved by the adoption of defensive avoidance as a coping strategy. Leaders commit themselves to a course of action and deny information that indicates that their policy might not succeed (Janis and Mann, 1977). In the Egyptian case, the decisional dilemma that prompted defensive avoidance was the result of incompatibility between domestic imperatives and foreign realities. The domestic threat, the political and economic losses, was the overriding consideration for Egyptian policymakers. Their estimates of their vulnerability motivated error and miscalculation and culminated in the failure of deterrence.

The Egyptian decision to use force in 1973 was even more damaging to the logic of deterrence than the motivated miscalculation in 1969. Egyptian leaders chose to use force in 1973 not because they miscalculated Israel's resolve or response but because they felt so intolerably vulnerable and constrained. If Egyptian leaders had miscalculated, proponents of deterrence might argue that human error accounted for its failure. Economists advance similar kinds of arguments: The strategy is not flawed, only the people who use it. Egypt's leaders decided to challenge deterrence not because they erred but because they considered the domestic and foreign costs of inaction unbearably high. They anticipated correctly a major military response by Israel and expected to suffer significant casualties and losses. Nevertheless, they planned a limited military action to disrupt the status quo and hoped for an internationally imposed cease-fire before their limited gains could be reversed. In 1973, Egyptian leaders considered their military capabilities inferior to those of Israel but chose to use force because they anticipated grave domestic and strategic consequences from continuing inaction.

The same domestic considerations that compelled Egyptian leaders to challenge Israel also provided the incentives for Egyptian military planners to devise a strategy that compensated for their military weakness. Human ingenuity and careful organization succeeded in exploiting the flexibility of multipurpose conventional weaponry to circumvent many of the constraints of military inferiority. Egyptian officers strove to achieve defensive superiority in what they planned to keep a limited battle zone (Stein, 1985a).

The Japanese decision to attack the United States in December 1941 seems analogous to the Egyptian decision of 1973. Like the Egyptians, the Japanese fully recognized the military superiority of their adversary, particularly the greater naval power and vastly superior economic base of the United States. The Japanese, nevertheless, felt compelled to attack the United States in the illusory hope that a limited victory would facilitate a favorable settlement of their festering and costly conflict with China.

As the Egyptians were to do more than 30 years later, the Japanese military devised an ingenious and daring strategy to compensate for their adversary's advantages; they relied on air power and surprise to neutralize U.S. naval power in the Pacific. They too deluded themselves that their foe would accept the political consequences of a disastrous initial defeat instead of fighting to regain the initiative. The Japanese strategy was an act of desperation. Japan's leaders opted for war only after they were persuaded that the military balance between themselves and their adversaries would never again be as favorable as it was in 1941; time was working against them. They were also convinced that they could not attain their objectives by diplomacy (Butow, 1961; Borg and Okamoto, 1973; Ienaga, 1978; Ike, 1967; Russett, 1967; Hosoya, 1968).

The Japanese case highlights the importance of an uncongenial strategic environment as an incentive for a challenge. Leaders who anticipate an unfavorable decline in the relative balance of power may see no alternative to military action. President Sadat, for example, estimated that the longer he postponed war, the stronger Israel would become. This assumption helped to create a mood of desperation in Cairo, so much so that Sadat repeatedly purged the Egyptian military command until he found generals who were confident that they could design around Israel's air and armored capability.

The Egyptian and Japanese cases indicate that a defender's capability and resolve are only some of the factors challengers consider when they contemplate war. They are also influenced by domestic political pressures that push them toward action and their judgments about future trends in the military balance. A pessimistic estimate of the probability of achieving important goals by peaceful means can also create frustration and constitute an incentive to act. This was very much so in Egypt in 1973 and in Japan in 1941. Both these cases illustrate how frustration, pessimism, and a sense of weakness in response to an unfavorable domestic and strategic environment can outweigh considerations of military inferiority.

## How Deterrence Can Backfire

When challengers are vulnerable or feel themselves vulnerable, a deterrer's effort to make important commitments more defensible and credible will have uncertain and unpredictable effects. At best, deterrence will be benign; it will simply have no effect. But it can also be malignant by intensifying precisely those pressures that are pushing leaders toward a choice of force. Japan offers an example.

The United States and other Western powers imposed first an asset freeze and then an oil embargo upon Japan in July–August 1941 in the hope of moderating Tokyo's policies. These actions were in fact the catalysts for Japan's decision to go to war. Her leaders feared that the embargo would deprive them of the means of continuing their struggle against China and would ultimately put them at the mercy of their adversaries. It accordingly fostered a mood of desperation in Tokyo, an essential precondition for the attack on Pearl Harbor that followed.

In his contribution to *Psychology and Deterrence*, Jack Snyder (1985:153–79) explores security dilemmas and their role in the outbreak of war in 1914. The distinguishing characteristic of a security dilemma is that behavior perceived by adversaries as threatening and aggressive is actually a defensive response to an inhospitable strategic environment. A "perceptual security dilemma" develops, Snyder argues, when strategic and psychological factors interact and strategic assessments are exaggerated or distorted by perceptual biases. In effect, leaders overrate the advantages of the offensive, the magnitude of power shifts, and the hostility of their adversaries.

In 1914, the major continental powers confronted elements of a security dilemma. As French fortifications improved in the 1880s, German security required the vulnerability of Russian forces in Poland; without this vulnerability, the German general staff feared that Russia and France could mobilize to full strength and then attack jointly. Russian security, however, excluded precisely such a weakness: Russia could not tolerate a decisive German advantage in a short war and so planned to increase her standing forces 40 percent by 1917. With French financial assistance, Russia also constructed new railways to transport these forces more rapidly to her western borders. Defensive preparations by Russia constituted an offensive threat to Germany, and conversely, a defensive strategy by Germany seemed to require offensives directed against France and Russia. Offense and defense thus became virtually indistinguishable.

Although the strategic environment was inhospitable and dangerous, Germany's military leaders greatly exaggerated the dangers and, as Snyder (1985:170) demonstrates, reasoned inside out. They overrated the hostility of their adversaries and consequently assumed the inevitability of a two-front war. Once they did, the attractiveness of a preventive war-fighting strategy became overwhelming; German military leaders saw preventive war as the only alternative to their vulnerability. Indeed, the general staff gave no serious consideration after 1890 to the possibility of a defensive strategy against Russia and France. From then until 1914, the German military did not overestimate their offensive capabilities and then choose force; on the contrary, they exaggerated the hostility of their adversaries in ways that psychological theories expect and then argued that an offensive capability was the least unsatisfactory option. Because of this choice, Germany's neighbors confronted a real security dilemma.

In this kind of strategic environment, the attempt to deter Germany was counterproductive. Threats of retaliation and shows of force by Russia and France only fueled German fears and, in so doing, further destabilized an already unstable environment. The Russian mobilization designed to deter, for example, could not help but alarm German military leaders committed to an offensive preemptive strategy. In 1914, when Germany's leaders chose to use force, they did so not because they saw an "opportunity" for gain but because they believed the strategic consequences of inaction would be catastrophic. In an environment where already unfavorable strategic assessments were overlain by exaggerated fear and a sense of vulnerability, deterrence could only provoke the use of force it was designed to prevent.

## Psychological Problems

The psychological component of this critique is also related to the motivation behind deterrence challenges. To the extent that policymakers believe in the necessity of challenging commitments of their adversaries, they become predisposed to see their objectives as attainable. Motivated error in the form of distorted threat assessments can result in the unrealistic expectation that an adversary will back down when challenged or, alternatively, that it will fight precisely the kind of war the challenger plans for. Once committed to a challenge, policymakers may also become insensitive to warnings that their chosen course of action is likely to result in disaster. In these circumstances, deterrence, no matter how well it is practiced, can be defeated by a challenger's wishful thinking.

## Flawed Assessments

I have already described Egypt's flawed assessments in 1969 and 1973. In 1969, the Egyptians convinced themselves that Israel would engage in a costly war of attrition along the canal, despite the well-known fact that Israeli strategy had always been premised on the need to avoid this kind of conflict. In 1973, the Egyptians assumed that Israel would accept the loss of her positions along the east bank of the Suez Canal as a fait accompli despite Egypt's own inability to do this for much the same reasons. Both expectations flew in the face of obvious political realities. They led to costly wars that very nearly ended in political disaster. Both resorts to force were a response to Egypt's leaders' need to reassert their strength at home and abroad, a need that prompted grossly distorted estimates of Israel's likely responses to a challenge.

The Japanese decision to attack Pearl Harbor is another example of a strategic decision based on wishful thinking. The Japanese military settled on a limited war strategy because they knew that it was the only kind of war they could hope to win against the United States, given the latter's superior economic and military power. They convinced themselves that a successful counterforce strike against U.S. naval units in the Pacific would convince Washington to withdraw from the Western Pacific and give Japan a free hand in the region. The American reaction was, of course, nothing of the kind. Public opinion in the United States was enraged by Japan's "sneak attack" and intent on waging war against her *a l'outrance*. President Roosevelt and Chairman of the Joint Chiefs of Staff George C. Marshall had a difficult time throughout the war in directing America's principal military effort against Germany, which they rightly concluded constituted the more serious threat, because public opinion was more interested in punishing Japan.

The origins of World War I offer a third example of how wishful thinking can defeat deterrence. German policy in the July crisis was based on a series of erroneous assumptions on the probable Russian, French, and British reaction to the destruction of Serbia by Austria–Hungary. German leaders were on the whole confident of their ability to localize an Austro–Serbian war despite all the indications to the contrary and, one fleeting moment of hesitation by the German chancellor aside, urged Vienna throughout the crisis to ignore all pleas for moderation.

Germany's strategy was remarkably shortsighted. Even if the unrealistic assumptions on which it was based had proved correct it still would have been self-defeating. Serbia's destruction would only have aggravated Russo–German hostility, making Russia even more dependent on France and Britain and setting the stage for a renewed and more intense clash between the two blocs. This outcome aside, all of the assumptions on which German policy was based proved ill-founded; Austria's declaration of war on Serbia triggered a series of responses that embroiled Germany in a war with Russia, France, Belgium, and Great Britain.

The German strategy only makes sense when it is understood as a response to the contradictions between the country's perceived strategic needs and perceived strategic realities. The former dictated support of Austria, Germany's principal ally, as a means of shoring up her self-confidence and maintaining the all-important alliance. The latter dictated caution because Germany's politicians shied away from responsibility for a European war while her generals were uncertain of their ability to win one. These contradictions were reconciled in a strategy premised on the illusion that Austria, with German support, could wage a limited war in the Balkans without provoking the intervention of the other great powers. German leaders were only disabused of their illusion after it was too late to alter the course of events (Lebow, 1981:26–29, 119–24; 1984).

## Challenger's Insensitivity to Warnings

Motivated errors can play a major role in blocking receptivity to signals. Once leaders have committed themselves to a challenge, efforts by defenders to impart credibility to their commitments will at best have a marginal impact on their adversaries' behavior. Even the most elaborate efforts to demonstrate prowess and resolve may prove insufficient to discourage a challenger who is convinced that a use of force is necessary to preserve vital strategic and political interests.

Irving Janis and Leon Mann (1977), in their analysis of decision making, argue that policymakers who contemplate a course of action, but recognize that their initiative entails serious risk, will experience psychological stress. They will become emotionally upset and preoccupied with finding a less-risky alternative. If, after further investigation, they conclude that it is unrealistic to hope for a better strategy, they will terminate their search despite their continuing dissatisfaction with available options. The result is a pattern of "defensive avoidance," characterized by efforts to avoid, dismiss, and deny warnings that increase anxiety and fear.

One of the three forms of defensive avoidance identified by Janis and Mann (1977:57–58, 107–33) is bolstering. It refers to a set of psychological tactics that policymakers may resort to to make a decision they are about to make, or have already made, more acceptable to themselves. Bolstering occurs when policymakers have lost hope of finding an altogether satisfactory policy option and are unable to postpone a decision or shift responsibility to others. Instead, they commit themselves to the least objectionable alternative and proceed to "spread the alternatives," that is, to exaggerate its positive consequences or minimize its costs. They may also deny the existence of aversive feelings, emphasize the remoteness of the consequence, or attempt to minimize personal responsibility for the decision once it is made. Policymakers continue to think about the problem but ward off anxiety by practicing selective attention and other forms of distorted information processing.

Bolstering can serve a useful purpose. It helps a policymaker forced to settle for a less than optimal course of action to overcome residual conflict and move more confidently toward decision and action. Bolstering can occur before and after a decision is made. When it takes place before, it discourages leaders from making a careful search of the alternatives. It subsequently lulls them into believing that they have made a good decision, when in fact they have avoided making a vigilant appraisal of the possible alternatives in order to escape from the conflict that would ensue. When leaders resort to bolstering after a decision it tends to blind to warnings that the course of action to which they are committed may prove unsatisfactory or even disastrous.

Janis and Mann (1977:74–79) consider insensitivity to warnings a hallmark of defensive avoidance. When this becomes the dominant pattern of coping, "the person tries to keep himself from being exposed to communications that might reveal the shortcomings of the course of action he has chosen." When actually confronted with disturbing information, leaders will alter its implications through a process of wishful thinking; they rationalize and deny the prospect of serious loss. Extraordinary circumstances with irrefutable negative feedback may be required to overcome such defenses.

Selective attention, denial, or almost any other psychological tactic used by policymakers to cope with critical information can be institutionalized. Merely by making their expectations or preferences known, policymakers encourage their subordinates to report or emphasize information supportive of those expectations and preferences. Policymakers can also purposely rig their intelligence networks and bureaucracies to achieve the same effect. Perspectives thus confirmed and reconfirmed over time become more and more resistant to discrepant information and more difficult to refute.

In an earlier study, I (1981:101–228) described in detail how this process occurred in Germany in 1914, in the United States in 1950 with regard to the possibility of Chinese entry into the Korean War, and in India in 1962 during its border dispute with China. In all three instances, policymakers, responding to perceived domestic and strategic imperatives, became committed to risky military policies in the face of efforts by others to deter them. They resorted to defensive avoidance to insulate themselves from the stress triggered by these warnings. They subsequently allowed or encouraged their respective political-military bureaucracies to submit reports supportive of the policies to which the leadership was committed. Institutionalized in this manner, defensive avoidance succeeded in blinding the policymakers to repeated warnings of impending disaster.

Motivated bias is a response to personal needs or external pressures. Evidence drawn from these cases suggests that at least one mediating condition of motivated bias is a choice by policymakers of a course of action that they recognize could result in substantial loss. Once challengers become committed to such an action, even the most strenuous efforts by a deterrer to define a commitment and give it credibility may have little impact. Motivated bias, in the form of faulty assessment of an adversary's resolve, overconfidence, and insensitivity to warnings, can defeat even well-articulated and well-executed deterrence.

## Problems in Applying Deterrence

Deterrence is beset by a host of practical problems. One of these is the difficulty of communicating capability and resolve to would-be challengers. Strategies of deterrence generally assume that everyone understands, so to speak, the meaning of barking guard dogs, barbed wire, and "No Trespassing" signs. This is not so. Signals only take on meaning in terms of the context in which they are interpreted. When sender and recipient use quite different contexts to frame, communicate, or interpret signals, the opportunities for miscalculation and misjudgment multiply. This problem is endemic to international relations and is not limited to deterrence (Jervis, 1979: 305–10; Lebow, 1985:204–11).

A second problem, and one that is more specific to deterrence, concerns the difficulty of reconstructing the cost–benefit calculus of another actor. Deterrence requires the party intent on forestalling a challenge to manipulate the cost–benefit calculus of a would-be challenger so that the expected costs of a challenge are judged to outweigh its expected benefits. If credible threats of punishment always increased the cost side of the ledger—something deterrence theory takes for granted—then it would be unnecessary for deterrers to understand the value hierarchy and outcome preferences of target states. This convenient assumption is not borne out in practice. Leaders may be driven not primarily by "opportunity" but rather by "vulnerability." When they are, increasing the costs of military action may have no effect on their unwillingness to tolerate the high costs of inaction.

Deterrent threats in these circumstances can also provoke the very behavior they are designed to prevent. This happens when, contrary to the deterrer's expectations, they intensify the pressures on the challenger to act. Unfortunately, the kinds of considerations that determine how a threat will influence an adversary's cost–benefit calculus are often invisible or not easily understood from the outside.

The Cuban Missile Crisis offers a striking example of this phenomenon. Scholars have advanced several hypotheses to explain why the Soviets placed missiles in Cuba in September and October of 1962. By far the most widely accepted is the perceived Soviet need to redress the strategic balance. The deployment was a reaction to American pronouncements of strategic superiority in the fall of 1961 (Horelick and Rush, 1966:141; Hilsman, 1967:200–2; Tatu, 1968; Abel, 1966; Allison, 171:52–56). At that time the Soviets possessed a very small fleet of long-range bombers, a sizable number of medium-range ballistic missiles (MRBMs) and intermediate-range ballistic missiles (IRBMs) and a small number of intercontinental ballistic missiles (ICBMs). All of these weapons were based in the Soviet Union and were of limited use in any retaliatory strike against the United States. The bombers were slow and easy to detect; they could not be expected to penetrate American air defenses. The medium- and intermediate-range ballistic missiles were excellent weapons but incapable of reaching the continental United States, and the first-generation ICBMs, for which the Soviets had great hopes, proved too unreliable and vulnerable to serve as a practical weapon. Only a few of them were actually deployed.

American estimates of the size and effectiveness of the Soviet missile force had been highly speculative after May 1960 when U-2 overflights of the Soviet Union had been discontinued. This situation was rectified in the late summer of 1961 by the introduction of satellite reconnaissance, which gave American intelligence a more accurate assessment of the number of Soviet missiles. At that time a far-reaching political decision was made to tell Moscow that Washington knew of its vulnerability.

The risk inherent in such a course of action was not fully appreciated by President Kennedy, who feared only that the Soviets would now speed up their ICBM program. The president and his advisers were more sensitive to the need to moderate Khrushchev's bellicosity, alarmingly manifest in his several Berlin ultimatums, and thought this could be accomplished by communicating their awareness of American strategic superiority. The message was first conveyed by Roswell Gilpatric, deputy secretary of defense, in a speech delivered in October 1961, and was subsequently reinforced through other channels.

For Soviet leaders, the political implications of this message must have been staggering. Almost overnight the Kremlin was confronted with the realization that its nuclear arsenal was not an effective deterrent. In the words of Roger Hilsman (1967:164):

> It was not so much the fact that the Americans had military superiority—that was not news to the Soviets. What was bound to frighten them most was that the Americans knew that they had military superiority. For the Soviets quickly realized that to have reached this conclusion, the Americans must have made an intelligence breakthrough and found a way to pinpoint the location of the Soviet missiles that had been deployed as well as to calculate their total numbers. A "soft" ICBM system with somewhat cumbersome launching techniques . . . is an effective weapon for both a first strike . . . and a second, retaliatory strike so long as the location of the launching pads can be kept secret. However, if the

enemy has a map with all the pads plotted, the system will retain some of its utility as a first-strike weapon, but almost none at all as a second-strike weapon. The whole Soviet ICBM system was suddenly obsolescent.

The Soviets were in a quandary. The missile gap could be closed by a crash program to develop more effective second-generation ICBMs and perhaps a submersible delivery system. Such an effort was extremely costly and likely to meet strong opposition within the Soviet hierarchy. More importantly, a crash program did nothing to solve the short-term but paralyzing Soviet strategic inferiority that could be exploited by American leaders. The deployment of missiles in Cuba can be viewed as a bold attempt to resolve this dilemma. If this interpretation is correct, the American warning had the paradoxical impact of provoking the action it was designed to deter.

For 25 years all interpretations of Soviet motives and policies in the missile crisis were speculative. Existing Soviet commentaries, among them Khrushchev's memoirs (1970, 1974) and Anatoly Gromyko's study of the crisis (1971), contained enough obvious falsehoods to make them highly suspect sources. In October 1987, an extraordinary meeting took place in Cambridge, Massachusetts. A small group of scholars—myself among them—and former Kennedy administration officials met with three Soviet officials to talk about the origins and politics of the missile crisis. The Soviet representatives were Georgi Shaknazarov, a member of the Central Committee, Fedor Burlatsky, a former Khrushchev speech writer, and Sergei Mikoyan, a foreign ministry official and son of former deputy prime minister, Anastas I. Mikoyan.

All three Soviets were remarkably forthcoming; they shared with us their personal memories and feelings about the crisis and also what they had learned from talking to other officials at the time and subsequently. They did not always agree among themselves about important aspects of the crisis and were careful to distinguish between fact and opinion and between what they had witnessed or learned about only secondhand. The American participants, some of whom, like Raymond L. Garthoff and Robert McNamara, had extensive prior experience with Soviet officials, came away convinced that the Soviets were telling us the truth as they understood it.

The Russians advanced three explanations for the Cuban missile deployment: the perceived need to deter an expected American invasion of Cuba, to overcome Soviet strategic inferiority, and to attain political–psychological equality with the United States. They disagreed among themselves about the relative importance of these objectives for Khrushchev and other top leaders.

Sergei Mikoyan (1987:20, 40, 45–47) maintained that "there were only two thoughts: defend Cuba and repair the [strategic nuclear] imbalance." "Our 'pentagon'," he reported, "thought the strategic balance was dangerous, and sought parity." Marshall Rodion Malinovsky, Soviet defense minister, was adamant about the need to secure a more credible second-strike capability. "Khrushchev," too, Mikoyan continued, "was very concerned about a possible American attack. He worried . . . that somebody in the United States might think that a 17-to-1 superiority would mean that a first strike was possible." Mikoyan insisted, however, that Khrushchev's primary objective was to prevent an American assault on Cuba, something the Soviet leadership believed to be imminent.

Fedor Burlatsky and Georgi Shaknazarov agreed that Khrushchev wanted to protect Castro but maintained that he was even more concerned to do something to redress the strategic imbalance. They gave somewhat different reasons for why Khrushchev sought to do this.

Georgi Shaknazarov (1987:17–18, 58, 75–76) emphasized the military consequences of American superiority. "The main idea," as he saw it, "was to publicly attain parity." This was critical "because there were circles in the United States who believed that war with the Soviet Union was possible and could be won." The Cuban missile deployment was accordingly attractive to Khrushchev because it offered an immediate solution to the strategic vulnerability problem at very little cost. "It was an attempt by Khrushchev to get parity without spending resources we did not have."

Burlatsky (1987:17–18, 30–31, 115–16; 1987a:22) agreed that Soviet leaders "had a long sense of nuclear inferiority, especially at this time." Many Soviet officials, he reported, really feared an American first strike. But Khrushchev did not. He worried instead about American efforts to exploit its superiority politically. Khrushchev was particularly aggrieved by the Kennedy administration's deployment of missiles in Turkey, missiles that, because of their vulnerability to air attack, could only be used for a first strike or political intimidation. "Why do the Americans have the right to encircle us with nuclear missile bases on all sides," he complained to Burlatsky, "yet we do not have that right?" Burlatsky believed that the Jupiter deployment in Turkey had been the catalyst for Khrushchev's decision to send missiles to Cuba. "These missiles were not needed for deterrence," he explained. "Our 300 were already more than enough to destroy the United States—more than enough. So it was a psychological thing. From my point of view, it was the first step to strategic parity."

The Kennedy administration officials at the Cambridge conference admitted in retrospect that the Jupiter deployment had been provocative and unwise. Kennedy, it is apparent, had gone ahead with the deployment in spite of considerable opposition to it within State and Defense where the missiles were viewed as obsolescent and provocative. He did so because he was afraid that Khrushchev would misinterpret cancellation of the proposed deployment as a sign of his weakness and lack of resolve and become more emboldened in his challenges of Western interests in Berlin and elsewhere (Lebow, forthcoming).

Robert McNamara, secretary of defense during the Cuban crisis, was surprised that Khrushchev worried about a Cuban invasion. McNamara (1987:59) assured the Russians "that we had *no* plan to attack Cuba, and I would have opposed the idea strongly, if it ever came up." But he acknowledged that he could understand why the Soviets could have concluded that an invasion was imminent. The covert military operations the administration was conducting against Castro's regime, he agreed, conveyed the wrong impression about American intentions. They were "stupid but our intent was not to invade." From the vantage point of a quarter-century, McNamara was struck by the irony of the situation. "We thought those covert operations were terribly ineffective," he mused, "and you thought they were ominous."

McNamara and former national security advisor, McGeorge Bundy, were also surprised that the Soviets could have worried about a first strike. They knew that the administration had no intention of carrying one out! McNamara (1987:76) asked Shaknazarov: "Did your leaders actually believe that some of us thought it would be in our interest to launch a first strike?" Shaknazarov: "Yes. That is why it seems to me Khrushchev decided to put missiles in Cuba" (1987:76). The Russians went on to explain that their fears of a first strike had been aroused by the Kennedy administration's strategic buildup, its stationing of first-strike weapons in Turkey, and claims by its defense and military leaders that they could destroy the Soviet Union without losing more than 25 percent of its own population in a counterblow.

Although none of the Soviets mentioned the Gilpatric speech, they all emphasized the extent to which American military preparations and assertions of strategic superiority exacerbated Soviet strategic insecurities and pushed Khrushchev toward more confrontational policies. From this it is clear the Gilpatric speech and related American attempts to manipulate the cost-calculus of Soviet leaders backfired. The Kennedy administration's efforts to increase the cost to the Soviet Union of any challenge had the real and undesired effect of making such a challenge more attractive to Soviet leaders.

The missile crisis indicates that deterrence, as practiced by *both* superpowers, was provocative instead of preventive. Khrushchev and other top Soviet leaders conceived of the Cuban missiles as a means of deterring American military and political threats to Cuba and the Soviet Union. The American actions that provoked Khrushchev had in turn been envisaged by President Kennedy as prudent, defensive measures against perceived Soviet threats. Both leaders, seeking to moderate the behavior of their adversary, helped to bring about the very kind of confrontation they were trying to prevent.

## The Primacy of Self

Deterrence purports to describe an *interactive* process between the defender of a commitment and a would-be challenger. The defending state is expected to define and publicize its commitment and do its best to make that commitment credible in the eyes of its adversary. Would-be challengers are expected to assess accurately the defender's capability and resolve. The repetitive cycle of test and challenge is expected to provide both sides with an increasingly sophisticated understanding of each other's interests, propensity for risk taking, threshold of provocation, and style of foreign policy behavior.

My analysis of adversarial relationships indicates that the expectations that deterrence has about deterrer and challenger bear little relationship to reality. Challengers frequently focus on their own needs and do not consider, or distort if they do, the needs, interests, and capabilities of their adversaries. Moreover, at times they are motivated not by "opportunity," as deterrence theory expects, but rather by "vulnerability" and perceived weakness. Deterrers, in turn, may interpret the motives or objectives of a challenger in a manner consistent with their expectations, with little regard to the competing expectations of the challenger. Both sides may also prove insensitive to each other's signals. Under these conditions, deterrence is likely to fail. Even recurrent deterrence episodes may not facilitate greater mutual understanding. On the contrary, experience may actually hinder learning to the extent that it encourages tautological confirmation of misleading or inappropriate lessons.

## Implications for Deterrence Theory

Some empiricists (Achen and Snidal, Tetlock, Huth and Russett) contend that Stein and I misunderstand the purpose of social science theory. They argue that its goal is to predict human behavior, not necessarily to explain why that behavior occurs. With respect to deterrence, they insist that our sample, based only on deterrence failures, significantly biases our results. If we looked at deterrence successes, they argue, we would discover that deterrence is more successful than not. This would confirm the validity of deterrence theory as a predictor of state behavior.

These criticisms are methodologically and conceptually misguided. No analyst has yet succeeded, or ever will, in identifying the relevant universe of cases. Some of the reasons for this were made clear in the introduction of the chapter (see also Lebow and Stein, 1987b). Chief among these is the difficulty of identifying deterrence successes. The more successful deterrence is, the fewer the behavioral traces it leaves behind. The assertion that deterrence theory is a better-than-average predictor of state behavior cannot be demonstrated. The several empirical studies that attempt to validate this claim do not come to grips with this and other methodological obstacles.

Because the universe of relevant deterrence cases can never be identified, the significance of the cases examined becomes critical. But aggregate data analyses have made no attempt to weight their cases in favor of those they deem the most important or critical. Instead, they treat them as equivalent in every respect. Analysts who use the case study approach, by contrast, make strenuous efforts to identify critical cases and to justify their choices. The case study literature on deterrence failure has now identified an impressive number of important deterrence failures. These cases, which led to major crises and wars, stand as a sharp challenge to the expectations of deterrence as a theory and its practice as a strategy.

These cases of deterrence failure reveal important common features. Flawed information gathering, evaluation, attribution, and decision making on the part of initiators were most often responsible for the miscalculations that defeated deterrence. These all-important processes cannot be captured by aggregate analysis. This requires in-depth study of individual cases of deterrence failure and success. As the old French saying goes, God is to be found in the details.

These same empiricists acknowledge the power of our argument about the importance of domestic politics and strategic vulnerabilities in pushing states toward military challenges. But they—and even some deterrence critics (George and Smoke, 1974)—believe that deterrence theory could accommodate these considerations. To do so, they propose expanding it to incorporate a much wider range of political factors. Utility estimates could then take domestic politics, strategic vulnerabilities, and other factors into account instead of being based solely on narrow, and admittedly misleading, calculations of the relative military balance. This is easier said than done.

The incorporation of new variables would require an entirely new set of propositions to guide their weighing. Just how much importance, for example, should be given to national honor in comparison to the domestic political interests of leaders, ideological goals, or allied obligations? Deterrence theory provides no guidance for discriminating among these variables in order to construct a weighted model. For this reason, the Lebow–Stein critique of deterrence strikes at the theory, not only at deterrence as a real-world strategy.

Even if this problem could somehow be solved, deterrence theory would confront another insuperable obstacle. The incorporation of additional, more political variables would not help deterrence theory come to grips with the evidence that leaders deviate significantly from the process of rational choice in making critical foreign policy decisions. It is these deviations that largely account for deterrence failures. Models based on rational choice cannot therefore predict strategic decisions with any impressive degree of success. Analysts interested in improving the predictive capability of their models must abandon rational choice or, at the very least, incorporate significant elements of nonrational processes into their models. They cannot do this and retain the core of deterrence theory.

## NOTES

This chapter is based on Part I of "Beyond Deterrence," coauthored with Janice Gross Stein, *Journal of Social Issues* (Winter 1987) 43, no. 4, 5–71. Research and writing of the paper were supported by grants from the Carnegie Corporation of New York to Richard Ned Lebow and the Canadian Institute of Peace and Security to Janice Gross Stein.

1. For a fuller treatment of the detrimental effects of nuclear deterrence between the superpowers, see Lebow (1987a).

2. The definition of adequate communication and apparent resolve is difficult. Students of deterrence have traditionally assessed credibility with reference to how a would-be challenger's leaders perceived the commitment in question. There is a serious problem with this approach; it risks making determinations of credibility tautological. If a commitment is challenged, it is assumed not to have been credible. This ignores the possibility that the commitment should have been seen as credible but was not for any one of a number of reasons independent of the defender's military capability or resolve. For this reason, the appropriate test of credibility must be the judgment of disinterested third parties and not that of the

would-be challenger. As I will show, a challenger's receptivity to communications and its judgment about a commitment's credibility can be impaired by motivated biases. Thus, deterrent threats that appear credible to third parties can fail to be perceived as such by leaders intent on a challenge.

3. George and Smoke (1974:519–20) argue that the outcome of a deterrence encounter can also be mixed. This occurs, in their opinion, when deterrence succeeds in dissuading a country's leaders from choosing certain options as too risky but does not prevent them from embarking upon another, less-risky challenge of the status quo. Such cases undoubtedly occur but I am not persuaded by the examples George and Smoke cite.

4. These cases are Fashoda (1898), Korea (1903–1904), Agadir (1911), July 1914, the Chinese entry into the Korean War (1950), Cuba (1962), the Sino–Indian crisis of 1962, and the Arab–Israeli wars of 1967, 1969, and 1973.

# REFERENCES

Abel, E., 1966. *The Missile Crisis*. Philadelphia: Lippincott, p. 28.

Achen, C. H., and Snidal, D., 1988. Rational deterrence theory and comparative case studies. *World Politics,* fall.

Allison, G., 1971. *Essence of Decision: Explaining the Cuban Missile Crisis*. Boston: Little, Brown, pp. 52–56, 237–44.

Borg, D., and Okamoto, S., eds., 1973. *Pearl Harbor as History: Japanese–American Relations, 1931–1941*. New York: Columbia University Press.

Brodie, B., 1959. The anatomy of deterrence. *World Politics* 11 (January):173–92.

Burlatsky, F., 1987. *Proceedings of the Cambridge Conference on the Cuban Missile Crisis*. Cambridge, Mass.: 11–12 October 1987, mimeograph.

——— 1987a. The Caribbean crisis and its lessons. *Literaturnaya Gazeta* 11 November 1987:14.

Butow, R., 1961. *Tojo and the Coming of the War*. Stanford, Calif.: Stanford University Press.

George, A. L., and Smoke, R., 1974. *Deterrence in American Foreign Policy: Theory and Practice*. New York: Columbia University Press.

Gromyko, A. A., 1971. The Caribbean crisis, 2 parts. *Voprosy istorii* Nos. 4 & 8, English translation in Ronald R. Pope, *Soviet Views on the Cuban Crisis: Myth and Reality in Foreign Policy Analysis*. Lanham, Md.: University Press of America, 1982: pp. 161–226.

Heller, M. A., 1984. *The Iran–Iraq War: Implications for Third Parties*. JCSS Paper No. 23. Tel Aviv and Cambridge: Jaffee Center for Strategic Studies and Harvard University Center for International Affairs.

Hilsman, R., 1967. *To Move a Nation*. Garden City, N.Y.: Doubleday, pp. 164, 200–20.

Horelick, A., and Rush, M., 1966. *Strategic Power and Soviet Foreign Policy*. Chicago: University of Chicago Press, p. 141.

Hosoya, C., 1968. Miscalculation in deterrence policy: Japanese–U.S. relations, 1938–1941. *Journal of Peace Research* 2:79–115.
Huth, P., and Russett, B., 1984. What makes deterrence work? Cases from 1900 to 1980. *World Politics* 36(July)(4):496–526.
Ienaga, S., 1978. *The Pacific War, 1931–1945*. New York: Pantheon.
Ike, N., 1967. *Japan's Decision for War, Records of 1941: Policy Conferences.* Stanford, Calif.: Stanford University Press.
Janis, I., and Mann, L., 1977. *Decision Making: A Psychological Analysis of Conflict, Choice, and Commitment.* New York: Free Press.
Jervis, R., 1979. Deterrence theory revisited. *World Politics* 31(January):289–324.
Jervis, R., Lebow, R. N., and Stein, J. G., 1985. *Psychology and Deterrence.* Baltimore: Johns Hopkins University Press.
Kaplan, M. A., 1958. The calculus of deterrence. *World Politics* 11(October):20–44.
Kaufmann, W. W., 1954. *The Requirements of Deterrence*. Princeton, N.J.: Center of International Studies.
Kissinger, H. A., 1960. *The Necessity of Choice*. New York: Harper, pp. 40–41.
Khrushchev, N. S., 1970, 1974. *Khrushchev Remembers*. 2 vols. Strobe Talbott, ed. and trans. Boston: Little, Brown, pp. 488–505, 509–14.
Lebow, R. N., 1981. *Between Peace and War: The Nature of International Crisis*. Baltimore: Johns Hopkins University Press, pp. 26–29, 48–51, 101–228.
——— 1984. Windows of opportunity: Do states jump through them? *International Security* 9(Summer):147–86.
——— 1985. Conclusions. *Psychology and Deterrence*. Baltimore: Johns Hopkins University Press, pp. 204–11.
——— 1987a. Conventional and nuclear deterrence: Are the lessons transferable? *Journal of Social Issues* 43(4):171–91.
——— 1987b. Deterrence failure revisited. *International Security* 12(Summer):197–213.
——— The Turkish missile deployment and the origins of the Cuban Missile Crisis, forthcoming.
Lebow, R. N., and Stein, J. G., 1987a. Beyond deterrence. *Journal of Social Issues* 43(4):5–71.
——— 1987b. Beyond deterrence: Building better theory. *Journal of Social Issues* 43(4):155–69.
McNamara, R., 1987. *Proceedings of the Cambridge Conference on the Cuban Missile Crisis*. Cambridge, Mass.: 11–12 October 1987, mimeograph.
Mikoyan, S., 1987. *Proceedings of the Cambridge Conference on the Cuban Missile Crisis*. Cambridge, Mass.: 11–12 October 1987, mimeograph.
Milburn, T. W., 1959. What constitutes effective deterrence? *Journal of Conflict Resolution* 3(June):138–46.
Orme, J., 1987. Deterrence failures: A second look. *International Security* (Spring):16–124.

Quester, G., 1966. *Deterrence Before Hiroshima: The Airpower Background to Modern Strategy.* New York: Wiley.

Russett, B., 1967. Pearl Harbor: Deterrence theory and decision theory. *Journal of Peace Research* 4(2):89–105.

Schelling, T., 1966. *Arms and Influence.* New Haven, Conn.: Yale University Press, p. 374.

Shaknazarov, G., 1987. *Proceedings of the Cambridge Conference on the Cuban Missile Crisis.* Cambridge, Mass.: 11–12 October 1987, mimeograph.

Snyder, G. H., and Diesing, P., 1977. *Conflict Among Nations: Bargaining, Decision Making and System Structure in International Crisis.* Princeton, N.J.: Princeton University Press.

Snyder, J., 1985. Perceptions of the security dilemma in 1914. In R. Jervis, R. N. Lebow, and J. G. Stein, eds., *Psychology and Deterrence.* Baltimore: Johns Hopkins University Press, pp. 153–79.

Stein, J. G., 1985a. Calculation, miscalculation, and conventional deterrence I: The view from Cairo. In R. Jervis, R. N. Lebow, and J. G. Stein, eds., *Psychology and Deterrence.* Baltimore: Johns Hopkins University Press, pp. 34–59.

——— 1985b. Calculation, miscalculation, and conventional deterrence II: The view from Jerusalem. In R. Jervis, R. N. Lebow, and J. G. Stein, eds., *Psychology and Deterrence.* Baltimore: Johns Hopkins University Press, pp. 60–88.

Tatu, M., 1968. *Power in the Kremlin: From Khrushchev's Decline to Collective Leadership.* trans. by H. Katel. London: Collins.

Tetlock, P. E. 1987. Testing deterrence theory: Some conceptual and methodological issues. *Journal of Social Issues* 43(4):85–92.

Tripp, C., 1986. Iraq—ambitions checked. *Survival* 28(November–December): 495–508.

# 3

# Some Thoughts on "Deterrence Failures"

## GEORGE H. QUESTER

The concept of deterrence draws a wide variety of criticisms these days, criticisms that are often partially correct but that may also be importantly wrong. At the very least, the criticisms are sometimes put forward in a form that can be substantially misleading. An attempt will be made here to lay out several kinds of skepticism about the deterrence model which thus tend to be overstated or misstated, and some possibilities of why there might be a net bias, among many analysts, toward understating the rationality of national political leaders.

### Uniquely American, Uniquely Nuclear?

It is often argued, especially by more "hawkish" commentators, that deterrence is basically only an American idea, so that it is somehow "ethnocentric" for us to impute any similar reasoning to the Soviets.[1] This might be so, in the sense that most of the elaboration and articulation of deterrence concepts since World War II has indeed come from American writers, with West Europeans trailing in the American wake, and with Soviet spokesmen only very grudgingly and belatedly moving to acknowledge any awareness of mutual deterrence or mutual assured destruction. Yet this is also a wrong generalization, in that one can indeed find examples of the concept of deterrence, and even very comparable wordings, enunciated by the British analysts considering the possibilities of air warfare between World Wars I and II.[2] The German 1939 attitude on the use of bombers against homelands similarly very much fitted our model of mutual deterrence; Goering's last message to the British, relayed to London by the Swedish intermediary Birger Dahlerus as war was about to be declared, was that Germany would not bomb British cities as long as the RAF did not bomb those of Germany.[3]

A slightly different kind of misstatement then emerges in the widespread assumption that deterrence is a very modern idea, indeed unique to the nuclear age. As Glenn Snyder demonstrated nearly three decades ago (1961), however, we have all along been aspiring to a "deterrence by denial" whenever we speak of defense (we do not really wish to have to use whatever forces and fortifications we have erected along our borders; we hope that our neighbor will be dissuaded —deterred— from testing these forces, by the prospect of gaining nothing and suffering the inherent costs of combat). "Deterrence by punishment," whereby the enemy could not be held back from his prospective gains but would instead be deterred by the additional punishment we could inflict, in going above or around his advancing forces, is indeed more new, the product of new technologies of weapons delivery. But this, as just noted, also has a track record going back beyond 1945. We might date modern concepts of deterrence to the introduction of Zeppelin airships and biplane aircraft in World War I;[4] or we even may have to go back further, to the intertwining of commercial activity in the economic interdependence which emerged in the nineteenth century; naval forces could attack the coastal cities and the general prosperity of the other side, without necessarily first having defeated that side's forces.

Sir Julian Corbett thus pointed out such distinctions between countervalue and counterforce attack already in 1911 (Corbett, 1911:94–95), in what was partially a rebuttal to Mahan's stress totally and purely on counterforce. Whereas Mahan (1957:119) had dismissed countervalue attacks as needlessly brutal, Corbett instead several times referred to the countervalue potential of naval force as a "deterrent" (1911:36, 95–96).

The slippery slope leading from countervalue naval operations (as exemplified by the British blockade of Germany in World War I) to conventional air operations as envisaged and practiced in both World Wars, and then to nuclear attacks is illustrated all too well in our retrospective debates about the necessity or morality of having used nuclear weapons against Hiroshima and Nagasaki. Critics of this first and only use of nuclear weapons in anger insist that Japan was about to surrender in any event, such that there was no need to destroy these two cities.[5] When pressed, however, as to what would have forced the Japanese to surrender, their explanation at first often points to the conventional air attacks already under way, air attacks that killed 100,000 in a single night at Tokyo, more than died at Hiroshima or Nagasaki. Are these raids so much less immoral or brutal or countervalue?

Do they not involve all of the same notions of motivation that are at the base of our current deterrence mechanisms?

Some critics of the nuclear air raids of August 1945 would thus extend their disapproval to these conventional air raids as well, contending then that the naval blockade of Japan would by itself have caused such a Japanese surrender. But what was there about this blockade that could have caused such a concession? If the blockade had not, like the British blockade of Germany that forced Germany's 1918 surrender, been torturing the Japanese population by halting even food shipments, is there any reason to believe that a purely counterforce interdiction of only the strictly military shipments would have led the Japanese army and the Emperor to become peace-minded?

Deterrence by punishment consists of getting the other side to avoid starting a war; if a war has already been begun, its logical twin amounts to imposing pain so as to make the other side sue for peace. None of this is a new idea, and none of it is basically untested or prone to failure in test after test.

But what if the other side does not surrender? Or what if it is not dissuaded from beginning a war? Does this mean that deterrence is a flawed idea? It will be argued here that the idea is not flawed at all, for the concept of deterrence has always included prerequisites that first have to be satisfied, without which no one would have predicted that the other side would prefer peace to war.

## "Deterrence Failures"?

When wars break out, we often speak of failures of deterrence. This may be an excessively rich phrase, however, combining several distinct possibilities that do not necessarily have to go together. In a tautological sense, deterrence has indeed "failed" whenever a war has broken out—if we think of deterrence as being exactly equivalent to preserving peace and precluding armed aggressions. But is there any more than this to the "failure" phrase? Do we have grounds for inferring that the theory has failed as well, or that human reasoning processes have failed?

In some cases, yes, and in other cases, no. The theory of deterrence has indeed failed when statesmen and military leaders fail to notice, and be deterred by, powerful modes of retaliation. But many wars may erupt simply because of inadequate retaliatory threats. Would it not thus be more careful, when considering a crisis that led to war, to begin by saying only that "deterrence was not accomplished"?

A theory of deterrence indeed stipulates some prerequisites for preventing war. The side in danger of attack has to be able to punish the attacker regardless of how the military battle goes, to punish him with a damage outweighing the gains of an aggression, within the aggressor's own preferences.[6] And the defenders have to have made it reasonably obvious that they intend to inflict such damage when they have no way of repulsing the attack.

If the punishment is not capable of being sufficiently severe, or if the chances are good that the aggressor can preempt and preclude the retaliatory punishment strikes, then there will be no deterrence. And if the aggressor has real reason to doubt the victim's willingness to escalate to massive degrees of retaliation, then there will also be no deterrence. Given that most renditions of deterrence theory have required that these conditions be satisfied, it would hardly be indicated, as soon as any war breaks out, that the theory has failed.

For the *concept* of deterrence to come into doubt, one would rather have to conclude that human beings typically and most often fail to see whatever retaliatory options are directed against them, and fail to see the willingness of an adversary to go through with such threats. If we were to conclude that such perceptual failures were common in *some* kinds of situations, we would find it useful to sort out and identify those particular situations, but we would hardly be justified in concluding that such failures were more generally so common.

We might thus begin by suggesting that the phrase "deterrence failure" has been used a little too often and too easily, a phrase that may imply and denote more than has been proved, a phrase that may lead us to throw the baby out with the bathwater as we hunt for devices around which to build our reinforcements for peace. If Pakistan could not muster the incentives to dissuade India from entering what is today Bangladesh, or if Portugal could not muster anything to keep India from seizing Goa, we would be playing a mental trick on ourselves if we inferentially let this build a skepticism on the general mechanism of deterrence.

## Understating Rationality

But does not the apparent evidence of blindness by the opposing sides in a full-blown crisis, as each side barrels ahead in a game of "Chicken," suggest that political leaders are generically not up to the cognitive demands of deterrence? If a crisis leads to war, or even when war is averted, we again and again encounter evidence that one side or both has misread the risks and opportunities involved and also misread the intentions and signals of the adversary. If our theories of deterrence presume that decision makers have an elementary awareness of the opportunities and risks they are facing, the theory would then seem to be in considerable trouble if there is such a great deal of incompetence and misperception and psychological confusion in place.[7]

But it will be argued here that one of our more difficult tasks, in the analysis of strategic interactions, arises precisely in determining how little each side understood of the situation. Here we might not just be playing a mental trick on ourselves; statesmen owe it to their countries to try to play tricks on all of us outsiders. One can indeed offer several arguments on why we should guard against underrating the perceptiveness of the leaders whose actions we are reviewing.

First, and most generally, deception can play a role in successful strategy. One typically does better if the other participants in the political process, domestically or internationally, cannot tell exactly what we are doing or what we are thinking. If we must conceal the reality, we must thus create an image that is different from such reality. It would then be argued here that it is relatively easy to look less intelligent and less perceptive than the actuality; and it is quite difficult to look more intelligent and perceptive than the actuality. An intelligent stage actor can look stupid. Can a stupid stage actor look intelligent? If we extracted inferences about life from the dramatic stage, would we not then conclude that humanity was less intelligent than the average for all stage actors? And the same holds for that most important "stage" of all, the communications arenas on which we play out extended nuclear deterrence, and basic nuclear deterrence, and crisis diplomacy, and ordinary diplomacy.

Our tendency to underrate the intelligence and the perceptiveness of our political leaders may be compounded by some psychological needs of the press and of academia, each of which will feel somewhat envious of those who, rather than merely writing about political events, actually win elections or command armies, each of which is instead dedicated (thank God they are) to information and education, and hence very inclined to assume a greater intelligence for themselves than for their subjects. The political science bookshelf holds countless volumes, with regard to all levels of politics, recounting the follies and mistakes of actual political decision makers. It has relatively few books concluding that the actual practitioners are just as intelligent and perceptive as academics or possibly even more intelligent and perceptive.

When we turn to crisis situations, in the form of the game of chicken, we then encounter an additional reinforcement for any of our tendencies toward underrating the rationality of political leaders. For, in the game of chicken, we may do somewhat better for our own side if we can convince the other that we are stupid or fanatic or unaware of the peril facing us, that is, incapable of altering course and making a concession.[8] If one wishes to renew extended deterrence, to renew the process by which the United States "foolishly and irrationally" plans to escalate to nuclear warfare if Western Europe is ever invaded by Soviet conventional forces, it may thus help to pretend to be foolish and irrational more generally.

This ploy of the "rationality of irrationality" has been understood for decades. It was not invented in the nuclear age, for it has been applied by the adversaries in earlier international military crises, indeed in every war that became stalemated into an endurance contest or contest of resolve, and it has been applied also by domestic adversaries (for example, in a strike or an argument between college roommates). What is easy to underrate for such crises, however, is how very much of the historical record and of personal memories has been polluted by the game of mutual bluff in an endurance contest. Even if every instance of deterrence success or deterrence failure (absence of deterrence) had in actuality been governed by perfect information about the situation (with each side simply having to guess about the other side's motivation), the written records and oral history records of such events would be replete with imputations of mistakes and misperceptions: "We're eyeball to eyeball, and he just blinked."

## Some Possibilities of Overstating Rationality

Anyone asserting that most important political interactions are indeed so carefully and accurately calculated has, of course, to be wary of tautology here. We can go too far by saying that everyone who seems to be stupid, or seems to be unaware, is actually very wise and very aware (and indeed superwise, in concealing his wisdom and awareness, so as to trick us and catch us by surprise). By this kind of test, the world is full of Machiavellian geniuses. At the end, we would have a very unsatisfying set of unfalsifiable propositions. Surface indications of substantial folly can be evidence of great wisdom, but we are stuck with the fact that such surface indications could as well be evidence of actual folly.

One can fall also into another logical trap, when human error has indeed definitely been documented, of responding that such error was simply rational by a higher and prior evaluation. "The actor decided that it wasn't to his interest to familiarize himself with the data relevant to his interest, etc., etc." This would amount to an endless regression whereby we always concluded that there was a rational calculation at the end of the trail, a calculation that we could never prove but always had to assume.

There is also, of course, some tendency that we all may have toward false rationalization, rationalization after the fact. If we did something mindlessly or inadvertently, we may feel sheepish for having done so. Given the time to concoct an explanation for our actions, we may be good at coming up with some cleverness that was never there at the time. We may only have had 10 seconds to think of what to do when we blunder into a bank robbery in progress. When we have hours afterward to think about our behavior, we can perhaps devise a quite complicated rationale for why we ran, why we took three minutes to dial the telephone calling the police, why we did not park our car so as to block the escape route for the bank robbers, and so on. Much of this devising of rationales after the event is thus perhaps to make us feel better about our own wisdom and acuity, and we find it all pleasantly persuasive.

But if we find it good for our self-esteem to impute such complicated calculations to ourselves, it is similarly good for our egos to deny such calculations to the minds of others. Relatively few of us, if we dislike someone else, react by claiming that "he is smarter than he lets on." Much more tempting is the conclusion that "he isn't half as smart as he pretends to be."

If there are thus instances in which we are led to exaggerate, rather than underrate, the wisdom and perceptiveness of the arrangers and the subjects of deterrence, it would be asserted here that such tendencies toward overstating crisis-decision-maker acuity are still minor, as compared to the temptations and tendencies we have toward understatement. Some of us may see elaborate schemes that were never really there, in the minds of decision makers. But most of us instead overrate the ignorance or proclivity to error in such people.

Staying away from the above traps of possible tautology, we might still make the empirical guess that very much of politically relevant behavior is motivated and calculated, with only a little being the opposite. A nice example of the *latter* would be the death of the Russian ambassador at the Congress of Vienna, whereupon one of the other participants was heard to respond: "Now, why did he choose to do that?" No one is very likely to believe that political figures *choose* to die (somehow calculating that mobilizing the bodily energies to ward off a disease had lesser utility than giving in). The important point about this story is that virtually everything else the Russian ambassador and all the other ambassadors were doing did have a "why" and that it was often a "why" that was not so easy to detect.

Much of what happens in strategy indeed happens precisely because the actors see linkages between certain actions and certain results; the actions are caused by anticipations. If one wishes to discuss the short-circuits in such processes, it may yet be very misleading to imply that the circuitry is not indeed there or that we have any good substitute for such circuitry.

## Social Science Casts of Mind

We might say something here about casts of mind in the social sciences, and about the prejudices these bring to bear in the analysis of nuclear deterrence. At some very substantial risk of oversimplification, one might conlude that political science is not itself a discipline but rather a subject area, an area ripe for occupation by one or the other of two conquering disciplinary armies: that of economics or that of sociology–psychology. The issue between these two disciplinary perspectives might then be almost exactly the issue we have been outlining here. Is most of politically important and interesting behavior to be explained best by perceptions about consequences, by expectations that stimulate actions by those experiencing such expectations?[9] Or is most of such behavior rather much more inadvertent and unanticipated, the sum total of a great deal of rubbing of shoulders, with strategy and expectations playing little or no role?

The economist, and any political scientist who thinks like an economist (a category that probably includes most strategists), thus believes in one form or another of "rationality."

We are not dealing here with any perfect sense of rationality, whereby correct information has been obtained by the decision maker on all relevant questions, and where such decision makers are totally free of neuroses and personality defects. Rather we are assuming a "bounded rationality," where such national leaders may indeed be guided by wrong information or imperfect information but where outsiders can make guesses about such information. (If someone holds up a bank using a wooden model of a gun, he is applying a rational model to deter the "misinformed" bank tellers from resisting his demands for money, while at the same time avoiding the risk of shooting and the higher criminal penalties that would come if he were apprehended carrying an actual deadly weapon.)

Similarly the degree of rationality presupposed for deterrence assumptions, and for most strategists' calculations, does not require any total mental health on the adversary side. Rather it presupposes some regularity of tastes and preferences, merely some predictability. And in the case of nuclear deterrence, it may presuppose nothing more than that the other side would prefer its cities *not* be destroyed by nuclear explosions. (If we ever find a national leader in charge of a national nuclear stockpile who is indifferent to such a destruction of his own cities, or who would welcome such destruction, for reasons of psychosis, or for any other reason, we would indeed have a deterrence failure of monumental proportions.)

Before one becomes too skeptical about the applicability of such rational models, one should consider the hundreds of mechanisms we encounter every day in the society around us that clearly presuppose the very same thing. Law enforcement, our commercial interactions, and our daily interactions with spouses and in-laws are replete with mechanisms whereby one party is trying to motivate the other by carrot-and-stick mechanisms, and where the other is trying to do the same in reverse.

The contrary emphasis of sociology or psychology tends to assert that the more interesting parts of our social processes are to be explained instead by missed signals and unanticipated consequences. In step with this, many of the discussions of "deterrence failure" are thus inclined to the possibility that messages have not been received in the same form as they were sent, that opposite sides have seen the costs of war or of crises very differently, that the two sides are generally more blind than perceptive as they walk through a crisis (and not only blind because they choose to be blind as some kind of bargaining ploy).

For this second, antirational perspective, the working assumption is thus more often that communications do not happen, that messages do not make a difference. Or at least the communications have a life of their own, out of the control of the sender and the receiver; the messages get garbled, in a pattern that only a specialist in the confusions and defects of mental and social processes could have predicted.

For the believer in rational models, this throws away too much. When deterrence does not happen, when wars break out, the standard strategist and the economist, and anyone with an economist's cast of mind, would tend more often to suspect that an insufficient message got sent or that a very complicated game was being played. Because deterrence theory specifies the shape of the correct message for dissuading an adversary from attacking, this would hardly amount to a failure of deterrence theory, any more than the coldness of a house without a furnace amounts to a failure in theory of physics (would we ever call it a "physics failure"?).

Neither of these dominant working perspectives has a monopoly of wisdom, of course (or else university deans could easily choose to fold their economics department or their department of sociology). There may indeed be portions of our deterrence phenomenon where one working bias or the other could be strongly recommended; our task has generally been to sort out the cases for which deterrence is more likely to "fail," and where it is quite likely succeed.

## Nuclear Deterrence Versus Conventional Deterrence

It has to be stressed that nuclear deterrence has not failed. Where nuclear threats have been in place, they have not been challenged (or else none of us would be here to discuss our logical doubts about the deterrence concept). We have rather here been contemplating how deterrence has several times indeed failed in *conventional* confrontations and making the pessimistic projection that this mechanism might therefore fail as well for the nuclear case.

Supporters of a reliance on *nuclear* deterrence might indeed argue that the retaliatory threats are simply much more awesome, and therefore more reliable and effective, in the nuclear case, so that inferences from any failures of conventional threats to dissuade an attacker would be very misleading. But skeptics about a reliance on nuclear deterrence could respond that the world has merely been lucky thus far, that the period of time for which we have been tracking this perfect record for nuclear deterrence has been much too short to amount to any kind of serious test.

In any event, the very same awesomeness of punishment that allegedly makes nuclear deterrence so much more reliable than conventional deterrence poses much more of a disaster for all of us, if deterrence here were ever to fail.

Psychologists and others would certainly not bet with certainty on any proposition that the larger the magnitude of the threatened punishment, the greater the effectiveness of the threat. Perhaps a greater scale of punishment will reach the minds that matter on the other side; but perhaps these minds will be so much repulsed by the horror of such punishments that they refuse to think about these realities and hence act as if the punishment were not at all there; such a repression possibility poses a major difficulty for any mechanism of deterrence and dissuasion.

What also can happen, with our "perfect scorecard of deterrence," is that skeptics begin to doubt and question whether there were ever any dangers of aggression to be deterred in the first place. Did Stalin ever really wish to send his troops into Bruxelles and Paris, deterred only by the retaliatory threats posed by U.S. nuclear weapons? Would the United States by now really have intervened to rescue the Hungarians and the Czechs and the Poles, being deterred only by the retaliatory threats of Soviet nuclear weapons? An assessment of nuclear deterrence is burdened not only by inferences from failures of conventional deterrence, for it is also likely to be denied credit for any successes, if analysts cannot prove to themselves that any aggressive tendencies needed to be deterred in the first place.

The irony is thus that mutual deterrence is so very self-punishing, in terms of the credits it gets for effectiveness. We never really know what this world's aggressors were planning and contemplating, except when they are defeated and forced to surrender "unconditionally," but the development of nuclear weapons has meant that the archives of Moscow and Washington will never be captured by hostile armies as were those of

Berlin and Tokyo. Because of Stalin's atomic bomb, we will never be sure about how much he was deterred by the U.S. atomic bomb.

For every case of a "deterrence success," the possibility will thus remain that no deterrence was needed, and that no effect was achieved, that no test was passed. NATO self-evaluations are too often treated with snickers, like the man who proclaims, "May this house be safe from tigers," with no tigers appearing thereafter. Perhaps the Russians never wished to impose Communist rule on Western Europe by force of arms. By contrast, a deterrence failure is there for all to see, as wars break out, as invasions roll ahead, as (if the instrument that was challenged was the nuclear force of either of the sides) the entire world might be destroyed.

There is nonetheless the possibility of a fairer test here, if we are only patient enough. If the world goes on for 100 years, instead of merely 40, at the current pace of challenges to nuclear deterrence and the current pace of nonuse of nuclear weapons, some of us will surely conclude that this was not merely a statistical fluke, based on insufficient evidence and insufficient testing, but rather a salient downturn in the frequency of warfare and in the proclivity of men to use weapons whenever they have built and deployed them.

If the next six decades at all match the past four, we will change our assessment of nuclear deterrence, of whether it is not saliently more reliable than conventional deterrence.

## Some Concluding Comments

In effect, this is an argument that the emperor sometimes indeed has clothes, and that a very clever emperor could even be better off pretending to be naked. This is particularly true whenever each side is up to playing games of deterrence and compellence, and where each side's commitment to whatever is at stake might be questioned and challenged by the other side. In a mature game of Chicken, the winner will often be the national leader who does the best job of pretending that he does not appreciate the disaster that is imminent or that he does not understand the threats and other messages the opposite side is transmitting. That is, the winner may be the leader who does the most to offer ammunition to those who question whether deterrence theories make sense.

If one has read Thomas Schelling (1960), an obvious lesson to be drawn is that one should pretend not to have read him or at least pretend not to understand his logic. A mature and rational understanding of all of the mechanisms of bargaining and deterrence suggests that one should conceal that understanding, that one should look irrational whenever this may frighten the other side into making a concession first.

Another way of phrasing our general analytical disagreement here would be as follows: Critics of deterrence theory imply that deterrence is actually quite difficult to achieve. But in truth, basic deterrence is very easy to accomplish. There is no doubt in anyone's mind that the Soviet Union will suffer terrible retaliation if it attacks the United States itself and that the United States will suffer similar retaliation if it attacks the Soviet Union. Where there is much more doubt comes in "extended deterrence," whether the United States would really retaliate if Moscow launched an invasion only of Western Europe or South Korea, or whether the Soviet Union would retaliate if the United States were intervening only in one of the East European satellites.[10]

The NATO countries and South Korea are not nearly as secure as some other areas valuable to Americans, for example, Japan, Britain, New Zealand, and Australia, where deterrence takes care of itself as "deterrence by denial." There is no real threat of a Soviet invasion of Japan, for the Japanese Self-Defense Forces, perhaps even the Japanese police forces, could cope with all the amphibious forces Moscow has developed. As a West German general put it, "The Sea of Japan is worth 90 divisions." Because South Korea and the NATO countries of Western Europe are in effect peninsulas sticking out from the Eurasian land mass, vulnerable to a possible conventional invasion, and because they are valuable to the United States but not quite as assuredly valuable as the state of Maryland, the risk of a "deterrence failure," that is, an absence of deterrence, would be predicted by deterrence theory itself.

It is in crises about places that are vulnerable in either direction and valuable, but not absolutely valuable, to the two sides that we thus get into exercises of "you may be deterred because I will not be deterred." It is well understood by game theorists and by those who simply use derivatives of game theoretical analysis to underpine deterrence reasoning that chicken is an underdetermined game. So be it; politicians have been playing this game for a long time.

## Notes

1. For an example of an argument that Americans are ethnocentric here, see Gray (1986).

2. Interwar British discussions of deterrence are to be found in Griffin (1938).

3. On the last-minute signals between Berlin and London on aerial bombardment, see Documents on British Foreign Policy (1949:636–38; 1954:485).

4. The air attacks of World War I are outlined in Charlton (1936).

5. For a detailed analysis of the Japanese surrender, see Butow (1954) and Feis (1961).

6. A succinct outline of the requirements of deterrence for rationality can be found in Ellsberg (1960).

7. For some examples of skepticism about rationality during crises, see Lebow (1981), Kinder and Weiss (1978), and Steinbruner (1974).

8. On the mechanisms of the game of Chicken, see Snyder (1971).

9. For a nice illustration of rational modeling explaining what might have looked unexplainable, see Brams (1976).

10. On the special burdens imposed by extended deterrence, see Pierre (1984).

## References

Brams, S. J., 1976. *Paradoxes in Politics*. New York: Macmillan.
Butow, R. C., 1954. *Japan's Decision to Surrender*. Palo Alto, Calif.: Stanford University Press.
Charlton, L. E. O., 1936. *War Over England*. London: Longmans Green and Co.
Corbett, Sir J., 1911. *Principles of Maritime Strategy*. London: Conway Maritime Press.
Documents on British Foreign Policy, 1949. *Third Series*, Vol. II. London: H.M.S.O.
——— 1954. *Third Series*, Vol. VII. London: H.M.S.O.
Ellsberg, D., 1960. *The Crude Analysis of Strategic Choices*. Santa Monica, Calif.: RAND Corporation Publication No. P-2183.
Feis, H., 1961. *Japan Subdued*. Princeton, N.J.: Princeton University Press.
Gray, C. S., 1986. *Nuclear Weapons and National Style*. Lanham, Md.: Hamilton Press.
Griffin, J., 1938. *Glass Houses and Modern War*. London: Chatto and Windus.
Kinder, D. R., and Weiss, J. A., 1978. In lieu of rationality. *Journal of Conflict Resolution* 22(4):707–35.
Lebow, R. N., 1981. *Between Peace and War*. Baltimore: Johns Hopkins University Press.
Mahan, A. T., 1957. *The Influence of Seapower Upon History: 1660–1783*. New York: Hill and Wang reprint (originally published 1890).
Pierre, A. J., ed., 1984. *Nuclear Weapons in Europe*. New York: Council on Foreign Relations.
Schelling, T. C., 1960. *The Strategy of Conflict*. Cambridge, Mass.: Harvard University Press.

Snyder, G., 1961. *Deterrence and Defense.* Princeton, N.J.: Princeton University Press.

——— 1971. "Prisoner's dilemma" and "chicken" models in international relations. *International Studies Quarterly* 15(1):66–103.

Steinbruner, J. D., 1974. *The Cybernetic Theory of Decision.* Princeton, N.J.: Princeton University Press.

# 4
# Failed Bargain Crises, Deterrence, and the International System

## PAUL W. SCHROEDER

This chapter represents a historian's contribution to the general effort at developing a satisfactory deterrence theory for the nuclear age. It attempts both to add something to the fund of information and categories political scientists and others use to analyze international crises and to urge a central idea. Though for certain purposes it may be useful to treat international crises as if they were bilateral encounters (aggressor versus defender, revisionists versus status quo powers, etc.), a satisfactory deterrence theory needs to go beyond this. International crises are really multilateral encounters in which the actions and reactions of powers outside the main confrontation are as important as those of the two opponents, and in which the kind of system or regime of international conduct prevailing at the time has as much to do with the success or failure of deterrence as do the deterrence methods and strategy themselves. Some may detect in this opening statement a prelude to the familiar complaint from historians against political scientists and others that in subjecting international politics to quantitative, behavioral, or other kinds of scientific analysis, they oversimplify and distort it, especially by treating it as behavior rather than conduct. This is not my purpose. For one thing, most behavioral scientists know what they are doing and have good reasons for their methods. For another, most analysts of international politics, including game theorists, treat it precisely as purposive conduct, not behavior. But most important, my argument is intended less to emphasize the role of individual calculation and action in international politics than to limit it, to stress how certain collective and institutional aspects of international politics control purposive acts of agency in it and help determine their outcome.

A good starting point for discussing international crises and deterrence is R. N. Lebow's interesting and instructive book, *Between Peace and War: The Nature of International Crisis* (1981). In this work Professor Lebow divides modern international crises into three categories—justification of hostility, spin-off, and brinkmanship—and concentrates on the latter category of brinkmanship crises in analyzing how and why deterrence succeeds or fails. Lebow's approach and much of his argument seem to me quite sound. For the purposes of this essay, one disagreement is important, concerning the origins and nature of the Bosnian crisis of 1908–1909. Lebow interprets it as a brinkmanship crisis. Broadly speaking, he contends that Austria–Hungary and its ally Germany engineered the crisis. By forcing Russia and Serbia to accept Austria's annexation of Bosnia–Herzegovina, they humiliated Serbia and imposed a diplomatic defeat and loss of prestige on Russia, so as to prove that the Austro–German alliance was more effective than the Franco–Russian one (Lebow, 1981:60–69). Clearly, the Bosnian crisis became a brinkmanship crisis in the course of its development and had some of the results Lebow describes. Its origins, however, involved not brinkmanship, but the reverse of it—a genuine effort at Austro–Russian rapprochement and cooperation. In September 1908 Counts Aehrenthal and Izvolski, the Austrian and Russian foreign ministers, reached agreement over how to settle the issues of Bosnia and the Turkish Straits in a mutually advantageous fashion. It was the breakdown of this bargain in the course of its implementation just a few days later that created a crisis that turned into a test of strength between the opposed alliance systems (Schmitt, 1937; Bridge, 1972; Carlgren, 1955).

If my interpretation is correct, it may suggest that Lebow's typology serves better for analyzing what crises develop into and what results they have in international politics, rather than how they arise and what causes and purposes are behind them. Be that as it may, many crises in modern history, like the Bosnian crisis, stem not from conflicting purposes but from cooperation or agreement, the breakdown of apparently successful bargains. In short, many crises are in origin and nature failed bargain crises.[1]

This calls for definition. A failed bargain crisis does not mean one arising from failure in bargaining. Virtually all crises by definition involve a failure or inability to reconcile crucial differences. Instead, a failed bargain crisis must be one in which a central cause of the crisis is the breakdown of a successfully negotiated agreement. And because all agreements break down or are revised sooner or later, the term will here be restricted to agreements that fail within a reasonably short time after their conclusion (at most two or three years).

Leaving aside for the moment the reasons why bargains fail and how this affects the resultant international crises, the first thing to establish is that failed bargain crises are commonplace, that failed bargains constitute the central factor in some international crises, are a major element in most, and are rarely entirely absent or unimportant. To show this, I will list 20 major crises between 1789 and 1914 that by the criteria stated qualify as failed bargain crises. The list, with just enough description of each to make it comprehensible, reads as follows:

1. The Austro–Prussian crises of 1793–1795, which brought the two countries to the brink of war in 1795. These arose over the breakdown of their alliance against France in 1792 and subsequent agreements on the conduct of the war and the compensations and indemnities each should receive (Sorel,1986 (1892–1913); Blanning, 1986; Lord, 1915).
2. The Austro–French crisis of 1798–1799 that led to renewed war. This arose directly from the breakdown of their peace treaty at Campo Formio in October 1797, particularly its provisions on Germany and Italy (Blanning, 1986; Schroeder, 1987).
3. The Anglo–Russian crisis and virtual war of 1800–1801, which originated in the breakdown of their wartime partnership against France in 1799 (Mackesy, 1974; 1984).
4. The Anglo–French crisis and renewed war in 1803, a product of the breakdown of the peace treaty of Amiens of 1802 over the British refusal to evacuate Malta as the treaty demanded, a stand prompted by a series of French expansionist moves in Europe and elsewhere (Lefebvre, 1969; Ziegler, 1965).
5. The Austro–French crisis and war of 1804–1805, involving the breakdown of the Peace of Luneville in late 1801 and of subsequent French assurances to Austria, particularly concerning Italy (Deutsch, 1938; Lefebvre, 1969).
6. The Franco–Prussian war in 1806, which arose out of the breakdown of their treaties of Schönbrunn and Paris in December 1805 and February 1806. The general issue was Prussian security in the face of French control of southern and western Germany; the particular quarrel concerned the extent of Prussia's zone of neutrality in northern Germany (Deutsch, 1938; Fugier, 1954).
7. The Russo–Turkish war in 1807, caused by the breakdown of their alliance against France and the agreements they had reached in 1806 over the Danubian Principalities (Saul, 1970; Puryear, 1951; Mouraviev, 1954).
8. The Franco–Russian crisis, beginning in late 1810 and culminating in Napoleon's invasion in 1812. This stemmed from the collapse of the Russo–French partnership established at Tilsit (1807) and Erfurt (1808)

and involved a series of failed bargains over Poland, the Continental System, and the Ottoman Empire (Vandal, 1891–1896).
9. The Polish–Saxon crisis at the Congress of Vienna in 1814–1815. This involved disputes over agreements on Poland reached between Austria, Russia, and Prussia at Reichenbach and Teplitz in 1813 (Kraehe, 1983).
10. The Russo–Turkish crisis of 1821–1823. This arose directly from Russia's agreeing in early 1821 to allow Turkey to occupy the Danubian Principalities and to crush an insurrection there and in Greece and from Turkish violations of the implicit and explicit terms of the agreement (Schroeder, 1962).
11. The Russo–Turkish war in 1828. It derived in major part from differences over the meaning of the Convention of Akkermann concluded by the two powers in 1826 (though the central cause was intervention by England, France, and Russia in the struggle between Turkey and Greece) (Crawley, 1930).
12. The Anglo–French crisis of 1840, caused by the breakdown of an Anglo–French understanding and partnership in the Near East reached in 1839 (Webster, 1951).
13. The Crimean War, pitting Britain, France, and Turkey against Russia in 1854. This involved the breakdown of at least one clear-cut agreement and several proposed agreements among the European powers in 1853 for settling the Russo–Turkish quarrel (Schroeder, 1972).
14. The Austro–Prussian crisis and war in 1866. This derived from the breakdown of their alliance of 1864 against Denmark and the Gastein Convention they had concluded in 1865 over Schleswig–Holstein and other German questions (Lutz, 1985).
15. The Austro–Russian crisis and near-war in 1877–1878. This grew out of a breakdown of their previous cooperation in the Balkans from 1875 on and particularly out of the violation by Russia of the Budapest Accords of early 1877 in the Russo–Turkish Treaty of San Stefano in 1878 (Rupp, 1941).
16. The prolonged crisis between Austria and Russia over Bulgaria in 1884–1886. This arose similarly out of the breakdown of their previous attempts as members of the Three Emperors Alliance to settle the Bulgarian problem in cooperation (Bridge, 1972).
17. The Anglo–French quarrel over the British occupation of Egypt from 1882 on, which ultimately led to a confrontation and threat of war at Fashoda in 1898. This resulted directly from the breakdown of previous Anglo–French arrangements for the Dual Control of Egypt from 1876 through early 1882 (Gifford and Louis, 1971; Ramm, 1971).

18. The Russo–Japanese War in 1904. Here a series of failed bargains was involved, including the Nishi–Rosen Agreement of 1898 and the Russo–Chinese convention of 1902 governing the Russian evacuation of Manchuria (Nish, 1985).
19. The Austro–Russian (Bosnian) crisis of 1908–1909—already discussed.
20. The Franco–German crisis of 1911 (Second Moroccan or Agadir crisis). So far as these two countries were concerned, the crisis was caused by the breakdown of their agreement for cooperation in Morocco at Casablanca in 1909 (Poidevin, 1969).

There is no reason to believe that failed bargain crises were particularly characteristic of nineteenth century international politics. The eighteenth century seems to have had even more,[2] and one can easily think of more recent crises that seem to fit the pattern—the failed bargain at Munich that led to the crises of March–April and August 1939, the failed Nazi–Soviet bargains of August–September 1939 leading to war in 1941, the failed wartime agreements among America, Britain, and Russia contributing to the Cold War, failed or failing ABM and SALT agreements promoting Soviet–American tensions today.

The analyst of international politics is not likely to feel particularly surprised or enlightened by all this. He already knew that failed bargains frequently cause serious trouble, and he may see here another historian insisting on his own taxonomic scheme out of concern for the purity of his art, regardless of its utility or lack of it for purposes of analysis. Moroever, he probably knows enough history to see that this list of alleged failed bargain crises does not present a relatively homogenous group of developments but a very mixed bag. In some instances, the cooperation and shared purposes involved in the initial bargains were minimal, far outweighed by latent conflict, where in others they were more genuine. The bargains failed for all sorts of reasons—a deliberate intent if not to break them at least to exploit one's own advantages to the hilt, clear-cut breaches of faith, misinterpretations or disputed interpretations, inability to fulfill commitments, changed circumstances, and more. How then is the concept of the failed bargain crisis useful for the general analysis of international politics, and how is it relevant to deterrence in particular?

I do not propose final answers to these questions but can offer at least a prima facie reply on the second one. Deterrence theory often seems to assume that it is possible to distinguish between powers seeking to alter the status quo and those defending it, those initiating a threat or an aggressive act and those seeking to deter it. Analysts undoubtedly know that these dichotomies are oversimplified for analytic purposes. Yet if failed bargains are as central to crises as it would seem, these already elastic and inexact distinctions between initiator and defender may stretch to the breaking point. Who is the aggressor in a case where the initiator of some coercive action against another state can plausibly claim that he is merely policing cooperation, enforcing conformity to a bargain? Who is defending the status quo and who threatening it when (as in the Bosnian crisis) the bargain the two actors had reached and over which they were now in conflict concerned precisely how to change the status quo in a peaceful, cooperative fashion? The practical implications of this problem are as disturbing for deterrence theory as its theoretical ones. It must make a great difference in the application and efficacy of a deterrent response, psychologically and otherwise, if an "aggressor" can plausibly claim that deterrence is only being used to keep him from receiving his share of a bargain—a claim often made and sometimes genuinely held.

The concept of the failed bargain crisis, unfortunately, may be relevant to deterrence theory without being useful, serving only to add additional complications. One might suppose that if the various kinds of failed bargain crises could be analyzed and classified according to the causes or grounds for their failure, this would help in deciding what kinds of deterrence would be most effective in different situations. For instance, if one side clearly violates a bargain or gives evidence of never having intended to observe it, stronger coercive measures against it might be considered necessary than in cases of plausible disagreement between the two sides over the terms of the bargain. In these latter instances, the goal might be to apply only enough deterrence to keep either side from imposing a unilateral solution until they could negotiate a settlement. This sounds like a good rule of thumb, but the difficulties involved in arriving at any principle or general rule for its application are staggering. Usually the difference between the two kinds of cases becomes apparent, if at all, only by hindsight. Even a notorious aggressor like Napoleon or a statesman like Bismarck who makes no secret of his desire to overthrow the status quo and his willingness to violate treaties can be adept at playing the role of the injured party and maneuvering his opponent into committing the first overt violation or aggressive act. Britain was the technical violator of the Treaty of Amiens in 1803; Prussia was the technical aggressor in 1806, Austria in 1809 and 1866. Few historians would argue that they were the real aggressors or the states that most needed deterring. Moreover, even where the real aggressor is clearly known, it is far from certain that massive threats will serve to deter him or even that the bargain or status quo being defended is worth defending. Part of the dilemma that German liberals and others faced in 1866 was that they knew that Prussia under Bismarck was pursuing a ruthless *Machtpolitik* and destroying all standards of international conduct. At the same time they believed on plausible grounds that the status quo in Germany was intolerable and untenable and that a victory for Austria would be a victory for reaction.

Furthermore, the very attempt to classify failed bargain crises according to the reasons for their failure appears on reflection impossible. In most instances the causes for failure are multiple and intertwined. Worse still, they change in the course of the dispute, so that it becomes virtually impossible to assign a principal ground for the breakdown. For example, though the Austro–Prussian alliance of 1792 was plagued from the outset by latent distrust and uncertainty over the terms of the agreement, both sides genuinely intended at first to maintain their bargain. Changed circumstances (military misfortune, financial exhaustion, unrest in Poland) quickly made the original bargain impossible to execute, and then bad faith (the desire to get out of the bargain and/or exploit it against one's partner) took over in both states, especially Prussia. This was certainly a failed bargain crisis, and it is important at least for the historian to see it as such. It helps demonstrate how the general character of international politics and the international system at that time made virtually any bargain, no matter how sincerely intended, almost impossible to sustain. But it seems arbitrary to designate just what made it fail, or what kind of failed bargain crisis it was.

A more hopeful line of inquiry might be to investigate how deterrence works in sustaining bargains or failing to do so. This would involve asking such questions as: How and why do states use threats to enforce bargains? What different reasons may they have for resorting to threats, and what different ends beyond simple compliance may these threats serve? How do varied circumstances affect the efficacy or inefficacy of such threats in failed bargain cases? How may they promote or deter conflict?

These are important questions and I see no reason why they could not be investigated systematically and fruitfully. That such investigation would lead to clear-cut theoretical or practical results, however, is doubtful. Even a superficial look at failed bargain crises reveals, as one would expect, that states employ a wide range of threats and inducements to enforce bargains, that they do so for a variety of motives, that many different circumstances influence their choice of means and their efficacy, and that various results, immediate and long-range, can and do occur. The trouble is that again no usable pattern seems to emerge from this bewildering variety. For example, states regularly attribute illegitimacy to the other side's actions in justifying their use of threats in failed bargain crises. But almost any argument for attributing illegitimacy or refuting the charge is likely to serve, however transparent it may be. One can distinguish in theory between threats made to police cooperation and threats made to ensure survival or secure gains, but in practice these aims tend to merge or change in the course of events. For example, in 1866 Austria initially mobilized against Prussia primarily for purposes of policing cooperation and defending the status quo. But having mobilized, the Austrians planned in case of war to strengthen their own position in Germany and to weaken greatly that of Prussia, thereby overthrowing the status quo. Plainly states attempt to enforce bargains through threats for additional reasons besides the intrinsic value of the original stakes—concern for reputation and honor, a desire to demonstrate resolve, the desire to shape the opponent's behavior in general, even a concern for international law or general rules of conduct. The difficulty as always is that in most cases many such reasons, these and others, can be detected. The more one finds, the more difficult it is to establish their relative importance. Worst of all, it is often impossible to determine clearly whether threats ostensibly made to enforce bargains really represent deterrence or aggression. After more than a century of investigation, historians are still not agreed on whether the threatening actions taken by Britain and France against Russia in late 1853 were designed to stop Russian aggression against Turkey and enforce compliance with the European Concert or were really intended to force Russia into war.[3]

One more problem must be kept in mind. Failed bargains clearly can and do produce crises, but not all crises involve failed bargains, and not all failed bargains result in crises. In the period 1789–1914 there were probably as many failed bargains that passed without serious consequences as those that caused important conflict. Nor does there seem to be a necessary or clear correlation between, on the one hand, the nature of the failed bargain and the intrinsic importance of the stakes involved, and on the other, the nature and gravity of the conflict engendered. The failed Anglo–French bargain on the Eastern Question in 1840, almost purely a question of French honor and prestige, produced a major crisis and threat of war; a similar failed Anglo–French bargain on the Spanish Marriages in 1845–1846, this time a question of British honor and prestige, produced strained relations but no important crisis.[4] Other examples could be cited.

So far, the concept of the failed bargain crisis seems to offer deterrence theory nothing but additional complications. Having volunteered to serve as a hewer of wood and bearer of water for analysts, I must produce at least a few sticks and a small pail. There is a connecting link, a similarity, tying together the failed bargain crises named earlier. All represent individual bargains reached between particular states. They are mostly bilateral agreements, occasionally trilateral, but never constitute part of a general scheme or agreement. Obviously these are not the only kinds of agreements subject to failure. General agreements, concerts, and multilateral treaty systems also break down. Nor should one automatically suspect such separate agreements of being inherently selfish, designed for special advantages at the expense of others or of the general system. That is often true, but not always. There are numerous examples of states entering into particular bargains with one or two others for the purpose of achieving or strengthening a general concert, or with the intent of extending their particular agreement to the community as a whole. What this does strongly suggest, however, is that bilateral or trilateral agreements are especially likely to fail and to produce crises, particularly if the bargaining partners try to exclude other states or fail to make the terms of the bargain acceptable to them.

This unsurprising observation is reinforced and sharpened by another one, equally a truism on the surface but having some useful implications. In all the instances of failed bargain crises cited, the reaction of other powers to each bargain was important either in helping cause the failure or in helping determine the dimensions of the ensuing crisis after the bargain failed, or both. In at least one case, the Bosnian crisis, the reaction of other powers directly and immediately caused the bargain to fail and ensured that a crisis would develop. It was Britain's and France's disapproval of the Aehrenthal–Izvolski deal and their refusal to consent to the compensations proposed for Russia that primarily caused the deal to break down, and it was Germany's firm support for Austria (despite the fact that Aehrenthal had made the deal with Izvolski behind Germany's back) that enabled Austria to break Russian and Serbian resistance to the annexation, thus "humiliating" Russia. Other instances are readily found where the reaction of other powers contributed heavily to the breakdown of bargains. France's eagerness to break up the partnership between Austria and Prussia helped Bismarck maneuver Austria into war in 1866. Tsar Nicholas I's determination to break up the Anglo–French entente contributed a great deal to the crisis of 1840. Even in instances where one might claim that bargains were doomed to fail from the outset because one party or both were insincere about maintaining them, the reaction of other powers still is important in affecting the outcome and dimensions of the resultant crisis. Neither France nor Austria in 1798–1799 were serious about maintaining the Peace of Campo Formio, but Austria probably would not have dared to fight had not Britain and Russia decided to push Austria into war for their own anti-French purposes. The reaction of other powers can work in the opposite direction as well, to sustain bargains or limit crises. An important reason why some failed bargains in our sample did not cause war was the intervention of powers not party to the failed bargain to control its results—Austria and England in the Russo–Turkish crisis of 1821–1823, Germany in the Austro–Russian crises of 1878 and 1884–1886, and so on.

All this, as said earlier, may seem to prove no more than that international politics is densely interconnected and that all actions have important side and ripple effects. But the implications for deterrence go somewhat further. The main reason why the success or failure of particular bargains depends so heavily on the attitudes and actions of outside actors is not the interconnectedness of actions in international politics but the very nature of international bargains. Every particular bargain in international politics is at least implicitly a challenge to outsiders, calling for a response to control its effects and protect their interests. It represents an incipient coalition that spurs others to join it, break it up, merge it into something wider, or form a countercoalition (Riker, 1962). No matter how sincere, well-intentioned, desirable, and fair an individual bargain may seem to be, if it does not allow for the reactions of other actors it is likely to fail. The diplomatic historian constantly encounters statesmen, particularly from great and superpowers, saying to their counterparts in some other great power, "If we two agree on this point, we can settle it without regard to anyone else." This almost always proves wrong and leads to trouble. Schemes for preserving world peace through a partnership or condominium of two or three superpowers have been commonplace, and remain so. They always break down when tried, usually quickly. This is true for a variety of reasons, the main and relevant one here being the inability even of great or superpowers to control the reactions of the many actors excluded from the bargain.

In other words, the durability of bargains depends not simply on their intrinsic character and the intentions behind them or the good faith with which they are executed but equally on whether and how they fit into the general international system and can be made part of a broad concert. This has important implications for deterrence theory and practice. A great deal of the analysis of deterrence by historians as well as other scholars concentrates on attempting to determine how deterrence can work to solve or manage individual crises, that is, what kinds of deterrent practices work best in particular confrontations to check an aggressor, prevent war, and preserve vital interests. If, however, confrontations and crises arise in great measure from failed bargains, and the success or failure of bargains depends heavily upon how they fit into a general system of international politics and become part of a general consensus, then the analysis of deterrence must be expanded beyond the study of individual crises and include how deterrence affects the whole international system and the system affects it.

By international system I do not mean simply the number of major actors in international politics and the distribution of power between them (Snyder and Diesing, 1977:28 passim). I assume rather that international politics represents a kind of anarchic society (Hedley Bull) that includes in modern times certain developing institutions and institutionalized practices; that it rests, like domestic politics but in a less-developed way, on a network of reigning assumptions, rules, practices, mutual understandings, learned responses, and collective outlooks constituting, in Michael Oakeshott's words, the language and practice of a civic association (Bull, 1977; Oakeshott, 1975).[5] The main burden of this essay is that deterrence theory and practice has to take the international system in this sense fully into account, understanding how they mutually affect each other.

An adequate exposition of this theme is obviously impossible here. Let me simply try to illustrate four points about it: (1) Given a certain kind of prevalent system, one can have effective deterrence without using any coercion or threats at all. (2) The range and types of deterrent measures available to statesmen and their efficacy depend heavily on the existing system; conversely, the use statesmen make of available deterrents helps determine their availability and usefulness thereafter. (3) A certain kind of international system can directly cause valuable bargains to fail and ensure that deterrent measures, even if they succeed in particular instances, will ultimately prove counterproductive. (4) Even a successful case of deterrence without apparent harmful side effects can have hidden and long-range systemic effects more important than its apparent immediate results.

On the first point, witness the way Russia was deterred from waging war on Turkey in 1821–1825. This deterrence or dissuasion, exercised by Austria and Britain, involved no coercion or threats of any kind. The worst sanction either power ever indicated it would impose on Russia if it went to war was a kind of passive moral disapproval, that is, a refusal itself to break relations with Turkey. The pressures that kept Russia from going to war despite its having unimpeachable legal justification for it and powerful parties and interests in favor of it was the argument that any war whether justified or not would wreck the existing system and cost Russia the general advantages it provided.

For evidence on the second point, how the system helps determine what kinds of deterrence practices are available to statesmen and how effective they will be, and vice versa, one can look to the Crimean War. In 1853 all the other great powers were agreed that Russia presented a clear threat to the independence and integrity of Turkey. The basic question they faced was how to deter Russia—by confrontation, as the Western powers preferred, or by grouping Russia in the concert, as Austria and Prussia urged.

One can debate which policy was more appropriate for solving that particular crisis. What is beyond question, however, is that when as a result of accident, drift, and design the policy of deterrence by confrontation won out and war ensued, the very possibility of any longer deterring Russia in the Near East by grouping it in a general European concert disappeared for the foreseeable future. The system that had helped manage European crises for four decades was thus vitally changed.

To see how a prevalent system of international politics can undermine valuable bargains and make even the most powerful deterrent measures useless or counterproductive, one need only look at the various Austro–Russian crises in the Balkans between 1908 and 1914. Despite the fundamental rivalry between these two powers in this area, which by 1914 was two centuries old and impossible to heal, Austria and Russia most of the time managed to cooperate to keep the Balkans quiet and avoid open war between themselves. From 1894 to 1907 they had followed this policy in a particularly striking way, especially over the Macedonian question, and while their relations had become somewhat strained in 1908, the bargain Aehrenthal and Izvolski struck in September 1908 was supposed to restore and continue it. What served to wreck this vital Austro–Russian working bargain and make it thereafter impossible to revive was not so much the Bosnian quarrel itself or its outcome. The actual concrete issues were not of crucial importance, and Russia's alleged humiliation by the German powers was at least as much a matter of Russian perception, actively promoted by Britain and France, as a matter of objective fact. The revival of the pattern of Austro–Russian mutual restraint and cooperation as rivals in the Balkans was prevented above all by a general change in the European system. A shift occurred in the main purpose and goal of high politics, one both produced and signaled by this crisis. Where formerly since the early 1890s European alliances and alignments had primarily served to provide the European powers' security and stability at home so that they could act more effectively in world politics abroad, now the overriding goal of European politics became to strengthen one's own alliance system in Europe and if possible to weaken the opposing one in preparation for an ultimate test of strength. France and England no longer were ready to allow or encourage a durable Russo–Austrian bargain in the Balkans because they feared it would revive the Three Emperors' League and weaken the Franco–Russian alliance and the Anglo–Russian and Anglo–French ententes. Germany in turn encouraged an Austro–Russian bargain in the Balkans only under its control, for the very purposes Britain and France feared. Italy, Austria's ally, wanted an Austro–Russian deadlock so as to make its position stronger vis-à-vis both sides. Thus the shared purposes and rules of European international politics directly worked against any stable Austro–Russian bargain that was required to make the general Balkan situation manageable.

Worse still, they also ensured that it would become increasingly difficult to deter Austria from making the kind of offensive move against its small enemy neighbor Serbia, which was most likely to turn the Austro–Russian deadlock into a general war. At least three times between 1909 and 1913 Austria seriously contemplated attacking Serbia and was successfully deterred. Each time the deterrence of Austria, carried out by Germany as well as Austria's opponents, rested on convincing Austria that system-conforming behavior on its part would protect its interests better than actions that risked war. But the only conceivable long-range security for Austria's interests in the Balkans (which involved its existence as a multinational state) lay in a European concert to guarantee those Austrian interests. That concert in turn would have to rest on some kind of Austro–Russian or Austro–Italio–Russian agreement and cooperation in the area. Everyone understood this; yet this kind of mutual restraint and cooperation among rivals, transcending and interpenetrating the rival alliance systems, was precisely what the current system of international politics was designed to prevent. Austrian leaders therefore ultimately became convinced that the only purpose served by Concert deterrence was to keep Austria quiescent until it collapsed. The more the deterrence of Austria was successfully practiced, the more likely it became that Austria would ultimately rebel against it. This is not to blame the Entente powers or anyone in particular; blame in such a situation is irrelevant. It is to point to a fundamental systemic breakdown, the ultimate form of the downward spiral described by Robert Jervis (1976).

Finally, the Fashoda crisis in 1898 serves to show how even a successful use of deterrence can have a crucial hidden impact on the international system. In this confrontation, the British government forced the French to retreat from their occupation of the Sudan and abandon their claim to it, accepting British claims both there and in Egypt without any concessions in return (e.g., Sanderson, 1965; Andrew, 1968; Brown, 1970; Michel, 1972; Gifford and Louis, 1971). The crisis is often seen as a good example of the beneficial effects of a clear deterrent stand, for supposedly it served to clear the air between Britain and France and promoted their later rapprochement in the Entente Cordiale of 1904.

The central puzzle for historians has always been to understand why the French government risked such a confrontation as this, which it did not want and could not possibly win, at a time of serious domestic crisis (the Dreyfus Affair), with a power that was not its enemy over a prize it always knew was worthless. The answer is partly that the French government, internally in disarray, failed to control various reckless subordinate officials. (A good way to understand the Iran–Contra debacle in American policy of the 1980s is to read about the Marchand mission that led to the Fashoda crisis.) A more important answer, however, lies deeper, in certain French assumptions about the prevailing European system. Historians and others have debated whether the British government gave France a clear and credible signal to warn it off the Sudan well in advance of the crisis. The more important question is whether, given the rules of the game as the French understood them, they could be expected to recognize and heed even a very clear signal from Britain. For as all recent historians agree, the French government risked a confrontation with Britain only because it assumed that no risk of *war* was involved. This was an African colonial question, which meant it was something that European great powers would compete, bargain, quarrel, or cooperate over, but that no one would make a *casus belli*. In the long series of Anglo–French colonial quarrels since 1815, some of them over issues far more important than this (e.g., Algeria, Morocco, or Egypt), the British had never threatened France with war. Nor had they done so with the Dutch, the Americans, or even the Russians over an issue outside Europe. The French government, once it had blundered into the Sudan, had normal political and diplomatic aims in mind—to pressure the British into an international conference over Egypt and ultimately to convince them that they needed a general entente with France. Suddenly the foreign minister Delcassé discovered that the rules were changed; the game of diplomatic chess had become Russian roulette.

Naturally British deterrence worked; the British held all the military cards. But the usual verdict, that this incident shows how a firm deterrent stand, even if it produces a momentary crisis, can promote a long-term improvement in relations, shows how one-sided and superficial a nonsystemic analysis can be. Though Fashoda eventually led to the entente with Britain France had been seeking all along, it can hardly be said to have caused it or speeded it up. Delcassé actually took 4 years to get over the humiliation of Fashoda, give up seeking revenge, and be ready for an entente on Britain's terms. Moreover, the main long-range effect of Fashoda was to change the rule in European politics prevailing since 1815 whereby European great powers did not resort to war with each other or threaten each other with it over colonial questions.[6] Fashoda was not the sole or main cause of this change, of course; given the accelerating competition in European and world politics, some development was bound to overturn it. But Fashoda was a catalyst, and it is not accidental that from this time onward colonial questions (South Africa, Morocco, the Baghdad

Railway, the Far East, Anatolia) became part and parcel of European power politics, including the mobilization and use of alliances. This shows how even successful deterrence can promote a downward spiral in the system.

This call for extending the analysis of deterrence to include its systemic effects in international politics clearly adds another factor or dimension to an already extremely complex and difficult calculus. But this is clearly not something new in deterrence theory, even in the nuclear age. When analysts of current deterrence theory and practice show how widely the desirable level of threats may vary from case to case and how difficult it is to determine what level is best for any occasion; or when they note how unpredictable the immediate and the long-range effects of strong or weak deterrent actions may be; or when they point out how many different perceptual and emotional as well as rational factors influence the outcome of deterrence, then they are clearly pointing not merely to individual but also systemic variables, and implicitly calling for a deterrence theory that takes the whole international system into account.

This would seem in fact to be a practical as well as scholarly necessity. Even if one sets the immediate goal for deterrence theory in the nuclear age in the narrowest practical terms (e.g., how to neutralize the Soviet nuclear threat in order to advance American interests around the globe), the awesome nature of the threat and the overriding interest involved in meeting it would seem to require going beyond any military–technological achievement or narrower political strategy and seeking a solution in the direction of a viable system of international order. In other words, not merely the theory of deterrence but its very purpose and practice require thinking in terms of the international system as a whole.

## NOTES

1. In the case of this crisis and all succeeding ones to be discussed, I will not attempt to "prove" the interpretations presented. This would require citing masses of evidence not only from the extensive literature on each of them, but also from published and unpublished documents, and would be impossibly long and distracting. Only a few works useful for the general reader will be cited.
2. For a good general overview, see McKay and Scott (1983).
3. My own verdict is that they were clearly the latter. A recent study that also reaches this conclusion is Rich (1985).
4. On the latter, see Bullen (1974).
5. What I here call "system" may be essentially what some political scientists

call "regime" and discuss in regime theory; but I am not familiar enough with the literature on the latter to be sure. *World Politics* 38:1 (October 1985) contains valuable articles on the theme of cooperation under anarchy (see Oye, 1986).

6. For a discussion of how this rule emerged in 1815, changing the system previously prevailing, see Schroeder (1986).

# REFERENCES

Andrew, C., 1968. *Theophile Delcassé and the Making of the Entente Cordiale.* New York: St. Martin's.

Blanning, T. C. W., 1986. *The Origins of the French Revolutionary Wars.* London: Longman.

Bridge, F. R., 1972a. *From Sadowa to Sarajevo: The Foreign Policy of Austria–Hungary, 1866–1914.* London: Routledge and Kegan Paul.

――― 1972b. *Great Britain and Austria–Hungary 1906–1914: A Diplomatic History.* London: Weidenfeld and Nicolson.

Brown, R., 1970. *Fashoda Reconsidered.* Baltimore: Johns Hopkins University Press.

Bull, H., 1977. *The Anarchical Society.* New York: Columbia University Press.

Bullen, R., 1974. *Palmerston, Guizot, and the Collapse of the Entente Cordiale.* London: Athlone.

Carlgren, W. M., 1955. *Iswolsky und Aehrenthal vor der bosnischen Annexionskrise.* Uppsala, Sweden: Almqvist and Wiksells.

Crawley, C. W., 1930. *The Question of Greek Independence.* Cambridge, Eng.: Cambridge University Press.

Deutsch, H. C., 1938. *The Genesis of Napoleonic Imperialism.* Cambridge, Mass.: Harvard University Press.

Fugier, A., 1954. *La révolution française et l'empire Napoléonien.* Paris: Hachette.

Gifford, P., and Louis, W. R., eds., 1971. *France and Britain in Africa: Imperial Rivalry and Colonial Rule.* New Haven, Conn.: Yale University Press.

Jervis, R., 1976. *Perception and Misperception in International Politics.* Princeton, N.J.: Princeton University Press.

Kraehe, E., 1983. *Metternich's German Policy.* Vol. II, Princeton, N.J.: Princeton University Press.

Lebow, R. N., 1981. *Between Peace and War: The Nature of International Crisis.* Baltimore: Johns Hopkins University Press.

Lefebvre, G., 1969. *Napoleon from 18 Brumaire to Tilsit 1799–1807*, trans. by Henry F. Stockhold. New York: Columbia University Press.

Lord, R. H. 1915. *The Second Partition of Poland.* Cambridge, Mass.: Harvard University Press.

Lutz, H., 1985. *Zwischen Habsburg und Preussen: Das Ringen um die Vormacht in Deutschland 1815–1866.* Berlin: Siedler.

Mackesy, P., 1974. *Statesmen at War: The Strategy of Overthrow, 1798–1799*. London: Longman.

——— 1984. *War Without Victory: The Downfall of Pitt, 1799–1802*. Oxford: Oxford University Press.

McKay, D., and Scott, H. M., 1983. *The Rise of the Great Powers, 1648–1815*. London: Longman.

Michel, M., 1972. *La mission Marchand 1895–1899*. Paris: Mouton.

Mouraviev, B., 1954. *L'Alliance russo–turque au milieu des guerres napoleoniennes*. Neuchatel: Baçonniere.

Nish, I., 1985. *The Origins of the Russo–Japanese War*. London: Longman.

Oakeshott, M., 1975. *On Human Conduct*. Oxford: Clarendon.

Oye, K. A., 1986. *Cooperation Under Anarchy*. Princeton, N.J.: Princeton University Press.

Poidevin, R., 1969. *Les rélations économiques et financières entre la France et l'Allemagne, 1898 à 1914*. Paris: A. Colin.

Puryear, V. J., 1951. *Napoleon and the Dardanelles*. Berkeley, Calif.: University of California Press.

Ramm, A., 1971. Great Britain and France in Egypt 1876–1882. In *France and Britain in Africa*. P. Gifford and W. R. Louis, eds. New Haven, Conn.: Yale University Press, pp. 73–119.

Rich, N., 1985. *Why the Crimean War?* Hanover, N.H.: University Press of New England.

Riker, W. H., 1962. *The Theory of Political Coalitions*. New Haven, Conn.: Yale University Press.

Rupp, G. H., 1941. *A Wavering Friendship: Russia and Austria, 1876–1878*. Cambridge, Mass.: Harvard University Press.

Sanderson, G. N., 1965. *England, Europe, and the Upper Nile, 1882–1899*. Edinburgh: University Press.

Saul, N. E., 1970. *Russia and the Mediterranean 1797–1807*. Chicago: University of Chicago Press.

Schmitt, B. E., 1937. *The Annexation of Bosnia, 1908–1909*. Cambridge, Engl.: Cambridge University Press.

Schroeder, P. W., 1962. *Metternich's Diplomacy at Its Zenith, 1820–1823*. Austin, Tex.: University of Texas Press.

——— 1972. *Austria, Great Britain and the Crimean War*. Ithaca, N.Y.: Cornell University Press.

——— 1986. The 19th century international system: Changes in the structure. *World Politics* 39(1):13–17.

——— 1987. The collapse of the second coalition. *Journal of Modern History* 59(2):244–90.

Snyder, G. H., and Diesing, P., 1977. *Conflict Among Nations*. Princeton, N.J.: Princeton University Press.

Sorel, A., 1986. *L'Europe et la révolution française*. (8 vols.), Paris: E. Plon, Nourrit (1892–1913), Vols. 2–3.)

Vandal, A., 1891–1896. *Napoleon et Alexandre Ier*. (3 vols), Paris: E. Plon, Nourrit.
Webster, C. K., 1951. *The Foreign Policy of Palmerston, 1830–1841*. (2 vols), London: G. Bell.
Ziegler, P., 1965. *Addington: A Life of Henry Addington, Viscount Sidmouth*. New York: John Day.

# 5

# Historians and Deterrence

## MICHAEL G. FRY

The archives of the United States and its allies, and of France, the records of the derivation and formulation of state policy and of the external behavior of states are, under the 30 years rule, beginning to disgorge the Cold War. The files for 1956 are now available for research; the Soviet archives remain closed. Historians of the nuclear age, challenged by the changing availability of evidence and working for the most part within the realist paradigm, face the formidable task of mastering a massive body of information deposited by complex industrial societies and their governments. It will be a test of stamina as well as of intellect, of courage as much as of sophistication. They will go about the task as always, reasoning adductively, seeking contingent relationships, and asking how could it be so, why did that outcome occur to the exclusion of other possible results?

A central question will be how and why has the management of global competition between the United States and the Soviet Union not resulted in nuclear war but seems to have helped ensure the perpetuation of conventional warfare and a resort to covert operations on an unprecedented scale. The role of nuclear deterrence lies at the core of this question but, without an example of nuclear war, without a precedent, the precise effect of nuclear deterrence is a counterfactual situation as well as a prime source of reductionism. To probe how deterrence works in the nuclear age one has the seductive, deductive elegance of game theory with "prisoners' dilemma" and "chicken" prominent, simulation, the conclusions of contemporary analysis from several disciplines, written from at least three ideological perspectives, and comparative reasoning of various types. One form of comparison is to evaluate the historical record of the behavior of modern industrialized states to look for enduring factors, valid patterns, and conclusions that retain significance across time and cultures and to ask, in effect, in what fundamental ways is the world since 1945 different from previous eras?

## Theoretical Considerations

The central question is grounded in several bodies of theory (Smart, 1975; Howard, 1983). Systems theory asks how the commanding structural property of the international state system, the distribution of power that constitutes bipolarity, contributes to stability and predictable behavior—how a degree of order prevails, how constructive change occurs in circumstances of anarchy, and whether a strategic regime in fact exists. Normative theory explores the role war continues to play in various cultures, whether war remains a legitimate instrument of policy and an acceptable agent of political change. Can a just war be launched by the Soviet Union or the United States against the other or against a third party? Theory about the nature of the state examines the properties of the national security state, societal–government relations, the policy consequences of political legitimation, and the internal processes of policy formulation.

Fourth, and at the core, stands the theoretical relation between military preparedness and the preservation of peace and, conversely, between the procurement of weapons and the incidence of war. This question, in effect about the causes of war, is fundamental because of the propositions derived from it. To some, the first relation between preparedness and peace is a contradiction and the second, between weaponry and war, a statement of a necessary condition. To others, both relations operate in the opposite direction. Thus, more *and* less weapons can be said to promote peace or cause war; higher *and* lower levels can seem intolerable or efficacious; rearmament *and* disarmament may contribute to stability. The security dilemma is a derivative of this reasoning where incremental, defensive, and seemingly justified steps actually decrease stability and reduce security because of the predictable, understandable reaction of the potential adversary. So is discussion about limited nuclear war and winning or surviving such conflicts.

These seemingly irreconcilable propositions, in defense of deterrence and in fear of spiraling arms races, relate directly to moral considerations which have, for example, helped persuade the Catholic Bishops of the United States to condemn nuclear war as a policy option and to embrace nuclear deterrence and what might be described as possession of a "Protestant" bomb for purely defensive purposes. Refinements of these propositions came from two sources—when weapons systems are assessed in terms of their type and nature and the rate and extent of technological change is measured as a source of instability, and when related questions concerning civil–military relations, interservice competition, the primacy of the political sphere in democratic and other societies, and the relationship of foreign to defense policy are explored.

Historians have rarely used deterrence theory formally as an organizing principle of their research into the external behavior of states since 1815. They have not done so particularly for the period before 1914 and for the most part only implicitly for the interwar years. The explanation for this neglect must be speculative. Many historians of international relations have seemingly a schizophrenic relationship to theory. They recognize that history is a major source of theory; they shy away from anything approaching historicism. Theory's tasks, to bring order to complexity, parsimony to explanation, and patterns to seeming irregularities offend against their concern to set out unparalleled complexity and richness in description and narrative and to offer competitive interpretation as explanation.

There has also tended to be, among historians, something of an intellectual divorce, born of specialization, between the four approaches to the subject represented by diplomatic history, military history, the history of dissent, disarmament, and pacifism, and the history of military preparedness in peacetime and the development of war economies. This compartmentalizing of historical scholarship has not been conducive to the testing of deterrence theory.

Diplomatic historians, for example, have pursued other questions. In their prolonged concern with the issue of responsibility they have made the history of the origins of World Wars I and II and the Cold War almost a quasi-judicial inquiry, and a sterile one at that. They have been affected excessively by the war guilt issue.

Recent scholarship, particularly on 1914, in a most encouraging trend, is escaping from this approach as the subject becomes shared in a mutually beneficial way with political scientists. International relations scholars now have a discrete, impressive, and plural body of theoretical and historical literature. Smith (1982) surveyed the theoretical work on deterrence, following the "three waves" identified by Robert Jervis. Lynn-Jones (1986) divides the literature on 1914 into four categories and demonstrates a sound, if not complete, grasp of historical and theoretical scholarship on the origins of the first World War. Sagan (1986) adds to the review of the literature by Lynn-Jones.

Finally, historians dealt with the problem of the relation between extant structures and individual behavior by writing first of deep underlying causes

*Historians and Deterrence*                                                87

and then of decision making in the final crisis, looking for error, miscalculation, loss of control, and aggressive risk taking. Deterrence theory was not irrelevant but was not the fundamental organizing principle.

## Deterrence and the Origins of the First World War

Steinberg (1965) is the only historian working in the English language who has used the word *deterrent* in the title of a book dealing with the origins of the first World War, and his interpretation of the period was both original and convincing. He was concerned with German naval policy in the Tirpitz era, with a "risk theory" and a "period of danger theory" that motivated the German government to create a High Seas Fleet, a naval deterrent, to encourage Britain to behave cooperatively and responsibly despite Germany's current naval inferiority and thus her susceptibility to British diplomatic pressure.

The High Seas Fleet was not meant to be a deterrent in the conventional sense. Rather, its construction was to induce Britain to seek a political agreement with Germany that would result in her support in international disputes, her compliance with German policy, and ultimately her neutrality in the event of a European war in which Germany was a belligerent. The immediate payoff would be diplomatic; the final benefit would be military, unless the record of Anglo–German cooperation deterred Germany's continental rivals from risking war with her and convinced them to acquiesce in her demands.

The German government, however, actually assumed that the very creation of a High Seas Fleet might convince Britain to risk a preemptive strike against the fleet while it was still under construction and incomplete. In other words, the act of building a fleet was understood to be a possible cause of a naval conflict, an incentive to Britain to act promptly to destroy incipient German naval power.

Once begun, the creation of the German fleet, despite the visible and sustained failure to secure its principal diplomatic purpose, could not be abandoned. Anglo–German relations deteriorated, but its construction became part of domestic political dogma and an important element in industrial policy. The building of the German fleet in fact altered British perceptions of her naval position, helped supplant France and Russia as Britain's most threatening naval rivals, and fueled what is seen as the classic arms race, the spiraling, persistent, and unresolved challenge, which made its contribution to the development of Anglo–German tension and the decision for war. Moreover, the German fleet that was built never matched the British fleet, at least in the perception of its creator. It was in the logic of that situation that Admiral Tirpitz opposed the decision to risk war with England in 1914.

Professor Steinberg in fact wrote about an arms race and its political consequences, about Anglo–German rivalry in the tradition of E. L. Woodward and others. His impressive work stands with scholarship on the military arms races and their deterrent functions and political ramifications, on alliance formation and consolidation, on war plans and strategic assumptions about the offensive, on crisis, escalation, and risk taking. It deals with bargains that broke down in an age when it could seem reasonable to prefer war earlier than later, and when the possible magnitude and duration of a war between the great powers was not fully understood and thus a form of optimism could prevail about its consequences.

Professor Steinberg's book, moreover, raises questions about the probable, almost inescapable, relation between the creation of a deterrent against a single opponent of similar, great power status and the instigation of an arms race, the former as purpose and the latter as consequence. This is an important issue, for the creation of a detterent is invariably meant to add stability to an arms race. Coercibility and the resolve to deter are the bedrock, twin assumptions of deterrence theory, and they are logically compatible. Both parties in the relation must share these characteristics equally and unswervingly, and in ways that contribute to stability if deterrence is to work. Arms races take much of their internal fuel from technological innovation, domestic imperatives, for reasons of status, and bureaucratic dynamics, but states historically have also raced to deter war from occurring at inopportune times, or at all, or to win the war that might occur, and in each situation to reap the current political and diplomatic benefits of preparedness. The outcome was always unpredictable. Today the Soviet Union and the United States seek to deter and are thus locked in an arms race, hoping that racing remains consistent with deterrence, that both remain coercible and yet resolved, that MAD means "mutually assured deterrence."

## Deterrence and the Origins of the Second World War

The interwar years up to 1939 or 1941 have been approached only implicitly and in part as exercises in disarmament and then deterrence, without the words *deterrent* or *deterrence* appearing in any book title. The four approaches to international history mentioned above with regard to the historiography of the origins of the first World War retained much of their discreteness. Historians asked other questions: The responsibility debate flourished, sometimes in bizarre fashion, and appeasement, the organizing principle of so much scholarship, was seen fairly narrowly as a condemnable political act in the face of an obvious threat to the values of western civilization.

Gradually, however, as the archives opened in the mid-1960s, appeasement was recognized as a product of the new imperialist mind attempting to grapple with the extraordinarily difficult and novel global predicament presented by the emergence almost simultaneously of three predators, Germany, Italy, and Japan, acting with a degree of menacing cooperation in Europe, the Mediterranean, the Middle East, and Asia (Pratt, 1975; Watt, 1976; Fry, 1986; Wark, 1986). The possession of empire by Britain and France was thus both a source of prestige and world power and the root of their vulnerability. In the shadow of the Versailles settlement, Britain and France resorted to a policy that offered seemingly reasonable and defensible concessions to the predators—economic, financial, diplomatic, strategic, and territorial (in and outside Europe)—for their dissatisfactions and discontent were seen as legitimate. The policy had, as a second indispensable component, the creation of armed forces that would both deter the predators from risking war and contribute to postcrisis stability. Together, this combination of diplomacy and rearmament seemed the way to orchestrate peaceful change and produce stability despite the current crisis atmosphere.

In the prevailing circumstances left by the legacies of the 1920s and given the state of weapons research and development, the debate over the respective value of various offensive and defensive weapons, the nature of prevailing rearmament cycles and procurement schedules, and obsolescence rates that initially reduced front-line strength as a state rearmed, resulting in a U-curve, military and air capabilities were required in Europe to deter Germany, air and naval forces in the Mediterranean to deter Italy, and naval and air forces in the Pacific to deter Japan. Insofar as deterrence rested on the strategic balance, deterrents of different composition were thus required to differing extents in each theater.

Yet, because a crisis of empire could be regional and global, because preoccupation with or losses in one theater could encourage hostile encroachment in another, deterrent capabilities had to be mobile and have global reach. Deterrence had to be divisible and indivisible. All this had to be accomplished in times of slow economic growth, financial stringency, without the United States and the Soviet Union, in an unpropitious public climate, with alliance relationships that were complicated and even tenuous, with varying colonial and dominion expectations, and when Germany, Japan, and even Italy were in their own way deterring their opponents by propaganda, blustering exaggerations of their rearmament, the successful management of diplomatic negotiations and crises, control of the timing and agenda of confrontation, and preemptive conduct.

The appeasers were balancing risks, weighing priorities, evaluating allies and neutrals, husbanding scarce resources, seeking to reduce liabilities, and attempting to ease the strain on limited capabilities. They were faced with cruel dilemmas and tragic predicaments, some of which were of their own making. They ended up offering guarantees to indefensible states.

But cunctation, misjudgment, and inconsistency marked their conduct of affairs far more than ignorance, spineless fear, and craven neglect. Appeasement was not meant to buy time in order to win a future war. Its practitioners saw it as a dynamic and creative policy that would establish a self-regulating European balance of power between four rearmed, satiated, and secure powers (Britain, France, Germany, and Italy), and result in a stable, global situation in which European empires could evolve peacefully. Creative diplomacy and deterrence would go forward hand-in-hand and prove efficacious. In fact, they did not; slow and faltering rearmament did not produce a credible deterrent before 1941 and accompanied vigorous but inadequate diplomacy. The two components of appeasement were out of step and balance, and provided Germany with a prime opportunity in Europe, Italy with a margin for maneuver in the Mediterranean, and Japan with a temporary, fragile opening in East Asia that an elite, guided by cultural imperatives and driven by gambling instincts, could not resist.

The historical literature on the 1930s is, therefore, implicitly and in part concerned with deterrence, but few if any historians seemingly have gone to the archives specifically to test deterrence theory and question its robustness. They should, because such inquiry would be quite a different intellectual exercise from that of political scientists investigating the origins of the second World War as a failure of deterrence using the published results of research by historians who were asking different questions and concerned with other problems.

Moreover, theoretically interested historians can learn from historically sensitive social scientists (Lebow, 1981; Mearsheimer, 1983; Jervis, Lebow, and Stein, 1985; Miller, 1985; Jervis, 1986; and Lebow, 1986). Mearsheimer (1983), for example, read British manuscript and published private and official files, German- and French-published primary sources, and some of the secondary literature in order to write on Anglo–French and German policies in 1939, specifically to explore the functioning of deterrence. Historians could tackle the crises of the 1930s as iterated exercises in the relation between general and crisis deterrence and between primary and extended deterrence.

Conversely, historical writing on the 1930s, even as it made appeasement the organizing principle, demonstrated that deterrence is not a function exclusively of the military balance, existing or potential. The conduct of diplomacy, the demonstration of resolve and firmness, and the development of reputations by individual leaders, governments, and societies all play a part and are interrelated as policy calculations are made and risks avoided or taken. Clearly, in prenuclear eras, even when perceptions of the destructive power of existing weapons were decidedly sobering, some leaders were simply not deterrable.

## Deterrence and the Bipolar World

And as one ponders the appeasers' dream of a stable, self-regulating balance of power, when appeasement had succeeded and four rearmed European powers lived in harmony, one must ask whether deterrence, as a decisive component of policy, can be a sound basis on which to build a stable future, given its assumptions and its unavoidable consequence—rearmament. These lines of enquiry are important in themselves and provide one of the bases for comparing the preserving of peace through deterrence in prenuclear and nuclear eras.

One should be, however, suitably cautious about the value of lessons and the relevance of prescriptions drawn from the pre-1941 international system to the nuclear age. Comparisons are valuable and provide insight but basic structural differences exist that give the post-1945 system a unique nature. They are of four kinds. First, the distribution of capabilities and resources in the contemporary international system has produced a bipolar world that is unprecedented in the history of modern industrialized states. The balance of power, the fundamental relationship between states, thus functions in a somewhat different fashion from earlier periods. Both the United States and the Soviet Union face the challenge of an apparently unambiguous opponent and enjoy the comfort of a degree of predictability.

There is a form of stability in that situation. In 1928, in contrast, the British government thought its most likely opponent in a future war would be France, Russia, or the United States. Moreover, before 1914 the European powers functioned with the knowledge that an external, albeit distant power, the United States, could intervene decisively in a war involving the two European alliances. Before 1941, the United States and the Soviet Union stood as potential external regulators. No such reservoir of uncommitted capabilities now exists. In addition, the balance of resources within the prevailing, commanding alliances has changed since 1945. Those who possess comprehensive nuclear weapons wield unprecedented influence.

Thus the alliances function somewhat differently than before 1941, and have different degrees of potential for internal restraint and coercion. The modern international system has always had its fundamental paradox—the impotence of the strong and the influence of the weak in certain circumstances. It still has, even in the presence of the two nuclear superpowers, but the consequences, should the paradox unfold, are more dramatic, threatening, and possibly unmanageable.

Second, nuclear weapons are a new parameter with major strategic and political consequences. They have radically revised strategic doctrine on the conduct of war. That is because nuclear weapons threaten an instantaneous terror and destruction, and become ever more reliable and accurate. War will be the Armageddon. Earlier generations may have *thought* they faced a similar tragedy; this generation *does*. Yet Winston Churchill proposed the use of nuclear weapons on one occasion against the Soviet Union while the West enjoyed a nuclear monopoly, and their use was debated in the United States seriously three times in the 1960s.

Moreover, arms systems are now arranged hierarchically in two tiers not one; there are nuclear and conventional weapons. Each have their own research and development paths, technologies, production cycles, procurement schedules, obsolescence rates, segments of defense budgets, and characteristics, and present special verification problems. They have, as weapons systems, complex relations to each other. Wars can now be fought with or without nuclear weapons, between nuclear states, between nonnuclear states, or involve one nuclear power. Nuclear weapons affect decisively the debate on the value of offensive as opposed to defensive weapons systems. They may have curbed the offensive will, but they have not provided an escape from the reasons to rearm. They have given deterrence a new and vital credibility by raising enormously the consequences of its failure, by massively increasing the penalties and limiting the rewards of war.

So much seems to depend on the efficient functioning of nuclear deterrence; so much stability seems to stem from the nuclear balance. It is entirely appropriate, therefore, that Basil Liddell Hart's distinction between strategy (i.e., "generalship") and the grand strategy of statesmanship has collapsed. Strategy has been politicized; the locus of strategic thought has moved from war to peace.

But serious questions remain about the wisdom of having the Soviet–American relationship founded so centrally on nuclear deterrence. And does each state require a deterrent capability in every weapons category? Can there not be effective deterrence at lower levels and in more constrained ways? Whatever the answer, the need for effective and accountable political control over nuclear strategy is evermore essential, complicating further the conduct of civil–military relations. This is particularly true because the presence of nuclear weapons has not made the resort to war between states less likely. Indeed, the institutionalization of primary nuclear deterrence may actually have undermined the prospects for extended deterrence and whetted certain appetites for low-intensity warfare.

Thus nuclear deterrence may be a source of stability in one realm and of instability in another. The role of force in the conduct of the international system may have increased. An adventurer may risk conflict at the nonnuclear level of violence precisely because escalation to the nuclear level seems improbable. This situation, affected decisively perhaps by the presence of nuclear weapons, thus relates to the prospects for the control of escalation, to the management of crises, and to forms of behavior that can be practiced safely or risked.

Third, state behavior in the nuclear age takes place in an intellectual climate where many of the questions asked are not new, but where the reasoning about them has changed. Peace is now to be preferred overwhelmingly, but has war been exorcised as a policy choice? And does the denial of war as a legitimate instrument of change reflect Western statist presumption? Will empires continue to rise and fall and bids for hegemony be made and defeated in the twin, reinforcing conditions of bipolarity and the possession of nuclear weapons? Will friends and enemies in the current international system remain permanent and be identifiable from their ideological preferences? Will states in relative decline still seem vulnerable and invite encroachment or remain dangerous because they continue to prefer to risk war earlier rather than later? Or does the possession of nuclear weapons offset the significance of erstwhile indicators of declining power? Are fewer values shared between the nuclear powers in their bipolar relationship than were shared between the great powers of earlier systems? Are nuclear armed ideologues basically less flexible tactically than their predecessors, or does pragmatism still flourish? The first World War and the Versailles Treaty of 1919 produced public and elite climates of opinion and a relationship between dissent and orthodox views that were different from those prevailing before 1914. Certain views have changed since 1945, certain debates have altered, and it is in that atmosphere that policy must find legitimation.

Finally, the central problem of the international system has changed since 1945, though this structural difference says more about the concluding theme of this chapter, the management of Soviet–American relations, than it does about deterrence. Between 1870 and 1945 management of the German problem was the most fundamental issue, exacerbated by the presence of untenable empires and the loss of effective middle powers that had helped cushion Europe against destabilizing shocks. Before the second World War the Russian policy of the United States was largely a function of its Germany policy. Now the reverse is true as Europe rests between the superpowers. The American problem that is Russia's concern has changed similarly, and Soviet leaders are not alone in seeing the United States as the principal threat to international society.

Understanding the management of Soviet–American relations on a global scale, probing the practices of nuclear deterrence, and comprehending the continued avoidance of nuclear war requires research into the history of the relation since 1917 and particularly from 1945. Much has been done, many works of careful scholarship have been published, yet several problems remain at issue.

The fact that many public servants in the United States, and presumably in the Soviet Union, continue to seem to prefer simplistic, ideologically driven, hostile explanations of the behavior of the other power makes this body of research and its adaptation for policy even more necessary. Scholarship, debate, and dissent do influence policy, if only indirectly and slowly. Seeking answers to certain questions about the Soviet Union must accompany inquiry into the record of Soviet–American relations. Does the Soviet Union share American views about nuclear deterrence and its contribution to stability, the dangers of arms races, and the relationship between the creation of deterrence capability and war preparedness? Is it clear that the Soviet Union prefers peaceful competition and orderly change and has relegated ideas of world power and preferences for belligerent policies to the level of oratory and posturing? Some might ask the same questions of the United States.

What kind of policy debate flourishes in the Soviet Union, how is dissent expressed, and what constraints exist because of the need for political legitimation? Is the Soviet Union, and do her leaders perceive her to be, captive of slow rates of economic growth and even in a state of economic and technological decline? Is she in consequence more vulnerable and dangerous? How much has she spent historically on armaments, how much can she sensibly devote to defense, and what does she currently spend as a proportion of available resources and with what degree of strain? What is the Soviet record on the conduct of civil–military relations as the military budget is constructed and policy implemented? What strategic doctrine governs policy? The work of Seweryn Bialer (1986) and Michael McGwire (1987) respectively are surely the points of departure on these subjects.

The history of Soviet external behavior generally must be considered and made more than merely the context of the unfolding of Soviet–American relations. Has the pattern and trend been one where defensive and responsible behavior predominates across regions and issues, and as leaders have changed? Have Soviet statesmen generally been careful in their calcula-

# Historians and Deterrence

tions about capabilities and goals, and about the value of short-run opportunism as opposed to longer-term policy consistency? As every crisis has both a history and a future, what reputation do Soviet governments deserve, use, and exploit? Has the Soviet Union tended to see opportunities rather than problems in Europe, the Middle East, Southeast Asia, Africa, and Latin America, and as foreign communist parties outside the bloc struggle for power and office?

In the light of answers to these and other questions research must give shape, form, and coherence to the specifics of Soviet–American relations. There is a record of functional cooperation and conflict, of alliance partnership and armed hostility, of the cumulative effect of sustained antagonism and periodic crises, of purposeful strategic choice about options and, no doubt, some less-than-rational behavior. Thus there is a record of decision making, bargaining, and negotiation, of analogical and precedential reasoning by officials and leaders of both states, and of significant failure to implement preferred policies.

The functioning of the balance of power in a bipolar, nuclear world is necessarily different than in previous eras. One rule of the classic theory, however—that no participant seeks to eliminate any other actor—and one characteristic of the system—that actors can pursue cooperation as well as power—are evermore relevant now. In 1919 the United States and her victorious allies pondered several options in order to construct a policy toward the Soviet Union. Invasion, rollback, containment, detente—pursued vigorously or more casually, selectively or generally—and, the ultimate in patience: waiting for and seeking to promote political change within the Soviet Union, to encourage a pink rather than a red or white Russia, all had their champions.

Some of those options were not necessarily discrete. Trade, technology transfer, functional cooperation, and normalized diplomatic relations could be utilized in various ways to facilitate certain ends. Today the sensible alternatives are fewer and less dramatic, although some words are now used differently—containment and rollback are, for some public servants in Washington apparently, ways of resisting the Soviet Union outside of Euro–Asia.

Detente, properly pursued, is meant to result in the increased security of both participants. Detente is not inconsistent with the maintenance of deterrence, which should be based on the lowest levels of those types of nuclear weapons that breed stability, though unyielding commitment to certain forms of deterrence, conducted in hostile tones, can undermine prospects for detente. Both the United States and the Soviet Union must be susceptible to coercion and resolved in their commitment to deter. It is a complex arrangement, and deterrence theory may possibly be flawed in fundamental ways. It has failed in the past. Deterrence should not be, therefore, an object of worship or a reason for closing the debate on how to manage the contemporary international system. It requires the most profound reasoning, for the consequences of failure will be complete.

## REFERENCES

Bialer, S., 1986. *The Soviet Paradox: External Expansion and Internal Decline.* New York: Knopf.
Fry, M. G., 1986. Appeasement: The Middle Eastern factor, 1933–1939. *Middle East Studies Journal* (UCLA) 1(1):23–42.
Howard, M., 1983. Weapons and peace. *Atlantic Quarterly* 1(1):45–60.
Jervis, R., 1986. Deterrence, the spiral model, and intentions of the adversary. In R. K. White, ed., *Psychology and the Prevention of Nuclear War.* New York: New York University Press, pp 107–30.
Jervis, R., Lebow, R. N., and Stein, J. G., 1985. *Psychology and Deterrence.* Baltimore: Johns Hopkins University Press.
Lebow, R. N., 1981. *Between Peace and War.* Baltimore: Johns Hopkins University Press.
——— 1986. Deterrence reconsidered: The challenge of recent research. In R. K. White, ed., *Psychology and the Prevention of Nuclear War.* New York: New York University Press, pp. 352–75.
Lynn-Jones, S. M., 1986. Detente and deterrence: Anglo–German relations, 1911–1914. *International Security* 11(2):121–50.
McGwire, M., 1987. *Military Objectives in Soviet Foreign Policy.* Washington, D.C.: Brookings Institution.
Mearsheimer, J. J., 1983. *Conventional Deterrence.* Ithaca, N.Y.: Cornell University Press.
Miller, S. E., ed., 1985. *Military Strategy and the Origins of the First World War.* Princeton, N.J.: Princeton University Press.
Pratt, L. R., 1975. *East of Malta, West of Suez. Britain's Mediterranean Crisis, 1936–1939.* Cambridge, Engl.: Cambridge University Press.
Sagan, S. D., 1986. 1914 Revisited: Allies, offense, and instability. *International Security* 11(2):151–76.
Smart, I., 1975. The study of strategy. In M. G. Fry, ed., *Freedom and Change: Essays in Honor of Lester B. Pearson.* Toronto: McClelland and Stewart, pp. 76–94.
Smith, T. C., 1982. *Trojan Peace: Some Deterrence Propositions Tested.* Denver, Colo.: University of Denver Press.
Steinberg, J., 1965. *Yesterday's Deterrent: Tirpitz and the Birth of the German Battlefleet.* London: Macdonald.

Wark, W. K., 1986. *The Ultimate Enemy: British Intelligence and Nazi Germany, 1933–1939*. Oxford: Oxford University Press.

Watt, Donald C., 1976. The historiography of appeasement. In A. Sked and C. Cook, eds., *Crisis and Controversy*. New York: St. Martin's Press, pp. 110–29.

# 6
# Quantitative Studies of Deterrence Success and Failure

## JACK S. LEVY

This chapter reviews some of the more important quantitative empirical literature on the effectiveness of deterrence threats. The central theoretical question concerns the conditions under which a deterrence threat is successful in persuading a potentially hostile adversary not to take certain actions that would be contrary to one's own interests and the conditions under which the deterrence threat fails to dissuade the adversary from taking the undesired action or actually provokes him into taking those actions. It is admittedly somewhat artificial to focus primarily on quantitative empirical studies of deterrence, while giving only minimal attention to the formal or nonformal theoretical literature from which hypotheses on deterrence are derived or to empirical analyses of these hypotheses through case study methodologies.[1] Much of this other literature, however, is covered elsewhere in this volume, and I will attempt to evaluate the assumptions and findings of quantitative empirical studies in terms of this broader theoretical and empirical literature.

In spite of its importance, the question of the conditions for deterrence has not received extensive treatment in the quantitative literature on international relations. The research most directly related to this question is that of Huth and Russett on extended deterrence, following up on Russett's influential piece on "The Calculus of Deterrence" in 1963, and their studies will be examined in detail. There has also been some interesting research on military threats and crisis behavior that does not focus specifically on deterrence but that has important implications for the question of the effectiveness of deterrent threats. This includes some of the work by North and his colleagues on the 1914 project; by Singer, Maoz, Leng, and others on recent extensions of the Correlates of War project; and by Karsten, Howell, and Allen in their historical study of military threats. I will examine these studies here and attempt to draw out their implications for the effectiveness of deterrence threats. It should be recognized, however, that because many of these studies were not designed specifically and solely to answer the theoretical question of the conditions affecting the success or failure of deterrence, my analysis of the bearing of these studies on that question should not be interpreted as a judgment of their overall merit.

The empirical findings from the quantitive empirical literature on deterrence cannot be easily summarized. They are sensitive to the empirical domain of the analysis, the selection of cases, the operational indicators of the independent and dependent variables, and to other aspects of the research design. Consequently, a meaningful analysis requires the specification of the theoretical questions toward which each study is directed and a discussion of the methodology by which it is carried out. For this reason I will examine a few important studies in some detail rather than present a laundry list of the empirical results of every study having something to do with deterrence.

One important theme in the literature concerns the relative importance of the dyadic balance of military capabilities in deterrence crises, and I will begin with that question. I will then examine in more detail the attempts of Karsten, Howell, and Allen and Huth and Russett to test a variety of hypotheses dealing with deterrence. Other empirical literature will be discussed where it has an important bearing on these other studies.

Before we begin it is necessary to make an important theoretical distinction between "general deterrence" and "immediate deterrence." Immediate deterrence refers to the relationship between opposing states "where at least one side is seriously considering an attack while the other is mounting a threat of retaliation in order to prevent it," whereas general deterrence refers to adversaries who "maintain armed forces to regulate their relationship even though neither is anywhere near mounting an attack" (Morgan, 1977: ch. 2). Immediate deterrence assumes the existence of a crisis or dispute in which military threats have been made and hence assumes the existence of the underlying conditions generating the crisis. General deterrence makes no assumption that there exists a crisis or serious dispute, that one state is seriously considering an attack on the other, or that a specific deterrent threat has been issued. Whereas general deterrence is concerned with the sources of crises as well as the conditions for crisis stability (stability within a crisis), immediate deterrence is concerned only with crisis stability. This study, and in fact most of the empirical literature on deterrence, is concerned with immediate deterrence rather than general deterrence, because the very question of the conditions under which deterrent threats are effective assumes the prior existence of a threat. As we will see, however, this distinction between general and immediate deterrence raises a difficult analytical problem.

## The Role of Capabilities

Deterrence can be defined as "the persuasion of one's opponent that the costs and/or risks of a given course of action he might take outweigh its benefits" (George and Smoke, 1974:11). Although there exists some disagreement regarding the precise requirements for effective deterrence, there is a consensus regarding some minimum conditions. A state must clearly define its commitment to defend a particular interest, communicate that commitment to the potential aggressor, possess a sufficiently potent military capability to impose costs on the adversary that exceed his expected gains, and demonstrate its resolve to implement the threat in spite of short-term costs to itself (Kaufmann, 1954; George and Smoke, 1974:ch.3; Lebow, 1981:84–85).

In spite of the numerous preconditions for successful deterrence, there are some proponents of a "power politics" model who focus primarily on military capabilities alone as the central element of deterrence. They assume that a state will not initiate a war that it expects to lose, so that the defender's possession of superior military capabilities (along with the adversary's recognition of that superiority) is a sufficient condition for deterrence. Although this is an ad hoc hypothesis that cannot technically be derived from any formal theory of deterrence, it has been accepted by some theorists as well as by statesmen and has also generated some interesting empirical research. This proposition is reflected in the old adage *si vis pacem para bellum* (if you want peace prepare for war, presumably by building up one's military capabilities), which has for centuries been used by statesmen to justify the expansion of their armaments programs. This proposition technically refers to sufficient rather than necessary conditions for deterrence: it does not say that the strong will always attack the weak, but only that the weak will never attack the strong in a situation isolated from the likely intervention of third states. Some adopt a stronger version of the hypothesis, however, and suggest that superior capabilities are a necessary as well as sufficient condition for deterrence, that the strong will attack the weak if there is nothing to prevent them from doing so. This is implied by the Athenians' argument to the Melians that "the strong do what they have the power to do and the weak accept what they have to accept" (Thucydides, 1954:V/89).

There are enough situations in which the strong do not attack the weak in spite of their ability to do so, as well as logical flaws in the argument, to cast serious doubt on the stronger version of the peace-through-strength hypothesis. Even the weaker version of the hypothesis, however, is flawed by serious logical problems in addition to some important contradictory cases. One problem is that it fails to incorporate the interests of the actors involved in the conflict. It is reasonable to assume that states consider the likely costs and benefits from war as well as the probability of victory based on the balance of dyadic capabilities, so that actions involving a low probability of success can be rationally undertaken if their potential benefits are sufficiently great and if there are some limits on the costs of defeat.[2] In addition, the costs and benefits of war should be compared to those of other alternatives, including the alternative of doing nothing. Consequently, weaker states may rationally initiate war if they believe that the existing status quo is so unacceptable that they have nothing to lose or that an attack by the adversary is imminent and that there are advantages in striking first.

In spite of these theoretical problems, the power politics hypothesis of deterrence has numerous advocates. The popularity of the hypothesis is suggested, perhaps, by the number of empirical studies designed to test it.[3]

## The North 1914 Studies

A fairly early study that has some bearing on the question of the importance of capabilities for the effectiveness of deterrent threats, though it was not designed to answer that specific theoretical question, is the 1961 article by Zinnes, North, and Koch, "Capability, Threat, and the Outbreak of War." Part of North's 1914 Project, this study uses content analysis of a fairly complete set of official diplomatic documents to examine the hypothesis that a state will not initiate a war if it perceives its (or its coalition's) military capabilities to be "significantly" inferior to those of its adversary. They offer an alternative hypothesis: "if a state's perception of injury (or frustration, dissatisfaction, hostility, or threat) to itself is 'sufficiently' great, this perception will offset perceptions of insufficient capability, . . . (and) under such circumstances, a state may go to war even though it perceives its power as relatively weak" (p. 470).[4] Here the independent variable is the perception of relative capabilities rather than an objective measure of capabilities.

The authors argue, with support from well-selected statements from high-ranking German or Austro–Hungarian political and military decision makers, that "both Austria and Germany possessed evidence of their own inadequate capabilities—yet they were not deterred" (p. 473). They report that their content analysis of approximately 3,000 documents demonstrates little German or Austrian concern with the balance of military capabilities until the last moment. Frequency counts of key indicators reveal that perceptions of (and, the authors imply, concern with) the adversary's hostility far exceeded perceptions of relative capabilities. The authors therefore reject the hypothesis that a state's military inferiority is sufficient to deter its initiation of a war and accept instead their alternative hypothesis. These results are supported by North's (1967) subsequent study, which uses events data on military actions ($N=354$) as well as perceptual data from the documents.

Space does not permit the exploration of alternative theoretical explanations of the findings of the 1914 studies with respect to the capabilities hypothesis or a review of some of the methodological limitations of these studies (Jervis, 1969; Hilton, 1970). One point should be mentioned, however, and that is the question of the validity of the use of frequency counts as a measure of the relative importance of perceptions of relative capabilities and adversary hostility. Jervis (1969) explains the greater frequency of perceptions of hostility by arguing that they change more rapidly than perceptions of capabilities and are in more need of constant updating, whereas capabilities are more constant and therefore less likely to be the focus of constant attention. Questions could also be raised about the validity of statements in official documents as measures of perceptions and intentions, given the multiple audiences toward which many of these statements are directed, and about the generalizability of the findings to other cases. In spite of its limitations, however, this study is still important. It was one of the first systematic empirical analyses to contradict the common assumption that perceptions of one's inferior capabilities will preclude one from initiating a war, that superior capabilities are always sufficient to deter an adversary from attacking. Its findings gain additional support from other studies that employ radically different methodologies to investigate similar theoretical questions.

## The "Correlates of War" Studies

Some of the work by Singer and his colleagues on the Militarized Interstate Dispute (MID) project (an extension of Singer's Correlates of War project) is relevant to the question of whether military superiority is sufficient for deterrence in international disputes, although they do not focus directly on deterrence per se. Maoz (1983) attempts to test a "capability model" versus a "resolve model" for all interstate disputes since the Congress of Vienna using the dispute data he collected with Gochman.[5] The capability/threat model predicts that the probability of victory for an initiator of a dispute (defined as "that state which has first committed a military confrontation action against another state") varies positively with the ratio of the initiator's capabilities to the target's capabilities, where capabilities are measured using the military expenditure and military personnel indicators from Singer's COW capability data.[6] The resolve model predicts that the outcome of the dispute is determined primarily by the resolve of the two parties, as measured by their relative levels of "hostility" reached during the dispute and by the extent to which one side undertakes "incidents" to maintain the initiative during the dispute (Maoz, 1983).

Maoz confirms the findings of others (Bueno de Mesquita, 1981) that initiators are disproportionately likely to emerge victorious in militarized disputes. His central empirical result is that the initiator's success is unrelated to the balance of military capabilities between initiator and target (or between the initiator's coalition and the target's coalition), thus disconfirming the predictions of the capability/threat model. The various resolve indicators, on the other hand, are significantly associated with dispute outcomes: Initiators tend to win when they display higher levels of hostility than their adversary or when they maintain control over the escalatory sequence of the dispute, lose when targets are more hostile or maintain the initiative, and tie when the two are matched on these indicators of resolve. Perhaps even more surprising, the resolve indicators have a greater impact on the outcome of disputes that escalate into wars than do the capability indicators. Maoz (1983:221) concludes that "initiators of serious interstate disputes tend to disproportionately emerge as victors not because they are stronger than targets but because they are able to demonstrate that the stakes of the dispute are more important to them than to their opponents."[7] He cautions, however, that whether this imbalance of resolve is real or whether it derives from the deceptive manipulation of risks by initiators needs to be analyzed. It should be emphasized that Maoz's findings suggest that the motivations and actions of the initiator of the dispute are more important than those of the defender in determining the outcome. This runs against the standard focus in classical deterrence theory on the importance of commitment, resolve, and signaling on the part of the defender. It is more consistent with the emphasis of George and Smoke (1974) on initiation theory and with a similar emphasis in the work of Lebow (1981) and Jervis, Lebow, and Stein (1985).[8]

Although this is not the place for a thorough critique of the Maoz (1983) article, it is important to point out some limitations of the study's relevance for the question of immediate deterrence (which, to repeat, was not its primary purpose). First, although all of the MID cases do involve situations in which at least one side has made a military threat against the other, they do not necessarily involve any specific attempt by the defender to deter the initiator from taking a specific action, so we could not necessarily conclude that any success by an initiator is a failure of deterrence. Second, Maoz does not differentiate between deterrence and compellence, which refers to the use of threats to induce an adversary to do something or to stop doing something rather than to refrain from doing something he has not yet done. Compellence is harder to implement than deterrence (Schelling, 1966:ch.2), so that the failure of compellence does not necessarily imply the failure of deterrence. Third, Maoz's operational indicators of resolve are highly questionable and fail to tap the importance of the stakes involved or the intensity of actors' commitments. Finally, Maoz's definition of success and failure is probably not appropriate for the analysis of the success or failure of deterrent threats. A dispute that escalates to war is coded as a success for the side that wins the war militarily (Maoz, 1982: appendix II). This may be useful for the theoretical questions he is asking, but from the perspective of deterrence such an outcome should be treated as a failure.

Wayman, Singer, and Goertz (1983) look at the impact of capabilities on the outcome of disputes from a slightly different perspective. They also use the MID data for the 1816–1976 period, but examine only disputes between the major powers ($N=101$). Their independent variables include both overall capability ratios, defined in terms of the COW project's six indicators of the demographic, economic/industrial, and military dimensions of national strength, and also the allocation of resources between the industrial and military sectors. Although the direct relevance of their findings for deterrence is limited by the same factors mentioned earlier with respect to Maoz's (1983) study—including the coding of a favorable war outcome as a success in the dispute for that actor (p. 501), the findings are nonetheless interesting. Overall superiority in military capabilities is advantageous in fighting a war, but industrial capabilities are more important than military preparedness (operationalized in terms of military expenditures and number of armed forces personnel). Moreover, initiators who overallocate in terms of expenditures vis-à-vis the industrial base have been defeated in war more often than they have been victorious. The value of military superiority in war (as long as it does not come at the expense of industrial might) disappears for disputes that do not escalate to war: The weaker party in terms of both personnel and expenditures tends to be more successful (pp. 504–10). The authors conclude (p. 513) by questioning the accuracy (at least for the post-Vienna period) of the statement by Frederick the Great that "God is always with the strongest battalions." (This theme is developed at length by Kennedy (1988) in his important study of the relationship between economic change and military power for the great powers over the last five centuries.)

In another study that uses the MID data but that is not part of the Correlates of War project, Bueno de Mesquita (1981:140–45) compares the relative predictive power of a power politics model with that of his expected utility model, which attempts to incorporate the interests of states (as measured by their alliance commitments) as well as their military capabilities. He examines the proportion of war initiators having superior military capabilities and the proportion having positive expected utility for the 1816 to 1974 period. Although the predictions of these models often overlap, under certain conditions they diverge, and consequently the percentage of correct predictions can be compared. Although war initiators tend disproportionately to be the stronger of two states, Bueno de Mesquita finds that the relationship between war initiation and states' expected utility for war is stronger than that between war initiation and relative capabilities. Moreover, the expected utility model is stable over time, whereas the predictive power of the power politics model is considerably weaker in the twentieth century than in the nineteenth century. Though Bueno de Mesquita's cases aren't restricted to situations involving deterrent threats, and though some might quarrel with his measurement of utilities solely in terms of alliance patterns, his findings provide further evidence against the proposition that one's military superiority is the primary determinant of the absence of aggression by the adversary. These and other findings suggest that deterrence practitioners should be at least as sensitive to the motivations of the potential aggressor as to the dyadic balance of military capabilities.[9]

## The Karsten, Howell, and Allen Study

In *Military Threats: A Systematic Historical Analysis of the Determinants of Success*, Karsten, Howell, and Allen (1984) make an explicit and comprehensive attempt to analyze the conditions contributing to the successful use of military threats and to determine whether these conditions have changed in the nuclear age. They include over 100 independent variables, grouped into categories of interests, objectives, capabilities, situational factors, clarity and accuracy of the threat, tactical variables, perceptions of the adversary, and others. A threat is defined to occur "only if leaders of one or more powers signaled clearly (either in public or in private) a willingness to use military force against one or more other nations in order to deter them from doing something or to compel them to do something" (p. 30).[10] A success (for either deterrence or compellence) occurs "only if the threatener's objectives are at least partially attained without recourse to fighting," and the seven-point scale for the dependent variable includes categories for total, substantial, and partial success. War is classified as a failure of deterrence, though the authors also include a category for whether or not the war results in the achievement of the threatener's political objectives. The empirical domain of the study includes 77 cases, from the beginning of the Peloponnesian War to the present. Cases involving threats that are a pretext for war (Lebow's [1981] "justification of hostility crises" are excluded). Regression analysis is used (after some needed justification) to determine the relationship between the predominantly ordinal independent and dependent variables.

The numerous findings are not all fully consistent, though some are particularly interesting. The balance of objective capabilities does not significantly affect the outcome of the crisis, and weaker or smaller states are no more likely to yield to threats than are stronger or larger states (pp. 54, 70). If the target perceives that the threatener has the capability to inflict serious damage, however, threats tend to succeed (pp. 69–70). On the other hand, the *threatener's* perceptions of the target's capabilities tend to be far less important (although this has changed in the nuclear age). In fact, there is a modest tendency, at least in the pre-1945 period, for threats to fail when the threatener perceived itself as superior and to succeed when it perceived itself as inferior (p. 83). This is explained in terms of the enormous importance of resolve and the threatener's perception of the extent to which the target's interests are at stake, although the target's perception of the extent to which the threatener's interests are at stake does not have a significant impact (p. 67). The authors conclude that neither the clarity of threats nor attempts to fine-tune threats have much impact on the outcome of the dispute.[11] They also argue that shows of force in support of a military threat are largely irrelevant to the outcome of the threat (pp. 73, 110). They criticize the common emphasis on the credibility, resolve, and signaling of the threatener and the common failure to recognize the importance of target goals and interests.

The validity of many of these findings is limited by some rather serious flaws in the research design. There is no clear theoretical framework guiding the study, and it is not obvious which of the 100 independent variables are most important or how they relate to one another. As a result, it is very difficult to interpret the findings or to determine the extent to which they are consistent. The 100 variables and 77 cases create serious problems of model specification and make it impossible to conduct a controlled empirical inquiry. The cases are not systematically selected from any well-defined population, so that it is difficult to generalize beyond the specific cases included in the study. Moreover, the criteria for the selection of the cases are not made explicit, so that it is difficult to estimate the biases that might affect the findings. It is also difficult to determine the extent to which the operational indicators are valid measures of the theoretical concepts, for the authors do not make many of their coding rules explicit (though they do recognize that "it is incumbent upon us to provide some illustrations of how we used evidence . . . " [p. 43]). Thus the book is quite uneven. The authors provide a reasonably sophisticated discussion of *some* of the conceptual and methodological issues involved in the empirical study of deterrence, and the more qualitative historical analysis in the study is impressive in breadth and quality, yet many aspects of the research design for their large-N empirical analysis do not inspire much confidence. For a more sophisticated large-N study of the efficacy of military threats, and one that focuses explicitly on deterrent threats, it would be useful to examine the Russett–Huth research program on extended deterrence.

## The Russett and Huth Studies

Of all the empirical studies of deterrence, those by Russett and Huth are in many respects the most relevant for our purposes. They focus explicitly on deterrence rather than on military threats in general, though they restrict themselves to the question of extended deterrence (deterrence of an attack against an ally) and do not examine the deterrence of a direct attack. Although their focus is on situational rather than decision-making variables, their most recent studies have begun to incorporate indicators of bargaining behavior, and by supplementing their quantitative analyses with case studies they have begun to examine some intervening perceptual variables. Their ongoing research program includes Russett's "The Calculus of Deterrence" (1963) and "Pearl Harbor: Deterrence Theory and Decision Theory" (1967); Huth and Russett's "What Makes Deterrence Work? Cases from 1900 to 1980" (1984), "After Deterrence Fails: Escalation to War?" (forthcoming), and "Deterrence Failure and Crisis Escalation (1988); and Huth's *Extended Deterrence and the Prevention of War* (1989) and "Extended Deterrence and the Outbreak of War" (1988). Although each study builds on the previous one it would be useful to consider each separately for several reasons. The evolution of this research program demonstrates the sensitivity of some empirical findings to the particular research design employed and also raises some important conceptual and methodological issues in the empirical study of deterrence. It also demonstrates the positive learning experience of the research program over time.[12]

## Russett, "The Calculus of Deterrence" (1963)

In his initial study of deterrence a quarter of a century ago, Russett frames his question of extended deterrence as follows: "How can a major power make credible an intent to defend a smaller ally from attack by another major power?" (p. 97). His objective is to identify the variables accounting for the success or failure of deterrent threats, and his method is a comparative study of "all the cases during the last three decades where a major power 'attacker' overtly threatened a pawn with military force, and where the defender either had given, prior to the crisis, some indication of an intent to protect the pawn or made a commitment in time to prevent the threatened attack." Russett generates 17 such cases from 1935 to 1961. He then measures several independent variables, including the importance of the pawn (pawn/defender ratio of both population and GNP); the presence or absence of a prior formal commitment by the defender; the dyadic balance of both overall strategic and local military power; the nature of the defender's political system (democratic or "totalitarian"); the extent of formal military cooperation between defender and pawn (arms transfers or military advisers); political interdependence between defender and pawn (defined generally in terms of a current or recent alliance, recent occupation, close ideological ties, etc.); and economic interdependence between defender and pawn (relative proportion of imports and exports). The dependent variable is deterrence success or failure, with success defined as "an instance when an attack on the pawn is prevented or repulsed without conflict between the attacking forces and regular combat units of the major power defender" (p. 98).

The comparative analysis is conducted without the use of formal statistical methods. It is found that the effectiveness of deterrent threats is unaffected by the size of the pawn, the existence of a formal commitment by the defender, or the strategic or local balance of military capabilities, though equality on at least one military dimension is a necessary (but not sufficient) condition for a deterrence success. Deterrent threats by democratic regimes are slightly less credible than those of nondemocratic regimes. Some level of military cooperation between defender and pawn appears to be a necessary condition for successful deterrence, but it is not sufficient. The existence of political ties is "helpful if not essential," and economic interdependence is "virtually essential" to successful deterrence (pp. 100–105). Russett then attempts to identify the factors associated with the defender's decision whether or not to go to war to defend the pawn once it has been attacked. Neither the size of the pawn, the military balance, nor the nature of the defender's regime has much of an impact on the defender's response, but bonds of economic, political, and military interdependence are quite important (as they were for the attacker's actions (pp. 105–106). Russett gives great emphasis to these bonds between defender and pawn and suggests that strengthening these ties is a means for the defender to increase the credibility of his deterrent threats. He fails to acknowledge, however, that increasing ties between defender and pawn to reinforce commitment and credibility may involve substantial costs.

Russett (1963:105–107) also presents a simple expected utility model (though he doesn't refer to it in those terms) to explain the actions of both attacker and defender, though this model appears in footnotes and is not fully integrated into the analysis as a whole. The defender will pursue a "firm" policy and attempt to deter the adversary if his prospective gains from successful deterrence, weighted by the probability of success and discounted by the cost and probability of war, exceed the losses of retreat (the failure to issue a deterrent threat). The adversary will attack in spite of the deterrent threat if the expected value of attacking (as determined by the value and expected probability of an attack that is not resisted by the deterrer and the cost and probability of war resulting from an attack that is resisted) exceeds the value of the status quo.[13]

There is little space here for an extended critique of Russett's article, but a few brief comments are in order, if only to demonstrate how some of the deficiencies are overcome in his subsequent studies. First, Russett's theoretical discussion is weakened by framing the question in terms of the credibility of the threat. Credibility is an intervening perceptual variable that may help explain, along with other variables, the effectiveness of the threat, but credibility is not equivalent to effectiveness. In fact, since Russett's expected-utility model includes the value of a successful (i.e., uncountered) attack, it implies that if the value of the target is important enough to the attacker, the existence of a credible threat by the defender will not be sufficient to deter. But Russett's analysis is not closely guided by the model he presents. He never directly tests whether or not the threat is believed (a perceptual variable), but only whether or not it leads to a successful outcome (a behavioral variable). It should be noted that this emphasis on the credibility of the threat affects the theoretical interpretation of the findings but not the validity of the observed empirical associations.[14]

A more serious problem from the perspective of the validity and generalizability of the empirical findings is the definition of deterrence success to include cases in which an attack on the pawn is repulsed without violent military conflict between the two major powers (p. 98). As a result, several cases that might normally be regarded as partial failures of deterrence are instead coded as instances of successful deterrence, including the Berlin Blockade (successful deterrence by the United States), Anglo–French attack on Egypt in 1956 (Soviet success), Chinese Communist artillery blockade of Quemoy in 1958, and Bay of Pigs (Soviet success) [George and Smoke, 1974:517]. To the extent that the 1948 Berlin crisis was a U.S. success, for example, it was a success of compellence after a partial failure of deterrence. Similarly, the successful U.S. threat against the Soviet Union in 1946 might be better classified as compellence than deterrence. The more general theoretical problem is the treatment of the dispute outcome (success–failure) as a dichotomous variable, whereas George and Smoke (1974) argue persuasively that deterrence can fail in a variety of different ways and that the initiator can often "design around" a deterrence threat. Though George and Smoke are undoubtedly correct on the theoretical level, I believe that for the purposes of a large-$N$ correlational study the dichotomous classification of the dependent variable is a reasonable first approximation, but one which ought to be refined in subsequent research.

Perhaps an even more serious problem with defining deterrence success is that the very concept implies a *causal* relationship, that the potential aggressor does not attack the pawn *because* of the defender's threat. The mere observation of nonattack is necessary but not sufficient to demonstrate this. One must also show that in the absence of such a threat the adversary would have attacked the pawn, and that the adversary was dissuaded by the defender's threat rather than something else (such as his domestic public opinion, anticipated diplomatic reaction, ability of the pawn to mount a successful or at least costly defense, etc.). This counterfactual hypothesis regarding what the adversary would have done in the absence of the deterrent threat involves a difficult analytical problem and substantial data requirements. Russett (and later Huth and Russett) attempts to deal with this problem by including the adversary's prior threat against the pawn as a definitional requirement for all cases, assuming such a threat to be a sufficient indicator of the adversary's intent to attack. Admittedly, this assumption is not always valid. An adversary may threaten a weaker ally not because it intends to attack but instead as a means to some other end: to win a concession on some other issue, to distract the defender's attention, or to induce him to divert vital military resources to the defense of the pawn (Fink, 1965). Such a threat may also be a product of the domestic or bureaucratic politics within the adversary's regime. A case study methodology can devote more attention to the motivations and intent of the potential attacker as a means of verifying the counterfactual, but even it can rarely be conclusive.[15] In any case, such intensive analysis is not feasible for a large-$N$ study of this kind.[16] My own view is that

Russett's assumption is reasonable as a first approximation but that additional work to confirm the validity of this indicator of the adversary's intent would be very valuable.

Thus in spite of its limitations Russett's 1963 study marks the initiation of an important research program. This program is particularly impressive because of Russett's recognition of the costs of excluding perceptual variables and the limitations of correlational analysis for making causal inferences. In a 1970 article he discusses the need to use both correlational and case study methods to complement each other for the purposes of the development of theory, and his case study of Pearl Harbor is consistent with this conception of theory building and cumulation in international research.

### Russett, "Pearl Harbor: Deterrence Theory and Decision Theory" (1967)

One of the main purposes of the Pearl Harbor study was to explore and validate some of the empirical associations uncovered in the earlier correlational analysis. Russett's (1963:106–7) earlier expected-utility model is used as a framework for the theoretical interpretation of Japan's decision for war. In spite of the absence of an explicit American deterrent threat, Russett (1967:94–96) argues, Japanese decision makers were fully convinced that the United States would respond militarily to a Japanese attack on Malaya and especially the Dutch East Indies because of the strategic and economic value of those colonies (pp. 94–96). This is consistent with Russett's (1963) argument that military, political, and economic ties reinforce commitment in a way that formal threats do not.[17] The fact that the Japanese perceived the U.S. threat to be highly credible but attacked anyway demonstrates the fallacy (in Russett's 1963 study) of equating the credibility of the threat with its effectiveness. Russett shows that the Japanese in fact perceived the military superiority of the United States and that the Japanese expected to lose a prolonged war *if* the United States chose to fight such a war (pp. 98–99). This is consistent with the findings of other studies surveyed above that the military superiority of the defender, even if accurately perceived, is not sufficient for deterrence. This is explained in part by the very low assessment of the value of the status quo, which was reinforced by domestic and bureaucratic political as well as strategic and economic considerations (pp. 96–98).

Thus Russett rejects the common argument that the Japanese attack on Pearl Harbor was an irrational action and argues that given Japanese preferences, expectations, and constraints, their behavior was consistent with a rational expected-utility calculus.[18] He acknowledges, however, that some departure from a rational model may be necessary to explain both Japan's assumption that the United States would prefer to reach a negotiated settlement recognizing Japanese hegemony in Southeast Asia than to fight a prolonged war, and their failure to explore the validity of that assumption. Finally, on the basis of this case Russett argues that a theory of extended deterrence must include in the set of possible outcomes a direct attack against the defender as well as inaction and an attack against the pawn.[19]

## Huth and Russett, "What Makes Deterrence Work?" (1984)

This article develops the expected-utility model from Russett (1963) and tests the model on cases of extended, immediate deterrence from 1900 to 1980. It makes a number of improvements on Russett's first study. It recognizes the problem of inferring the success of deterrence and argues that by explicitly focusing on immediate deterrence the problem is reduced though not eliminated (p. 497). By extending the temporal domain of the study back to 1900 and forward to 1980, it significantly increases the number of cases to 54. This permits the use of more formal statistical methods, which were not used in Russett's 1963 study. Deterrence failure occurs if there is an attack against the protégé, operationally defined as "a government-sanctioned engagement of its regular armed forces in combat with the regular armed forces of the protégé and/or its defender, resulting in more than 250 fatalities." Cases in which the attacker gains its principal goals or occupies the territory of the protégé in spite of minimal fatalities are also classified as failures of deterrence. All other cases are classified as deterrence successes, which include 57 percent of the total number of cases (Huth and Russett, 1984:505).

This study also introduces some new independent variables and refines some of the operational indicators for variables used in earlier studies. Hypotheses based on five different dimensions of relative military capabilities are now tested: overall military and economic capabilities, or military potential; overall existing military capabilities; potential local capabilities proximate to the protégé (in a semantic change, the authors refer to the "protégé" rather than the "pawn"); existing local capabilities; and defender's possession or nonpossession of nuclear weapons. (There is no indicator tapping whether or not the initiator has nuclear weapons, and thus whether the crisis involves a confrontation between two nuclear powers.) Economic and military capabilities are measured using the Correlates of War capability data (Singer, Bremer, and Stuckey, 1972), with a loss-of-strength gradient introduced for local capabilities (p. 510). The effect of the defender's previous behavior is introduced through dummy variables tapping whether or not the defender had fought on behalf of the protégé in the previous deterrent situation (against any adversary). The presence or absence of a formal military alliance between defender and protégé is also included. Economic ties are measured by the protégé's share of the defender's total merchandise exports and imports, and political–military ties are measured by a four-point scale of the percentage share of major weapons systems imported by the protégé from the defender. The strategic importance of the protégé to the defender is measured (as before) by the ratio of the protégé's capabilities (on the various dimensions) to those of the defender, and whether or not they shared a common border. Although the Pearl Harbor study demonstrated the critical importance of the expected utility of peace to the attacker, this variable is very difficult to measure and is not incorporated into the model, which is a serious limitation and one acknowledged by the authors (p. 514). Each of the just-named factors is an independent variable in a linear model predicting the success or failure of deterrence. The relationships are analyzed by the technique of probit analysis, which is similar to regression analysis but more appropriate in the case of a dichotomous dependent variable.

The model predicts 78 percent of all cases correctly. The variables having a significant ($p < .10$) impact on deterrence success or failure include economic and political ties (trade and arms transfers) and the local military balance. The existence of a formal military alliance (formed *prior* to the aggressor's initial threat) between defender and protégé is moderately important but tends to *reduce* the likelihood of successful deterrence.[20] The overall strategic balance and the defender's behavior in previous crises, however, appear to have little impact on the effectiveness of deterrence. Moreover, the defender's possession of nuclear weapons has only a "marginal" impact on outcomes. This leads Huth and Russett (1984:516–18) to conclude that "local military capabilities (of the defender and protégé combined) seem to have more to do with successful deterrence than do strategic capabilities, and both may be less important than having a dense network of political and economic bonds between defender and protégé." This is consistent with the findings of other studies previously surveyed that the balance of military capabilities is not the primary determinant of deterrence.[21]

After examining the sources of deterrence success and failure, Huth and Russett (1984:520–23) analyze the factors determining whether the defender will fight to defend its protégé, which happened in 15 of their 23 cases. The defender is more likely to fight if the protégé is important in terms of its relative military capability, and particularly if there exists a military alliance between defender and protégé. However, the dyadic military balance between defender and attacker, geographical contiguity, and the defender's past behavior are not associated with the occurrence or nonoccurrence of war.

It is important to note that the variables associated with deterrence success and those associated with the defender's decision to fight if deterrence fails are not the same. The only factor important in both decisions is the existence of a military alliance between defender and protégé, the effect of which reverses direction in the second decision. This is a particularly dangerous combination and leads Huth and Russett (1984:522) to conclude, again emphasizing the importance of economic and political ties between defender and protégé, that "a military alliance not backed up by more tangible linkages . . . may *increase* the danger that a defender will be drawn into war." The tendency for alliances to encourage the adversary to attack the protégé and then to lead the defender to intervene would appear to imply a mismatch between the calculations of the attacker and the defender, but Huth and Russett (1984:522–23) suggest an alternative interpretation in which economic and political ties are the primary influence on the attacker's decision and alliances are more important for the defender's decision.[22]

## Huth and Russett, "After Deterrence Fails: Escalation to War?" (1988)[23]

This paper, like the previous one, deals with both the determinants of the success of immediate extended deterrence and with the determinants of escalation to war in the event that deterrence fails. It goes beyond the previous study by suggesting additional hypotheses, introducing new variables and conceptualizing others, modifying some definitional criteria and empirical indicators, extending the temporal domain, and by making the corresponding changes in the data base. As a result, there are some new empirical findings.

More specifically, the temporal domain of the study is extended back until 1885. This, plus further additions and deletions based on the examination of previously unused sources, results in an increase in the number of cases from 54 to 58.[24] In one particularly significant change from the 1984 study, the measure of the past behavior of the defender (whether or not it came to the defense of the protégé) is altered to tap its behavior in the last deterrent situation with the *same* adversary rather than with any adversary. The concept of relative military capabilities (and hypotheses related to them) is also modified and improved and now includes immediate, short-term, and long-term dimensions, plus the defender's possession/nonpossession of nuclear weapons. The immediate balance, measured by forces currently and proximately available to attack or defend the protégé, are hypothesized to be the most important for both deterrence success and for the defender's decision whether to intervene in the case of deterrence failure. The short-term balance consists of all active-duty forces and readily available reserves. The long-term military balance is defined as all existing military forces and national mobilization capabilities (economic, industrial, demographic) for fighting a protracted war.[25] It is hypothesized that the attacker does not usually expect a long war of attrition and therefore discounts the importance of the long-term balance of capabilities and that he may attack in spite of his inferiority in long-term forces as long as he has superiority in immediate or even short-term forces. The long-term balance is hypothesized to be important only for the defender's decision regarding whether to intervene to save the protégé after the failure of deterrence, but even that is qualified.

The most significant theoretical change from the earlier Russett–Huth studies is the inclusion of the bargaining behavior of the adversaries into the model. The basic hypothesis is that the effectiveness of diplomatic and military techniques used by the adversaries to influence each other is a nonlinear function of the firmness of one's bargaining behavior, with threats of moderate firmness being the most effective. Excessively conciliatory bargaining behavior undermines credibility and therefore deterrence, and excessively hostile threats provoke equally hostile responses and trigger an upward spiral of escalation. Drawing on some of Leng's early work on the Behavioral Correlates of War project, Huth and Russett have compiled chronological summaries of the diplomatic and military actions of both defender and attacker for each case of attempted deterrence.[26] The diplomatic responses of the defender are coded according to the degree of cooperation and flexibility, and the military actions of attacker and defender are coded by a six-point scale of escalation. The military responses of the defender are then classified as to whether they matched, exceeded, or failed to match the attacker's level of escalation at each stage in the crisis. These many pairs of actions over the course of the crisis are then aggregated into a single measure reflecting the "predominant influence strategy" (Leng and Wheeler, 1979) of a state on both diplomatic and military dimensions. Diplomatic strategies are classified as bullying, conciliatory, or firm-but-fair, and military actions are classified as either policies of strength, weakness, or tit-for-tat.

The definition of deterrence success or failure is the same as for the 1984 study. Failure is defined as "an attack on the protégé by regular military forces resulting in more than 250 fatalities, where the attacker gained its principal political or territorial goals even though fatalities were minimal, or where the attacker occupied territory of the protégé for several years" (Huth and Russett, forthcoming). Success is the absence of such an attack. This implies that an attack that is repulsed with minimal casualties by the protégé or the deterrer is defined as a deterrent success. Thus the 1948 Berlin case is still classified as a deterrent success for the United States, which illustrates the problem of failing to include a category for the partial failure of deterrence. Another limitation of the 1984 study that is not corrected here is the failure to incorporate the attacker's evaluation of the acceptability of the status quo, the importance of which was demonstrated by Russett's (1967) case study on Pearl Harbor.[27]

Applying probit analysis to the data, Huth and Russett (forthcoming) find that successful deterrence is associated with an immediate or short-term balance of forces favoring the defender ($p < .05$), with the long-term balance being only weakly associated with the outcome.[28] The defender's possession of nuclear weapons, or an overt threat to use them, has no impact on the outcome of the crisis.[29] In the most surprising finding, and one contrary to the central result of the 1963 and 1984 studies, economic and political-military ties between defender and protégé are found to be unrelated to the success or failure of deterrence. Unfortunately, the authors make little effort to explain this dramatic change from their previous studies, though they do assert that it derives from the introduction of crisis-bargaining variables into the analysis.[30] These bargaining variables are found to be significantly correlated with the success or failure of deterrence. As hypothesized, reciprocal strategies are found to be associated with successful outcomes. Deterrence is likely to succeed if the defender follows a firm-but-fair diplomatic strategy, and likely to fail for defenders following conciliatory or bullying strategies ($p < .01$). Similarly, tit-for-tat policies of military actions are usually successful, whereas excessively firm or cautious policies are not ($p < .025$).[31]

Another finding that runs contrary to the results of the 1984 study is that the reputation of the defender, defined here as its behavior in the last crisis against the same adversary,[32] is correlated with the outcome of a crisis.[33] Both backing down and prevailing in the last crisis against the same adversary are associated with the failure of deterrence, leading Huth and Russett (forthcoming) to conclude that "a stalemate is a safer outcome." This conclusion, however, must be regarded with a certain amount of skepticism in the absence of further research. The sensitivity of many of these empirical findings to relatively minor changes in the operationalizations of certain variables or to the addition of new variables is one ground for caution. In addition, the failure to examine alternative explanations for the selection of different bargaining strategies raises the possibility of spurious inferences regarding the causal impact of these strategies.[34] Huth and Russett (forthcoming) conclude that the attacker's decision appears to be based primarily on short-term considerations, particularly military ones, and that long-term military power avails little. What is important is the defender's ability to prevent a quick seizure of territory or to roll back that seizure relatively promptly, not the threat of future retaliation. They infer from this that deterrence by denial is more critical than deterrence by punishment (Snyder, 1961) for immediate extended deterrence.

Now let us consider the conditions affecting the defender's decision to go to war in the event that deterrence fails. The model correctly postdicts 83 percent of these cases ($n = 24$). The short-term balance of military forces in being is statistically significant, and the long-term balance is nearly significant. The defender's ties with the protégé are also important, particularly formal alliances and geographic proximity. Crisis-bargaining behavior is statistically significant ($p = .10$).

Thus several factors that appear to be important in the attacker's decision whether or not to defy a deterrent threat are relatively unimportant or less important in the defender's decision whether to fight in the event that deterrence fails. The immediate balance of military forces and the past behavior of the defender are no longer important, and the crisis-bargaining behavior of the defender is slightly less important than that of the initiator. The less-immediate dimensions of military power are more significant, as are the nature and strength of linkages between defender and protégé. The fact that the decisions of the attacker and defender are influenced by such different criteria increases their insensitivity to the cost–benefit calculations made by the other. States are particularly likely to underestimate the adversary's perceived costs of retreat, and the attacker is likely to underestimate the importance of defender–protégé bonds to the defender. This increases the likelihood of serious misperceptions of adversary intentions and consequently increases the likelihood of war (Levy, 1983).

## Back to Capabilities: The Problem of Selection Bias

One of the themes emerging from most of the studies surveyed above is that the possession of military superiority by the defender is no guarantee that deterrence will work. The overall (long-term) balance of military capabilities between two states does not have a significant impact on the success or failure of immediate deterrence (and perhaps on the effectiveness of military threats in general). Moreover, although strategic deterrence may be effective in regulating the behavior of nuclear states toward each other, there is little evidence that nuclear weapons (in the hands of the defender) affect the success or failure of extended deterrence of attacks on allies.[35] Several studies suggest, however, that the balance of conventional capabilities in proximity to the target does play an important role in extended deterrence. Taken together, these findings are consistent with a more general theme emphasized by George and Smoke (1974) and by George (1984) in his work on crisis management: The utility of military threats, whether deterrent or compellent in nature, depends on the threatener's possession of a spectrum of military capabilities and options appropriate to the level of the threat and the behavior it is attempting to influence.

It is essential to recognize, however, that there is a serious but perhaps unavoidable flaw in these research designs regarding the role of military capabilities in immediate deterrence, and that it is difficult to assess the extent to which this biases the empirical findings. In order to lend plausibility to the inference that the absence of a military attack constitutes an indicator of successful deterrence, there needs to be some evidence that the potential attacker would have attacked in the absence of a deterrent threat, that he was seriously considering military action. Several studies fail to provide such evidence, and this limits the relevance of their results for the question of immediate deterrence. The Huth and Russett studies attempt to deal with this problem by requiring the existence of the aggressor's prior threat against the protégé as a definitional requirement for a deterrence situation and assume such a threat implies that the attacker intended to act militarily. Although some assumption of this kind may be necessary, it may result in a *biased selection of cases* included in the study and consequently an *underestimation of the importance of military capabilities in immediate deterrence*.

The problem is that a research design incorporating the assumption of a prior threat permits an analysis of the conditions for the success or failure of immediate deterrence but not of the conditions under which the attacker makes the threat that initiates the crisis and thus qualifies the case for inclusion.[36] If the attacker makes threats only in those instances in which its expected probability of success (as determined by the balance of military capabilities) is sufficiently high, then because of selection bias the importance of capabilities may not be reflected in an analysis of the attacker's later decision whether or not to defy the deterrence threat and attack. There are different dimensions of military capabilities, of course.

The problem of selection bias occurs whenever the same dimension or combination of dimensions of military strength (whether it be long-term, immediate, or local) affects both the initiator's original threat (which determines case selection) and his decision regarding whether or not to implement the threat.[37] If threats are made and carried out primarily by the strong on the basis of their military strength (however they define it), that might not be detected by Huth and Russett or by others studying disputes involving a prior threat.[38]

A similar problem would arise in an analysis of the importance of the protégé to the attacker in immediate deterrence,[39] because to the extent that the initial threat is made only against important targets, selection bias will result in an underestimation of the impact of this variable in immediate deterrence. Combining the capability (which affects expected probability of success) and value variables, we see that the problem of selection bias precludes a straightforward analysis of the role of the initiator's expected utility of attack in immediate deterrence.

The potential seriousness of the problem of selection bias is demonstrated by the finding that deterrence is significantly more likely to fail if the protégé has a preexisting military alliance with its major power defender.[40] As Huth and Russett (1984:17) recognize, the very fact that the aggressor makes a threat under such conditions suggests its determination to carry out the threat regardless of any attempt by the protégé's major defender to deter that action. This sugggests that the critical variables affecting both the decision to issue the initial threat and the decision to attack are the interests and motivations of the aggressor rather than the presence or absence of alliances and that the failure to incorporate these variables into the analysis may result in spurious inferences.[41]

Both the Karsten, Howell, and Allen (1984:31–32) and Huth and Russett (1984:524) studies acknowledge this general problem. The latter caution that "these findings apply only to cases of immediate deterrence . . . in which an overt military threat from a potential attacker has already become manifest. Perhaps this kind of case understates the value of military strength in general deterrence. If military power were overwhelming, possibly no aggressor would ever rise to the level of making the overt challenge that characterizes these cases" (p. 524). I would argue, however, that this selection bias affects not only the analysis of general deterrence but also the interpretation of the results in cases of immediate deterrence, because spurious inferences from observed correlations cannot be ruled out. This problem concerns any variable that affects both the criteria upon which the case selection is based and the success or failure of immediate deterrence. We are caught in a difficult dilemma. If we make the distinction between general and immediate deterrence and examine only those cases in which there is some indication of a prior intention to attack, we risk introducing serious selection biases into the analysis. If, on the other hand, we make no distinction between general and immediate deterrence, we seriously diminish our ability to make the causal inference that the absence of an attack is due to successful deterrence.

Although Huth and Russett not only acknowledge this dilemma but also deal with it in a reasonable manner, there may be alternative methodologies for dealing with the problem of selection bias, and the exploration of these constitutes an important avenue for further research. One potentially fruitful approach would be the application of some sophisticated new statistical methods developed for quasi-experimental research designs utilizing nonrandom samples (Achen, 1986). Another possibility would be to supplement the analysis of immediate deterrence with a separate analysis of the conditions under which military threats are initially made or, more generally, of the conditions under which one state seriously considers an attack against another.[42]

## Conclusions

The quantitative empirical studies surveyed above deal with different aspects of the question of when deterrence works and identify different independent variables. They also utilize different operational indicators, temporal domains, types of data, and methods of analysis. Yet several general themes do emerge. One concerns the role of military capabilities in deterrence. We have seen that the overall (long-term) balance of military capabilities between two states has at most a secondary impact on the success or failure of immediate deterrence (and on the effectiveness of military threats in general), though this finding must be regarded as tentative until the magnitude of selection biases can be assessed. Several studies suggest, however, that the balance of conventional capabilities in proximity to the target does play an important role in extending deterrence. Taken together, these findings are consistent with a more general theme emphasized by George and Smoke (1974) and by George (1984) in his work on crisis management: The utility of military threats, whether deterrent or compellent in nature, depends on the threatener's possession of a spectrum of military capabilities and options appropriate to the level of the threat and the behavior it is attempting to influence.

The finding that superior military capabilities alone are not necessarily sufficient for deterrence can be explained in part by the tremendous importance of the interests and resolve of the initiator of the crisis, which is another theme emerging from several of these studies. Bueno de Mesquita (1981) demonstrates the superiority of an expected utility model incorporating the initiator's utility for war as well as its expected probability of success. Maoz (1983) and Karsten, Howell, and Allen (1984) go further and give greater emphasis to the motivations and behavior of the initiator than to the capabilities, commitment, and signaling of the defender. These factors are difficult to operationalize in large-N studies, however, for their measurement often requires a fairly intensive examination of individual cases. For this reason, the quantitative empirical literature on deterrence has generally been less successful than the case study literature (George and Smoke, 1974:Chapter 17; Lebow, 1981; Jervis, Lebow, and Stein, 1985; Betts, 1987; Russett, 1967) in dealing with the motivations and perceptions of the initiator. The quantitative literature has also given far too little attention to the domestic incentives that often lead states to take military action in spite of a credible deterrent threat by the defender (Lebow, 1981; Levy, 1988a, 1989).

Another important theme emerging from several of these studies concerns the stabilizing effects of reciprocity in the interaction between adversaries. These are important findings, particularly since they are reinforced by other social scientific research on reciprocity (Axelrod, 1984). Although these studies are reasonably rigorous and systematic, the operationalization of reciprocity in large-N studies is a difficult task, and this is a sufficiently important theoretical question to require further research from several different theoretical and methodological perspectives. Another aspect of deterrence theory requiring further research is the role of reputation, or the impact of the past behavior of the adversaries. This variable has received little attention in the quantitative empirical literature on deterrence, not only because of the difficulty of constructing an operational indicator for a large-N study but also because of the limited development of this variable in the theoretical literature. One particularly interesting but highly tentative finding emerging from the Huth and Russett (1984, forthcoming) studies is that the success or failure of deterrence is associated with the defender's response in the previous deterrence situation with the same adversary but not with its behavior against another adversary. If confirmed, this finding would suggest that reputation must be treated as a multidimensional concept.

This review of quantitative empirical studies of deterrence has demonstrated that this is not an isolated body of literature, but instead has substantial intellectual interconnections with both rational deterrence theory and with the case study literature on deterrence. Many of the hypotheses that it has systematically tested were derived from these other bodies of literature, and the quantitative empirical literature has in turn contributed to the development of theoretical generalizations regarding when deterrence works. New developments in both the formal and nonformal theoretical literature on deterrence provide a rich source of important hypotheses that should now be tested empirically by systematic quantitative analysis as well as by case study methods. In addition, some of the findings from quantitative empirical studies represent interesting theoretical anomalies and ought to stimulate additional theoretical analysis. The broader literature on deterrence provides a useful model of how formal theoretical, quantitative empirical, and case study methodologies can supplement each other to enhance our understanding of important theoretical questions that also have undeniable implications for contemporary international security.

## NOTES

This research has been supported by the Stanford Center for International Security and Arms Control, the Carnegie Corporation, and by a Social Science Research Council/MacArthur Foundation Fellowship in International Peace and Security. The views expressed here do not necessarily represent those of the Center, Council, or either Foundation. This study has benefited from the comments and criticisms of Christopher Achen, Robert Jervis, Kimberly Marten, John Mearsheimer, Paul Stern, Steven Weber, and especially Alexander George.

1. For a classification of the literature addressing the general theoretical question of when deterrence works, and a brief comparison of classical deterrence theory, the case study literature on deterrence, and the quantitative empirical literature, see Levy (1988c). See also Chapter 1 of this volume.

2. The importance of the balance of interests at stake in a conflict is emphasized by George and Smoke (1974) in their concept of asymmetry of motivation and by Jervis (1979:314–17) in his concept of "intrinsic interests." Both the probability of victory or defeat and the value of those outcomes have been integrated into an expected utility theory of war by Bueno de Mesquita (1981).

3. Dyadic-level studies of the "parity hypothesis" and the "power preponderance hypothesis," which concern the relationship between the distribution of capabilities between pairs of states and the frequency of war between them, are more relevant to the question of general deterrence than immediate deterrence, because they are not concerned with the question of whether one state is even considering aggression against another. Consequently, these studies will not be examined here. It should be noted, however, that although some of these studies do support the dyadic preponderance hypothesis (Garnham, 1976; Organski and

Kugler, 1980), the bulk of the evidence runs against it. See Ferris (1973), Siverson and Sullivan (1983), and (in the anthropological literature) Naroll, Bullough, and Naroll (1974).

4. Note that unless the qualifier "sufficiently" is operationally defined, its inclusion seriously reduces the explanatory and predictive power of the hypothesis by making it nearly nonfalsifiable.

5. The Militarized Interstate Dispute project (MID) was designed to help answer the question of why some interstate disputes escalate to war while others do not. The project and the data set it has generated are summarized in Gochman and Maoz (1984) and in Maoz (1982). This is probably the most widely used data set in quantitative international conflict studies today. A militarized interstate dispute is defined as "a set of interactions between or among states involving threats to use military force, displays of military force, or actual uses of military force. . . . [they are] explicit, overt, nonaccidental, and government sanctioned." Gochman and Maoz define 14 types of military acts, classified as threats, displays, and uses of force, and identify 960 militarized disputes from 1816 to 1976. These studies focus on objective military capabilities rather than on decision makers' perceptions of those capabilities. Note that not all disputes reach a level of intensity sufficient to qualify as a crisis; crises are subsets of disputes.

6. I use "capability/threat model" to refer to Maoz's "threat model," because the former is more descriptively accurate. Maoz also suggests another capability model, the power transition model, for which the key independent variable is change in relative military capabilities. This may be an important variable in the process leading to war (Levy, 1987), but is not normally included in the theoretical or empirical literature on deterrence and will not be examined here.

7. An important exception is that capability ratios do have a significant impact on the outcome of disputes and wars between major powers, though it is not indicated in the article whether the resolve indicators have an even greater impact.

8. Maoz's results are consistent with those of Blechman and Kaplan (1978) in their study of 12 cases since World War II in which the United States threatened the use of force against the Soviet Union. They find that demonstrating resolve is more important for a successful outcome than regional or global military superiority.

9. The argument that overall military capabilities have only a secondary impact on immediate deterrence would seem to be strengthened by the fact that most empirical studies of the relationship between the dyadic balance of military capabilities and war support the "parity hypothesis" rather than the "power preponderance" hypothesis (see footnote 3). The relationship between these studies and our ability to make inferences is complicated by the fact that they focus on slightly different sets of cases. The latter set of studies focus on the direct relationship between pairs of states, whereas the Russett–Huth analyses focus on a more restricted set of cases involving the existence of (1) a prior threat and (2) one that is directed against a third party. Further research is clearly needed on the relationship between these different dimensions of deterrence.

10. The authors are explicit in focusing on "direct" as opposed to "indirect" threats. The former are linked to clearly stated objectives and are temporally limited, whereas the latter are designed to "deter certain types of issues from being raised" (Karsten, Howell, and Allen, 1984:4). This is similar to Morgan's (1977) distinction between immediate and general deterrence.

11. Whether clear and specific threats are more effective than more ambiguous and general threats is an important question. Leng's data-based studies of interstate crisis behavior (see my summary of his Behavioral Correlates of War project in Note 26) are consistent with the Karsten, Howell, and Allen findings. He finds, in a study of a stratified random sample of 14 crises since 1850 (Leng, 1980) as well as in a more specific study of recent U.S.–Soviet behavior (Leng, 1984), that the more specific the threat the greater the likelihood of a defiant response. Presumably, some degree of vagueness facilitates the target's compliance with the threat by avoiding the appearance of being bullied. Leng agrees with Snyder and Diesing (1977) and others that face-saving is a critical dimension in the resolution of any dispute, even where one party is militarily dominant. George and Smoke (1974: ch. 17) suggest another reason precise threats may fail: The target is frequently able to "design around" a deterrent threat, particularly if that state has multiple options by which to achieve its objectives.

12. I will make some references to Huth's recent article and book (1988, 1989) but will not examine them in detail, because at the time of this writing they have not yet been published. I will not focus on the third Huth and Russett (1988) article because it does not go significantly beyond the second one (forthcoming).

13. Formally, the defender will pursue a firm policy and attempt to deter a possible attack only if, in his calculation,

$$V_f * s + V_w * (1 - s) > V_r$$

where

$V_f$ = the value of successful firmness (deterrence without war)
$V_w$ = the value (usually negative) of the failure of firmness (war)
$V_r$ = the value (usually negative) of retreat (no attempt to deter an attack)
$s$  = the probability that firmness will be successful.

The initiator will attack only if

$$V_a * t + V_c * (1 - t) > V_o$$

where

$V_a$ = the value of a successful attack (defender does not intervene)
$V_c$ = the value (usually negative) of an attack that is countered (war)
$V_o$ = the value of doing nothing (i.e., the status quo)
$t$  = the probability of a successful (uncountered) attack.

14. For further discussion of this problem, and a simple derivation from the expected utility model of the conditions under which a credible threat will be a necessary and sufficient condition for deterrence, see the critique by Fink (1965).

15. This problem of identifying genuine deterrence success led George and Smoke (1974) to restrict their study to cases of deterrence failure. This was reasonable for the purposes of their study, which is concerned with constructing a typological theory of deterrence failure. Ultimately, however, the success or failure of deterrence cannot be fully *explained* without a fully controlled study that includes cases of deterrence success as well as failure.

16. Admittedly, Russett's $N$ of 17 cases is too small to capture all of the advantages of a large-$N$ correlational analysis (and probably too large to permit a very intensive analysis of individual cases), but the number of cases is increased in his later studies.

17. This is reminiscent of Jervis's (1970) distinction between signals and indices.

18. Russett's classification of this case as a deterrent failure gives insufficient attention to the fact that U.S. threats involved compellence as well as deterrence. The United States attempted not only to deter the Japanese from moving into Southeast Asia but also to compel them to withdraw from China and used a highly coercive oil embargo to enforce this policy. This case involved the backfiring of a strategy of compellence as much as the failure of deterrence.

19. In the nuclear age a direct attack against a major power defender rather than its pawn is unlikely to be a viable option.

20. Huth and Russett (1984:517) explain this by arguing that if an adversary threatens a protégé that is formally allied to the defender, that adversary has already decided to stand firm and carry out the threat.

21. Blechman and Kaplan (1978:527) reach similar conclusions regarding the outcomes of cases involving the threat or use of force short of war since World War II. They find, both from their aggregate analysis and from their case studies, no evidence that crisis decisions are strongly influenced by aggregate strategic capabilities and argue that the local balance of conventional power tends to be more important. Organski and Kugler (1980:ch. 4) reach similar conclusions from their examination of 14 cases of deterrence since 1945. They find that nuclear powers have prevailed in only about half of these but that conventional superiority does make a difference. Kugler (1984) presents comparable results and finds that even a nuclear monopoly has brought a favorable outcome only about half the time. Weede (1983), however, finds that mutual nuclear deterrence has reduced the risk of war not only between superpowers but also between allies in opposing blocs.

22. They hypothesize, in the ellipses in the quoted passage, that these linkages "perhaps give the defender some control to prevent adventurism by a protégé." Alternative explanations would have to be considered, however, including selection bias, a point to which I will return. I should note that the statement quoted in the text is not technically supported by their analysis. It implies an interaction effect between military alliances and tangible (i.e., economic or political) linkages, but no such term is formally incorporated into their model.

23. Since this study has not yet been published, I have not referred to specific page numbers. The quoted passages are taken from the authors' May 1986 confer-

ence paper (University of British Columbia, Vancouver) and from several revised versions of it. The authors have been kind enough to point out aspects of earlier versions of my review that have been affected by their revisions, and I have made changes where appropriate.

24. Some cases were deleted because of the ambiguity regarding whether a prior threat of attack actually existed (and thus whether this was actually a case of immediate deterrence). Other cases were deleted because the intervention of the defender occurred after hostilities (between attacker and protégé) had already escalated to the level of large-scale armed conflict, leading to the classification of the case as compellence rather than deterrence (Huth, 1989).

25. The immediate balance corresponds to the "existing local" balance in the 1984 study; the short-term balance to the "existing overall" balance; and the long-term balance to the "potential overall" balance.

26. The Behavioral Correlates of War project (BCOW) is not restricted to cases of deterrence and does not deal directly enough (for our purposes) with the central hypotheses in the theoretical and empirical literature on deterrence to be thoroughly analyzed here, given space constraints. It is, however, a very important ongoing research program on crisis-bargaining behavior, in part because it demonstrates the potential utility of a large-N quantitative analysis of the role of behavioral variables in the bargaining process. Consequently, it would be useful to summarize the project briefly here and subsequently make a few references to some of its major findings where appropriate in the remainder of this study.

BCOW is the most recent extension (along with the Militarized Interstate Dispute project) of Singer's Correlates of War project. It was developed to facilitate the testing of a wide range of hypotheses dealing with bargaining in interstate crises and particularly the propensity of certain kinds of bargaining behavior to result in war. A typology of state actions was constructed and utilized for the generation of events data on a set of interstate crises. Unlike most events data sets, BCOW includes secondary historical sources as well as newspaper accounts. The data base currently (1988) consists of a stratified random sample of 38 militarized interstate disputes from the period 1816–1975, designed to include sufficient war and non-war cases and sufficient cases from the periods 1816–1919, 1920–1945, and 1946–1975. The sampling is done from the nearly 1,000 disputes identified by the Military Interstate Dispute project (see Note 5). The project is summarized in Leng and Singer (1988), and a selected list of BCOW studies of crisis bargaining can be found under Leng in the reference section.

27. Huth and Russett would argue that some aspects of the initiator's evaluation of the status quo are incorporated into the analysis indirectly through bargaining behavior and reputation. One reason why bullying strategies are hypothesized to be ineffective is the high diplomatic and domestic political costs of retreating from the status quo. The costs of retreat are particularly serious for a state that had been forced to back down in a previous crisis, for a prior humiliation produces a strong disinclination to back down again.

Although a prospective loss from a *retreat* from the status quo is weighed heavily by decision makers, it is analytically distinct from the *value* of the status quo itself. A retreat involves reputational and perhaps domestic political costs regardless of the utility or desirability of the original status quo. The fact of making the initial threat in itself changes the status quo by creating additional reputational interests. In this sense the value of the original status quo has *not* been incorporated into the analysis by Huth and Russett.

This raises two very interesting and important theoretical questions. One is whether states evaluate prospective gains and losses in terms of the utility of the outcome or final asset position, as classical microeconomic-utility theory assumes, or whether calculations are based on the magnitude and direction of the *change* in utility. (The truth, of course, is probably more complex, and the more appropriate and also more difficult question would be the relative weights given to final asset or utility positions and to changes in utilities.) A related question concerns the definition of the status quo by the initiator. Does the initiator, having made the threat, conceive of a prospective retreat as a retreat *from* the (new) status quo or a retreat *to* the old status quo. That is, would a retreat be seen as a loss or the absence of a gain? (Note that because of its focus on absolute utilities, expected-utility theory denies the significance of this question.) There is good reason to believe that this makes a difference in international politics: States appear to go to greater efforts to maintain an existing status quo than to change the status quo in their favor. Thus the question of how the decision is *framed* may be critical. There is substantial evidence in social psychology that this is true for individual behavior. It is found that individuals weigh losses more heavily than gains, that they are risk-acceptant when faced with lossess and risk-averse when faced with gains, and that framing is critical (Tversky and Kahneman, 1986). These behavioral findings constitute the assumptions of prospect theory (Kahneman and Tversky, 1979), which is an axiomatically based alternative to expected-utility theory.

These considerations take us back to Russett's original expected-utility equations (see Note 13), which suggest that the initiator will attack only if the expected utility of attacking exceeds the expected utility of the status quo. This appears straightforward enough. But what is the status quo? Although Huth and Russett (and earlier Russett) do not address this question, the implication is that the status quo is what exists prior to the initiator's initial threat. If my argument is correct, however, the fact of making the threat changes the status quo, so that an analysis of the decision to implement the threat requires that the status quo be defined in terms of the situation existing after the initial threat is made. Thus Huth and Russett are correct in emphasizing the bargaining variables and the reputational and domestic political concerns that underlie them, not because they reflect the value of the old status quo but instead because they capture one important component of the *new* status quo. (Note that Huth and Russett are precluded from measuring the status quo existing prior to the initial threat, because that threat is a definitional requirement for case selection.)

28. Only the statistically significant (at $p = .10$) probit coefficients are reported, so I must rely on the authors' interpretation of the results.

29. The authors acknowledge that the generalizability of this finding is restricted by the limited number of cases involved (18 with nuclear defenders, four with overt nuclear threats).

30. If the defender's bargaining strategy were a function of the extent of defender-protégé bonds (i.e., the stronger the ties the more coercive the bargaining), the resulting multicollinearity would account for the drop in significance of those ties. Huth (1989:ch. 4) reports, however, that the correlations between these two sets of variables are very low and suggests an alternative explanation for the decline in significance of the ties between a protégé and its protector.

31. This finding of the effectiveness of reciprocal strategies is consistent with a growing body of theoretical and experimental work by social scientists (Axelrod, 1984; Gouldner, 1960). It is also consistent with empirical findings from Leng's BCOW project. Leng and Wheeler (1979) define four predominant influence strategies: bullying, reciprocating, appeasing, and trial-and-error. Reciprocating strategies combine positive initiatives with firm responses (including counterthreats) to the coercive actions of the adversary, whereas bullying strategies are primarily coercive. Leng and Wheeler (1979) find, in their data-based analysis of 20 crises since 1900, that reciprocating strategies are the most successful, particularly against an adversary employing a bullying strategy. Bullying strategies, on the other hand, are the most likely of the four to result in war. The tendency of bullying strategies to generate coercive counterthreats rather than compliance also emerges in Leng's (1984) subsequent study of U.S.–Soviet interaction patterns in the Berlin crises of 1948 and 1961 and the Cuban Missile Crisis of 1962. Leng notes that his data-based findings regarding crisis-bargaining behavior are similar to those of Snyder and Diesing (1977) in their qualitative studies of many of the same cases.

32. In their 1984 study, Huth and Russett defined the defender's reputation in terms of its behavior in the previous crisis with *any* adversary and found that it has no significant impact on the outcome of a current crisis.

33. The effect of behavior in one crisis on behavior in the following crisis between the same two adversaries is also analyzed by Leng (1983). He examines 18 crises since 1900, selected to include three successive crises between six pairs of states of relatively equal strength (a useful restriction for our purposes). The six sets of cases are important and include France–Germany (1905–1914), Austria–Russia (1908–1914), Britain–Germany (1936–1939), India–Pakistan (1948–1971), Egypt–Israel (1947–1967), and Soviet Union–United States (1948–1962). He finds that the diplomatic victor in one dispute tends to utilize the same (successful) influence strategy in the next crisis, unless the adversary adopts a more coercive strategy, in which case (and only under such conditions) the previous winner would also adopt a more coercive strategy. The loser, assuming that its diplomatic defeat was due to the failure to demonstrate resolve, tends to adopt a more coercive

strategy in the next crisis. A diplomatic compromise also tends to result in more coercive influence strategies by both parties in the next crisis. Crises ending in war tend to result in more coercive strategies in the next crisis *unless* a state perceives that the war had been "unwanted" (i.e., one's behavior was overly coercive, leading the adversary to preempt), in which case a more accommodative strategy is adopted. To the extent that states learn from their past experience, therefore, they have a general tendency to adopt more coercive bargaining the next time.

34. This finding raises another question. If "stalemate" is defined as a possible outcome of previous crises, utilized in the statistical analysis, and found to be associated with successful deterrence in a current crisis, that is not made explicit in this study. And if outcomes can be adequately measured trichotomously for use as an independent variable predicting the behavior and outcomes in the next crisis, this new measure should be utilized as the dependent variable in all crises, replacing the problematic success–failure dichotomy. A technical methodological point is also in order. Statistical inference generally requires the independence of cases. If the outcome of one case is affected by the outcome of the previous case, the assumption of independence is violated, and more sophisticated statistical procedures are normally required.

35. We would have more confidence in this result if there were a control for whether or not the initiator also possesses nuclear weapons.

36. Because these studies deal only with those cases in which threats of force have already been made, general deterrence has already failed, but that failure does not necessarily imply the failure of immediate deterrence. Thus, the conditions for the success of immediate deterrence are not necessarily the same as those for the success of general deterrence, and vice versa. Overall military capabilities may be more important for general deterrence than for immediate deterrence.

37. Selection bias would not arise, for example, if the inital threat were made on the basis of one's overall military strength and if the actual attack were made on the basis of the initiator's expectation of a fait accompli based on immediate available military forces, or vice versa.

38. For this reason, the Huth–Russett finding that the short-term military balance is important probably *underestimates* its true impact.

39. As noted, Huth and Russett (1984, forthcoming) do *not* include this variable.

40. Another clear example of likely selection bias is the Karsten, Howell, and Allen (1984:83) finding that threats fail when the threatener sees itself as stronger and succeed when it perceives itself as the weaker party.

41. One possible way to circumvent this problem would be to analyze those cases in which alliances are formed *after* the initial threat but before an attack. This would not fully deal with the problem of selection bias, however, because the alliance formation would probably be the causal result of the protégé's (or defender's) anticipation of an attack (based on the initiator's prior threat). For a more general discussion of the causal relationship between alliances and war, see Levy (1981:603–13).

42. The potential utility of case studies for this purpose should not be underestimated (George and McKeown, 1985). Intensive analyses of individual cases may be particularly useful in determining the presumed aggressor's prior motivations and intent regarding the possible use of force and thus serve as a validity check on the operational indicators used in the Huth and Russett or other aggregate studies. On the limitations of case studies, see Achen and Snidal (1989).

# REFERENCES

Achen, C. H., 1986. *The Statistical Analysis of Quasi-Experiments*. Berkeley: University of California Press.

Achen, C. H., and Snidal, D., 1989. Rational deterrence theory and comparative case studies. *World Politics*.

Axelrod, R. A., 1984. *The Evolution of Cooperation*. New York: Basic Books.

Betts, R. K., 1987. *Nuclear Blackmail and Nuclear Balance*. Washington, D.C.: Brookings.

Blechman, B. M., and Kaplan, S. S., 1978. *Force Without War: U.S. Armed Forces as a Political Instrument*. Washington, D.C.: Brookings.

Bueno de Mesquita, B., 1981. *The War Trap*. New Haven, Conn.: Yale University Press.

Ferris, W., 1973. *The Power Capabilities of Nation States*. Lexington, Mass.: Lexington Books.

Fink, C. F., 1965. More calculations about deterrence. *Journal of Conflict Resolution* 9 (March):54–65.

Garnham, D., 1976. Dyadic international war, 1816–1965. *Western Political Quarterly* 29:231–42.

George, A. L., 1984. Crisis management: The interaction of political and military considerations. *Survival* (September–October):323–34.

George, A. L., and McKeown, T. J., 1985. Case studies and theories of organizational decision making. *Advances in Information Processes in Organizations* 2:21–58.

George, A. L., and Smoke, R., 1974. *Deterrence in American Foreign Policy*. New York: Columbia University Press.

Gochman, C. S., and Maoz, Z., 1984. Militarized interstate disputes, 1816–1976. *Journal of Conflict Resolution* 28(December):585–616.

Gouldner, A. W., 1960. The norm of reciprocity: A preliminary statement. *American Sociological Review* 25:161–78.

Hilton, G., 1970. The 1914 studies: A reassessment of the evidence and some further thoughts. *Peace Research Society (International) Papers* 13:117–41.

Huth, P. K., 1989. *Extended Deterrence and the Prevention of War*. New Haven, Conn.: Yale University Press.

―――― 1988. Extended deterrence and the outbreak of war. *American Political Science Review* 82(June).
Huth, P., and Russett, B., 1984. What makes deterrence work? Cases from 1900 to 1980. *World Politics* 36(July):496–526.
―――― 1988. Deterrence failure and crisis escalation. *International Studies Quarterly* 32(March):29–46.
―――― forthcoming. After deterrence fails: Escalation to war? In M. Wallace, ed., *Accidental Nuclear War: A Growing Risk?* London: Butterworth.
Jervis, R., 1969. The costs of the quantitative study of international relations. In K. Knorr and J. N. Rosenau, eds., *Contending Approaches to International Politics*. Princeton, N.J.: Princeton University Press, pp. 177–217.
―――― 1970. *The Logic of Images in International Relations*. Princeton, N.J.: Princeton University Press.
―――― 1979. Deterrence theory revisited. *World Politics* 31(January):289–324.
Jervis, R., Lebow, R. N., and Stein, J., 1985. *The Psychology of Deterrence*. Baltimore: Johns Hopkins University Press.
Karsten, P., Howell, P. D., and Allen, A. F., 1984. *Military Threats: A Systematic Historical Analysis of the Determinants of Success*. Westport, Conn.: Greenwood Press.
Kahneman, D., and Tversky, A., 1979. Prospect theory: An analysis of decisions under risk. *Econometrica* 47(March):273–91.
Kaufmann, W. W., 1954. *The Requirements of Deterrence*. Princeton, N.J.: Center of International Studies.
Kennedy, P., 1988. *The Rise and Fall of the Great Powers: Economic Change and Military Conflict from 1500 to 2000*. New York: Random House.
Kugler, J., 1984. Terror without deterrence: Reassessing the role of nuclear deterrence. *Journal of Conflict Resolution* 28(September):470–506.
Lebow, R. N., 1981. *Between Peace and War: The Nature of International Crises*. Baltimore: Johns Hopkins University Press.
Leng, R. J., 1980. Influence strategies and interstate conflict. In J. D. Singer, ed., *The Correlates of War: II*. New York: Free Press, pp. 124–57.
―――― 1983. When will they ever learn? Coercive bargaining in recurrent crises. *Journal of Conflict Resolution* 27(September):379–419.
―――― 1984. Reagan and the Russians: Crisis-bargaining beliefs and the historical record. *American Political Science Review* 78(June):338–55.
Leng, R. J., and Singer, J. D., 1988. Militarized interstate crises: The BCOW typology and its applications. *International Studies Quarterly* 32(June):155–73.
Leng, R. J., and Wheeler, H. G., 1979. Influence strategies, success, and war. *Journal of Conflict Resolution* 23(December):655–84.
Levy, J. S., 1981. Alliance formation and war behavior: An analysis of the great powers, 1495–1975. *Journal of Conflict Resolution* 25(December):581–614.

―――― 1983. Misperception and the causes of war. *World Politics* 35(October): 76–99.

―――― 1987. Declining power and the preventive motivation for war. *World Politics* 40(October):82–107.

―――― 1988a. Domestic politics and war. *Journal of Interdisciplinary History* 18 (Spring):653–73.

―――― 1988b. When do deterrent threats work? *British Journal of Political Science* 18(October):433–60.

―――― 1989. The diversionary theory of war. In M. I. Midlarsky, ed., *Handbook of War Studies*. Winchester, Mass.: Allen and Unwin. Forthcoming.

Maoz, Z., 1982. *Paths to Conflict: International Dispute Initiation, 1816–1976*. Boulder, Colo.: Westview.

―――― 1983. Resolve, capabilities, and the outcomes of interstate disputes, 1816–1976. *Journal of Conflict Resolution* 27(June):195–229.

Morgan, P. M., 1977. *Deterrence: A Conceptual Analysis*. Beverly Hills, Calif.: Sage.

Naroll, R., Bullough, V. L., and Naroll, F., 1974. *Military Deterrence in History: A Pilot Cross-Historical Survey*. Albany, N.Y.: State University of New York Press.

North, R. C., 1967. Perception and action in the 1914 crisis. *Journal of International Affairs* 21:103–22.

Organski, A. F. K., and Kugler, J., 1980. *The War Ledger*. Chicago: University of Chicago Press.

Russett, B. M., 1963. The calculus of deterrence. *Journal of Conflict Resolution* 7 (June):97–109.

―――― 1967. Pearl Harbor: Deterrence theory and decision theory. *Journal of Peace Research* 4:89–105.

―――― 1970. International behavior research: Case studies and cumulation. In M. Haas and H. S. Kariel, eds., *Approaches to the Study of Political Science*. Scranton, Penn.: Chandler, pp. 425–43.

Schelling, T. C., 1966. *Arms and Influence*. New Haven, Conn.: Yale University Press.

Singer, J. D., Bremer, S., and Stuckey, J., 1972. Capability distribution, uncertainty, and major power war, 1820–1965. In B. Russett, ed., *War, Peace, and Numbers*. Beverly Hills, Calif.: Sage, pp. 19–48.

Siverson, R. M., and Sullivan, M. P., 1983. The distribution of power and the onset of war. *Journal of Conflict Resolution* 27(September):473–94.

Snyder, G. H., 1961. *Deterrence and Defense*. Princeton, N.J.: Princeton University Press.

Snyder, G. H., and Diesing, P., 1977. *Conflict Among Nations*. Princeton, N.J.: Princeton University Press.

Thucydides, 1954. *History of the Peloponnesian War*, trans. by R. Warner. New York: Penguin.

Tversky, A., and Kahneman, D., 1986. The framing of decisions and the psychology of choice. In J. Elster, ed., *Rational Choice*. New York: New York University Press.

Wayman, F. J., and Singer, J. D., and Goertz, G., 1983. Capabilities, military allocations, and success in militarized disputes. *International Studies Quarterly* 27(December):497–515.

Weede, E., 1983. Extended deterrence by superpower alliance. *Journal of Conflict Resolution* 27(June):231–54.

Zinnes, D. A., North, R. C., and Koch, H. E., Jr., 1961. Capability, threat, and the outbreak of war. In J. N. Rosenau, ed., *International Politics and Foreign Policy*. New York: Free Press, pp. 469–82.

# 7

# Game Theory and the Study of the Deterrence of War

## BARRY O'NEILL

Lawrence Freedman (1981) characterized the concept of deterrence as a "gift to strategists in that its nature and working remain so elusive and so imperfectly understood as to permit endless speculation with little danger of empirical refutation justifying the maintenance of almost any military capability on the grounds that it might be doing good and we could well be worse off without it." Because game theory is the formal theory of strategic interaction, it may have the potential to solve some puzzles of deterrence. In this chapter I examine how far game theory has fulfilled this hope. The next section describes some purposes game-theory models have served in the study of war deterrence, and the final section gives a brief history of the game theory–deterrence theory interaction and suggests some future possibilities.

Our concept of *deterrence* will cover attempts to use negative sanctions to induce another not to initiate or escalate a conflict. Analyses of the arms race using game theory are numerous but will not be covered, nor will experimental gaming on deterrence and game-theoretical analyses of military tactics.[1]

*Game theory* is the section of mathematical decision theory that studies optimal strategy when two or more decision makers make choices that interact and when they use knowledge of this interaction to optimize their choices. The difference between decision theory and game theory is exemplified by some models that analyze a potential attacker's decision to go to war. In some models the attacker's probability of success is regarded as given or is calculated without analyzing the strategies and counterstrategies that are available to the two sides, without considering how each might outguess the other. These studies are only decision theoretic. However if the attacker is viewed as anticipating the preparations of the defender, and the defender considers the viewpoint of the attacker in choosing a degree of preparation, then the model is fully game theoretic because their knowledge that their choices are intertwined influences their decisions.

Game theory ranges from the use of two-by-two matrices to sophisticated mathematics, and we will divide the literature into three types of applications, in order of increasing sophistication: proto-game theory, low-game theory, and high-game theory.

*Proto-game theory* is the use of game theory simply for its concepts or formal structure, without the calculation of optimal behavior ("solutions") or the proof of general theorems. When one encounters a matrix in a political science journal or text it is most likely to be an instance of proto-game theory. This class includes, for example, Snyder and Diesing's work (1977) and the deterrence model of Ellsberg (1960, 1961), who sets up the problem as a game matrix but does not calculate solutions according to the theory of games. The name tries to suggest that the application has only the beginnings of a full game-theoretical model.

*Low-game theory* investigates specific games or restricted classes and their solutions. Examples in the area of deterrence are the recent models by Brams and Kilgour (1985a,b, 1987a–c, 1988a,b).

*High-game theory* involves the proof of general theorems covering broad classes of games. Being a primarily mathematical enterprise it will tolerate unrealistic assumptions. Typical paper titles show that high-game theory operates several levels of abstraction away from operational variables: "Selective strategies in loopy partizan graph games," "Extension of the Aumann–Shapley value concept to functions on arbitrary Banach spaces."

In the next section, which outlines various applications of game theory to deterrence, we will continually ask what is the right level of sophistication for a given application. A valid high-game-theory model would be ideal, but general theorems cannot be devised to order, and they seldom have relevance to real situations. Proto-game-theory models are "safe" but weak in the sense that they produce fewer formally supported conclusions. Low-game theory combines the best and worst features of the two adjacent levels. We specify numbers but cannot be sure the numbers or assumptions fit the world and cannot prove a general theorem to show that the conclusions are robust with regard to the model's assumptions and parameters. By moving up the ladder one understands more and more about an abstract entity that is less and less like the real world.

## Some Purposes of Game-Theory Models

### Purpose 1. To Collect Situations with the Same "Skeletal Structure"

The first step in generating new knowledge is choosing the class of phenomena to be investigated. This involves a leap of intuition because one can never know whether there are valid generalizations that describe the class. Game theory can play the role of a taxonomy here and group events according to their deeper structure.

For example, Jervis's 1978 article, "Cooperation Under the Security Dilemma," described the two-by-two games "Stag Hunt" and "Prisoners' Dilemma" as representative of situations in which two governments may move into a state of mutual cooperation or mutual threat. By grouping real situations according to their game representation, Jervis listed types of government actions that correspond to noncooperative moves and thus undermine the peaceful outcome, for example, striving for external territory to enhance one's security, building weapons with both offensive and defensive potential, using technologies that give a first-strike advantage, and so forth.

Game-theory concepts had more than a taxonomic role in Jervis's work, however, in that they matched features across different situations as strategically equivalent. Extending a railway line up to the border of a neighbor during the nineteenth century may correspond currently to installing multiple warheads on missiles, by virtue of similar effects on payoffs in the matrix. Game theory showed the isomorphism among situations that had the same conflict structure. By collecting situations Jervis enlarged his database and drew conclusions concerning the degree of tension in the system, the tendencies to form alliances, and other variables. His analysis has influenced much subsequent work on the security dilemma (Levy, 1984; Snyder, 1984; Van Evera, 1985; Hopmann, 1987).

This pattern of collecting strategically equivalent actions or situations is evident also in Ellsberg's 1960 RAND Report, *The Crude Analysis of Strategic Choices,* in which he grouped changes in nuclear weapons systems by their influence on the payoff matrix and thereby on the maximum risk of the other attacking that a government will tolerate before it decides to preempt. Another example in this class is the work of Snyder and Diesing (1977), who interpreted 16 historical crisis situations as one or another of a set of matrix games. Two-by-two games have been used by Stein (1982) to study patterns of misperception in a crisis, by Sharp (1986) and Snyder (1984) for the factors in a decision to form an alliance, and by

Klitgaard (1971) and Chatterjee (1974) to explicate Gandhi's theory of nonviolent action. Another body of work in this category is the use of game theory to elucidate the ethics of deterrence, for example, by Hardin (1983, 1986) and Danielson (1984).

In what could be regarded as an initial step to the goal of classification, some researchers have described a game based on a single situation, for example, the 1973 Israeli decision to mobilize (Ravid, 1980), the Middle East War of 1967 (Zagare, 1981, 1987), the alert decision of 1973 (Zagare, 1983, 1987), the Berlin crisis (Zagare, 1987), the U.S.–Soviet strategic relationship (Zagare, 1987), and the Cuban Missile Crisis and the confrontation between Solidarity and the Polish government (Brams, 1985a, ch. 1; 1985b, ch. 6). Investigations applying a non-standard-solution concept to specific deterrence situations are Richelson (1979) on Russian nuclear strategy and Fraser and Hipel (1983) and Hipel and Fraser (1984) on the Cuban Missile Crisis.

Another group of papers have added to the theoretical basis of this work by classifying two-by-two games by their deterrent properties, for example, Moulin (1981) and Brams and Hessel (1984). Brams and Zagare's work previously cited is in this theoretical class and is based on a different interpretation of the meaning of two-by-two games—the numbers denote rates of payoff rather than single payoffs, with players moving around within the matrix. They develop this concept as the *theory of moves*.

This purpose, collecting situations with a similar structure, can be achieved within the domain of proto-game theory, and indeed most of the above researchers do not investigate the solutions of their games. Perhaps they are dissuaded by the problem of measuring accurate utilities for the parties. However, we believe one should give a game's solution whenever possible. One cannot be sure that the game chosen is a valid representation of the real situation, and examining the solution provides a clue. Surprises can occur. For example, a facedown in a crisis is sometimes depicted by the two-by-two game "Chicken," with moves defined as yielding or not yielding. Each side chooses a certain risk of yielding, so the account goes, this risk being the probability assigned to not yielding in the mixed strategy equilibrium in the two-by-two game of "Chicken." However, calculating the mixed strategy equilibrium for Chicken, one finds that the worse your opponent's payoff in the both-don't-yield outcome, the higher should be your probability of yielding. This flies against common sense, for surely the worse the disaster outcome is for the opponent, the more confident you can be that the opponent will back down, and the more you will tend to hold fast. Either common sense is wrong, the solution concept is wrong, or the simultaneous move two-by-two game is an invalid model. We draw the moral that even conceptual applications would do well to solve the games they postulate.

## Purpose 2. To Organize the Analysis of a Single Situation

Here the theory of games is used to set an agenda, to dissect a complicated situation into small pieces for separate consideration. An example was the top secret 1959 RAND Corporation report, *The Deterrence and Strategy of Total War, 1959–1961: A Method of Analysis*. Its authors were Herbert Goldhamer, a founder of political gaming, Andrew Marshall, an economist, later director of Net Assessment at the Pentagon, and Nathan Leites, a Sovietologist. Fred Kaplan obtained the report under the Freedom of Information Act for his narrative book on the history of nuclear strategic thinking, *Wizards of Armageddon* (1983).

The authors anticipated later themes in American policy by arguing that the types of weapons needed for a retaliatory deterrence policy are also those for conducting a war, that strategists should plan beyond the first day of a nuclear war, looking at intrawar threats and communication as tools to end the war. In their model, the Soviet Union has the option of a sneak attack on Strategic Air Command bomber and tanker bases followed by an all-out attack on cities or military targets. The United States can respond by attacking military targets, possibly with ground-burst explosions that cause massive civilian damage. Another U.S. option is to withhold two-thirds of its surviving strategic forces as a threat to induce the Soviet Union to cancel the second attack. If warning arrives early enough, the United States might withhold all its retaliation in hopes of having the Soviet Union recall even the first attack.

Rather than focus on the authors' conclusions, we look at the benefits of game theory for their study. Game concepts provided the organizing scheme of their presentation—chapter titles included "The Soviet Utility Matrix," "Soviet Probability Calculations," "The U.S. Utility Matrix," and so on. Mapping world events into game-theory variables allowed them to clarify the influence structure of the situation by showing which certain considerations affected which others. Sixty-three end positions were differentiated on the game tree and the authors, with help from their colleagues, estimated hypothetical utilities based on the resulting military and civilian damage. Their view of the war's possible courses is so explicit that we can draw a game tree, Figure 7.1. Their method has the advantage over almost all other strategic analyses in that they define the possible moves and associated available information clearly, making their reasoning clearer, allowing a sceptic to spot the source of the disagreement. Kaplan states that

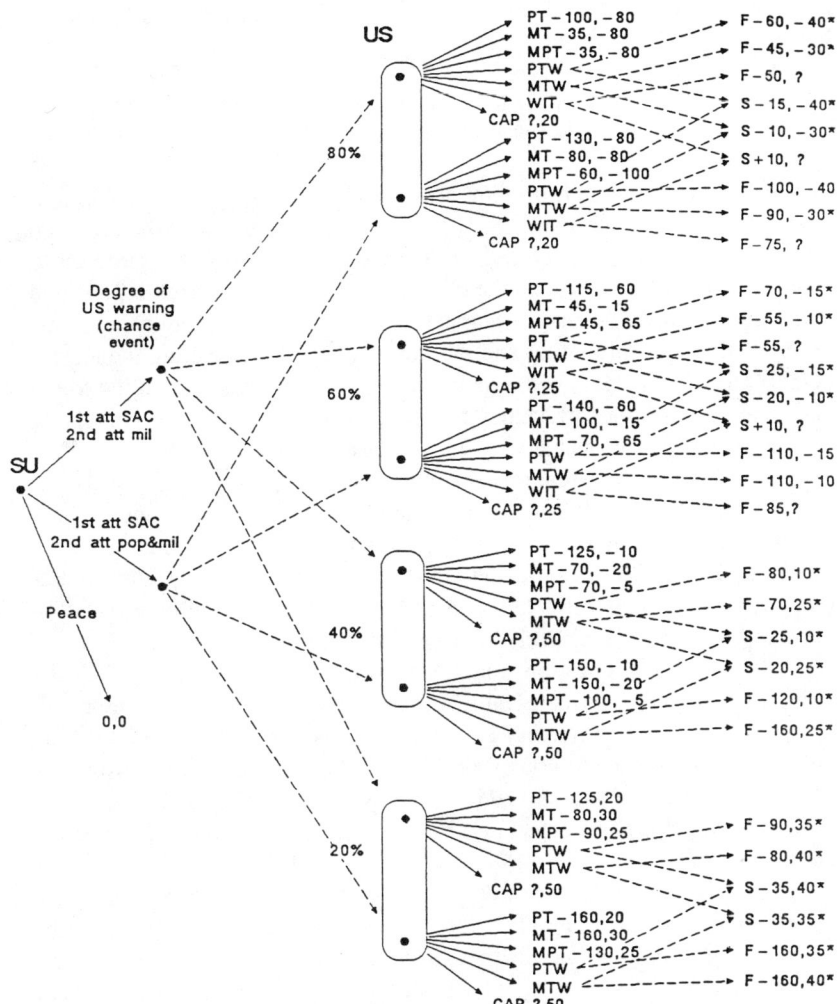

**Figure 7.1.** Game tree for a U.S.–Soviet Union nuclear war. (Constructed from Goldhamer et al., 1959). The Soviet Union chooses peace, or a small strike against SAC with a larger second attack against only military installations, or a small first strike against SAC with the second against both military and population targets. The United States receives a degree of warning determined by chance, expressed in the figure as the percentage of SAC aircraft that would survive if the Soviet first attack continues as planned (20 percent, 40 percent, 60 percent, or 80 percent). The United States learns its degree of warning but does not know whether the Soviet Union's further strike will include population targets. The United States responds by retaliating against Soviet population targets (PT), or against military targets (MT), or against both (MPT), or withholding two-thirds of its forces to induce the

the extensiveness of the analysis and its quantitative approach made it influential in shifting opinion at RAND toward counterforce weaponry, which has since become the prominent element in U.S. strategic nuclear policy.

Like the first function of game theory described earlier, this methodology exemplifies proto-game theory, and, as before, we raise the criticism that the study should have defined the game completely and gone on to solve it. The authors omitted the game tree, Figure 7.1, in their report, and the figure makes clear that certain parameters are missing, for example, the U.S. utility for capitulating and the Soviet utility for canceling the attack. Oddly, the authors assigned hypothetical utilities but were unwilling to put any values or ranges of values to chance events such as the percent of damage of the Soviet attack or the success of the U.S. threat strategies. Without these numbers the reader cannot solve the tree to answer questions like: Does the model lead to conclusions other than those the authors present, conclusions that are strongly counterintuitive and thus make the assumptions suspect? Could the United States credibly make the threats they recommend? Is the likelihood of war substantial within the model— that is, does the model itself imply that the problem is urgent?

Asking this last question might have been especially useful. Near the time of this study Herman Kahn and Thomas Schelling polled their colleagues at RAND and found that a surprise attack was judged the least likely start of a war, although almost all RAND studies began from this premise (Herken, 1985, p. 205). Solving Goldhamer et al.'s game tree might have helped strategists turn to more justified worries like escalation or crisis instability.

A study with this degree of detail rolls over the line between conceptual clarification and specific policy recommendations. We think that only the former use is appropriate. Although the authors detailed strategies, outcomes, and utilities, they spent very little space examining whether their

---

Soviet Union to call off the second wave and sending the other one-third against population (PTW) or military targets (MTW). If warning is early enough the United States might choose to withhold (WIT) all its forces to induce the Soviet Union to call off both the first and second attacks. A final alternative is to announce capitulation (CAP), perhaps insincerely. Threats based on withholding may succeed (S) or fail (F), again a chance event. Payoffs are shown in the order: U.S. payoff, Soviet payoff, and those with an asterisk are weighted averages of payoffs associated with the success or failure of the United States demand to call off the second attack, weighted by the probabilities. Some payoffs ("?") were not specified by the authors.

structure was valid. A game in which each government knows the other's goals and the available moves completely may not have been an accurate model of each side's cognition. The study warns about the hypothetical nature of the numbers but goes on to make many policy suggestions. To follow through and solve the game in this context would imply excessive trust in the model and its parameters, but had the authors limited their goals to establishing conceptual connections, solving the game would have spotted inconsistencies in beliefs.

In their study, proto-game theory becomes a tool of systems analysis. There seem to be few such instances in the unclassified literature, perhaps because of the atheoretical nature of the work and its need for many details, but one example is the paper of Phillips and Hayes (1978), who analyze the effect of an antisubmarine-warfare breakthrough on arms control, deterrence, and war, drawing out a game tree with no fewer than 340 different positions. A study at a lower level of detail is Kaplan's argument (1958) for proportional reprisals to a Soviet attack.

## Purpose 3. To Provide Examples that Show Elementary Facts or Counterexamples that Refute Elementary Fallacies

In this role games are specimens that illustrate simple ideas. The following are some notions that game theory has helped to spread:

- Conflictual and cooperative motives can coexist in a situation, an antidote to the attitude that "what is good for them is bad for us." Many non-zero-sum games, especially "Prisoners' Dilemma," show this.
- The structure of a situation can entrap intelligent, aware protagonists by inducing them to act to their mutual disadvantage ("Prisoners' Dilemma," "Stag Hunt"). The naïve attitude is that social inefficiencies are due to flaws in judgment, perception, or motives. Social psychologists have demonstrated the tendency to ignore situational variables as causes of human action and labeled it the "fundamental error of attribution."
- One can be worse off from having more options. The attitude that more choices always helps seems to be an unstated assumption behind the general enthusiasm for technology. It is true if only one decision maker is present but false in multiactor contexts, as shown by games like "Chicken" and "Stag Hunt."
- One can benefit by being or appearing irrational, exemplified by "Chicken," the repeated "Prisoners' Dilemma," and the "Chain Store Paradox" (Selten, 1978). Hersh (1983) recounts evidence that Ellsberg's writings on this subject influenced Richard Nixon's policy toward North Vietnam.

- More weapons can result in lower security even when the opponent's weapons are held constant (Ellsberg, 1960), in that they may force the other to strike first.

Many analyses in the political science literature perform this illustrative function, typically using two-by-two matrix games. Examples are Kaplan (1957) and Russett (1983).

## Purpose 4. To Define Rational Behavior to the End of Establishing a Baseline Prediction and Spot Factors that Should Be Added to the Model

A frequent complaint against game theory is that it assumes rationality. "Rationality" comprises two ideas: that players engage in foresightful planning and that they seek consistent goals. Game-theory models do postulate foresight and consistency, but the enterprise can lead one to appreciate the limits of these assumptions. We calculate optimal behavior in the situation and try to discern what nonrational factors we must add to explain the difference. Sceptics may assert that behavior is at bottom irrational, but "irrational" acquires meaning only if one can specify rational behavior. A game-theory prediction allows us to identify the deviation and gives us something to explain.

In the dollar auction game, for example, two players bid in turns for a dollar bill. The higher bidder pays the amount bid, receives the dollar, and the bidder who dropped out at a lower bid must also pay that bid although that player receives no prize. The dollar auction differs from normal auctions in this regard but seems to fit the dilemma of two countries caught in an escalatory war, because the government that withdraws does not receive its investment back.

The dollar auction is an effective trap. In laboratory experiments and classroom demonstrations students have bid several times the amount of prize, unwilling to write off their investment. What is rational behavior in this situation? O'Neill (1986) derives the following conclusions when bids are in nickels: If players each have $2.50 in their pockets, for example, the first player should bid 60 cents and the second bidder drop out. This is a result of playing the unique perfect equilibrium, meaning roughly the pair of moves that involves rationality, expectations of the other's future rationality, and, as a secondary goal, minimum vulnerability to possible small mistakes of the opponent. If instead of $2.50 each they both possess $2.55, the first should bid 65 cents and the second drop out. At $2.90 each, the best opening bid drops to 5 cents. This solution is logically sound but so unintuitive that one must explain the difference between rational players of the dollar auction on the one hand and laboratory subject and governments escalating a war on the other. What ingredients should we add to the model to predict the facts: that the latter groups waste their resources?

A prominent example of this use of game theory is the experimental work by Rapoport and others on repeated plays of the "Prisoners' Dilemma" (Rapoport and Chammah, 1965), which according to theory should be totally noncooperative. Maynard-Smith (1982) and Axelrod (1984) followed up on this puzzle by theorizing on the evolution of cooperative behavior.

## Purpose 5. To Generate Measures for Variables

A measure that grows out of a formal theory can be stated axiomatically to allow the investigator to examine each axiom separately, accepting it or modifying it. Generating a measure from a well-understood body of research like game theory gives another advantage: There is less danger that some unintended artifact in the measure is behind the results. By using game theory one is making the strong and not totally justified assumption that people act "rationally," that is, consistently and with foresight, but this assumption is at least partially true, and if one insists on a unique measure based on well-understood assumptions, there is usually no alternative—the contrary assumption, that someone acts "irrationally," is not specific enough to yield a measure.

One example arises in the current debate on antimissile systems, whether such weapons generate crisis instability. Defenses would lessen the incentives for a first strike in that they protect some land-based missiles for retaliation, but they would also increase these incentives by allowing the first striker to ward off retaliating missiles from both silos and submarines. A mathematical model can estimate which of these two opposing effects would predominate, and at least a dozen formal studies have been conducted at military-analysis institutes. This enterprise requires a way to measure stability, and researchers have proposed a number of formulas (e.g., Grotte, 1980; Chrzanowski, 1986; Reinhardt and Squire, 1982; Reinhardt, 1984; Wilkening and Watman, 1986, App. B), but some of these lead to consequences probably not anticipated by the authors: The values become negative when there is still a danger of crisis instability or stay positive when there is no danger. O'Neill (1987a) argues that crisis instability can be represented by the following game, an instance of "Stag Hunt," in which the rows and columns correspond to planning not to attack, or to attack, when a specified crisis situation arises.

|  | 2's policy | |
|---|---|---|
| **1's policy** | don't attack | attack |
| don't attack | *peace*<br>1 gets $p_1$ (best)<br>2 gets $p_2$ (best) | *2 preempts*<br>1 gets $s_1$ (worst)<br>2 gets $f_2$ (2nd best) |
| attack | *1 preempts*<br>1 gets $f_1$ (2nd best)<br>2 gets $s_2$ (worst) | *both try to preempt*<br>1's expectation: $b_1$ (3rd best)<br>2's expectation: $b_2$ for both |

A set of axioms for reasonable strategic behavior leads to the following measure as the unique appropriate one for the relative danger of war in different situations:

$$\text{Crisis Instability Index} = \frac{b_1 - s_1}{p_1 - f_1} \frac{b_2 - s_2}{p_2 - f_2}$$

This formula can be interpreted as the product of two ratios, one for each player, involving the motive to attack if the other is known to be about to attack ($b_i - s_i$), divided by the motive to stay at peace if it is known the other is not attacking ($p_i - f_i$). The axioms guarantee that it is free of certain counterintuitive behaviors shown by past measures.

Another use of game theory to generate measures is Axelrod's formula for the conflict of interest inherent in a situation based on its game representation (Axelrod, 1967, 1969).

Harsanyi (1962) presents a definition of deterrent or compellent power based on the costs and benefits to the source and the target of the influence attempt, of bestowing the reward, of carrying out the threat, and of complying. His model includes a notion of partial compliance in which the target performs the action part way, or with a certain probability, or for a certain proportion of the time. Following previous formal analyses, he defines power as the change in probability or proportion of times that the target performs the action, and regarding this probability as a matter of negotiation between the source and target of influence he uses a game-theoretical model of bargaining to predict the agreement. In deterrence terms, if the payoff difference from a successful deterrence attempt is $x^*$ for the source and $x$ for the target, if the reward is worth $r^*$ and $r$, respectively, and if the threat costs are $t^*$ and $t$, where these costs are positive, then the power of the source over the target is found to be

$$\frac{r + t}{2x} - \frac{t^* - r^*}{2x^*}$$

In spite of the large list of measures of the "strategic balance," there are almost no game-theoretical approaches, or at least none in the open literature. Perhaps the reason is that game-theoretical techniques expose the essential flaw of static indicators: They ignore the dependence of the "effectiveness" of a weapon on the dynamics of a particular war. An exception is the discussion of Grotte and Brooks (1983), who chose a context where a game-theory measure seems more appropriate—the deployment of aircraft carriers forces—to suggest a measure of "naval presence."

## Purpose 6. To Formalize Ideas About the Dynamics of Strategic Interactions

A common debate in strategic analysis is whether a certain behavior is reasonable or whether it makes sense to expect a certain response. Here a game-theory model functions like an inventor's prototype to show whether rational actors would behave that way. It requires the level of low- or high-game theory because one must calculate solutions. The papers in this group are more sophisticated mathematically than two-by-two matrices, often involving continuous choices of strategies, a sequence of moves, or incomplete information.

Brams and Kilgour, for example, have provided several analyses of deterrence and escalation. In one model (Brams, 1985a, ch. 1) a government must balance the effectiveness of a deterrent threat in terms of harm to the target, against the threat's credibility, meaning the cost of carrying it out. He derives the optimal threat, which often involves less than 100 percent certainty of retaliation. Brams draws parallels between this partial probability of retaliation and the uncertainties that exist in a leader's resolve, the reliability of weapons and command and control.

Another group of models finds the response that best reestablishes stable deterrence after conflict has escalated to a certain level (Brams and Kilgour, 1985a,b, 1987a–c, 1988a,b). Here threats are made continuous by introducing not probabilities but degrees of conflictual behavior. A player must choose a deterrent threat or action in midcrisis, balancing its dissuasive effects against its tendency to evoke a further response.

Several models have paid attention to the effect of incomplete information on government's behavior. Guth (1986) extends some commonly used two-by-two game analyses to include uncertainty about each other's motive to attack. In that paper and an earlier one (1985) he states a bargaining model for the deployment of U.S. missiles in Europe in which each superpower is uncertain of Europe's willingness to accept the missiles.

Powell (1987a, 1987b) compares two games in which governments pressure each other by tolerating an increasing risk of disaster. By setting up two models, one with and one without uncertainty about the opponent's goals, he argues that with complete knowledge of the goals one side will yield before there is danger of war. However, with uncertainty rational behavior can lead to a crisis.

Morrow (1987) states a model of bargaining in the context of deterrence in which each side is uncertain not about goals but about its own and the other's potential for success in a war. Each gains partial information about its military ability and can cede or hold firm on that basis.

Nalebuff (1982, 1987) confronts Snyder's stability–instability paradox, the notion that when the disaster of total war becomes worse, governments' increased caution may be negated by a tendency to act more recklessly, each being more confident that the other will back down. He postulates that each is uncertain about the other's motive to win and also to tolerate the pain of continued conflict and, in the later model, suggests that these effects exactly cancel.

Credibility, a central issue in deterrence theory, has been difficult to incorporate in game models because they either disallow any threat that would be costly to carry out or trivialize credibility in the opposite direction by adding options of total precommitment at the time the threat is made. Selten's (1979) model provides a middle course, describing a kidnapper who, if the ransom is not paid, may become irrational and commit the murder with a probability depending on the size of utility loss when the ransom demand was frustrated. Threats thus vary in credibility, and the kidnapper's demand is chosen with an eye on the credibility of that player's future threat. If the ransom demand is frustrated, a player may display irrational behavior, but the likelihood of this still depends on a decision-theoretic variable, utility. O'Neill (1987b) applies Selten's approach to examine the rationale for deployment of intermediate range missiles in Europe.

A related function is the use of the theory of games to establish definitions for basic terms. Here one embeds the definition in a model to show that it is a sensible one. An example is Zagare's step-by-step derivation of a proper representation of deterrence as a game (Zagare, 1985a, 1985b; Zagare, forthcoming) and Sobel's analysis of coercion (1972).

Schelling's analysis (1958, 1960) of deterrence instability belongs here. In spite of the superiority of peace, each side entertains a fear of irrational attack by the other. Solutions are investigated as functions of this probability of irrational attack, and the effect of a partially reliable warning system is discussed. Selten and Tietz (1972) discuss a very abstracted

# Game Theory and the Study of the Deterrence of War

$N$-country model relating stockpiles of weapons, government's utilities, and stability. Wagner (1982) addresses the important question of the significance of "nuclear superiority" and uses a model of intrawar bargaining, distinguishing escalation based on attrition of forces from escalation based on increasing risk.

Finally, we will describe a model from our current work that gives a different answer to the question implicitly addressed by Wagner: Why has each superpower deployed approximately 10,000 strategic nuclear weapons at enormous cost when a small fraction of this number would devastate the other's country beyond any historical precedent? Standard justifications, such as the danger of losing ICBMs in a first strike, escalation dominance, or the need to credibly threaten a limited nuclear attack, seem unconvincing. The following model formalizes the concept of "demonstrating resolve" and backs up the counterintuitive idea that the purpose of these weapons is not to build military capability but to publicly display the infliction of hardship on oneself by throwing away money. The model will be given in detail as it illustrates some recent theoretical developments to be discussed in the next section.

The game has two players and two stages. In the first stage each player chooses either to commit a "self-damage" action or chooses not to. These moves are made simultaneously and observed immediately afterward by the other player. Not self-damaging costs \$0, and self-damaging is valued at $-\$30$, equivalent to deliberately throwing away \$30.

At the second stage each player makes a demand for some portion of a prize. Only three demand levels are possible, proportion 0, $\frac{1}{2}$, or 1. If the players' demands total no more than the available prize, they receive the amount demanded, plus half the surplus if any. For example, if the respective demands are $\frac{1}{2}$ and 0, then player A receives $\frac{1}{2} + \frac{1}{4} = \frac{3}{4}$, and player B receives $0 + \frac{1}{4} = \frac{1}{4}$ of the prize. If the demands sum to more than the prize, however, each receives no share, in fact, each must pay a conflict penalty of $-\$20$, which is independent of the specific demands. The prize may be regarded as getting one's way in some dispute beyond one's territory (successful extended deterrence), and the conflict payoff is the expected cost of a fight.

Each player may be one of two types: a weakly motivated ("weak") player or a strongly motivated ("strong") one. A strong player values the prize at \$100, but a weak player values it at only \$50. The players know their own types but are ignorant of the other's, and with no other information they hold the chance of the other being weak or strong as 50 percent.

What is an equilibrium in this game? By definition an *equilibrium* will comprise two plans of action, one for each player, such that player A has no incentive to change, given A expects B to follow B's plan, and, likewise, B has no incentive to change if B expects A to follow A's plan. Clearly one equilibrium is that a player of either type does not self-damage and then demands $\frac{1}{2}$. It is an equilibrium because any deviation by a single player would lead to a worse outcome: Self-damaging would be a waste, and demanding more or less than $\frac{1}{2}$ would cause either a conflict or a reduction of one's prize.

Are there any equilibria that involve the seemingly senseless move of self-damage? It is easy to verify that the following is an equilibrium: A weak player does not self-damage, a strong player does; at the second stage a weak player demands $\frac{1}{2}$ or 0 according to whether the other did not or did self-damage; a strong player demands 1 or $\frac{1}{2}$, respectively, in these cases. To check that this is indeed an equilibrium, note that a strong player choosing not to self-damage would then face a more demanding opponent and lose more than the cost of self-damaging. The strong player is paying $30 to gain $50. However a weak player's motivations are such that it would not pay to bluff by self-damaging; the gain would be only $25. Self-damaging becomes a signal of strength and of intention in the next stage, a strong player saying in effect, "If I didn't really want the prize, would I be doing this to prove I do?"

Comparing this equilibrium with the previous one, that is, the one where both do not self-damage and then demand $\frac{1}{2}$, one might hope that players would recognize the benefits of no self-damage and an even split. However further strategic arguments show that rational players will choose the self-damage equilibrium. Suppose player A intends to use the first equilibrium and expects B to do so. Accordingly at the first stage A does not self-damage, but is surprised to see B self-damage. What must A conclude? There is only one plausible rationale for B's action in the first stage: It is that B is strong and also intends to demand all the prize in the second stage. Player A, whether weak or strong, had thus better demand 0 in the second stage. The outcome will be a net gain for a strong player B. So even before the first stage, A knows that B, if strong, will not play the first equilibrium, and thus A should not use it either. Though formally an equilibrium, the 50/50 split collapses when the self-damage move is available.

This approach suggests that nuclear arms spending is a public show of resolve hinging on the sacrifice a government makes for the armaments. The military capacity conferred by further nuclear arms is negligible and irrelevant. Of course there are many ways for a nation to inflict suffering on itself, but the course of history makes arms spending the most natural. Before the nuclear era a strongly motivated government spent more because military forces had an instrumental relationship to its goals. Now technology has changed, but it is natural that governments choose military spending to examine who gets his way in a conflict.

## Trends in the Use of Game Theory to Study Deterrence

The essential idea of game theory was stated by Borel in 1924, but it was the 1944 publication of von Neumann and Morgenstern's *Theory of Games and Economic Behavior* that really sparked enthusiasm and interest, with a front-page story in the *New York Times*. The book's unreadability did not lessen its influence, and its size was evidence that the field was mathematically fertile. It seemed natural that this theory might provide the key to the military dilemma of the new weapons, devices so powerful as to be incapable of promoting any traditional goal of war. The weapons had to be "used" politically without going to war, and the new theory offered the hope of integrating military and political aspects of the problem. Hopes for military applications led to the incorporation of a strong game-theory section in the RAND Corporation, but almost all of the work was either mathematical–theoretical or military tactics. The political–strategic combination work of Goldhamer et al. described above was an exception.

During the 1960s interest grew in another direction of application, employing game theory in the search for cooperative solutions to the arms race. The general conceptual writings of Rapoport, Boulding, Schelling, and others, especially in the *Journal of Conflict Resolution,* were supplemented by game experimentation and the critique of strategic analysis through its comparison with game theory. Examples of the latter are the books *Strategy and Conscience* by Anatol Rapoport (1964) and *Deadly Logic* by Phillip Green (1966). Rapoport's attitude was that the fault lay not with the theory of games but with its exploiters in the strategic-analysis community. He called for a reorientation toward a study of cooperative solution concepts. Rapoport predicted that the efforts of those using game theory as an instrument of national power would backfire. He hoped that the necessary step of putting oneself in the opponents' shoes to discern their goals would force one to reexamine the malevolent image of the opponent constructed to serve the cold war mentality. If economics is "the dismal science," he dubbed game theory "the subversive science."

Researchers in the Eastern Bloc also showed interest in game-theory applications. Robinson (1970) translated the work of six Soviet social scientists and mathematicians, who were enthusiastic for the theory as a tool in their disciplines but distrusted its association with American nuclear strategists.

An important event in the interaction of game theory and deterrence came in the mid-1960s with the Arms Control and Disarmament Agency's initiative to fund theoretical work (Aumann et al., 1966, 1967, 1968). ACDA Director Herbert Scoville sponsored the collaboration through Mathematica, Inc., at Princeton with Harold Kuhn and Thomas Saaty, who assembled theoreticians of the first magnitude. Contexts of application included theories of negotiation, stability, definition of national-utility functions, and procedures for reducing weapons in small steps while maintaining deterrence. The analysis was at a highly theoretical level but was presented to regular ACDA personnel at several conferences. The project ended after ACDA's funding for research was cut and Scoville retired. Because of the high level of abstractness in the models and small circulation of the reports, the work has had no effect on the political science literature. However, the authors continued to develop their theories, and these had enormous impact, both in the mathematical theory of repeated games with incomplete information and in mathematical economics. During the 1970s, game-theoretical applications in deterrence theory seemed to be at a low point, but the 1980s have seen a resurgence, as evidenced by the large number of citations in the references. Perhaps researchers have been encouraged by the burgeoning use in economics. A number of new theoretical developments promise a further expansion, and we will list some of them now.

*Games of incomplete information* involve some players who are uncertain of the other's utility assignments. Examples are Guth's, Morrow's, Nalebuff's and Powell's models in the last section, as well as the self-damage game. Methods for these games allow the investigation of signaling, in which a player tries to convince the opponent of the player's goal. A relevant theme for a game played repeatedly is the analysis of how to maintain a reputation for having a certain goal. Typically one must forego some immediate gains to invest in long-term benefits of keeping a reputation (Wilson, 1985), as in the self damage game.

*Games involving bounded rationality* are a further new area. In principle any limitation on intelligence or inconsistency of goals can be incorporated in game theory by changing the rules—for example, if real humans have limited ability to plan ahead we define a game whose rules state that future possible moves are unknown. Similarly varying goals may be modeled by replacing a single player with several who share some interests but not all. In practice, however, this approach leads to unsolvable mathematical problems, so other ways have been sought to represent limited rationality or changes in utilities. One fast-growing area is the study of games between automata that have finite memory and planning ability. This area was suggested first by Aumann (1985), and work in the area is growing rapidly (see for example, Neyman, 1986, and Rubenstein, 1986). Its present direction is to draw on the theory of computation for the limits on processing that it postulates and ignore cognitive psychology, but perhaps it will inspire work that has more application to human behavior.

Another body of work in the artificial intelligence literature abstracts the design of computer chess programs and promises to clarify the case of limitations on ability to look down the tree of responses and counter-responses. Pearl (1984) gives a summary and references.

*Games in extensive form,* those involving successive moves over time, have received more study with regard to the proper definition of an equilibrium. Solution concepts such as sequential equilibria (Kreps and Wilson, 1982) or strategically stable equilibria (Kohlberg and Mertens, 1986) are in development and have focused attention on the course of play through time, especially on the role of reasonable change in beliefs (as opposed to reasonable actions) in the definition of rationality.

Much of this research can be traced back to the work at ACDA, and I hope the knowledge will return to be used again. The likelihood of useful findings depends on the willingness of political scientists to learn the newer techniques of game theory and in turn depends on the willingness of game theorists to acquaint themselves in a more sophisticated way with social sciences, politics, and military systems.

## NOTES

The author would like to thank Anatol Rapoport, Steve van Evera, Jim Mayberry, Roger Myerson, Dov Samet, Bruce Anderson, and Jerry Bracken for enjoyable and helpful discussions.

1. Other relevant general studies on the application of game theory are P. Bracken (1984), Hirshleifer (1987), Intriligator (1982), Maoz (1985), Shubik (1968, 1984, 1985, 1987), Snydal (1985), Wagner (1983), and Zagare (1986).

Some representative topics and papers in the game-theory analysis of strategic military planning are the study of attack-and-defense allocations (Eckler and Burr, 1972; Karr, 1981; Bracken, Brooks, and Falk, 1986) and nuclear exchange models. In the latter each side is attempting to maximize some stated function of its own and the other's damage (Bracken, Falk, and Miercort, 1977). These applications usually involve maximin techniques: The first government moves such that a function will be as high as possible after the other has observed the move and tried to minimize the function. Another game application is the problem of coordinating retaliation when communication between silos has been partially destroyed (Weiss, 1983).

# REFERENCES

Aumann, R., 1985. Repeated games. In G. Feiwel, ed., *Issues in Contemporary Microeconomics and Welfare*. London: Macmillan.
Aumann, R., Harsanyi, J., Maschler, M., O'Brien, G., Radner, R., and Shubik, M., 1966. Development of Utility Theory for Arms Control and Disarmament. Final Report by Mathematica to the U.S. Arms Control and Disarmament Agency. Contract ACDA/ST-80.
Aumann, R., Harsanyi, J., Maschler, M., Radner, R., Mayberry, J. P., Scarf, H. E., Selten, R., and Stearns, R., 1968. The Indirect Measurement of Utility. Final Report by Mathematica to the U.S. Arms Control and Disarmament Agency. Contract ACDA/ST-143.
Aumann, R., Harsanyi, J., Mayberry, J., Maschler, M., Scarf, H., Selten, R., and Stearns, R., 1967. Models of the Gradual Reduction of Arms. Final Report by Mathematica to the U.S. Arms Control and Disarmament Agency. Contract ACDA/ST-116.
Axelrod, R., 1967. Conflict of interest: An axiomatic treatment. *Journal of Conflict Resolution* 11:87–99.
———— 1969. *Conflict of Interest*. Chicago: Markham.
———— 1984. *The Evolution of Cooperation*. New York: Basic Books.
Borel, E., 1924. Sur les jeux ou interviennent le hasard et l'habilité des joueurs. In E. Borel, *Elements de la Theorie des Probabilites*. Third Edition. Paris: Librairie Scientifique.
Bracken, P., 1984. Deterrence, gaming, and game theory. *Orbis* 27:790–802.
Bracken, J., Brooks, P., and Falk, J., 1986. Robust preallocated preferential defense. Institute for Defense Analyses Paper P-1816.
Bracken, J., Falk, J., and Miercort, J., 1977. A strategic weapons exchange allocation model. *Operations Research* 25:968–76.
Brams, S. J., 1985a. *Superpower Games: Applying Game Theory to Superpower Conflict*. New Haven: Yale University Press.
———— 1985b. *Rational Politics: Decisions, Games, and Strategy*. Washington: CQ Press.
Brams, S. J., and Hessel, M., 1984. Threat power in sequential games. *International Studies Quarterly* 28:15–36.
Brams, S. J., and Kilgour, M., 1985a. Optimal deterrence. *Social Philosophy and Policy* 3:118–35.
———— 1985b. The path to stable deterrence. In U. Luterbacher and M. Ward, eds., *Dynamic Models of International Conflict*. Boulder: Lynn Rienner.
———— 1987a. Optimal threats. *Operations Research* 35:524-36.
———— 1987b. Threat escalation and crisis stability: A game-theoretic analysis. *American Political Science Review* 81:833–50.
———— 1987c. Winding down if preemption or escalation occurs: A game-theoretic analysis. *Journal of Conflict Resolution* 31:547–72.
———— 1988a. Deterrence versus defense: A game-theoretic analysis of Star Wars. *International Studies Quarterly* 32.

——— 1988b. *Game Theory and National Security*. New York: Basil Blackwell.
Chatterjee, B., 1974. Search for an appropriate game model of Satyagraha. *Journal of Peace Research* 11:21–29.
Chrzanowski, P., 1986. *Strategic Defense and Crisis Stability*. Lawrence Livermore National Laboratory, UCID 20699.
Danielson, P., 1984. Rationality and ultimate commitment. Mimeo. York University, Toronto, Department of Philosophy.
Eckler, R. A., and Burr, S., 1972. *Mathematical Models of Target Coverage and Missile Allocation*. Washington: Military Operations Research Society of America.
Ellsberg, D., 1960. *The Crude Analysis of Strategic Choices*. P-2183. Santa Monica, Calif.: The Rand Corporation, December 15.
——— 1961. The crude analysis of strategic choices. *American Economic Review Proceedings* 51:472–78.
Fraser, N., and Hipel, K., 1983. Dynamic modeling of the Cuban Missile Crisis. *Conflict Management and Peace Science* 6:1–18.
Freedman, L., 1981. The rationale for medium-sized deterrent forces. In C. Bertram, ed., *The Future of Strategic Deterrence*. Hamden, Conn.: Archon Books.
Goldhamer, H., Marshall, A., and Leites, N., 1959. *The Deterrence and Strategy of Total War, 1959–1961: A Method of Analysis*. RN-2301. Santa Monica, Calif.: Rand Corporation.
Green, P., 1966. *Deadly Logic*. Columbus: Ohio State University Press.
Grotte, J., 1980. Measuring strategic stability with a two-sided nuclear exchange model. *Journal of Conflict Resolution* 24:213–39.
Grotte, J., and Brooks, P. S., 1983. Measuring naval presence using Blotto games. *International Journal of Game Theory* 12:225–36.
Guth, W., 1985. An extensive game approach to model the nuclear deterrence debate. *Zeitschrift für die gesamte Staatswissenschaft/Journal of Institutional and Theoretical Economics* 140:525–38.
——— 1986. Deterrence and incomplete information: The game theory approach. In R. Avenhaus, R. K. Huber, and J. D. Kettelle, eds., *Modeling and Analysis in Arms Control*. New York: Springer-Verlag.
Hardin, R., 1983. Unilateral versus mutual disarmament. *Philosophy and Public Affairs* 12:236–54.
——— 1986. Risking Armageddon. In A. Cohen and S. Lee, eds., *Nuclear Weapons and the Future of Humanity: The Fundamental Questions*. New York: Rowman and Allanheld.
Harsanyi, J. C., 1962. Measurement of social power opportunity costs and the theory of two-person bargaining games. *Behavioral Science* 7:67–80.
Herken, G., 1985. *Counsels of War*. New York: Knopf.
Hersh, S., 1983. *The Price of Power: Kissinger in the Nixon White House*. New York: Summit.
Hipel, K., and Fraser, N., 1984. *Conflict Analysis: Models and Resolutions*. New York: North Holland.

Hirshleifer, J., 1987. Conflict and settlement. In *The New Palgrave Dictionary of Economics*, vol. 1. London: Macmillan.

Hopmann, P. T., 1987. The security dilemma and arms control in Europe. In F. Barnaby and P. T. Hopmann, eds., *Rethinking the Nuclear Weapons Dilemma in Europe*. New York: St. Martin's Press.

Intriligator, M., 1982. Research on conflict theory: Analytic approaches and areas of application. *Journal of Conflict Resolution* 26:307–27.

Jervis. R., 1978. Cooperation under the security dilemma. *World Politics* 30:289–24.

Kaplan, F., 1983. *The Wizards of Armageddon*. New York: Simon and Schuster.

Kaplan, M., 1957. *System and Process in International Politics*. New York: Wiley.

——— 1958. The calculus of nuclear deterrence. *World Politics* 11:20–43.

Karr, A., 1981. Nationwide Defense Against Nuclear Weapons: Properties of Prim-Read Deployments. Institute for Defense Analyses, P-1395.

Klitgaard, N., 1971. Gandi's nonviolence as a tactic. *Journal of Peace Research* 8:143–53.

Kohlberg, E., and Mertens, J. F., 1986. On the strategic stability of equilibria. *Econometrica* 54:1003–1037.

Kreps, D., and Wilson, R., 1982a. Sequential equilibria. *Econometrica* 50:862–87.

Levy, J., 1984. The offensive–defensive balance of military technology: A theoretical and historical analysis. *International Studies Quarterly* 28:219–38.

Maoz, Z., 1985. Decision-theoretic and game-theoretic models of international conflict. In U. Luterbacher and M. Ward, eds., *Dynamic Models of International Conflict*. Boulder, Colo.: Lynne Rienner.

Maynard-Smith, J., 1982. *Evolution and the Theory of Games*. New York: Cambridge University Press.

Morrow, J., 1987. A limited information model of crisis bargaining. Paper presented at the 1987 Annual Meeting of the International Studies Association, Washington, D.C.

Moulin, H., 1981. Deterrence and cooperation: A classification of two-person games. *European Economic Review* 15:179–93.

Nalebuff, B., 1982. Brinkmanship, in *Prizes and Incentives*, unpublished dissertation. Oxford, Engl.: Nuffield College.

——— 1987. Brinkmanship and Nuclear Deterrence: The Neutrality of Escalation. Princeton University Discussion Papers in Economics, No. 125.

Neyman, A., 1986. Bounded complexity justifies cooperation in the finitely repeated Prisoners' Dilemma. *Economic Letters* 19:227–29.

O'Neill, B., 1986. The dollar auction and international escalation. *Journal of Conflict Resolution* 30:33–50.

——— 1987a. A measure for crisis instability with applications to space-based missile defenses. *Journal of Conflict Resolution* 31(4):631–72.

———— 1987b. Game theory and the U.S. Euromissiles. Paper presented at Annual Meeting, American Association for the Advancement of Science, Chicago, Illinois, February, 1987.

Pearl, J., 1984. *Heuristics: Strategies for Computer Problem Solving*. Reading, Mass.: Addison-Wesley.

Phillips, W. R., and Hayes, R., 1978. Linking forecasting to policy planning: An application of the theory of noncooperative games. In W. Hollist, ed., *Exploring Competitive Arms Processes*. New York: Dekker.

Powell, R., 1987a. Crisis bargaining, escalation, and MAD. *American Political Science Review* 81(3):717–35.

———— 1987b. Nuclear Brinkmanship with Two-Sided Incomplete Information. Mimeo. Harvard University, Center for International Affairs.

Rapoport, A., 1964. *Strategy and Conscience*. New York: Harper and Row.

Rapoport, A., and Chammah, A., 1965. *Prisoner's Dilemma*. Ann Arbor: University of Michigan.

Ravid, I., 1980. To mobilize or not to mobilize, October 1973. Mimeo. Centre for Military Analyses, Tel Aviv, Israel.

Reinhardt, G. C., 1984. On Exchange Simulation and Crisis Stability. Lawrence Livermore National Laboratory, UCRL-53585.

Reinhardt, G. C., and Squire, R. K., 1982. Using Game Theory to Evaluate the Stability of Strategic Forces. Lawrence Livermore National Laboratory, UCID-19297.

Richelson, J., 1979. Soviet strategic posture and limited nuclear operations: A metagame analysis. *Journal of Conflict Resolution* 23:326–36.

Robinson, T. W., 1970. Game Theory and Politics: Recent Soviet Views. RAND RM-5839. Santa Monica, Calif.: RAND Corporation.

Rubenstein, A., 1986. Finite automata play the repeated Prisoner's Dilemma. *Journal of Economic Theory* 39:83–96.

Russett, B., 1983. *Prisoners of Insecurity*. San Francisco: Freeman.

Schelling, T. C., 1958. The Reciprocal Fear of Surprise Attack. RAND P-1342. Santa Monica, Calif.: RAND Corporation.

———— 1960. *The Strategy of Conflict*. Cambridge, Mass.: Harvard University Press.

Selten, R., 1978. The chain store paradox. *Theory and Decision* 9:27–159.

———— 1979. A simple model of kidnapping. In S. J. Brams, A. Schotter, and G. Schwodiauer, eds., *Applied Game Theory: Proceedings of a Conference at the Institute for Advanced Studies, Vienna*. Wurzburg, FDR: Physica-Verlag.

Selten, R., and Tietz, R., 1972. Security equilibria. In R. Rosecrance, ed., *Future of the International Strategic System*. San Francisco: Chandler.

Sharp, J., 1986. Alliance security dilemmas. Mimeo. Harvard University, Center for European Studies.

Shubik, M., 1968. On the study of disarmament and escalation. *Journal of Conflict Resolution* 12:83–101.

―――― 1984. Game theory: The language of strategy. In M. Shubik, ed., *Mathematics of Conflict*. Amsterdam: Elsevier.

―――― 1985. The Uses, Value, and Limitations of Game-Theoretic Methods in Defense Analysis. Cowles Foundation Discussion Paper No. 766, Yale University.

―――― 1987. Game-Theory Models of Strategic Behavior and Nuclear Deterrence. Cowles Foundation Discussion Paper No. 829, Yale University.

Snidal, D., 1985. The game *theory* of international politics. *World Politics* 38:25–57.

Snyder, G., 1984. The security dilemma in alliance politics. *World Politics* 36:461–95.

Snyder, G., and Diesing, P., 1977. *Conflict Among Nations: Bargaining, Decision Making and Systems Structure in International Crises*. Princeton, N.J.: Princeton University Press.

Sobel, J. H., 1972. The need for coercion. In J. R. Pennock and J. W. Chapman, eds., *Coercion*. Chicago: Aldine-Atherton.

Van Evera, S., 1985. Why cooperation failed in 1914. *World Politics* 38:81–117.

von Neumann, J., and Morgenstern, O., 1944. *Theory of Games and Economic Behavior*. Princeton, N.J.: Princeton University Press.

Wagner, R. H., 1982. Deterrence and bargaining. *Journal of Conflict Resolution* 26:329–58.

―――― 1983. The theory of games and the problem of international cooperation. *American Political Science Review* 77:330–46.

Weiss, M. P., 1983. Two Game-Theoretic Studies of Military Command and Control. Ph.D. dissertation, Evanston, Ill.: Northwestern University.

Wilkening, D., and Watman, K., 1986. Strategic Defenses and First-Strike Stability. RAND R-3412-FF/RC. Santa Monica, Calif.: RAND Corporation.

Wilson, R., 1985. Reputations in games and markets. In A. Roth, ed., *Game-Theoretic Models of Bargaining*. New York: Cambridge University Press.

Zagare, F., 1981. Non-myopic equilibria and the Middle East Crisis of 1967. *Conflict Management and Peace Science* 5:139–62.

―――― 1983. A game-theoretic analysis of the cease-fire alert decision of 1973. *Journal of Peace Research* 20:73–86.

―――― 1985a. The pathologies of unilateral deterrence. In U. Luterbacher and M. Ward, eds., *Dynamic Models of International Conflict*. Boulder, Colo.: Lynne Rienner.

―――― 1985b. Toward a reformulation of the theory of mutual deterrence. *International Studies Quarterly* 29:155–70.

―――― 1986. Recent advances in game theory and political science. In S. Long, ed., *Annual Review of Political Science*. Norwood, N.J.: Ablex.

―――― 1987. *The Dynamics of Deterrence*. Chicago: University of Chicago Press.

# 8

# Deterrence in Oligopolistic Competition

## ROBERT WILSON

The purpose of this chapter is to report on theoretical studies of deterrence in the economics literature. The role of deterrence in market competition provides, in a familiar mundane context, a partial analogy that can be useful for studying propositions about deterrence in military and political contexts. In both environments, the methodology of game theory has been an important analytical tool. Consequently, critical examination of the strengths and weaknesses of this methodology in the economic context may be instructive. Similarly, empirical and experimental studies of deterrence in market settings are easier.

Deterrence in market contexts differs markedly from political contexts, so the validity of extrapolating *positive* propositions from an economic to a political context is doubtful. An economic context remains useful nevertheless for refuting purported generalizations. Further, the applications of game theory developed in this context potentially have heuristic value for studies of military and political strategies. I will emphasize the main concepts that have proved useful in unraveling the many complexities of competitive behavior, but I also focus selectively on those that might be transferable to political environments. For example, I describe the important roles in economic contexts of repeated encounters and private information and the strong interaction effects when these two features occur together; it seems likely that these have counterparts in political contexts.

One could construe deterrence broadly to encompass nearly any action taken by an incumbent to forestall, thwart, modify, or ameliorate the effects of others' actions that jeopardize the incumbent's interests; thus, essentially all "protective" strategies would be included. This broad interpretation applies to some of the studies reviewed here, but in the economics literature a narrower interpretation usually applies that focuses on the preservation of monopoly power, which is the ultimate source of most supranormal profits. That is, the focus is on avoiding entry or investment in the incumbent's industry and on wresting market share from other established firms.

Further, there is a primary emphasis on altering others' incentives or perceptions so as to preclude their initiation of moves that will be costly, perhaps too costly, for the incumbent to counter. This emphasis accounts for two preoccupations: one is with the immediate credibility of the incumbent's strategy, and the other is with the demonstration effect on subsequent transgressors. Credibility refers both to the signaling interpretation of the incumbent's preemptive moves, designed to alter perceptions, and to the incumbent's incentives to carry out threatened responses to intrusions, designed to alter incentives. One stratagem to ensure credibility is commitment, typically via irrevocable investments in durable equipment that reduce irreversibly the incumbent's subsequent costs. More generally, threatened actions are credible that, in the event of an intrusion, are in the best interests of the incumbent to carry out. In economic contexts, the demonstration effect refers to the possibility that an aggressive response to one intrusion may deter subsequent intrusions—not unlike the domino effect in political contexts.

In economic contexts, deterrence is primarily an aspect of the competitive process among firms maneuvering for advantage, or simply for a foothold, in an oligopolistic market. Competitive battles for entry into a market, and subsequently for market shares or continued survival, include in modified forms many of the features that arise in military and political contexts. An incumbent firm often has a variety of tactics available that enable it to threaten credibly to retaliate against incursions by opponents that would affect adversely the profitability of the incumbent. Some of the conditions that make a threat both credible and effective have analogs in political situations. For example, an incentive to maintain a reputation for capability and willingness to snuff out invaders can be an effective deterrent: even if an aggressive response is not cost-effective myopically, the demonstration effect can make it worthwhile from a longer-term perspective—and the existence of the incentive itself can mean that potential intruders never choose to test the incumbent's resolve.

In sum, a deterrent strategy is a plan of action to preserve market power.

The role of game theory is to establish in simple models which strategies are optimal and, importantly, credible.

Within the economics literature, studies of oligopolistic competition are mostly included within the field of "industrial organization" and, especially, the topic called the structure of industries, which examines the factors that influence the number, size, and products of firms in a static or cross-sectional view, as well as the dynamics of the competitive interactions among firms within an industry.

The next section discusses the issues in the field of industrial organization, with particular reference to the topic of deterrence. Following it is a brief discussion of the strengths and limitations of the game-theoretic methodology that is the chief instrument in analytical studies. The subsequent section summarizes the main theoretical conclusions about deterrence in oligopolistic competition that have been derived from simple game-theoretic models. These conclusions are amplified in an Appendix that describes typical models and results, first for the case that participants have the same information, and then for the more realistic case that some have private information.

Because the literature relies on institutional features peculiar to market competition among firms, the available case studies and statistical evidence are not described here. They have less transferable value for studies of military deterrence than direct political and military histories. For an admirably realistic and comprehensive examination of oligopolistic competition, I refer the reader to Scherer (1980), who includes generous citations to the evidence. Compendia of recent theoretical results are in Fudenberg and Tirole (1986, 1987), Roberts (1987), Schmalansee (1982), and Wilson (1985, 1987). Experimental methodology and results are reviewed by Plott (1982), and with special relevance to deterrence by Isaac and Smith (1985). Policy concerns are summarized in Salop (1981).

The reader will likely conclude that all of the material included here reveals its vulnerability to the sorts of criticism directed at deterrence theory in the other chapters in this volume and in the earlier literature (e.g., George and Smoke (1974); Jervis, Lebow, and Stein (1985)). In particular, the theoretical models rely on strong assumptions of rationality and common knowledge. Nevertheless, by delineating conditions under which deterrence succeeds or fails to be credible and effective, even with such strong assumptions, these models serve at least to narrow the domain in which behavioral factors must be invoked to constrain the implementation of deterrent strategies. Furthermore, these models provide benchmarks for more realistic empirical and experimental studies.

## Background

An oligopoly comprises the firms in an industry. The firms compete (or collude) continually via product designs, delivery conditions, and prices. Investments in factor supplies, plants and sites, R&D, and production technology and equipment have long-term effects on firms' options and their costs. Firms are interested primarily in (the expected present value of) profits, comprising both revenue (prices times quantities) and costs (investments in capacity plus operating costs).

The salient case involves one or a few firms whose products are close substitutes, and other industries that offer weak substitutes, plus possibly some potential entrants. Entrants are other firms that might enter the market in competition with the present incumbents, which is usually detrimental to the incumbents. Each firm can affect its market conditions through discretionary pricing, product designs, and productive investments. These also significantly affect the opportunities available to its competitors and to potential entrants; thus, firms' decisions are strongly interactive. Firms' behaviors are motivated, therefore, by strategic considerations derived from their mutual interdependence. In the United States, at least, collusion is illegal and subject to civil liability, and contracts to that end are unenforceable.[1] Hence, noncooperative behavior predominates, and in any case cooperative arrangements must be self-enforcing. If there is any predictable stable outcome, it necessarily results from an "equilibrium" among the firms' strategies.

Dating from Adam Smith in the eighteenth century, casual empiricism has provided many "stylized facts" about oligopolistic competition. Systematic expositions date mainly from the 1930s, but without substantial empirical studies. Bain (1956) initiated what has become a continuing enterprise, studying empirically the "structure, conduct, and performance" of industries—a theme that dominates the journal literature. Some of this literature is statistical; some of it studies industries longitudinally, replete with blow-by-blow histories. Other sources include antitrust cases, Federal Trade Commission dockets, teaching cases (mainly written at Harvard Business School), and a few data bases; also, many authors bring firsthand experience from consulting, expert testimony, or service with government regulatory agencies. Recent texts, notably Scherer (1980), accompany expositions of the theory with ample references to empirical evidence and the body of legal precedent and interpretations from antitrust cases. The gap between the theory developed for simple models and the complexities of a case study can be great, however. Close examination of actual behavior has been rare, perhaps because such information is usually proprietary, but recently experimental methods have been used to examine behavioral aspects; consult Plott (1982). Few attempts have been made to examine empirically the effects of such features of preferences as risk aversion and intertemporal impatience.

Some economists argue that the "oligopoly problem" is fundamentally indeterminate, but the main view is that theoretical models can provide salient, albeit rough, predictions about the processes and outcomes of competition. The theoretical literature, dating from Cournot (1838), is predominantly deductive and positive. That is, plausible assumptions are invoked to obtain predictions that are compared qualitatively against the stylized facts. Occasionally, predictions are estimated or tested econometrically and, recently, experimentally. Because a model comprises many assumptions applied in concert, such studies test a complicated joint hypothesis that rarely allows separation of effects and identification of causal relationships. Theoretical constructions greatly exceed tests; explicit tests of underlying assumptions are rare.

## The Role of Deterrence

In studies of oligopolistic competition among firms, mention of deterrence usually refers to the context of potential entry. Because profits accrue to monopoly power, incumbents want to prevent expansion of each other's market share and as well to deter entries of other firms into their industry. Entry involves investments in capacity, product design and differentiation, spatial location and delivery conditions, and so on. Deterrent strategies of incumbents likewise involve preemptive capacity expansion that irreversibly alters their costs and potential output, threats of price wars that could make entry unprofitable, and the like. Thus, deterrence affects industry structure: the number, size, technology, products, and prices of firms.

As mentioned, the interpretation of deterrence could be so broad as to include any context jeopardizing the profitability of an incumbent, but studies focus primarily on the asymmetry between an established incumbent and a potential entrant who must incur sunk costs to enter. These costs represent the unfavorable outcome for an entrant whose maneuver fails and who is forced to exit or to sell out to an incumbent. Such costs are unrecoverable either because they are dissipated in administrative and operating expenses or because they are invested irreversibly in specialized equipment or knowledge with limited mobility or resale possibilities. Unsuccessful entry can be expensive for an incumbent, too, if driving out the entrant entails costly actions, such as a price war, and in any case an incumbent usually experiences a temporarily reduced market share and price. The consequences of successful entry are continuing market share and profits for the entrant and resulting reductions for the incumbents. The ensuing sustained competition typically entails lower prices, so aggregate profits in the industry decrease; but market penetration, consumers' benefits, and total surplus increase—which is the reason why competition generally and entry in particular are socially condoned.

The means of deterrence vary greatly: preemptive investments in plant sites, equipment, production technologies, and product designs; signaling via "limit pricing" (as explained later); and threats of price wars. (For example, preemptive siting of stores was the basis for an antitrust suit against Safeway in Canada.) Durable investments that alter irreversibly the incumbent's technology and costs are means of commitment: They ensure that the incumbent has the capacity and the cost structure to ensure domination of the market. (This was the basis for a successful antitrust suit against Alcoa in 1945. Dupont's early and large investments in capacity in various segments of the chemical industry have been examined from this perspective.) Pricing and other actions (e.g., advertising) having less durable effects are interpreted partly as signals. The inferences others draw from signaling behavior are the durable consequences of signaling and account for some of the important reputational effects in dynamic models of deterrence. In other cases, however, deterrence is plain vanilla: The copper industry in the United States long held to stable prices set at approximately the long-run average full cost for the efficient scale of operations, thus requiring an entrant to have a superior technology to make a profit.

The role of signaling derives from asymmetries in firms' information about each others' technologies, costs, and demand conditions. Typically a firm has private information about various attributes of its own circumstances, such as its costs, and incomplete information about others' attributes; thus, the firm has at best a probability assessment about every other firm's attributes. Often the firm's private information is valuable in the competitive process and is kept proprietary, and similarly its comparative ignorance about others' attributes is a potentially expensive vulnerability. The firm's strategy specifies its actions (such as choices of technology, products, outputs, or prices) as a function of its private information, its probability assessments about others' attributes, and its expectations about others' strategies. Because this is true of others' strategies as well, the firm can use its observations of others' actions to obtain revised probability assessments about their attributes. Further, anticipating that others are also making such inferences from its own actions, the firm's strategy must take account of the information conveyed to others by its actions. The choice of informational content of each firm's actions reflects the signaling component of its strategy. In some circumstances the strategy may convey substantially all of its private information, but in other cases the firm's behavior may (or may be designed) to preclude others from inferring significant information. For example, an extreme case of full revelation is one in which a firm's unit cost can be inferred from its choice of its price; an extreme case of the opposite occurs when the firm finds it advantageous to offer the same price regardless of its unit cost, in which case observations of its price yield no improvement in others' assessments. In signaling contexts, credibility is attached to actions that are in the best interests of the actor: Mere "speeches" or threats of purported intent are empty; it is actions that count. Others' inferences are based on inverting the causal connection between the actor's private information and its optimal actions.

In dynamic contexts, one kind of reputation effects involves repeated signaling. A firm invests in costly signals, such as aggressive pricing in response to entry, in order to build or maintain a reputation that it might have superior technology or resources; this is a version of the demonstration effect. The payoff from an investment in reputation is the anticipation of a reduced chance later of further incursions. The so-called deep pocket hypothesis argues further that large firms operating in many markets have both the resources and the strongest incentives to develop such reputations. For example, this is an oft-cited explanation for IBM's response to the incursions by the other mainframe and plug-compatible peripheral equipment manufacturers in the 1970s.

Failed deterrence may result in accommodation, meaning "normal" competition for market shares and profits in which each firm accepts the continuing presence of the other. *War* is a term often reserved for battles for survival. In a war of attrition, the incumbent and the entrant battle to determine whether the entrant's costs are sufficiently low (and its financial resources sufficiently large), or the reverse for the incumbent, for the entrant to gain accommodation from the incumbent; otherwise the entrant exits after a duration sufficiently long to conclude that the chances of eventual success are small. (For example, in the early 1980s Eastern Airlines eventually abandoned its entry into the transcontinental market after a protracted struggle complicated by its battle with New York Air to maintain its share of the East Coast market.) Essentially, such continuing games of "Chicken" are a protracted negotiation over division of the spoils from monopoly power. Anticipation of a war of attrition may itself deter entry. The incumbent can credibly threaten a costly price war if such a battle would reduce the chance of successful entry now; but even if it would not, the demonstration effect on other firms with later opportunities to enter might deter subsequent entries.

Other more symmetric wars of attrition occur in natural monopolies and declining industries when the firms are too numerous for all to recover their fixed costs of operation and their opportunity costs of redeploying assets into other markets; the continuing exit of firms from the steel and airline industries is the most obvious example. Competitive battles for market shares can also take this form: The net effect is to reveal which firms are stronger in terms of costs and products and can therefore sustain claims to larger shares. (The surplus of optical-fiber capacity installed by competing long-distance telephone companies indicates a battle in the making.)

Wars of the above kinds are predictable features of the competitive process. In theories that construct equilibrium strategies, such wars are part of the sorting process that selects the more efficient firms for survival or larger market shares. Their occurrence in equilibrium stems from private information: Models without informational asymmetries typically predict immediate capitulation by the weaker firm. One can interpret competitive battles as akin to bargaining under incomplete information in which the only credible communication is persistence in the struggle. In an economic context, the sorting process selects efficient firms and promotes efficient production and pricing to the benefit of consumers. There is no evident analog to these efficiency properties in a military or political context because there are no third-party beneficiaries.

Also possible are roughly two kinds of disequilibrium wars, possibly triggered by "mistaken" entry. In one version, an incumbent firm can, in equilibrium, have an incentive to sustain its reputation for likely being "strong" (having low costs, etc.) by imposing severe losses on an entrant, even if the incumbent incurs losses from the price war or other means used. Again, such losses are an investment whose payoff subsequently is a chance the entrant will exit or a reduced chance of further entry. Such anticompetitive (or at least, entry-discouraging) aggressive behavior motivated by the prospect of inducing exit or deterring subsequent entry is often called "predatory." Although there is no presumed rapacious motive to "consume" the prey, the successful incumbent often acquires the assets of the defeated entrant. For example, in the last quarter of the nineteenth century, Standard Oil acquired a dominant position in the petroleum-refining industry by aggressive practices against competitors that often culminated in mergers. On the other hand, in the mid-1970s Folger's simply retreated from its attempt to enter the East Coast retail coffee markets dominated by General Foods after encountering greatly lowered prices and enlarged promotional expenditures. Both of these episodes are described by Scherer (1980, chapter 12).

In another version, the prospect of price wars and other noncooperative behavior is the credible threat that sustains equilibrium behavior that is either explicitly or implicitly collusive among incumbents. Wars that police such equilibria by punishing defectors can be triggered by deviant or errant behavior, or by noisy observations (such as imperfect observations of market prices or firms' quantities of output) that allow an inference that collusive arrangements might have been breached. One study concluded that this is a possible explanation for the apparent price war in the automobile industry in 1955; see Bresnahan (1980).

Lesser punishments than war are integral parts of the disequilibrium behaviors in many theories of equilibrium among firms. Whenever the equilibrium of a repeated encounter does not induce equilibria in the constituent stages, it is sustained by the prospect of a "less-cooperative" punishment phase if some firm deviates. One such punishment is reversion to a less-profitable equilibrium, and another is the familiar tit-for-tat strategy that reciprocates deviations exactly.

## Methodology

The analytical methodology is invariably based on game theory, which was employed in rudimentary forms even by nineteenth century authors. By modern standards much of the early work was incomplete or based on overly simplified models. Recent work focuses on models replete with dynamics, private information, and other realistic complicating features. The game-theoretic view emphasizes that the outcome of the competitive process results from an equilibrium among firms' strategies (customers are passive in most models) and possibly occasionally from disequilibrium.

Game theory offers an impressively flexible methodology, but it imposes severe limitations. Besides the evident assumption of consistent maximizing behavior, the most important is the requirement that the "rules of the game" are common knowledge. An event is common knowledge if each player in the game knows its, each knows that the other knows it, and so on ad infinitum. For example, a fact could become common knowledge if it were announced publicly to the assembled players, so that each could observe that the others heard the same announcement, as in some experimental settings. The results of studies that assume that each protagonist's actions, information, and preferences are common knowledge are usually not robust to variations that allow some features to be privately known.

It is unclear to what extent these limitations are peculiar to the special methodology of game theory and to what extent they reflect conundrums inherent in oligopolistic competition. That is, possibly the game-theoretic models represent the only (and unrealistic) contexts that oligopoly problems are solvable, whereas in reality most situations are fundamentally indeterminate, depending in each instance on the peculiarities of attitudes and behavior. In any case, the fundamental difficulties in employing game theory to study oligopolistic competition raise questions about whether game-theoretic models can possibly be accurate descriptions of firms' decision processes. In the absence of descriptive validity and verification of the super-rationality and common-knowledge assumptions, there are few normative prescriptions.

## The Game-Theoretic Apparatus

The theoretical constructions are based on a few key principles. Of course, one is that players are "unitary" and thoroughly rational according to the axioms of decision theory. What other disciplines might interpret as irrational or nonrational behavior, is here explained explicitly by preferences (e.g., risk aversion, impatience), limitations of information or memory, or complicated implications of equilibrium.

Peculiar to game theory is the requirement that a model must encompass all that is common knowledge among the participants; indeed, the formal "rules of the game" are equivalent to the body of common knowledge. (The "rules of the game" constitute the description of the situation; there is no implication that a participant adheres to any agreement or norm of acceptable behavior.) Relevant information is rarely common knowledge in practice, but the assumption of common knowledge is often invoked as a modeling device to obtain a tractable approximation. (However, as an approximation this tactic fails in the many models that are quite sensitive to common-knowledge assumptions: Several of these models are included in the Appendix.) The models used are therefore invariably afflicted by strong assumptions as to what is common knowledge. For example, models with private information typically assume that the probability distribution of this information is common knowledge. A major endeavor of theoretical studies is progressively to weaken the assumed base of common knowledge—but the regress is potentially infinite.

This endeavor is motivated by the fact that in most models of competitive battles among firms the effects of private information are severe, and the variety of predictable behaviors expands greatly with each successive relaxation of common-knowledge assumptions. The obverse is true as well: Many models yield implausible predictions when private information is deleted and predict recognizable behaviors when it is added. Casual empiricism suggests, too, that firms perceive their proprietary information

# Deterrence in Oligopolistic Competition

to be among their major assets and their uncertainties about other firms' private information to be among their greatest risks. Examples include tangible facts such as market data, production costs, credit reserves, and opportunities for investment or redeployment of mobile equipment; as well as intangibles such as forecasting skills, risk aversion, and time preferences (impatience). The gist is that among competing firms, much of the relevant information is proprietary, and the consequences are pronounced.

The raison d'être of the theory is to construct an equilibrium; that is, a strategy for each player that is optimal against the others' strategies. (Some predictions weaker than equilibria have been proposed; e.g., equilibria in correlated strategies and "rationalizable strategies.") Unlike equilibria and strategies in some other disciplines, here a strategy must specify the player's action in every possible contingency, even those unexpected in equilibrium, because equilibria are sustained by expectations about the consequences of deviant behavior. Of course, firms' strategies interact with the market structure to determine eventual outcomes, including quantities, prices, and profits, but in addition they specify the tactical means employed in each contingency to affect these outcomes.

Major mileposts of the theory are largely identified with discoveries of practically interesting games that have unique equilibria or unique equilibria subject to plausible selection criteria. Often these equilibria reveal important aspects of strategic behavior. A salient example is the demonstration from models of bargaining that the parties' relative impatience is a major determinant of the division of the gains from trade, or in models of entry deterrence that the incentive to sustain a reputation for aggressive behavior can be paramount.

Finitely repeated games pose paradoxes in some examples, however, because "subgame-perfect" equilibria can fail to manifest intuitively plausible behavior. A subgame-perfect equilibrium has the stronger property that each player's strategy remains optimal in every subgame. For example, in the penultimate stage of a repeated game, players' actions must be optimal, given that each player anticipates optimal play by himself as well as others in the final stage. The culprit in such examples is usually an overly strong common-knowledge assumption: This allows a backward induction that taxes plausibility. A familiar examples if the finitely repeated "Prisoners' Dilemma" game, for which the unique subgame-perfect equilibrium precludes cooperation regardless of the number of repetitions.

A major failing (some say strength[2]) of the theory is that often there are multiple equilibria: Selecting among these is a winnowing process in which plausible criteria are invoked to exclude equilibria deemed deficient. Some of these criteria invoke behavioral features, but mainly criteria are justified by an extended interpretation of rationality. Some of these criteria have considerable generality; others are peculiar to the context in which the model is interpreted. One general criterion aims to exclude implicit incredible threats: A strategy must be optimal in every subgame; or stronger, a strategy must be justified by probability assessments that are consistent with Bayes' rule for inference via conditional probability, and such that in every contingency the strategy is optimal for the remainder of the game. (Recall the distinction between a strategy and an action: a strategy specifies in *each* contingency the action to take.) These probability assessments are subject to further criteria of plausibility based on signaling interpretations of other players' observed actions. Related criteria exclude weakly or iteratively dominated strategies. A second criterion enforces minimal memory requirements and ideally prefers strategies that depend only on those parts of prior history that are payoff-relevant for the future (e.g., stationary or Markovian strategies in a stationary environment). Additional criteria invoke various kinds of stability, robustness under perturbations and related continuity considerations, and invariance to embeddings in larger games. These selection criteria are highly vulnerable to the requirement of game theory that the equilibrium selected must itself be common knowledge among the players. An exception is the "forward induction" criterion: As the players move in sequence, the actions of each player signal the equilibrium continuation that serves that player's own interests.

The empirical ramifications of game theory are exhausted by the joint implications of common knowledge of the rules, expected utility maximization, and (a selection of an) equilibrium. It is less a "theory," therefore, than a method. Properly, theories are constructed on a game-theoretic foundation by formulating and testing models. The theory of oligopolistic competition presently comprises mostly its collection of models and the assorted facts used to motivate and test them.

In the formulation of models, game theory brings the special advantage that it elicits the implications of a precise and complete specification of "who knows what when" and each player's possible actions in each contingency.[3] The recent theory has emphasized particularly the implications of dispersed private information among the players and the consequences of repeated encounters among the same players. Analyses of these features provide reasoned explanations of the role of credible commitments, threats, signaling, and reputations. The interesting results focus on two extremes: explanations of severely noncooperative behavior and, alternatively, maintenance of cooperative behavior in the absence of enforceable contracts. Interpreting equilibria in familiar terms (price wars, implicit collusion, etc.) is occasionally problematic, but artistic license is allowed.

The implications of game-theoretic models for empirical studies are distressing. The range of possible phenomena in or out of equilibria can be extreme, and no realistic model provides a simple regression for estimation—at the very least, a complicated time-series structure is implied, usually with many omitted explanatory variables. Matters are better regarding experimental studies: Some simple experimental designs admit specific predictions about a few key measures.

For matters of public policy, the variety and complexity of phenomena predicted by game-theoretic models are useful to justify what might happen and equally discouraging of attempts to justify exclusion of what might not happen. Adversial protagonists or a policy can construct models to justify nearly any prediction. There is therefore considerable emphasis on identifying general features whose predictions have wide applicability.

## Main Conclusions of the Theoretical Models

In the field of industrial organization, models and their predictions are presented as deductive exercises of the "if $M$ then $P$" variety. Actually, scholars search for plausible $M$s that yield $P$s approximating observations or stylized facts. Thus the field's research is mostly a summary of what observations can be approximated by the predictions of plausible models. A more general enterprise seeks to identify the ingredients of models that produce consistently interesting predictions. There seem to be few predictions that cannot be derived from some model; therefore, there is an understandable interest in finding plausible ingredients whose predictions have wide validity. I mention several ingredients here; the Appendix provides more details. The most interesting predictions are those that entail severe episodic competitive battles, and those that entail sustained cooperation, because these features are the ones that cannot be explained adequately by simple models of ongoing daily competition.

As mentioned previously, one important ingredient is an equilibrium-selection criterion that enforces some version of sequential rationality. That is, each player's equilibrium strategy is in every contingency optimal for the remainder of the game. Moreover, it is usually necessary to impose plausibility restrictions on a player's probability assessments entertained after observation of an event deemed to have zero probability according to the equilibrium strategies. Without such criteria, there are often many equilibria that are vulnerable to the criticism that they reflect implicit commitments, incredible threats, unenforceable contracts, or "threatening with absurd beliefs"—that is, probability assessments that reflect implausible inferences from disequilibrium behavior.

It is important to model commitment explicitly via irreversible investments in durable equipment, and so forth. But too-strong commitments can be noxious as well; for example, ignoring the time phasing of incremental investments precludes implicitly cooperative equilibria that depend on mutual expectations of restraint. Similarly, opportunities to preempt must be modeled explicitly (who moves first, etc.), or the several equilibria will reflect the several possibilities of who preempts first or a collision.

Ideally, a model and its accompanying equilibrium-selection criterion admit a single equilibrium. But as mentioned previously, this is a disadvantage if uniqueness hinges on an incredible backward induction. Multiple equilibria have a fundamental importance in dynamic games, moreover. Monopoly power or cooperation in an oligopoly is sometimes sustained by expectations that deviations will result in reversion to a less-profitable equilibrium, at least for a duration sufficient to deter deviations. For example, cartels can be sustained by expectations that deviations will dissolve the arrangement and result in the lower profits from competitive behavior (OPEC is a modern example, and the Joint Economic Committee of the railroads in the nineteenth century is another well-studied example).

Repeated encounters, and dynamic games generally, often provide an embarrassing wealth of equilibria. Finite repetition of a single stage-game need not add equilibria (e.g., the "Prisoners' Dilemma"), but in some cases the effects are appreciable, especially if the stage-game itself has multiple equilibria. Generally, repeated encounters add new possibilities for cooperation sustained by mutual expectations of punishments for deviations. In the extreme case of a single stage-game repeated infinitely often, essentially all feasible average payoffs are possible equilibrium outcomes.

Policing deviations from cooperative behavior can be problematic in the theory as well as in real life. In some equilibria, the incentives that motivate "punishers" depend on further punishments for noncompliance. In such cases, there is a potentially infinite regress in which the execution of each punishment depends on an expectation that failure to comply will be met with the next level of punishment: If the latter punishments require the participation of the original deviant, then these equilibria may be fragile in practice and could easily collapse if the predicted expectations are not sustained. Equilibria in which punishment of a deviator reaps an immediate benefit for the punisher(s) seem, plausibly, to be more robust in practice.

Equilibria can be greatly restricted by confining strategies to plausible behaviors, such as stationarity or dependence only on payoff-relevant history, bounded memory, and so on. Conversely, seemingly small powers of

## Deterrence in Oligopolistic Competition

commitment added to a dynamic game can sustain cooperative behavior even with narrowly restricted strategies. For instance, the Appendix describes a simple example in which firms alternate setting prices, so that each is committed to its price for two periods: Thus a price cut by one can be countered by a more severe cut by the other that for one period leaves the first without a market share, which tends to dampen its incentives to cut its price initially. In this example the monopoly price prevails in the stationary equilibrium, which may be one of the more unintuitive results from game theory.

Limitations on the players' common knowledge and, particularly, possession of private information can have dramatic effects in dynamic games. A main effect in finite games is to obviate the possibility of paradoxical backward inductions. Signaling and reputation effects can be the paramount motivation for limit pricing, wars of attrition, predatory price wars, bargaining delays and strikes, and presumably a host of other costly or dissipative behaviors that are inexplicable otherwise. Sometimes the only effect is the need to signal accurately to forestall reactions that are mutually unprofitable.

A recurrent feature is that a small dose of incomplete information allows commitment or credibility to be attached to behaviors that otherwise could not be optimal in equilibrium; moreover, these effects escalate as the number of repeated encounters increases. For example, others' perceptions that there is a small chance that one might immediately profit from aggressive predatory behavior provide one a strong incentive to sustain these perceptions by acting aggressively, even if such imitation is costly, if these perceptions might deter future incursions.

In repeated encounters, whenever a player's preferences (motivations, intentions) are privately known, there is an incentive to maintain a reputation (for reckless or benign intent) via behaviors that sustain opponents' beliefs or suggest misleading inferences: Offsetting the cost of reputation building via myopically nonoptimal behavior is the prospect that it will engender favorable reactions in the future or set the stage for exploitation of a more profitable opportunity later. For example, "Prisoners' Dilemma" offers rich opportunities to imitate the benign intent of a tit-for-tat player. In many models, private information is eventually revealed by the players' actions as the game unfolds, but in the interim private information is a major source of profitability.

On the other hand, limited common knowledge can also *necessitate* cooperation through reputation effects that engender imitative behavior, most notably in "Prisoners' Dilemma" and related coordination games. In these games, each player has an incentive to cooperate if there is a chance others will reciprocate and to reciprocate if it will sustain others' beliefs that there is such a chance of reciprocity.

## Remarks

Oligopolistic competition has been a main proving ground for development of game-theoretic methods and models—more so than military and political deterrence, to my knowledge. Game theory has been enriched by the encounter with difficult problems, and the subject has been enriched with models that offer explanations of puzzling phenomena. Most valuable have been the demonstrations that a wide variety of behavior previously deemed "irrational" or idiosyncratic can also be explained as the consequences of rational behavior in sufficiently rich models. That the explanations center on the role of repeated encounters and private information offers prospects of an eventual synthesis. Also, it has become abundantly clear that an equilibrium is a subtle and complicated construction whose ultimate implications for behavior need not be obvious.

On the other hand, game theory suffers from extreme rationality and informational assumptions, and little has been done to establish an empirical basis for these assumptions. The actual decision processes and behaviors of the firms it purports to describe have rarely been examined closely, and few inferences from case studies can claim transferability or generality. The substantive empirical basis of the theory still depends mainly on traditional statistical studies of industries and close examination of legal and regulatory cases. Experimental methods offer one route to examine behavior in greater depth; and one can hope that new econometric methods will provide more direct tests of the predictions derived from game-theoretic models.

For studies of deterrence in military and political spheres, there may be useful lessons that can be drawn from studies of oligopolistic competition. The best game-theoretic models mostly verify features that could be perceived directly by serious students of the subject using sufficient care; the worst amply demonstrate that a poorly formulated model can severely distort important features and easily miss the main point altogether. Nevertheless, the models enable analytical studies to be conducted within a consistent logical framework.

For example, in an ongoing relationship between two parties, each with private information, the extant models verify the variety of competitive regimes that can occur, including stable competition, dissipative battles for entry or shares of the spoils, or "predatory" attempts to acquire or maintain dominance via credible threats motivated by reputational effects. And as well, they verify possibilities for sustained cooperation by self-enforcing collusive agreements and by mutual incentives to sustain incentives for reciprocity. Because these features depend subtly on the structure of the situation (the "rules of the game"), and particularly on the structure of information and rewards and the dynamics of the parties' interaction, reliance on a systematic methodology is apparently essential for analytical studies.

The likely consequence is a more thorough understanding of the processes of competition and cooperation. Novel policy recommendations seem unlikely, because such studies can at most add further substance to conclusions derived from centuries of military engagements, diplomatic history, and political science.

## Appendix: Illustrative Game-Theoretic Models and Results

This appendix provides a selection of some of the models and results about oligopolistic competition among firms. The selection is intended to illustrate both the general spectrum of topics, models, and methods used in the game-theoretic study of oligopolistic competition and to illustrate the basis for the various generalizations offered in the text.

These results are all derived by the methods of noncooperative game theory. The noncooperative aspect of this theory derives from the assumption that the participants have no opportunities to enter into binding or enforceable contracts that are not modeled explicitly in the description of the game; that is, firms are assumed to act solely in their own interests, and any agreements or understandings among them must be self-enforcing for each one through the incentives arising from the structure of payoffs and others' strategies. Most of the results also exclude so-called correlated strategies, in which firms coordinate their strategies by conditioning their actions on exogenous observations that may be correlated in the statistical sense.

The first section examines only the case that there is no private information among the firms: All information is common knowledge. In this context, an equilibrium is assumed to be a subgame-perfect equilibrium: The equilibrium induces an equilibrium in every subgame. This restriction is intended to exclude implicit incredible threats. The second section allows that some of the participants have private information; however, it is still restricted by a common knowledge assumption (e.g., the probability distribution of private information is usually assumed to be common knowledge). In this context, an equilibrium is assumed to be (at least) a sequential equilibrium: Every action is part of an optimal strategy for the remainder of the game, based on probability assessments that are consistent with the rules of conditional probability and the structure of the game.

## Games with Complete Information

### Strategic Substitutes and Complements

The recent literature on oligopolistic competition emphasizes the distinction between strategic substitutes and complements. This distinction may explain the qualitative differences between deterrence models in economic and military contexts. Two firms' outputs, for example, are (roughly speaking) strategic substitutes if an increase in one's output reduces the other's optimal output in response; that is, the static reaction function is downward sloping. Strategic complements are analogous: The reaction function slopes upward. Of course, it is possible that one firm's reaction function slopes downward, and the other's, upward; or that a reaction function slopes upward initially and then downward, etc. In economic models it is fairly natural to specify that firms' outputs are strategic substitutes, and in some contexts that their prices are strategic complements. The recent literature indicates that these specifications account substantially for the qualitative nature of the results obtained from dynamic models of oligopolistic competition. In particular, several authors assume that outputs are strategic substitutes in the course of deriving the prediction that, in equilibrium, firms will not install excess durable capacity. On the other hand, examples have been given in which outputs are strategic complements and firms are predicted to install excess capacity in order to deter entry of other firms.

The analogy between excess capacity and armaments that are unused in equilibrium, but exist to deter invasions, is inexact. However, it is probable that realistic models of arms races would naturally assume that armaments are strategic complements: One's optimal defensive capability is an increasing function of the other's capability. One would expect, therefore, that the predictions derived would correspond more closely to those derived from economic models that similarly assume strategic complementarity. Such models are rare, except in the familiar case that the strategic variables are prices, and only the first of the following referenced authors provides examples that illustrate strategic complements in the context of capacity. *References*: Bulow, Geankoplos, and Klemperer (1985a,b), Dixit (1979, 1980), Eaton and Ware (1987), Fudenberg and Tirole (1986, Section 2; 1987).

### "Expectational" Equilibria of Dynamic Expansion Games

Continuing with the imperfect analogy between economic capacity and war-making capability, I mention a result that reveals some of the potential for implicit cooperation afforded by dynamic interactions. Consider the game between two firms competing for shares of a new market by installing durable capacity.[4] Assume that capacity costs and long-run profits are such that the firms' capacities are strategic substitutes. Each firm can continuously install capacity at a bounded rate. In one equilibrium, the firms install capacity until they reach one of the reaction functions; if firm 1 has a lead on firm 2 then it stops expansion early to induce 2 to stop at 1's optimal point on 2's reaction function. This equilibrium corresponds essentially to the result of the static game in which firms choose directly their final capacities (but recognizing the advantage of the leader). The dynamic game, however, has other equilibria resulting in smaller capacities and larger profits. These equilibria are sustained by mutual expectations about each other's retaliatory strategy. Both firms expand up to a mutually anticipated point; thereafter, each expands further up to one of the reaction functions if and only if the other continues expansion. These other equilibria are possible only in the dynamic formulation that admits the possibility of contingent retaliation. Other than direct communication, it is unclear how firms might coordinate on these equilibria.

The implication of these results is that incremental commitments offer more potential for cooperation by admitting a role for retaliation to police defections from mutually expected actions. *References*: Fudenberg and Tirole (1983, 1986), Spence (1979).

### Cooperative Outcomes Sustained by Expectations of Retaliation

A basic result in game theory is the "folk theorem" for infinite repetition of a single-stage game. For the case in which each of two players is interested in its average payoff, this theorem asserts that any pair of feasible stage-game payoffs, provided they give each player at least what that player could guarantee (by a maximin strategy), are the average payoffs from some equilibrium. Indeed, such payoffs are approximated by an equilibrium of a sufficiently long finite repetition, provided that in the stage game the worst and best each player could get from equilibria of the stage game are not the same. These equilibria are sustained by expectations of more or less credible retaliatory punishment phases ("trigger strategies," "three-phase punishments"). Or, more dramatically, efficient payoffs can be approximated, provided (among other conditions) that the stage game has three equilibria for which the players' preferences are in reverse order, in which case tit-for-tat strategies suffice and retaliation is not costly to the retaliator. (The provisos exclude the repeated "Prisoners' Dilemma" stage game.) Also, for some games, such as the repeated "Prisoners' Dilemma," $\epsilon$-equilibria achieve superior outcomes (an $\epsilon$-equilibrium is one for which each player's strategy comes within some small amount $\epsilon$ of achieving the maximal payoff that the player could have obtained by using its optimal strategy).

These results highlight the cooperative possibilities enabled by repetitive interactions, but they also admit inefficient outcomes. *References*: Abreu (1983), Benoit and Krishna (1985), Friedman (1977), Fudenberg and Maskin (1986), Radner (1980), Rubinstein (1979).

The special structure of particular games affords further insight. I illustrate with a simple example in which in each stage the players move sequentially as follows: The seller names a price, then the buyer accepts or rejects, then the seller chooses the quality to be high or low. Note that the buyer learns the quality only after paying the price. Assume a positive interest rate and suppose that high quality costs the seller more but is valued even more by the buyer; thus, high quality is efficient. In the only equilibrium of the stage game, the seller provides low quality, so expecting this the buyer is willing to pay only for low quality. In the game with infinitely many stages, the interesting equilibria can be interpreted in terms of the length of the buyer's memory. If the buyer has no memory, then the previously described stage-game equilibrium results. If the buyer remembers only the previous quality then there is an additional (pure strategy) equilibrium in which the buyer plays tit-for-tat: The buyer expects today the quality provided yesterday, and therefore the seller provides high quality continually. Each additional bit of memory adds an additional efficient equilibrium: Among all these, the one-bit memory is best for the buyer, because the buyer pays the least price for high quality. This example gives only a flavor of a newly flourishing approach to game theory that models players as finite automata having memory or information-processing capability that is limited. One genre of results shows that such limitations enforce a selection among the many possible equilibria. *Reference*: Abreu and Rubinstein (1986).

*Cooperative Outcomes Sustained by Small Powers of Commitment*

Outside the realm of repeated games there are other interesting models of sustained cooperation. I mention one in which a small degree of commitment suffices. Consider a duopoly in which each firm, in alternating periods, picks a price from a finite set to which it is committed for two periods. In a wide class of examples, the unique Markov[5] equilibrium predicts the monopoly price. This is sustained by the prospect that if one firm lowers its price then the other follows suit, resulting in a spiraling price war that ends only when one firm returns to the monopoly price; the duration of the price war is random because the return decision is randomized, but the expected duration is sufficient to deter deviations. Interestingly, after a price war starts, neither player prefers to return to the monopoly price until the price hits bottom one step above marginal cost; thus, there is a positive minimum duration. An implication of this kind of example is that in continuing encounters with retaliatory possibilities, a small degree of commitment can sustain cooperative outcomes. *References*: Fudenberg and Tirole (1986: Section 5), Maskin and Tirole (1988:Part II).

*Contestability of Markets*

The literature on contestability studies competition for the incumbent's role in a natural monopoly, in which potential profits are sufficient to cover the fixed costs of operation for one firm but not two. In one model, in alternating periods each of two firms commits for two periods either to exit or to entry and a production level. In the unique Markov equilibrium, a firm with an initial monopoly chooses a production level large enough (and therefore a price low enough) to deter entry that (in equilibrium) would result in its own subsequent exit. Starting from a duopoly, however, a competitive battle ensues that may take several periods to induce one or the other to exit. When fixed costs are small, the persistent threat of entry, even of the hit-and-run variety, keeps the incumbent monopolist's price and profit low.

These results are closely akin to limit pricing: The persistent threat of entry erodes monopoly power, keeping prices low and output high. *Reference*: Maskin and Tirole (1988:Part I).

A variation on this theme has been called "judo economics," and I am tempted to add "guerilla warfare" or "terrorism." An incumbent monopolist may have an incentive to engage an entrant in a competitive battle (e.g., price cuts) only if the scale of entry is sufficiently large; hence, small-scale entry can be profitable and not elicit a competitive response. An illustration refers to a large resort hotel beside which a small pension is built: Because the hotel gets the overflow from the pension in any case, the hotel prefers to retain monopoly pricing for its residual demand. More cleverly, the pension could sell advance reservation coupons for rooms at a stated price, which (if the price were above the hotel's marginal cost) the hotel would want to honor.[6] Indeed, with this form of "blackmail," the pension can in principle extract all of the profit from entry via its revenues from coupons and never need to serve a customer—although of course it must stand ready to serve to make the coupons credible.

These results are indicative of a general apprehension that the full panoply of competitive tactics has yet to be cataloged. Are monopoly profits subject to "blackmail"? *Reference*: Gelman and Salop (1983).

*The Coase Conjecture*

Coase (1972) offered the conjecture that a monopolist selling a durable good produced (or stored) at constant marginal cost would have little ability to price-discriminate intertemporally if customers were quite patient. It has been shown recently that this conjecture is true of the "stationary" subgame-perfect equilibria of the game among the seller and the buyers; moreover, if the seller's cost is less than all the buyer's valuations, then all subgame-perfect equilibria are stationary in the required sense that the buyers' use a reservation-price strategy. This result, that monopoly power is eroded by the buyers' patience, carries over to bargaining games between a seller and a buyer whose valuation is privately known, but it is sure that there are gains from trade: In a stationary sequential equilibrium, the seller is unable to screen profitably among the buyer's types (cf. "Bargaining," to follow).

This result indicates that customary notions of monopoly power that depend on intertemporal discrimination must be strongly qualified. When customers are included among the players in the game and they are patient (they use a small interest rate to discount gains from trade), then intertemporal discrimination is not credible. Customers anticipate correctly that the seller's prices will decline, and therefore they wait for favorable terms. Interestingly, this analysis does not apply to oligopolies, because the expectation of price wars in response to price cutting can sustain high prices that effectively discriminate. *References*: Bulow (1982); Coase (1972); Gul, Sonnenschein, and Wilson (1986).

## Games with Private Information

*Communication and Signaling*

Little of the literature deals directly with communication, because the prevailing view is that actions, which "speak louder than words," are the principal credible signals. There are, however, several results to report.

The first considers a game in which one player (the sender) first observes privately the realization of a real-valued random variable (the signal) and then chooses a real-valued action (the message) that is observed by the other player (the receiver), who then chooses an action. Assume that the players' payoffs depend only on the signal and the receiver's action, but differently for the two players, so that given any signal they prefer different actions; and for each the optimal action is a monotone function of the signal. There are many equilibria of this game, but surprisingly they are ordered by the fineness or accuracy of the message; moreover, one that is finer than another yields Pareto-superior outcomes. The unique finest equilibrium still yields imperfect communication: The sender's message enables the receiver to locate the signal only within an interval of positive length. Precise communication is precluded by the difference in the players' preferences. *Reference*: Crawford and Sobel (1982).

The second considers more general models in which the sender can make statements to the receiver. It has been argued (not deduced) that among the many equilibria it is plausible to select those that satisfy the following criterion: The receiver should believe a statement such that, if it is believed, the subsequent action benefits the sender if the statement is true and harms the sender if it is false. Several similar criteria have been invoked to select among equilibria of games involving signaling. A typical example involves bargaining between a seller and a buyer whose valuation of the item might be high or low. Suppose that the buyer is impatient and chooses to delay making a counteroffer so long as to make its acceptance unprofitable (compared to accepting immediately the seller's initial offer) if and only if the buyer's valuation is high: Then the seller concludes that the buyer's valuation is low.

This literature emphasizes on the one hand that costless signals must meet severe tests to be credible, and on the other, that one can select among equilibria on the basis of the plausibility of the inferences drawn from observations that have potential signaling content. However, one recent result shows that costless signals (communication) in a preplay stage of a bargaining game can substantially alter the equilibrium of the subsequent negotiation process if they affect the parties' estimates of the chance that gains from trade exist; see Farrell and Gibbons (1986). *References*: Bernheim (1984); Farrell (1984); Farrell and Gibbons (1986); Cho and Kreps (1985, 1987); Grossman and Perry (1986).

One example of reputation effects in communication might be called the "George Smiley" game. A spymaster (George) repeatedly receives reports from a spy with privileged information who might be loyal but might possibly be a mole. A loyal spy shares George's interests, whereas a mole's interests are directly opposed. In equilibrium, the mole's (randomized) strategy is to send accurate reports until a sufficiently important opportunity arrives to deceive George. Recognizing this, George's actions reflect probability assessments that the agent is a mole that decrease with the length of the history of accurate reports, weighted by the magnitude of the gain a mole could obtain from deception. If George ever discovers a deception, however, then he immediately concludes that the agent is a mole and acts accordingly thereafter. *References*: Axelrod (1979), Sobel (1985).

*Limit Pricing*

Limit pricing refers to the practice by an incumbent monopolist of keeping its price low in order to deter subsequent entry. Assuming that the current price has no effect on the profit an entrant might earn subsequently (e.g., it does not constrain the incumbent's future choices), one supposes that preentry pricing is mainly a means of communication, a credible signal to warn potential entrants against entry that would be unprofitable for both parties. The signal is credible because it is costly (a low price reduces the incumbent's present profits), but it is worthwhile to signal if it reduces the chance of entry.

An illustrative model assumes that both firms have private information about their costs of production. A potential entrant infers the incumbent's cost from observation of the incumbent's price and then enters if the inferred cost is sufficiently high to enable the entrant to reap a profit. Several kinds of equilibria can arise in this game, including the so-called pooling equilibrium in which neither the incumbent nor the entrant attach a signaling interpretation to the price. More interesting is the so-called separating equilibrium in which both parties anticipate that the incumbent's price reveals its cost. Thus, in a separating equilibrium it can be that entry occurs under precisely the same cost conditions as it would if the entrant knew the incumbent's cost. In this case, the advantage of limit pricing for the incumbent is to discourage entry by a firm with costs too high to make it profitable, yet whose very presence in the market would affect the incumbent's profits adversely.

A main conclusion from this literature is that limit pricing has a kind of inevitability, at least in those cases where the pooling equilibrium is not the only possible one. Were the incumbent to ignore the threat of entry and choose the ordinary monopoly price corresponding to its true costs, then an entrant would likely conclude that the incumbent's costs are higher than they really are, and this could precipitate uneconomical entry that would be costly for the incumbent. Similarly, the entrant cannot ignore the possibility that the price observed reflects limit pricing, because the entrant can anticipate that were it naively to assume that the observed price is the incumbent's ordinary monopoly price then the incumbent would find it advantageous to cut its price in order to stave off entry that would be profitable for the entrant. Thus whenever the incumbent has private information relevant to the profitability of entry, one must expect that its observable interim actions, such as prices, have a substantial signaling motivation. *References*: Milgrom and Roberts (1982), Ramey (1987).

*Bargaining*

A prototype for communication is bargaining in which the language of negotiation consists only of offers. In the economics literature a "standard" model considers bargaining between a buyer and a seller over the price of an item. The two parties alternate making offers until one accepts the other's offer, or there is no trade if offers continue forever. A central aspect of the formulation is that each party is impatient for an agreement; that is, each discounts gains from trade at some positive interest rate. If the gains from trade are known to both parties, then this game has a unique equilibrium: Trade occurs immediately at a price that, if preferences are linear in the price, divides the gains approximately in inverse proportion to their interest rates. Matters are greatly different if one party's valuation of the item is privately known: There are many sequential equilibria, but all the stationary ones have the property that if the interest rates are small or the interval between offers is short, then the informed party captures most of those gains in excess of the minimal possible gain, and again trade occurs quickly. This "quick-trade" result disappears if the informed party can choose his delay in responding with a counteroffer, in which case delay retains its signaling role.

The principal conclusion from this literature is that patience and private information are major advantages in negotiations. For example, a plausible extrapolation is that in negotiations between a union and a firm, one party (especially one with inferior information) might elect a strike or lockout in order to impose delay costs on the other to make it relatively more impatient for an agreement. *References*: Admati and Perry (1986); Rubinstein (1982); Grossman and Perry (1986b); Gul and Sonnenschein (1988); Gul, Sonnenschein, and Wilson (1986).

*Wars of Attrition*

A war of attrition is another mode of implicit bargaining in which costly persistence in the struggle is the only credible signal. Wars of attrition are contests for a prize (such as survival in a market) in which the struggle reveals which of the contestants is stronger (having lower costs or greater financial resources, etc.). Typically each side has private information about its own strength but is uncertain about the other's. The fight continues until one party infers that its chance of winning the prize is insufficient to justify further expense in the quest.

The main result of this literature is that costly battles are a predictable consequence of mutual uncertainties about each other's competitive strength. The outcome of the struggle reveals which contestant is stronger and can therefore claim the prize, but much of the value of the prize is dissipated in the process. Essentially the prize is sold at auction, but each contestant pays the second highest bid (namely, the cumulative costs incurred until capitulation) whether he or she wins or not. In an economic context, this double payment is the source of the benefits to consumers from competition; in a military context, presumably, there are no third-party winners. *Reference*: Fudenberg and Tirole (1986).

*Predation and Price Wars*

Predation usually refers to competitive tactics (e.g., a price war) whose advantages depend on increasing the likelihood that an entrant will exit; that is, they are anticompetitive to the extent they are designed to recoup monopoly power. The alternative to predation is accommodation: the normal pricing and other tactics based on an assumption that the entrant will persist if it has a viable technology. Predation is not applied to ordinary wars of attrition fought to determine which firm has the superior technology to be the surviving firm in a natural monopoly. It is more usually applied in the context that predation is the threat used to deter or defeat entry. In this context the main issue is whether predation is a credible threat: Can it be in the interest of an incumbent to incur losses battling a firm whose entry is a fait accompli? This issue is particularly complex when there is no chance that the battle will induce the entrant to exit.

One strand in the analysis examines the so-called deep pocket hypothesis; namely, that an incumbent with greater financial resources can drive an entrant to exit, and indeed, thereby prevent entry initially. A simple model supposes that initially the entrant can sustain losses for at most, say, 10 periods, whereas the incumbent is willing to impose these losses for one period if the reward is the entrant's exit. Then the entrant foregoes entry; or if it enters then it exits immediately! The argument is by backward induction: With one period's reserves remaining, the entrant anticipates that the incumbent will fight, after which the entrant will be forced to exit, so the entrant exits immediately. But anticipating this, with two periods' reserves remaining, the entrant expects the incumbent to fight because it will induce exit next period, so again the entrant exits immediately. And so on: Regardless of the reserves remaining, the entrant exits immediately; or better, never enters initially. This kind of conclusion is often called paradoxical, presumably because it precludes entry by an entrant with vast but finite financial reserves. The source of the conclusion is the reasoning by backward induction. The inductive steps can be invalidated by introducing some incomplete information into the model (as will be illustrated for a related model, to follow) with the result that the entrant may gain accommodation from the incumbent.

Some argue that clobbering an entrant must be irrational if it is costly and there is no chance that the entrant will exit. The counterargument is that the costs incurred are merely an investment in deterring subsequent entrants: This is the so-called demonstration effect. The prototypical paradoxical example runs as follows. An incumbent operating in several product markets anticipates the possibility of entry into each of its markets. Assume that these entry opportunities occur sequentially. Moreover, assume that in each market separately the incumbent prefers no entry, but given entry it prefers to accommodate, although it has available a (predatory) tactic that would make entry unprofitable for the entrant and itself. The unique equilibrium of this game predicts that the incumbent will acquiesce to entry in every market, and therefore every entrant will enter: Again the argument is by backward induction. This conclusion affronts intuition, at least if the number of markets is very large: The counterargument, appealing vaguely to the demonstration effect, is that clobbering a few of the early entrants might induce sufficiently many of the later ones to forego entry to make it worthwhile for the incumbent to incur the necessary losses early on.

To give substance to the demonstration effect and to invalidate the backward induction, it suffices to remove the hidden assumption that the model as postulated is common knowledge. Consider just two entrants and assume that individually each entrant and the incumbent know the facts stated above. However, suppose that the incumbent is unsure whether the second entrant knows that the incumbent's best response to entry is accommodation rather than predation. Now it is possible that in equilibrium the incumbent will clobber the hapless first entrant if it enters (so it won't), simply on the chance that this will sustain the second entrant's belief that the incumbent might prefer predation and therefore deter its entry—although in fact the second entrant knows that accommodation can be expected and will therefore enter.

The gist of this example is that predation is a credible threat if it might sustain the incumbent's reputation (in the mind of the second entrant, were it to be uncertain about the incumbent's preferences) that it might prefer predation. Moreover, predation could occur even though both the predator and the prey know that it is unprofitable for both, and the prey knows that actually it is ineffective in deterring the second entrant. All of this illustrates that informational effects due to limited common knowledge can be very complicated.

Another example illustrates that the effects of limited common knowledge escalate as the number of encounters increases. For this example, assume that the entrants are unsure whether the incumbent's best response to entry is accommodation or predation; in particular, suppose that initially they all assess a very small probability $p$ that it prefers predation, whereas acting in isolation each entrant would be willing to run the risk of entry if this probability were anything less than some large probability $q$. The claim is that, in equilibrium, all but a few entrants will forego entry. That is, if there are many entrants then all but the last few (the number depending only on $p$ and $q$) will pass up the opportunity to enter even though $p$ is small relative to $q$. This claim derives from a demonstration that when there are many entrants remaining, the incumbent who prefers accommodation will nevertheless want to meet entry with predation in order to sustain its reputation that it might prefer predation; indeed, if it were not to prey on an entrant then surely all the remaining entrants would enter. One method of proof is again a backward induction, this time showing that when $n$ entrants remain, the accommodating incumbent would nevertheless do best to meet entry with predation if $p > q^{N-1}$. Note that $n$ need not be very large for it to be optimal for the accommodating incumbent to "imitate" the behavior of a predatory one. Its motive can be simply explained as an investment decision: The cost of predation now is fully recouped by deterring entry of some of the subsequent entrants; predation deters by sustaining its reputation, interpreted as the probability that it might profit from predation. Other interpretations come to mind; for example, the predatory type of the incumbent might reflect the remote possibility that the incumbent is irrational or motivated by factors excluded from the model.

A sequence of entrants is used above only for expository purposes; the same result obtains if there is a single entrant with repeated opportunities to enter. In this case, it is of further interest to consider the case that also the incumbent is unsure whether the entrant is hurt sufficiently by predation to make entry unprofitable. The equilibrium now assumes the form of a war of attrition or a game of "Chicken." Following entry, the incumbent responds with predation, and as this continues both parties revise their probability assessments: The incumbent becomes increasingly convinced that the entrant can sustain predation, and the entrant becomes increasingly convinced that the incumbent profits from predation. The incumbent, if it is accommodating and the entrant has not exited, is all the while incurring losses and so eventually it succumbs and stops preying on the entrant; or the entrant, if it is hurt by predation and the incumbent has not reverted to accommodation, is all the while incurring losses so eventually it succumbs and exits. If they are both "strong" competitors, then they realize this after a limited duration; if only one is strong, then it surely "wins" the encounter; if both are weak, then one or the other wins according to their (randomized) choices of stopping times for capitulation.

The thrust of these several examples is that, in repeated encounters affected by private information, costly competitive battles may be undertaken as an investment in sustaining one's reputation. The benefits of building or maintaining a reputation derive from the prospect of deterring future entry, inducing exit or accommodation from a competitor (if there is a probability that it is 'weak'), and so on.

An important generalization of the folk theorem shows fairly generally that a small dose of incomplete information, added in appropriate ways to a model of a repeated game, can generate equilibria whose payoffs approximate any desired feasible outcome. *References*: Benoit (1984), Kreps and Wilson (1982), Maskin and Fudenberg (1986), Milgrom and Roberts (1982a,b). See Isaac and Smith (1985) for some disconfirming experimental evidence (the predicted amount of predatory behavior was not observed).

*Cooperation in the Finitely Repeated "Prisoners' Dilemma"*

One of the more dramatic instances of reputation effects occurs in the finitely repeated "Prisoners' Dilemma" game. The claim is that if there is a small chance that one of the players (say player 2) is an automaton that mechanically plays the tit-for-tat strategy, then an equilibrium necessarily entails cooperative play for all but the last few periods. The proof relies on the fact that tit-for-tat guarantees its user that its payoff will differ from its opponent's payoff by no more than an amount that is independent of the number of periods; that is, tit-for-tat is a good second-best strategy—which is one reason it fares well in tournaments. However, the intuition behind the result is plain. If it knew it was playing with an automaton, then player 1 would surely cooperate until near the end because it would be assured that cooperation would be reciprocated. With many periods to go, therefore, player 1 wants to cooperate until 2 defects, just on the chance that it is playing with an automaton. The nonautomaton player 2, moreover, wants to imitate the automaton's behavior (by scrupulous adherence to tit-for-tat) in order to promote this behavior by 1; indeed, were 2 ever to deviate from tit-for-tat its identity would be revealed and play would revert thereafter to strictly noncooperative behavior.

Recent results indicate that this conclusion can be generalized. One version, so far proved only for finitely repeated games of coordination, shows a comparable result for the case that there is a chance that one player is possibly any finite automaton with bounded memory. The key feature of this result is that efficient outcomes during most of the game are a necessary implication of equilibrium.

The main implication of these results is that cooperative behavior can be "bootstrapped" by adding some role for imitation of benign intentions, provided it is reinforced by reputational effects. An important feature is that cooperation for most of the history is a necessary consequence of equilibrium. An ideal result would characterize situations in which even scoundrels find it advantageous to imitate angels. *References*: Aumann and Sorin (1986); Kreps, Milgrom, Roberts, and Wilson (1982).

The infinitely repeated "Prisoners' Dilemma" allows essentially any outcome to be the result of equilibrium strategies, if there is no private information and the future is not discounted greatly. As in the folk theorem mentioned previously, nearly any behaviors can be sustained: Credible expectations that any deviation will be followed by noncooperation thereafter suffice to maintain incentives to continue cooperation.

## NOTES

I am indebted to Robert Axelrod for comments on an earlier draft. Research support from the National Science Foundation (SES 8605666) and the Office of Naval Research (N0014-79-C-0685 and N0014-K-0216) is gratefully acknowledged.

1. Note that the absence of enforceable contracts that would ensure cooperative behavior is due substantially to statutes that prohibit collusion. In international affairs the absence of enforcing agencies requires agreements and treaties to provide self-enforcing incentives.

2. For example, one line of analysis demonstrates that the several equilibria are the "shadows" cast by the equilibria of the various larger games in which the present game might be embedded. Multiple equilibria may therefore reflect realistically an inherent indeterminancy. Similarly, criteria that select among equilibria to find ones that are "stable" depend on the class of perturbations of the game that are entertained. Indeed, all equilibria are stable in the strongest sense that they are limits of "strict" equilibria in perturbed games obtained by modifying information sets.

3. On the other hand, this is also why game theory is ill-adapted to analyze communication via natural language, particularly where it is subject to uncertain interpretation.

4. Irreversible durable capacity is equivalent to a cost-reducing innovation. In both cases the effect is to enable production at costs no greater than and possibly less than previously. It is also formally equivalent in many contexts to an explicit observable irrevocable commitment.

5. That is, each firm ignores prior history that is payoff-irrelevant for the future.

6. Recall the coupon war among the major airlines: Eastern's coupons for transcontinental flights, issued on its eastern seaboard flights as part of its competitive battle with New York Air, were honored by the other major carriers, so in fact Eastern did not need to allocate many planes to the transcontinental routes.

## REFERENCES AND SELECTIVE BIBLIOGRAPHY

Abreu, D., 1983. Repeated Games with Discounting. Ph.D. dissertation, Princeton University.

Abreu, D., and Rubinstein, A., 1986. The Structure of Nash Equilibria in Repeated Games with Finite Automata. Harvard University.

Admati, A., and Perry, M., 1986. Strategic Delay in Bargaining. Stanford Business School.

Aumann, R., 1981. Survey of Repeated Games. In *Essays in Game Theory and Mathematical Economics in Honor of Oskar Morgenstern*. Wissenschaftsverlag, Bibliographissches Institut, Mannheim.

Aumann, R., and Sorin, S., 1986. Cooperation and Bounded Rationality. Hebrew University.

Axelrod, R., 1979. The rational timing of surprise. *World Politics* 31:228–46.

Bain, J. S., 1956. *Barriers to New Competition*. Harvard University Press.

Benoit, J., 1984. Financially constrained entry in a game with incomplete information. *Rand Journal of Economics* 15:490–99.

Benoit, J., and Krishna, V., 1985. Finitely repeated games. *Econometrica* 53:890–904.

Bernheim, B. D., 1984. Strategic deterrence of sequential entry into an industry. *Rand Journal of Economics* 15:1–11.

Bernheim, B. D., 1984. Rationalizable strategic behavior. *Econometrica* 52:1007–28.

Bresnahan, T., 1980. Competition and Collusion in the American Automobile Industry. Stanford University.

Bulow, J., 1982. Durable-goods monopolists. *Journal of Political Economy* 90:314–32.

Bulow, J., Geanakoplos, J., and Klemperer, P., 1985a. Holding idle capacity to deter entry. *Economic Journal* 95:178–82.

——— 1985b. Multimarket oligopoly: Strategic substitutes and complements. *Journal of Political Economy* 93:488–511.

Cho, I.-K., and Kreps, D., 1985. More Signaling Games and Stable Equilibria. Stanford Business School.

——— 1987. Signaling games and stable equilibria. *Quarterly Journal of Economics* 102:179–222.

Coase, R., 1972. Durability and monopoly. *Journal of Law and Economics* 15:143–49.

Cournot, A., 1838. Researches into the Mathematical Principles of the Theory of Wealth. N. T. Bacon (trans.). Homewood, Ill.: Richard D. Irwin, Inc., 1963.

Crawford, V., and Sobel, J., 1982. Strategic information transmission. *Econometrica* 50:1431–52.

Dixit, A., 1979. A model of duopoly suggesting a theory of entry barriers. *Bell Journal of Economics* 10:20–32.

——— 1980. The role of investment in entry deterrence. *Economic Journal* 90:95–106.

Eaton, C., and Lipsey, R. G., 1979. The theory of market preemption. *Econometrica* 46:149–58.

Eaton, C., and Ware, R., 1987. A theory of market structure with sequential entry. *Rand Journal of Economics* 18:1–16.

Farrell, J., 1984. Credible Neologisms in Games with Communication. MIT.

Farrell, J., and Gibbons, R., 1986. Cheap Talk in Bargaining Games. MIT No. 422.

Friedman, J., 1977. *Oligopoly and the Theory of Games*. Amsterdam: North-Holland.

Fudenberg, D., and Kreps, D., 1986. Reputation with multiple opponents. *Review of Economic Studies*, in press.

Fudenberg, D., Kreps, D., and Levine, D., 1986. On the Robustness of Equilibrium Refinements. Stanford University.

Fudenberg, D., and Maskin, E., 1986. The folk theorem in repeated games with discounting and with incomplete information. *Econometrica* 54:533–54.

Fudenberg, D., and Tirole, J., 1983. Capital as commitment: Strategic investment to deter mobility. *Journal of Economic Theory* 31:227–50.

——— 1986. *Dynamic Models of Oligopoly*. London: Harwood Academic Publishers.

——— 1987. Game theory for industrial organization: Introduction and overview. *Handbook of Industrial Organization*, in press.

Gelman, J., and Salop, S., 1983. Judo economics: Capacity limitation and coupon competition. *Bell Journal of Economics* 14:315–25.

George, A. L., and Smoke, R., 1974. *Deterrence in American Foreign Policy*. New York: Columbia University Press.

Grossman, S., and Perry, M., 1986a. Perfect sequential equilibrium. *Journal of Economic Theory* 39:97–119.

——— 1986b. Sequential bargaining under asymmetric information. *Journal of Economic Theory* 39:120–54.

Gul, F., and Sonnenschein, H., 1988. On delay in bargaining with one-sided uncertainty. *Econometrica* 56:601–12.

Gul, F., Sonnenschein, H., and Wilson, R., 1986. Foundations of dynamic monopoly and the Coase conjecture. *Journal of Economic Theory* 39:155–90.

Isaac, R. M., and Smith, V. L., 1985. In search of predatory pricing. *Journal of Political Economy* 93:320–45.

Jervis, R., Lebow, R. N., and Stein, J., 1985. *The Psychology of Deterrence.* Baltimore: Johns Hopkins University Press.

Kohlberg, E., and Mertens, J., 1986. On the strategic stability of equilibria. *Econometrica* 54:1003–38.

Kreps, D., Milgrom, P., Roberts, J., and Wilson, R., 1982. Rational cooperation in the finitely repeated "prisoners' dilemma." *Journal of Economic Theory* 27:245–52.

Kreps, D., and Wilson, R., 1982. Reputation and imperfect information. *Journal of Economic Theory* 27:253–78.

Kreps, D., and Wilson, R., 1982. Sequential equilibria. *Econometrica* 50:863–94.

Maskin, E., and Fudenberg, D., 1986. The folk theorem for repeated games with discounting or with incomplete information. *Econometrica* 54:533–54.

Maskin, E., and Tirole, J., 1988. A theory of dynamic oligopoly: I, II. *Econometrica* 56:549–600.

Milgrom, P., 1981. An axiomatic characterization of common knowledge. *Econometrica* 49:219–22.

Milgrom, P., and Roberts, J., 1982a. Limit pricing and entry under incomplete information: An equilibrium analysis. *Econometrica* 50:443–60.

——— 1982b. Predation, reputation, and entry deterrence. *Journal of Economic Theory* 27:280–312.

Myerson, R., 1978. Refinement of the Nash equilibrium concept. *International Journal of Game Theory* 7:73–80.

Pearce, D., 1984. Rationalizable strategic behavior and the problem of perfection. *Econometrica* 52:1029–50.

Plott, C. R., 1982. Industrial organization theory and experimental economics. *Journal of Economic Literature* 20:1485–1527.

Radner, R., 1980. Collusive behavior in noncooperative epsilon-equilibria in oligopolies with long but finite lives. *Journal of Economic Theory* 22:289–303.

Raiffa, H., 1982. *The Art and Science of Negotiation.* Cambridge, Mass.: Harvard University Press.

Ramey, G., 1987. Limit Pricing and Sequential Capacity Choice. Stanford University.

Roberts, D. J., 1987. Battles for market share. In *Advances in Economic Theory 1985*, T. Bewley, ed., New York: Cambridge University Press.

Rubinstein, A., 1979. Equilibria in supergames with the overtaking criterion. *Journal of Economic Theory* 21:1–9. See also Equilibria in Supergames, Hebrew University, 1977.

———— 1982. Perfect equilibrium in a bargaining model. *Econometrica* 50:97–110.

———— 1986. Finite automata play the repeated "Prisoner's Dilemma." *Journal of Economic Theory* 39:83–96.

Salop, S., ed., 1981. *Strategy, Predation, and Antitrust Analysis.* Washington, D.C.: Federal Trade Commission.

Scherer, F., 1980. *Industrial Market Structure and Economic Performance,* Second Edition. Rand-McNally.

Schmalansee, R., 1982. The new industrial organization and the economic analysis of modern markets. In *Advances in Economic Theory,* W. Hildenbrand, ed., Cambridge: Cambridge University Press.

Selten, R., 1975. Re-examination of the perfectness concept for equilibrium points in extensive games. *International Journal of Game Theory* 4:24–55.

———— 1978. The chain store paradox. *Theory and Decision* 9:127–59.

Smith, V. L., 1982. Microeconomic systems as an experimental science. *American Economic Review* 72:923–55.

———— 1986. Experimental methods in the political economy of exchange. *Science* (October 10) 167–73.

Sobel, J., 1985. A theory of credibility. *Review of Economic Studies* 52:557–74.

Spence, A. M., 1977. Entry, capacity, investment, and oligopolistic pricing. *Bell Journal of Economics* 8:534–44.

———— 1979. Investment strategy and growth in a new market. *Bell Journal of Economics* 10:1–19.

Wilson, R., 1985. Reputations in games and markets. In *Game-Theoretic Models of Bargaining,* A. Roth, ed., Cambridge: Cambridge University Press.

———— 1988. Entry and exit. In *The Economics of Imperfect Competition and Employment,* G. R. Feiwel, ed., London: Macmillan Press Ltd., in press. Available also as Technical Report 510, Institute for Mathematical Studies in the Social Sciences, Stanford University, March 1987.

# 9

# The Use of Deterrent Threats in International Trade Conflicts

## JOHN A. C. CONYBEARE

Military war and trade war are very different phenomena, yet both involve the application of similar underlying concepts of what makes threats both credible and effective. An examination of the theory and use of deterrent threats in trade wars may help clarify both the nature of these fundamental issues and the specific ways in which the use of deterrent threats in trade wars may be expected to differ from their use in military conflicts.

The approach used here will be to consider first a pure economic analysis of trade wars, examining the theory of optimal tariffs and strategic trade policy, inferring from this literature the kinds of factors that may be predictors of threat effectiveness in trade conflict. In summarizing this first part of the chapter, I conclude that if threats are effective, a purely economic theory of trade conflict would predict that trade wars would not occur, or would at least be very short. The explication of ineffective threats and long trade wars usually requires explanatory factors beyond the normal confines of trade theory. The identification of these supplementary variables is discussed at some length in the second half of the chapter, both because it is necessary in order to develop a predictive theory of trade wars and because these factors (iteration of conflicts, numbers of actors, linkage of trade to other issues, and cognitive distortions) are all analytic problems that may also be encountered in the analysis of military conflicts.

Finally, I conclude with some cautionary remarks on the comparison of deterrent threats in trade and military situations. Trade wars may bear a strong resemblance to arms-race problems, but exemplify at least six fundamental differences from actual nuclear war scenarios; these I discuss in the penultimate section of the chapter.

## Optimal Tariffs

### Large Countries

The earliest body of economic theory on trade conflict (aside from mercantilist balance-of-trade arguments) is that on optimal tariffs. Assuming two large, income-maximizing states, each may improve its welfare by applying an optimal tariff to its imports, changing the prices of traded goods (i.e., the terms of trade) in its favor. By a process of retaliation and counterretaliation, they will eventually reach an equilibrium in which both are worse off than at free trade. The pure theory of trade assumes that no bargaining takes place during this process and makes no predictions about how bargaining will proceed after they reach the postretaliatory equilibrium at which neither can make any further unilateral gains from higher tariffs. Because the structure of payoffs is that of an iterated "Prisoners' Dilemma" game, a tactic of contingent retaliation, using both deterrence and compellence (the latter being a threat to continue an action taken, until the desired behavior is forthcoming), should eventually lead both back to freer trade.[1]

It is not hard to find interactions between large countries that are consistent with this model. England and France fought a long trade war from the middle of the seventeenth century, until mutual recognition of its deleterious effects led to a treaty of economic peace (the Eden Treaty of 1786). Interrupted by the Napoleonic Wars, the two again gradually moved toward tariff disarmament, culminating in the Cobden–Chevalier Treaty of 1860. During the 1930s, both Britain and the United States implemented the high-tariff strategies appropriate to large countries, but took note of their power to damage each other, and concluded a tariff treaty in 1938. The pasta war of 1985–1986, between the European Economic Community (EEC) and the United States, ended with cooperation. The EEC and the United States have, in the past 20 years, both been concerned to establish a reputation for reliability in retaliating against predatory trade measures by the other.

Bargaining at most General Agreement on Tariffs and Trade (GATT) negotiations since 1948 has been between large countries offering concessions to each other, on a principal supplier basis (i.e., each large country will only give concessions to another large country that is its principal supplier of a particular import, because any concessions granted must be extended to all other members of GATT). Such behavior is consistent with the large-country optimal-tariff model. During the Tokyo Round of GATT negotiations, the veto power of each of the major participants (the United

States, Canada, EEC, and Japan) compelled them to find a formula that divided the benefits of concessions fairly equally among them (see Chan, 1985), presumably at the expense of other GATT participants.

However, there are also cases where large trading powers have become embroiled in trade wars that did not end in the mutual withdrawal of trade barriers. The trade wars between Venice and Genoa in the twelfth and thirteenth centuries were terminated only by the exclusion of Genoa from the eastern Mediterranean. The competition between England and the Hanseatic League for the Baltic trade routes, from the fourteenth to the seventeenth century, ended only with the collapse of the League, in the aftermath of the Thirty Years' War. The Anglo–Dutch wars of the seventeenth century eventually produced a cooperative economic relationship, but only after the Dutch had been militarily defeated. During the 1960s, the Chicken War between the United States and the EEC ended with the EEC retaining its higher tariff on U.S. chickens, and the United States implementing GATT-sanctioned retaliatory tariffs. In 1983 the United States raised import barriers against specialty steel, the EEC retaliated, and no agreement was forthcoming.

## Asymmetries of Size

Johnson's (1954) original synthesis of the problem pointed out that elasticity[2] conditions may result in a large country being better off after engaging in a tariff war with a smaller country. The small country may be unable to affect the terms of trade with the larger country. The latter may then impose a tariff, change the terms of trade, and extract gains from the small country that are less than fully offset by retaliation.

Factors other than size, such as the geographic and commodity concentration of trade, can also produce these elasticity conditions.[3] Size may be an important determinant of who wins a tariff war independent of elasticities (see Kennan and Riezman, 1984).

In Figure 9.1 the utilities ($U_L$, $U_S$) are for combinations of tariff (T) and no tariff (NT) for a very large country (L) in a tariff war with a very small country (S). L is better off at the postretaliation outcome ($T_L T_S$) than at free trade, and has a preference that Snyder and Diesing (1977:45) call "Deadlock."[4] S cannot change its terms of trade, and can only hurt itself by imposing a tariff on L, regardless of whether the latter has a tariff. S is better off being exploited, even though L can be hurt by retaliation.[5]

Small powers have generally recognized such asymmetries in bargaining power and made concessions accordingly. Tariff wars between France and Italy (1886–1898), France and Switzerland (1892–1895), and Germany

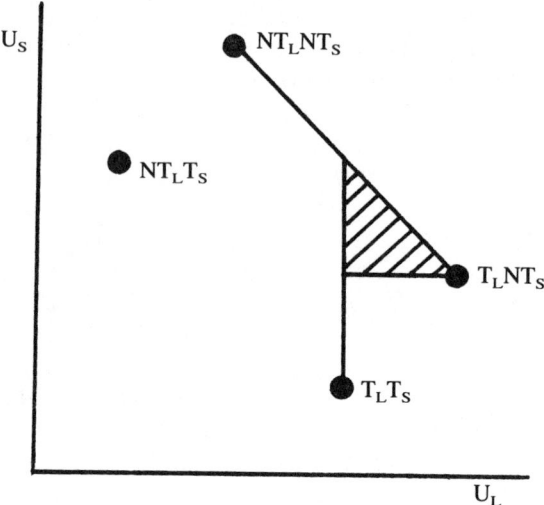

**Figure 9.1.** Payoffs in an asymmetric optimal tariff war.

and Russia (1893–1894) all resulted in the smaller country making concessions in order to return the trade relationship to a semblance of cooperation. During the Smoot–Hawley tariff wars of the 1930s, most small countries behaved with great circumspection in dealing with larger powers, often sought the protection of a benevolent regional *hegemon*, and sometimes attempted (mostly unsuccessfully, because it was discouraged by large countries' threats of retaliation) to create regional unions of small countries to offset their lack of bargaining power.

The optimal-tariff literature has nothing explicit to say about threat effectiveness. The theory leads our attention to size as the key variable. Large countries can make credible threats of contingent retaliation. In asymmetric situations, the large country's commitment to impose a tariff on the small country will be highly credible, because the small country only hurts itself by retaliating. The small country's dominating strategy is no-tariff regardless of what the big country does.

Only if it can credibly convince the large country that it is willing to hurt itself to punish the large country can the small country possibly change the large country's behavior. This would be similar to the chain-store problem discussed, involving commitment to a short-term policy that generates losses in the hope of securing a longer-term gain. The small country might threaten to put the game at $T_L T_S$ unless the large country agreed to an outcome within the shaded triangle of Figure 9.1, leaving the small country better off than at $T_L NT_S$ and the large country better off than if the small country held to its threat. Such tactics are unlikely to succeed, especially if the large country has trade relations with a number of small powers and cannot afford to set a precedent of giving in to one of them. As an example, Switzerland retaliated against the Smoot–Hawley tariff, to no effect.

## Strategic Industry Policy

If the traded-goods sector is oligopolistic,[6] there are "pools" of profits that are supernormal (i.e., larger than would exist in a perfectly competitive market), of which the state may act to secure a larger share for "our" firms. The literature on this problem (see essays in Krugman, 1986; Grossman and Richardson, 1986) start with a Cournot duopoly model in which each firm has a "zero" conjecture (i.e., it sets output assuming that the other firm's output will remain constant), and the firms' reaction functions lead them to an equilibrium from which neither will have an incentive to deviate. Any threat to increase output will not be credible and will therefore not induce the other firm to reduce output. The firm that increases output, in order to get a larger market share, will reduce its profits. (This literature appears to ignore the possibility that a firm may take a short-term loss if it thinks it can push the other out of the market.) The state may alter the situation by subsidizing its own oligopoly, causing the firm to increase its production, forcing the foreign firm to reduce production until a new equilibrium is reached in which our firm has a larger share of the pool of profits and our national income is increased. The gains to our national income must be large enough to offset any "deadweight" or efficiency losses caused by the price-distorting effects of the subsidy.

## Variations on the Strategic Industry Theme

The following are variations on the theme, drawn from the essays in Krugman (1986):

1. The particular behavioral conjecture attributed to the foreign firm is important. If our firm overestimates the aggressiveness of the foreign firm, an export subsidy will enhance national income, but if we underestimate the willingness of the foreign firm to resist production cuts, the subsidy will hurt us.

2. Protection of domestic firms may be of benefit if there are economies of scale in production or learning. Even where marginal costs do not diminish, if the industry has large fixed costs, protection will reduce the average costs of our firms.
3. If there are no domestic firms, we can extract rents from foreign oligopolies through a tariff. Up to a point, the foreign firm will not raise prices for fear of local entry.

## Limitations on Strategic Industry Policy

Such policies demand that governments acquire and use a large amount of information that may not be available and, if available, may not be correctly used (e.g., if strategic industry policy is influenced by rent-seeking oligopolists).[7] Aside from such practical difficulties, the theory is sensitive to key assumptions (see Krugman, 1986):

1. Specification of firms' reaction functions: for each conjecture on foreign firm behavior, there is a different optimal U.S. policy, ranging from export subsidy to export tax!
2. If there is more than one U.S. firm facing the foreigners, our firms will produce too much and not maximize our share of the profit. Again, the appropriate policy may be an export tax, rather than a subsidy.
3. The pool of supernormal profits may only exist temporarily, because it will draw in new firms (ours and theirs). Also, what appears to be supernormal profit may just be a normal rate of return in high-risk industries, where some firms have failed along the way to marketing the product. If you average in the losses of firms that don't make it, the industry may have a pool of losses rather than profits. In industries with subnormal profits, we should be taxing our firms to get them out, rather than subsidizing them.[8]
4. Subsidizing our oligopolist may increase the prices of scarce factors of production and hurt other domestic firms, causing a net loss to national income.
5. Our domestic consumers suffer from the cost of the subsidy, and perhaps from the cartel behavior that may be encouraged by a strategic-industry policy.
6. In a world of interdependent capital markets, it may not be clear what are "our" firms. As a shareholder in Glaxo Holdings, I would benefit from any strategic-industry policy adopted by the British government to increase the market share of "its" drug companies.

## International Bargaining

An obvious problem with strategic-industry policy, as with optimal tariffs, is that other states can do the same, and the result may be mutual losses. The literature does not as yet deal systematically with this issue, beyond mentioning that it may create "Prisoners' Dilemma"–type problems (e.g., Krugman, 1986:38–42). There have been a few recent exceptions. Dixit and Kyle (1985) specify the outcomes that occur under different sequences of moves and different assumptions about what each state has "committed" itself to do (e.g., protecting its firm's domestic market and/or subsidizing its firm's fixed costs), but they do not discuss threats and bargaining. Dixit (1987:265–79) includes a short discussion of bargaining issues related to strategic industry policies.

One may infer that size should again be a good initial predictor of threat credibility. Two large countries, each subsidizing or protecting their firms, should be in a "Prisoners' Dilemma" situation from which both will eventually extract themselves. In the early 1980s, the United States, EEC, and Japan reached such a cooperative state by dividing up their steel markets, after pursuing the strategic industry policies of protection and subsidization for about 15 years. In the international air passenger market, similar market-sharing agreements are reached, again after the United States has helped its airlines by restricting foreign carriers' access to U.S. gateway cities, and foreign governments have subsidized their carriers (e.g., the Bermuda II agreement between Britain and the United States in 1977). The current agricultural export subsidy wars should lead to similar restraint. A newly emerging issue with the same type of payoff structure is the conflict between the United States and the EEC over the market for wide-bodied passenger aircraft, and particularly over the EEC subsidies for the Airbus.

The case of an asymmetric strategic industry conflict will be slightly different from the optimal tariff case, because the small country should gain from an unreciprocated subsidy of its own oligopolist (unlike the optimal-tariff case in Figure 9.1, where the small country hurts itself with an unreciprocated tariff). The rest of the payoff structure is the same as Figure 9.1. In a mutual-subsidy war, the smaller country will have a higher opportunity cost per dollar of subsidy funds, and it will run out of subsidy funds sooner, than the larger country. If the large country can always "out-subsidize" the small country, the latter is better off giving up and allowing the large country to take its larger share of the market (i.e., it is better off being exploited than retaliating). The payoff structure here is identical to that which Snyder and Diesing (1977:46–7) refer to as "Called Bluff" or "Bully" (the latter if the large country is better off after a subsidy war than with free trade). I do not know of any subsidy wars between big and small countries, which is not surprising, because the theory predicts that such wars should not occur.

If each is trying to subsidize its oligopolists indirectly, through protecting domestic markets, the payoff structure will be different again. The small country can gain from unreciprocated protection of its domestic market, but may lose (relative to free trade) if it protects its oligopolist's domestic market at the expense of being excluded from the market of the large country. Nevertheless, it is better off under mutual protection than allowing the large country to protect its market without retaliating, because retaliation will at least allow its home firm to keep its small domestic market. The large country should be better off with mutual protection than with free trade, because its oligopolist will prefer all of its domestic market to half its domestic market and half the market of the smaller country. The payoff structure in the game is likely to look like that in Figure 9.2, where P and NP refer to protection or nonprotection of the domestic market. The game is constant sum (viz., the sum of the two domestic markets); there is little basis for cooperation and therefore little opportunity for making threats. (I should emphasize that the discussion of the last two paragraphs

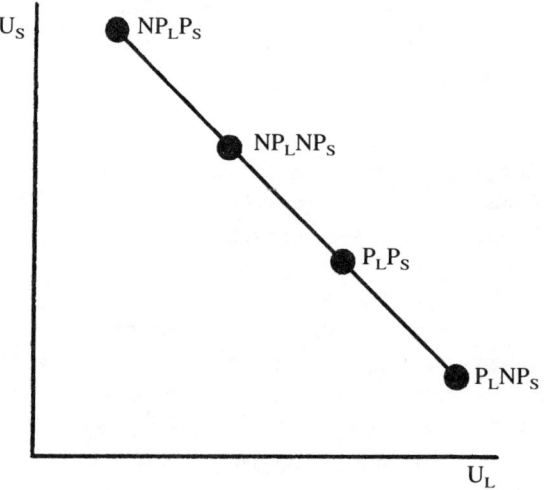

**Figure 9.2.** An asymmetric market protection war.

is speculative and not derived from any rigorous model. As far as I am aware, the strategic-industry literature has not yet dealt with asymmetric cases.)

The airline industry again may be an example. Australia would be better off if its carriers had half the Australian domestic market and half the U.S. domestic market ($NP_L NP_S$), assuming that Australian carriers could compete in the U.S. market. Given that the United States protects its domestic market against foreign carriers, Australia is better off doing the same ($P_L P_S$). U.S. carriers are better off with mutual protection, preferring all the U.S. market than half of both (i.e., the U.S. preference is $P_L P_S >$ $NP_L NP_S$). The current policy of shutting out developing-country steel producers from U.S. markets may be similarly explained.

## Size and Other Threat Variables

Neither optimal-tariff nor strategic-industry theory explicitly discusses the question of threat effectiveness in any detail. When threats are discussed, it is either as inferences from marginal cost principles (e.g., at a Cournot equilibrium, a threat to expand output will not be credible, because the firm would reduce its profits) or as exogenously determined assumptions in a strategic choice (e.g., if the United States precommits itself to a certain tariff policy, what is the optimal policy for the EEC?). General works on oligopoly theory, such as Friedman's (1983) survey, have few references to the issue of threat credibility: He notes, for example, that a threat to punish defectors from a collusive agreement may not be credible if the punishment hurts the enforcer more than doing nothing (1983:131). I suggested earlier that one may infer relative size to be a major influence on threat effectiveness.

A theory of international economic conflict based on relative size would predict that such conflicts should rarely escalate into sustained trade wars (i.e., periods of repeated, prolonged, and high-intensity mutual retaliation). This should be true because of the ease of conveying threats that are both credible and effective—either because strategies of contingent retaliation will quickly remove the gains from predatory policies between large countries, or else because asymmetry will be quickly manifested in a manner that will induce the weaker party to back down and accept the best deal it can get. This generalization is historically well supported: Trade conflicts rarely do escalate to the point of trade war. Yet it is also true that the size-based prediction of cooperative conflict resolution is not always consistent with outcomes. Credible threats do not always work, and in order to explain why trade conflict may escalate into war, one may need to introduce other variables that affect outcomes.

## Time

Though time may help threat credibility by providing the opportunity for retaliation, its effects are ambiguous. First, where the structure of outcomes remains constant, time may increase or reduce the credibility of threats. Consider the chain-store paradox, in which a large firm sees its long-term interest as being maximized by putting new entrants out of business, at some cost to itself, rather than following its short-term interest in collusive market sharing with new entrants (see Selton, 1978). In such cases the dynamic nature of the interaction increases the credibility of the chain store's threat to punish small entrants, even though this is more costly (in the short term) than cooperating with them. Conversely, the threat of small entrants to come into the market is less credible. In the late nineteenth century tariff wars, large countries (France, in particular) used this argument: We cannot make concessions to one small country (viz., Italy or Switzerland), because then all of our other small trading partners will expect the same.

Where there are no asymmetries of size, the same kind of factor may reduce the effectiveness of tit-for-tat types of threats to induce cooperation, even though the threat itself may be perfectly credible. Oligopolists and states may cooperate after hurting each other, but they may also keep going and try to put each other out of business. From the late medieval period to the eighteenth century, long trade wars between Venice and Genoa, England and the Hanse, and England and Holland all ended with one party being put out of the game.

Actors may see payoffs changing over time, in ways that make it advantageous to continue hostile action, even though the threat to retaliate may be credible. A country may chose to fight a trade war because its relative position is deteriorating, and it is better off fighting sooner rather than later. Germany's tariff war with Russia in 1893–1894 had been brewing for some time, and one reason for the latter's choice of initiating the war may have been that Germany was in the process of diversifying its sources of grain, reducing what little economic leverage Russia had in what would have been an asymmetric tariff war in any case. Russia waited too long, and Germany had already concluded agricultural treaties with Austria–Hungary, Italy, the United States, and other countries in 1891–1892. Russia had to resort to a military alliance with France to bring a settlement (see the following). One may initiate a war even if one knows that defeat is likely—better to lose than to lose really badly. In the Franco–Italian tariff war of the same period, French protectionist interests were gradually raising barriers to Italian agricultural products and, again, Italy may have provoked a tariff war thinking it was better off fighting while it still had a significant market share.

## Large Numbers of Actors

Large numbers of actors may reduce the effectiveness of threats by creating a situation in which everyone has an incentive not to cooperate but noncooperators cannot be individually punished. Such situations are quasi-public-good problems, because they exhibit one aspect of a public good: The inability to exclude noncooperators from enjoying the benefits of free-riding on the rest of the community. A common name for the problem is the Tragedy of the Commons, named after the parable of the farmers who all graze their cattle on the common land, cannot restrict each others' grazing, and hence all overgraze, quickly denuding the commons. Littering, crowding and pollution are other examples. The result is a "Prisoners' Dilemma" game (viz., each actor's dominant strategy is noncooperation, regardless of his conjecture about the behavior of others) that cannot iterate to cooperation, or even a "Deadlock" game, if mutual noncooperation by all still leaves some actors better off than if all cooperated. The failure of iteration to induce cooperation is precisely because of the large numbers and the inability of actors to practice a strategy of contingent retaliation for acts of noncooperation. Trade exhibits two forms of this problem.

First, Most Favored Nation (MFN) norms make it advantageous for large states to keep their tariffs high and refuse to negotiate tariff concessions, while still receiving the benefits of everyone else's negotiations. The MFN norm obliges states to extend bilaterally negotiated tariff concessions to all other states with which they have MFN treaty relations. Hence countries that may benefit from high tariffs will have a strong incentive to engage in such free-riding behavior. If many states follow their interest in this manner, the volume of international trade will diminish as the average global tariff levels increase. The United States did this during the 1920s and was followed by most other countries after 1929. The effectiveness of retaliatory threats may easily be restored by denying MFN treatment to the offending country; GATT does allow MFN to be suspended in GATT-sanctioned retaliations (Damm, 1970:104). MFN norms may also be circumvented by principal supplier rules and quotas, as has been the practice since the 1920s.

Second, a situation with many domestic, import-competing interest groups may make foreign threats of retaliation ineffective. Even if each individual group is worse off after foreign retaliation, there is no incentive for any one group to restrain its protectionist demands. Foreign retaliation will be diffused throughout all the groups, and restraint by any one of a large number of groups will not affect the outcome. Even worse, it is likely that such groups will face a Deadlock incentive (viz., they prefer mutual noncooperation with foreign countries to mutual cooperation), whereby they are still better off after foreign retaliation, because retaliation can rarely be directed against those groups (even in the aggregate), and they are hurt only very indirectly, by reductions in national income.

When fourteenth century English privateers took Hanse ships, and the Hanse seized the property of English merchants in retaliation, I have no doubt that the privateers were still better off, although there may have been more privateering than would have maximized the return to the industry as a whole, as predicted by the Tragedy of the Commons scenario. Similarly, the U.S. steel industry is better off being protected, even if other industries do the same, and the EEC retaliates against U.S. export industries. The EEC cannot retaliate against the U.S. steel industry because the United States exports no steel to the EEC, and U.S. steel firms can be hurt only indirectly by reductions in U.S. national income caused by EEC retaliation against other U.S. interests. EEC poultry producers preferred the mutual retaliation outcome of the Chicken War for the same reason. Lebow (1986:361) observes the same problem in military deterrence—domestic groups may gain from challenging credible foreign commitments. A credible threat may be ineffective, in trade as in military affairs.

## Linkage to Political Goals

One of the difficulties of the pure economic theory of trade wars is that it assumes the goal of such conflicts to be national welfare maximization. Economic goals are often linked to nonpecuniary objectives. Unfortunately, there is nothing that one can predict a priori about linkage, because issue linkage in a two-by-two game can change any of the four outcomes in any direction in the utility space. Linkage of a trade issue to a perfectly divisible system of side payments, with no transaction costs in making, monitoring, and enforcing agreements, should make threats largely irrelevant, because (by definition) the parties will automatically attain their joint optimum (though there may be threats used to determine which optimum is reached).[9] However, transaction costs are usually positive, and linkage to political issues is lumpy;[10] hence linkage can just as easily destroy zones of agreement and make threats less effective (e.g., by raising the other side's cost of giving in). The most I can do is to offer a few empirical observations from my "Trade Wars" (1987).

First, linkage is usually used as a threat to increase the other side's cost of not cooperating. The United States threatened to link the Chicken War to NATO, and the EEC counterthreatened to sabotage the Kennedy Round. France attempted to use its trade war with Italy in the 1880s to force the latter out of the Triple Alliance. In the 1980s Brazil has threatened not to pay its bank debt if shut out of the U.S. steel market.

Second, linkages rarely work (none of the above did). The tactic creates transaction costs, noise, and taxes the cognitive capacity of policymakers. Linkage may create such large and unpredictable risks that it is not taken seriously (e.g., the Chicken War and NATO) or would have major long-term consequences if it were taken seriously (e.g., had Italy allowed itself to be forced out of the Triple Alliance by French tariff policy; the tariff war did not end until France decoupled tariffs and the Alliance, though Italy still had to make large tariff concessions). Questions of legitimacy may also be invoked by linkage tactics. Linkage most often seems to destroy zones of agreement, reducing the effectiveness of threats, whether or not the threats are credible.

Third, linkage may constitute an effective threat when it creates large, asymmetric, and credible changes in payoffs. France was able to retrieve its Rainbow Warrior bombers from New Zealand by threatening the latter's access to EEC markets. Germany ended its tariff war with Russia after the latter entered a military alliance with France. The Kaiser reportedly intervened in the tariff war because he said he would not risk a military clash for the sake of "a hundred crazy Junkers" (a domestic group with a "Deadlock" preference, for both military and economic reasons). However, the Russians still had to make large economic concessions in order to reach a settlement.

## Cognitive Factors

The two aspects of cognition familiar to economists are transaction costs and conjectures about the responses of other actors to one's own behavior. Transaction costs may inhibit the making of threats or their effectiveness, by reducing the net gain from compliance. One reason why premodern trade wars could be so long-lasting was not so much that threats were not credible, but that the process of making, negotiating, monitoring, and enforcing threats was long and costly. During the late medieval Anglo–Hanse wars, the origin of predatory acts was often unclear, negotiations took years to complete (and were physically dangerous for the negotiators), and enforcement was difficult (both because of multiple actors and overlapping arenas of authority on both sides, and because a typical means of enforcement was the "letter of reprisal,"[11] which produced rapid escalation of disputes). Transaction costs may increase the effectiveness of a threat if the threat itself imposes transaction costs. Importers to the United States may choose to raise their prices rather than fight a long and costly battle against an antidumping or countervailing duty action.

The conjectural-variations approach that economists use to specify cognitive features of interaction may be used to make some inferences about threats. The "negative" conjecture is that a threat to be tough will be met by restraint; the "positive" conjecture is that such threats will meet like threats. However, these are simply beliefs that one has about the other party, and specifying a conjecture does not tell us how effective a threat will be. To do this we need ask whether the conjecture is correct ("consistent," to use the economist's term) or incorrect (e.g., a mistaken negative conjecture will produce an ineffective threat). The conjectures literature has little to say about threats as such and normally predicts only the output and welfare effects of different conjectures. There are a large number of permutations of correct and incorrect conjectures on even a few simple types of trade interaction.

As an empirical observation, I would say that misperception (wrong conjectures) rarely has a lasting effect on threats in trade situations. The iterated nature of the conflicts and the high degree of transparency of actions and goals produces consistent conjectures as the actors develop rational expectations.[12] Cognitive biases are hard to sustain in economic conflicts, and there is probably less motivated bias[13] to begin with, since fundamental political goals are rarely at stake. In the Franco–Italian tariff war of the 1880s, Italy expected a quick victory, (wishfully?) thinking that France was critically dependent on Italian agricultural exports. It soon discovered this conjecture to be mistaken and asked for peace, but found that France had raised its demands.

As a result of the factors just mentioned, ambitious attempts to override the underlying structure of payoffs with demonstrations of resolve, which a small power can sometimes use with success in military affairs, are rarely useful in trade conflicts. In the early 1890s, Switzerland initiated a tariff war with France, in order to demonstrate resolve in its refusal to accept the high rates of the new Meline tariff. This tactic of self-mutilation did not work, and the Swiss simply ended up making more concessions to France in order to end the war!

Economists do not usually consider the basic norms and values that affect threats. Risk aversion on the part of the actor being threatened, for example, may increase the effectiveness of threats (Jervis, 1986:124). Yet if risk aversion is very high, the party being threatened may adopt a maximin tactic (i.e., maximizing its worst payoff) which, in a Prisoners' Dilemma game, will prevent the evolution of cooperation by making retaliatory threats ineffective. Maximin tactics may be more feasible in economic games, where the costs of mutual noncooperation are lower than in military games.

Issues of legitimacy are likely to be less important than in military questions, because few economic goals are generally accepted as being illegitimate, even though they may produce severe distributional conflict. Nevertheless, there are several types of circumstance in which judgments of legitimacy may affect either the credibility of a threat or the propensity to make concessions or retaliate. One reason why linkage threats do not seem to work might be that such linkages are perceived as a violation of sovereignty, notably in the case of the French attempt to use a tariff war to force Italy out of the Triple Alliance. If the asymmetry is large enough, one's sense of sovereignty may have to be sacrificed, as in the case cited earlier of France and New Zealand.

A large, predatory increase in protection by a major economic power may lead to global retaliation irrespective of the normal collective-action problems that one would usually expect to vitiate such action. During historical periods when there are significant efforts in the direction of global cooperation, large-power predation may be perceived as such a massive norm violation that small countries retaliate even though it is not in their individual interest to do so. Ironically, if they do ignore their individual interest and retaliate, the collective effect of their retaliation will hurt the large country and be in the collective interest of the smaller countries, because they will improve their collective terms of trade. In other words, issues of legitimacy may help overcome the large-number (or quasi-public-good) problem that would normally inhibit retaliation against a large economic predator. The Smoot–Hawley tariff of the United States invoked such a response: Most countries (though not many small ones) retaliated against the United States.

Domestic economic regulations that are clearly disguised trade barriers seem to illicit a much higher degree of outrage and determination to retaliate on the part of the affected parties. In recent years, when the British government has banned the import of French turkeys (just before Christmas!) for "health" reasons, the French immediately banned the import of British lamb on similar grounds. When the Japanese government, in 1986, changed the safety specifications for ski equipment, solely for the purpose of excluding European manufacturers from the Japanese market, the cries of outrage were far louder than if the Japanese had merely imposed a tariff. Countries are usually less inclined to defend regulations that are so obviously nothing more than disguised trade barriers. Domestic measures that indirectly affect trade are, however, perceived as quite legitimate, often fiercely defended (e.g., the EEC practice of rebating Value Added Tax on exports), and less likely to be challenged by other countries.

Finally, institutions or sets of rules may have cognitive implications that affect the results of threats. Chan (1985) suggests that the outcomes of GATT negotiations are determined largely by a norm of distributional equality, enforced by individual veto powers. GATT's norms of reciprocity and retaliation increase the credibility (though not necessarily the effectiveness) of threats by providing both a mechanism and legitimacy for retaliation. However, insofar as GATT encapsulates conflicts, both preventing rounds of tit-for-tat retaliation and isolating them from other issues, the effectiveness of threats may be reduced. GATT's intervention helped the Chicken War to terminate at a point of mutual tariff war, rather than allowing the parties to explore further threats that might have produced cooperation.

## Trade War and Nuclear War

Although trade and military conflicts may both exhibit the same types of bargaining issues, there may also be significant differences that caution against any direct comparison of outcomes. This is especially true if one wishes to compare trade war with nuclear war. It is obvious that the kinds of threats used in trade conflicts should display differences from the threats that one would observe in nuclear strategy problems:

1. High stakes in a nuclear war produce a situation where mutual non-cooperation is disastrous (jointly and individually the least preferred outcome) and pure deterrence threats are the appropriate tactic, each actor wishing to avoid both disaster and being exploited. Trade wars have lower stakes, because of the lesser magnitude of the measures taken, and because the measures are themselves reversible (unlike a nuclear explosion). The welfare effects of a major tariff war would cost the United States little more than 2 percent of its national income (Whalley, 1985:248). In addition, trade conflict produces situations where at least one side initially has a dominating strategy of non-cooperation.
2. The dynamic process of trade conflicts is more analogous to arms races,

rather than nuclear wars. The contrast is implied in Jervis's characterization of spiral and deterrence models: The former applies to arms races that approximate the kind of Prisoners' Dilemma found in trade wars, and the latter applies to nuclear war situations, which are better described as a symmetric "Chicken" game in which pure deterrence strategies are most relevant (see also Lebow, 1986:370). A typical trade threat will have aspects of both deterrence and compellence (e.g., the United States threatens, and then applies, a penalty tariff to EEC pasta, until the latter eases restrictions on U.S. agricultural products). Tit-for-tat is common in trade and is a form of contingent retaliation that may begin as a deterrent threat but easily defaults to a compellence tactic.

3. The relative equality of power in a nuclear exchange is not found in many trade conflicts, where asymmetry produces a richer array of possible outcomes, including those in which one side gains in spite of mutual noncooperation. There is no analogous outcome in nuclear war (though there may be in arms races), unless one believes that it is possible for one side to "win" a nuclear exchange.

4. The absence of any international organization with power to mediate nuclear war issues may also be an important difference. Though one should not exaggerate the powers of GATT, it does provide norms (e.g., reciprocity and retaliation) and dispute-settlement procedures that influence the effectiveness of threats. A threat of geographically discriminatory tariff protection may be less credible than it would otherwise be, because it violates a norm of GATT. A threat to invoke an emergency protectionist measure may be more credible if it falls within the GATT rules for such actions.

5. Nuclear strategists must interpret complex political culture and psychological variables (e.g., what is Soviet nuclear strategy?) that create ambiguities about basic goals and processes, making it hard to impute outcomes to different bargaining scenarios. In trade conflicts it is often safe to assume that each party is maximizing something that is primarily pecuniary (e.g., national income, employment, balance of trade, market share). Though there may still be problems of linkage, transparency (e.g., phony health regulations), and deception (e.g., misrepresentation of country of origin), once a goal is established, prediction of the range of outcomes is fairly determinate.

6. Trade conflicts, unlike nuclear deterrence, often have more than two actors, creating public-good problems that inhibit threat effectiveness. Nuclear deterrence may create free-riding opportunities for small alliance members, but this has little effect on the credibility of the primary bilateral deterrent relationship between the superpowers. In trade

games, it is the largest trading powers that have the most incentive to free ride and refuse to negotiate reductions in trade barriers; hence the negative impact on global cooperation is much greater.

## Conclusions

Economic theories of trade war currently say little about what makes threats effective, beyond distinguishing between the costs of different actions (e.g., my threat to hurt you is ineffective, if carrying out the threat hurts me more than doing nothing). Nevertheless, the theories contain a clear basis for making inferences about what factors cause these cost differences, and I have suggested that relative size is one of them. Others (e.g., dynamic considerations, rent-seeking, and institutional constraints) need to be added in. A more basic problem is the assumption of national welfare maximization as the goal in trade wars. Nonpecuniary objectives may be introduced as linkage tactics, but because it is hard to make predictions about such things, linkage explanations are largely ad hoc. Furthermore, within the realm of purely economic objectives, the models (and the conditions for making threats) may well be altered by specifying different goals (e.g., revenue, employment).

The relevance of the theories of trade war for military deterrence partly depends on the type of military conflict with which one might wish to make comparisons. Many of the basic bargaining variables are common to both categories of conflict, both in specifying the underlying structure of payoffs (e.g., Prisoners' Dilemmas may be found in both) and explaining the process of escalation and resolution (e.g., the influence of iteration and norms of legitimacy). Trade wars are noticeably similar to arms races. However, comparison with nuclear war may be misleading, because the outcome of joint noncooperation in the latter case is radically different. The only trade war situation in which noncooperation can be disastrous is for a small country preyed upon by a large country, but even here the disaster is one-sided and of a lesser magnitude than nuclear war.

## NOTES

1. Infinitely divisible side payments (e.g., money), in the absence of transaction costs, should achieve the same result. Because a tariff will always result in some net social loss, the amount of income that one country can transfer to itself from

another by imposing a tariff should be less than the amount that the other would be willing to pay to avoid suffering the tariff. Another way of making the same point is that if two countries are in the tariff-ridden equilibrium of a Prisoners' Dilemma game, both will be willing to make payments to each other (in exchange for tariff reductions) in order to improve their joint and individual welfare. If side payments are not very divisible, this may reduce the scope for cooperation, if bargaining over tariffs alone is not feasible. See the following discussion on linkage.

2. Elasticity here refers to the responsiveness of the quantities of goods traded to changes in tariffs. Elasticities determine whether or not a country can affect the prices of its traded goods, and therefore also determine the optimal tariff and whether or not a country gains or loses from applying a tariff.

3. Russia, in its tariff war with Germany during the 1890s, should be considered a "small" country. A large part of its trade was with Germany; its imports from Germany were vital manufactured goods, and its exports to Germany were agricultural products for which Germany had easy substitutes.

4. The preference ordering for Deadlock is similar to Prisoners' Dilemma, except that in Deadlock mutual noncooperation is preferred to mutual cooperation.

5. The payoff structure in Figure 9.1 may be derived from the optimal tariff formula, $1/(D - 1)$, where D is the foreign country's elasticity of demand for imports. Because the very large country's elasticity will tend to infinity, the optimal tariff for the small country will be zero, and it will reduce its welfare with any positive tariff. The small country's elasticity will be low, and the large country will be better off (relative to free trade) imposing a tariff, even if the small country retaliates.

6. An industry may be considered oligopolistic when the number of firms in the industry is small enough for the actions of any one firm to have a significant effect on the profits and market shares of all other firms.

7. Rent seeking refers to the manipulation of the political process in order to transfer income among individuals or groups.

8. If capital markets are perfectly efficient, competition for funds should eliminate such industries, obviating the need for a tax.

9. This is simply a restatement of the tautology that is known to economists as the Coase Theorem: In the absence of transaction costs, infinitely divisible side payments will enable all externalities, or inefficiencies, to be bargained away.

10. Lumpy issues are imperfectly divisible. A threat to raise tariffs against a country if it does not join a defense alliance will be lumpy because the national security issue has only two options.

11. Letters of reprisal entitled aggrieved parties to seize the goods of any citizen from the country of origin of the predatory act.

12. *Rational expectations* is the economist's term for the assumption that people have the right theories and the right information with which to make predictions.

13. Biases that are motivated, or due to norm- or value-based beliefs, will be more difficult to correct than biases that are merely due to incorrect information.

# REFERENCES

Chan, K. S., 1985. The international negotiation game: Some evidence from the Tokyo round. *Review of Economics and Statistics* 67(August):456–64.
Conybeare, J. A. C., 1987. *Trade Wars: The Theory and Practice of Commercial Rivalry*. New York: Columbia University Press.
Damm, K., 1970. *The GATT*. Chicago: University of Chicago Press.
Dixit, A., 1987. How should the United States respond to other countries' trade policies? In R. M. Stern, ed., *U.S. Trade Policies in a Changing World Economy*. Cambridge, Mass.: MIT Press, pp. 245–82.
Dixit, A., and Kyle, A., 1985. The use of protection and subsidies for entry promotion and deterrence. *American Economic Review* 75(March):139–52.
Friedman, J., 1983. *Oligopoly Theory*. New York: Cambridge University Press.
Grossman, G., and Richardson, J. D., 1986. Strategic trade policy: A survey of the issues and early analysis. In R. Baldwin and J. D. Richardson, eds., *International Trade and Finance*, Third Edition. Boston: Little, Brown, pp. 95–113.
Jervis, R., 1986. Deterrence, the spiral model, and the intentions of the adversary. In R. White, ed., *Psychology and the Prevention of Nuclear War*. New York: NYU Press, pp. 107–30.
Johnson, H. G., 1954. Optimum tariffs and retaliation. *Review of Economic Studies* 21:142–53.
Kennan, J., and Riezman, R., 1984. Do big countries win tariff wars? Working Paper Series, No. 84-83. University of Iowa, College of Business Administration.
Krugman, P., ed., 1986. *Strategic Trade Policy and the New International Economics*. Cambridge, Mass.: MIT Press.
Lebow, R., 1986. Deterrence reconsidered. In R. White, ed., *Psychology and the Prevention of Nuclear War*. New York: NYU Press, pp. 352–75.
Selton, R., 1978. The chain-store paradox. *Theory and Decision* 9:127–59.
Snyder, G., and Diesing, P., 1977. *Conflict Among Nations*. Princeton, N.J.: Princeton University Press.
Whalley, J., 1985. *Trade Liberalization Among Major World Trading Areas*. Cambridge, Mass.: MIT Press.

# 10

# The Empirical Study of Trade Deterrence

## DAVID B. YOFFIE

Generalizing about the use of deterrence in international trade to the realm of nuclear conflict is a challenging if not impossible task. As John Conybeare has pointed out in his chapter, international trade theory offers very little insight and relatively few analogies for nuclear deterrence. With this caveat in mind, I will outline in this chapter the dangers associated with applying trade deterrence to the nuclear arena; the possible areas where the theory of international trade might offer limited insights; and finally suggest how empirical research on international trade conflicts could highlight areas of interest for the future study of deterrence in both the nuclear and trade arenas.

First, it is important to note the two most important conditions that make the theory and practice of trade conflict different from nuclear war. To begin with, trade decisions, unlike nuclear decisions, are reversible and generally much less costly. A country can impose a trade barrier at one point in time and eliminate it at little or no cost a short time later. For instance, imagine that the United States announced a tariff on products shipped from the European Community. Such an announcement would be considered an aggressive trade act. Whereas target countries of a nuclear strike would have to respond immediately to a similarly provocative act, targets of a trade action (in this case European exporters) would have no need to respond immediately, and in fact might not be able to even verify the threat. The United States could decide never to collect the tax or to reverse the decision while the goods were in transit over the Atlantic Ocean. Similarly, the United States could decide to collect the tax on a particular date and rebate the tax at a later time. Such a reversal might create limited diplomatic problems, but it would have relatively little economic impact.[1] Nuclear action, on the other hand, would have irreversible consequences on the target. Hence, the potential impact of trade deterrence or ignoring a threat of deterrence is significantly lower in trade than in nuclear conflicts. As a result, the decision to impose trade sanctions or trade barriers on a trading partner may not be comparable to a decision to use military and especially nuclear force.

Second, the utility of the theory of international trade for the study of deterrence is low because the theory itself is normative. Trade theory does not specifically address deterrence. Instead, trade theory extols the virtue of trade "peace" and free trade by specifying that trade barriers will always have negative consequences for the players. Trade theory also makes no effort to distinguish between compellence and deterrence: Many cases of trade deterrence could fit into Schelling's (1960) definition of compellence.

One area in which theory may offer some insights is in the strategic trade policy literature (Krugman, 1986). Yet even here the strategic-trade literature does not offer an original contribution to the study of deterrence. Strategic-trade policy is an effort to apply insights from industrial-organization literature, game theory (Axelrod, 1984), and models of oligopolistic competition. Another area of potential learning might come from the political economy of trade literature that focuses on regimes and the role of the General Agreement on Tariffs and Trade. The GATT can be seen as a system of deterrence: Its primary purpose is to reduce the incidence of trade conflict. Within the literature on GATT and regimes, the most valuable insights come from the discussions of reciprocity and the role of norms in affecting trade behavior (Keohane, 1986). But here again, the theory of trade regimes and reciprocity offers little insight into the generic problem of deterrence. To date, the literature on reciprocity and norms in international trade has been more descriptive and normative than an effort to build positive theory.

Given the weakness of trade theory for learning about deterrence, it may be more fruitful to explore other avenues. The most promising contribution of the study of international trade to the understanding of nuclear deterrence may come from the empirical research on international trade conflict rather than the theoretical research. Whereas most scholars who write on international trade, trade conflicts, and trade wars have not focused explicitly on the problem of trade deterrence, there is a growing body of rich case studies that describes the trade bargaining and negotiation between countries in conflict over trade matters. What is especially puzzling about these case studies from a deterrence perspective is that many, if not the vast majority, of the trade conflicts over manufactured goods in the postwar period have been resolved without escalation to trade wars.[2] In the more than 40 section 301 cases (unfair competition) filed by American manufacturing firms or the American government between 1976 and 1982, only one case ended in retaliation (Fisher and Steinhardt, 1982). In more than 50 individual cases that I have studied in industries ranging from textiles and apparel to videocassette recorders and semiconductors, all involved the use of threats by one party to impose trade sanctions on another party, but the vast majority were resolved without a "shot being fired" (i.e., a trade barrier being unilaterally imposed). In a systematic study of 20 trade conflicts since the 1950s, Rhodes-Jones similarly found that "cooperation was the most frequent outcome" (Rhodes-Jones, 1986:323). If we can uncover the reasons for successful application of deterrence in international trade, then it would be possible to generate conditional hypotheses that could shed light on nuclear cases.

To demonstrate the potential usefulness of this approach for the general study of deterrence, I will outline two trade conflicts from my research. The two conflicts are not necessarily a representative sample, but rather illustrate the richness of the cases and reveal the potential such an approach could offer for a deeper, systematic investigation of trade deterrence. I have chosen two cases involving the United States and Japan, actors that are relatively symmetrical. Although there are few cases of true parity in international trade in the postwar period, U.S.–Japan and U.S.–European relations come closest to the symmetry in U.S.–Soviet nuclear relations.

The two cases are the U.S.–Japanese textile negotiations of 1969–1971 that led to retaliation by the United States against Japan and the 1985–1986 U.S.–Japanese negotiations in semiconductors that were initially settled without escalating into punitive action. The two cases bolster several of the hypotheses that have been surfacing in the literature about the role of commitments and *domestic politics* in facilitating successful deterrence, and the role of decoupling issues or *issue linkage*.

## Thumbnail Sketch of the Two Cases

### The 1969–1971 Textile Case[3]

In 1969 the American textile and apparel industry successfully persuaded the Nixon administration to restrict the import of manmade and wool fibers from Japan. The president, not wanting to act unilaterally in violation of the GATT, directed his secretary of commerce to negotiate agreements with the leading exporters in East Asia. Several problems greatly complicated the negotiating effort. First, under American trade law at the time, there were no formal rules or regulations that gave the administration the legal rights to impose sanctions or even negotiate an agreement with the Japanese. Second, the United States was in the midst of negotiating several other important deals at the time, including the reversion of Okinawa to Japanese sovereignty and the revaluation of the yen–dollar exchange rate. As a result, there was great dissension within the government about the appropriateness of the textile negotiations. Several high members of the administration, including Henry Kissinger, felt that other issues should take priority; at the same time, the textile lobby was exerting tremendous pressure on the Congress and selected administration officials to take immediate action.

For the following two years, there was virtually constant negotiation. The Japanese bureaucracy, unconvinced that the American administration would be able to find a consensus on retaliation, blocked every effort—including efforts by the Japanese prime minister—to settle the dispute. Even after the U.S. House of Representatives passed a restrictive trade bill in retaliation for the failure in the negotiations, and the bill only narrowly escaped a vote in the Senate through a filibuster, Japanese bureaucrats remained convinced that the U.S. government would not retaliate because of the numerous free traders within the government and the lack of clear authority.

During the summer of 1971 Japanese intransigence ended after the United States invoked the Trading with the Enemy Act of 1917 and then imposed a variety of retaliatory trade measures, including a 10 percent surcharge.[4] Two months later the Japanese finally agreed to settle the dispute in exchange for the 10 percent surcharge not being applied to textile and apparel products.

For several years following this textile dispute, the United States and Japan had no further significant conflicts in textile trade. The final agreement that was reached 10 weeks after the Nixon shocks was relatively easy to implement and monitor. The two countries continued to bargain over textile quotas throughout the 1970s but without intense confrontation.

## 1986 U.S.–Japan Semiconductor Agreement

In June of 1985 the American Semiconductor Industry Association filed an unfair trade practices case (known as a section 301 case) against the Japanese semiconductor industry (Yoffie, 1987). In the suit, the association claimed that Japan had unfairly restricted the sale of American products into the Japanese market and were engaging in predatory pricing in the American market. Under the provisions of section 301, the Reagan administration had wide-ranging powers to retaliate against trading partners: Section 301 stipulated that if foreign access was being unfairly denied to American firms, the president could restrict any number of products of comparable value. In addition to the 301 suit, three dumping suits were filed in the fall of 1985 against the major Japanese semiconductor manufacturers. If the Commerce Department and the International Trade Commission found merit in the petitions, the U.S. government was obligated by the law to impose high duties on selected Japanese products.

In both the 301 and dumping cases, the relevant agencies within the United States government found merit to the charges. As a result, the administration not only had the authority to act, but it would have been obligated by law to impose sanctions in the dumping case in the absence of a settlement. The credibility of the threat that the president would take even stronger action was further enhanced because of the absence of the usual objections by the State Department. In an unusual turn of events, Secretary of State George Schultz reportedly supported the industry petition in the belief that the Japanese had violated American law and had engaged in unfair trade practices.[5]

The negotiations between the United States and Japan were conducted over a period of 10 months and appeared to be close to breakdown several times. Threats of retaliation by the United States were common throughout. Had an agreement not been reached in July 1986, the administration was ready to impose dumping duties on a variety of products on August 1, 1986. In addition, the administration threatened to impose other sanctions on related products to force compliance. At the end of July, an accord was finally reached, whereby the Japanese agreed to stop their predatory pricing behavior and to grant further access to the Japanese market by American semiconductor manufacturers.

Ironically, the aftermath of this "peaceful" settlement in semiconductors was much more conflictual than was the case in textiles. In the months following the semiconductor accord, the American industry claimed that Japan was violating the basic principles of the agreement. American threats of possible retaliation again made the front pages of the national press. At one point, the U.S. Senate voted 93–0 to retaliate against Japan because of the apparent violations. The very complex nature of the agreement made it difficult for the Japanese government to comply immediately with the Senate's demands. Furthermore, even if Japanese firms did begin to heed their government's wishes, the Americans would require time to confirm compliance. Orders by the Ministry of International Trade and Industry to cut production capacity would take several weeks, if not months, to have a significant impact on prices. In addition, the agreement specified that American manufacturers would increase their market share in Japan: After eight months of inaction, no short-term buying by Japanese customers could convince the U.S. industry or government that Japan was honoring its commitment. The result was a subsequent failure of deterrence: Despite numerous American threats that were taken seriously by the Japanese government,[6] Japan was not able to respond quickly enough to avoid U.S. sanctions.

In April of 1987, President Reagan imposed a 100 percent tariff on $300 million of Japanese imports. Lifting of the sanctions was contingent upon evidence that Japan was complying with the agreement. Two months later the president eliminated the duties on $130 million worth of imports, citing evidence that the Japanese were no longer dumping. The other $170 million in goods subject to tariffs would be lifted only after Japan demonstrated improved market access for American products.

One important similarity between these two cases is worth noting. In both periods—1971 and 1986—the United States had serious trade problems with Japan that went beyond the conflicts in textiles and semiconductors. In the earlier period, the United States wanted Japan to revalue the yen; in the latter period, the United States wanted Japan to take macroeconomic and trade-liberalizing measures to alleviate the nearly $70 billion bilateral trade deficit. Because the overall trade environments were similar during the two periods, we must look toward other variables to explain the failure of deterrence in one case and the success of deterrence in the other.

## Tentative Hypotheses

*Hypothesis #1:* Commitments to deterrence by the sender are made more credible (and thereby increase the probability of success) if there is a strong domestic political consensus in favor of retaliation and clear administrative authority for such retaliating.

One of the most striking differences between 1971 and 1986 was that in the earlier period the Japanese were not convinced that Richard Nixon had a consensus to force Japan to back down, nor did he have clear authority to impose a solution on Japan. Discussions by the Japanese press and Japanese policymakers during that period clearly suggested that they perceived the Nixon administration to be hamstrung by internal divisions and inadequate executive powers. Because Nixon could not cite a positive administrative decision in favor of the domestic textile industry with which to bolster the credibility of his threats, and because Nixon's own advisers were giving the president conflicting advice—sometimes in public—the Japanese government assumed that the president would not respond.

By contrast, there was virtually unanimous consensus within the Congress and the Executive Branch that forceful action should be taken on semiconductors if the Japanese did not agree to meet American demands. Furthermore, whereas the textile industry had secured no administrative authority to allow for retaliation or unilateral imposition of trade barriers, the semiconductor industry had given the Executive Branch the authority to respond two different ways: The affirmative 301 case allowed the president to impose virtually any sanction upon the Japanese without violating American law (although some options were constrained by the GATT); and the affirmative dumping suits mandated action unless the president could negotiate an agreement. Under these conditions, the Japanese perceived much greater risk in ignoring the signals being sent from the United States in 1986. The irony is that Japan perceived the probability of retaliation to be low in 1971, while the possibility of severe action was great; yet when the Japanese knew that the United States would take action in 1986, there was a lower probability that Reagan would broadly retaliate as Nixon had done 15 years earlier.

*Hypothesis #2:* Decoupling deterrence threats increases the probability of successful deterrence; linking threats to unrelated issues will decrease the probability of successful deterrence.

Another clear difference between the 1971 and 1986 trade conflicts was the manner in which issues were linked in the first episode compared to the decoupling of issues in the second episode. In 1971 the conflict over textiles was linked implicitly (and sometimes explicitly) to the devaluation of the yen and (at times) the reversion of Okinawa to Japanese sovereignty. The linked issues made it more difficult for the Japanese to respond positively in textiles because they feared that concession in one arena would inevitably lead to pressure in other issue areas. The result was much greater Japanese intransigence.

The semiconductor conflict, on the other hand, was treated in isolation from other issues. Despite the broad variety of potential trade items that could have been linked to semiconductors, no effort was made by the Executive Branch to extract concessions by threatening unrelated action: All deterrence threats were directly related to the semiconductor dispute. Here again there was an irony: In 1986, Japan was more willing to make concessions on semiconductors as a way to forestall action on other issues; yet in 1971, Japan was unwilling to make concessions because decision makers believed that any concession would precipitate further American demands.

## Other Observations

Several additional interesting questions are raised by these and other cases of deterrence in international trade. For instance, many more trade conflicts in agriculture have led to deterrence failures than has been the case in conflicts over manufactured goods. One could suggest two hypotheses to address this puzzle. The first would relate to the role of international norms: The stronger the international norms against retaliation, the greater the probability that deterrence threats will conclude in negotiated settlement rather than retaliation; the weaker the norms, the greater the probability of deterrence failure. In agricultural trade, the General Agreement on Tariffs and Trade has been notoriously weak because there were abundant exceptions for agriculture incorporated into the original GATT codes. Whereas the GATT sought to eliminate virtually all barriers to trade in manufacturers, GATT had special provisions for agricultural products that permitted quantitative restrictions (Article XI), domestic subsidies (Article XVI), and some export subsidies (Article XVI). Even the United States, the supposed defender of free trade, never felt constrained by GATT agricultural codes after the United States received a waiver from agricultural rules in 1955. In manufactured goods, on the other hand, international rules within the GATT were much stronger. Even though those rules have weakened over time, the GATT has continued to be cited by American decision makers as a constraint against retaliation in manufactured goods. The American fear is that if the United States ignores the rules of GATT, international trade in manufactures will become a free-for-all.

A second hypothesis about the difference between deterrence in agriculture and deterrence in manufactures focuses on the role of centralized versus decentralized decision making: Decisions in agricultural trade are typically made by the Department of Agriculture; decisions taken in manufactures trade are spread throughout the Executive Branch. Therefore, one might hypothesize from the trade experience that centralized decision-making units have a greater propensity to retaliate whereas decentralized decision-making entities are more prone to rely on deterrence threats and seek negotiated settlements. Trade conflicts in agriculture often have the character of action–reaction models: The United States threatens retaliation against Europe if it imposes a new duty on American farm products, negotiations take place, deterrence fails, the United States immediately retaliates, Europe counters with further sanctions, negotiations begin again, and ultimately a settlement is reached. The quick responsiveness of the United States in agriculture is in large measure due to the centralized decision-making process.

The use of deterrence in manufactures trade has a completely different dynamic. The United States government is usually hamstrung by the complicated, decentralized decision-making process. Resistance against retaliation by departments such as State and Treasury are highly predictable. As a result, every effort is made to seek negotiated settlements rather than take unilateral action. This tendency toward inaction creates an interesting paradox from the perspective of deterrence theory: Internal divisions will inevitably reduce the credibility of deterrence threats (as they did in 1971 in Japan), but at the same time the decentralized decision making tends to create greater patience and willingness to continue using deterrence. Hence, the United States was willing to bargain with Japan for two years over textiles before taking unilateral action.

## Conclusion

Despite the weakness of international trade theory for the study of deterrence, analysts have yet to tap the rich body of empirical research on trade conflict. Systematic, controlled comparisons of deterrence success as well as deterrence failure in international trade could yield new insights about nuclear deterrence in addition to providing a laboratory for testing older ideas.

In this chapter, I have attempted to illustrate in a very preliminary way how the empirical study of international trade might accomplish this goal. By examining the practice of deterrence in two episodes—the 1969–1971 U.S.–Japan dispute over textiles and the 1985–1986 U.S.–Japan conflict over semiconductors—one can see some of the dynamics that produced failed deterrence in one case and success in the other. The cases illustrated the potential importance of domestic consensus and administrative authority in creating credible threats and the potentially destructive role that linking unrelated issues can have on compliance.

Examining the differences between trade in agriculture and trade in manufactures provided yet another cut at the problem of deterrence. Such a perspective highlights the importance of international norms and rules and the possible role of centralized versus decentralized decision-making processes.

## NOTES

1. An example of this type of phenomenon occurred in 1986 in a dispute between the United States and Europe over agricultural trade. The United States announced quotas on imports, but these quotas would only limit imports at some future level. Before that level was reached and the action became restrictive, the two countries reached an interim agreement, suspending the retaliation. In effect, the United States reversed its penalties before they had any impact (European Community Office of Press and Public Affairs, 1987).

2. Before the 1950s, the American practice of reciprocity led to frequent trade conflicts. At the very least, from the 1880s through the 1930s American threats to impose trade barriers were frequently carried out without negotiated settlement (Rhodes-Jones, 1986).

3. The description of this case is taken from Yoffie (1983); see also Destler, Fukui, and Sato (1979).

4. The package of trade sanctions was part of a larger program, known as the "Nixon shocks," designed to force currency revaluation by America's trade partners. However, my research, as well as research by Mac Destler, confirms that the textile dispute was central in the retaliation.

5. Interviews with government and industry participants.

6. On March 20, 1987, the Japanese press ran a story over the Kyodo News Wire stating that "Japan has reacted with strong concern about the U.S. Senate resolution calling for retaliation against Japan for failing to honor the bilateral pact on orderly trade in semiconductors. . . . [The] Minister of International Trade and Ministry asked representatives of 10 major Japanese chipmakers to ensure there are no exceptions to the agreement. . . ."

## REFERENCES

Axelrod, R., 1984. *The Evolution of Cooperation.* New York: Basic Books.

Destler, I. M., Fukui, H., and Sato, H., 1979. *The Textile Wrangle: Conflict in Japanese–American Relations, 1969–1971.* Ithaca, N.Y.: Cornell University Press.

European Community Office of Press and Public Affairs, 1987. *European Community News* No. 1(January 8).

Fisher, B. S., and Steinhardt, R. G., III, 1982. Section 301 of the Trade Act of 1974: Protection for U.S. exporters of goods, services, and capital. *Law and Policy in International Business* 14:569–701.

Keohane, R. O., 1986. Reciprocity in international relations. *International Organization* 40:1–27.

Krugman, P. R., 1986. Introduction: New thinking about trade policy. In P. R. Krugman, ed., *Strategic Trade Policy and the New International Economics.* Cambridge, Mass.: MIT Press, pp. 1–22.

Rhodes-Jones, C., 1986. Reciprocity, U.S. Trade Policy, and the GATT Regime. Unpublished Ph.D. dissertation. Brandeis University, Department of Politics.

Schelling, T. C., 1960. *The Strategy of Conflict.* Cambridge, Mass.: Harvard University Press.

Yoffie, D. B., 1983. *Power and Protectionism: Strategies of the Newly Industrializing Countries.* New York: Columbia University Press.

Yoffie, D. B., 1987. The Semiconductor Industry Association and the Trade Dispute with Japan (A). Harvard Business School case, no. 0-387-205.

# 11

# Deterrence in Rebellions and Revolutions

## JACK A. GOLDSTONE

Rebellions and revolutions pose a problem for the theory of deterrence. This is because the state, whose failure to deter its opponents provides the opening for revolution, almost always begins the struggle in a much stronger position than its adversaries.[1] Of course, the historical record is largely one of successful deterrence. Even highly unpopular regimes—notably the current white minority regime in South Africa—have had more success than failure in deterring major uprisings. Yet rebellions and revolutions do occur, and examining the circumstances in which they arise may offer insight into the conditions for the success or failure of deterrence.

"Successful deterrence" is difficult to specify, except with hindsight. In the context of rebellion and revolution, I use the terms as follows: Rebellion is an attempt to change the policies or the makeup of the government by illegal means (demonstrations, violence, or seizure of power by nonruling groups); revolution is a successful attempt that gives political power to groups that were formally excluded.[2]

Historically, rebellion and revolution usually develop incrementally: A series of incidents—popular riots or elite protests that testify to the desire of some groups for political changes that they are unable to achieve by legal processes—increase in frequency and intensity, attracting more support, until the government is faced with a rebellion that is beyond its means to suppress. The increase is typically exponential, so that in a short period the incidents move from sporadic protests to national uprisings. For example, the French Revolution was preceded by popular riots in the 1770s and elite protests throughout the 1770s and 1780s; the English Revolution of

1640 was preceded by popular riots in the 1630s and an elite tax strike in 1639. Often it is failure of the government's ability to respond effectively to rebellious actions, rather than changes in the nature of the opposition, that lead to the explosive growth of protest.

I speak of revolution having been "deterred" if, once rebellious acts have occurred, the exponential increase in frequency and intensity of rebellious acts typical of revolution is averted. I speak of rebellion having been "deterred" if groups that once undertook rebellious acts cease to undertake them. Thus, empirically, the mark of successful deterrence of rebellion and revolution is a petering out of rebellious acts against a government.

My use of the term *deterrence* is always specific to a particular period. One may say of South Africa that, by preventing the Soweto riots of 1976 from spreading, it successfully deterred revolution in that year. Similarly South Africa successfully deterred revolution following the 1984–1985 riots triggered by the elections held under its new constitution. In the intervening period, from 1980 to 1984, even acts of rebellion were rare, and the government thus can be said in this period to have deterred rebellion. On the whole, I thus speak of the decade 1977–1987 as a period in which South Africa deterred revolution. South Africa failed to deter rebellion in 1976–1977 and 1984–1985, but quickly restored deterrence in both instances, as rebellion petered out.

In general, in this essay I use the term *deterrence failure* to denote the outbreak and spread of rebellious acts after a period of quiescence; I use the term *successful deterrence* to mean the restoration and maintenance of a period of quiescence, despite the continued presence of groups that have evidenced their opposition to the current regime.

## Theories of Rebellion and Revolution

Opponents of rebellion and revolution have often painted these acts as pathological, irrational behavior by distressed or frustrated individuals. However, systematic study has revealed that there is far more to rebellion and revolution than merely misery, poverty, or injustice.[3] Indeed, distress and injustice, grievances and conflicts, are to be found in all real-world societies, yet rebellion and revolution are relatively rare. Thus, understanding their occurrence depends on identifying the conditions under which grievances and conflicts of interest lead to overt action.

Tilly (1978) has persuasively argued that it is wrong to consider rebellion simply as an aggregate of violent actions by dissatisfied individuals. Instead, rebellion and revolution are the result of individuals acting in *groups*.[4] These may be occupational, ethnic, religious, or regional groupings—peasants or nobles, provincials or urban workers, members of an ethnic group or dwellers in a particular neighborhood or community (Calhoun, 1982). What is important is that the group provides a framework for mobilization and leadership of rebellious activity. Thus rebellion and revolution are only likely when there exist groups that not only have grievances, but that have the resources—in organization, money, arms, manpower, or strategic location—to challenge the state, and that moreover do not have a more effective alternative means of pursuing their goals. Rudé (1964), who has studied revolutionary crowds, and Muller (1972), who has studied violent political protesters, have found that their subjects were not an impoverished or criminal riffraff; instead rebellious actors were well-established, often well-educated, craftsmen, shopkeepers, and students who had a clear goal of improving the conditions of their community by their acts. Skocpol (1979) and Walton (1984) have further demonstrated that the weakness of the state and its policy choices are often the critical factor in setting the stage for a confrontation between rulers and potential rebels. There is thus a fairly widespread consensus among theorists of revolution that rebellious activity is best viewed as purposeful behavior aimed at changing the actions or organization of the state.

This is of course *not* to say that all revolutions were intended. On many occasions in history, such as the English and French revolutions, diverse groups rebelled for different reasons—peasants to free themselves from feudal dues, townsmen to obtain cheaper bread, nobles and landowners to protect themselves from arbitrary taxation—and the combination of such varied revolts overwhelmed the state, a result that no one had foreseen. This is only to say that revolutions originate in actions by groups that aim to influence the state, and that such overt acts of rebellion are likely to occur when potentially rebellious groups judge that their acts will have such influence.

In sum, revolution, like war, is in Clausewitz's famous dictum "politics by other means." Many of the conditions of deterrence of rebellious action thus are applicable to considerations of international conflict. In particular, the key factor is the judgment, by potentially rebellious groups, that their acts will be effective in pursuing change.

The theoretical framework for this chapter is thus one of modified rational choice. "Rational choice" implies that acts of rebellion are only undertaken when the actor judges that the probable benefits of his act, in terms of changing state policy or organization, will outweigh the probable costs. However, historical evidence requires several modifications of the manner in which rational choice is usually construed.

In economic and political theory, rational choice generally refers to the acts of individuals and focuses on how individual actions lead to, or depart from, optimal outcomes. In reality, the relevant actors in political struggles are not individuals but organized groups—either the state and its personnel or opposition groups. Moreover, the question of "optimal" outcomes rarely arises. Instead, both states and opposition groups appear willing to choose any strategy that seems to offer an advantage over their adversary, or movement toward their own goals, without concern for whether that strategy is "optimal." Opportunism and a positive cost–benefit calculus, rather than systematic pursuit of an optimum outcome, appear to govern the relationships between states and their opponents.

Two further modifications are necessary. States and their opponents are not the exclusive players in political conflict. States and their opponents are embedded in the larger society, which in turn is embedded in the international arena. Thus to understand the origins of rebellion and revolution one cannot simply focus on the consequences of a given act for the state and its opponents; one must also consider the reactions of third parties, both other groups within the society and other states. Finally, one must allow for the presence of some actors who are truly "irrational"; that is, groups that will undertake costly acts even though their probable impact on state policy and organization is nil. Fanatical religious or terrorist organizations that believe that it is better to die fighting against a hated state, even if one is unlikely to achieve change, rather than to endorse the status quo by passive acceptance, do exist (e.g., extreme wings of the Irish, Syrian, and Palestinian resistance, the Japanese Red Army and the American Weather Underground). For such groups, deterrence is largely a matter of removing opportunities for them to act and reducing their ability to attract a larger following, rather than dissuading them from acting.

To sum up, the theoretical model that seems to best encompass the empirical evidence on rebellion and revolution, and which I use in examining the conditions for deterrence success and failure, assumes (1) that states and their opponents will seek to improve their access to power and the implementation of favorable policies in a cost-effective, although not optimal, manner; (2) that the ability of the state and its opponents to pursue their goals depends on the resources—including leadership, manpower, arms, money, effective organization—that they can mobilize and bring to bear in their conflicts; (3) that political conflicts are not merely between a state and its opponents, but are embedded in a multiactor environment; and (4) that some, generally small, groups do act irrationally.

## Successful Deterrence

Successful deterrence is thus generally achieved if, for any potential opponent of the regime, the expected costs of initiating overt conflict are clearly greater than the expected gains. Though this seems straightforward, this situation can be difficult for a regime to sustain, for the potential gains to adversaries are highly varied. Opponents need not topple the regime in order to achieve success. Even if defeated, regime opponents might gain by (1) forcing the government to reveal its willingness and ability to use repressive measures; (2) impressing third parties—potential allies of the regime or of the rebels—with the courage and strength of the rebels, or the limited ability and strength of the regime; (3) demonstrating that the costs of overt confrontation are so great that it would be less costly to the regime to make some concessions; or (4) demonstrating that some new act or policy is so resented that its implementation will be far more difficult or expensive than anticipated.

Thwarting these possible gains requires the regime to maintain several conditions. First, the state must be willing and able to deploy force to convincingly defeat the rebels in such a manner that the state will not lose allies nor the rebels gain them. This means that the state must have sufficient control of the symbols of legitimacy and of the communications media that the defeat of the rebels can be persuasively presented as deserved punishment for criminal action, rather than as undeserved (or undeservedly brutal and severe) repression of honorable and courageous critics. It also means that the state's repressive measures must be controlled and proportionate to the rebellion (Muller, 1985). This involves clearly separating the rebels from neutral groups and harshly repressing the rebels with clearly targeted and well-administered force. This was the pattern of successful antiguerilla campaigns waged by the British in southeast Asia after World War II and by various Latin American governments in the 1960s (Chaliand, 1977). In addition, successful deterrence involves preventing the regime's opponents from organizing, arming, and forming links to potential allies (Stinchcombe, 1965, 1975). This is the key element in South Africa's strategy for deterring its nonwhite population from armed revolt. On the other hand, where the rebels are not clearly separated from the population and repressive measures are poorly controlled, the government's actions are liable to produce further defections to the rebels, whose added strength will encourage further conflict. Successful deterrence thus requires armed forces that are organized, disciplined, used with precise targeting, and facing isolated opponents (Chorley, 1973; Russell, 1974). Where the regime lacks these qualities, deterrence fails, as occurred in

China under Chiang Kai-shek, in Cuba under Batista, in Iran under the Shah, and in Nicaragua under Somoza (Goldstone, 1986b).

Second, the state must demonstrate that its commitment to the status quo is so great that it is willing to expend its fullest energies to maintain it. This usually means that, for certain clearly specified aspects of the status quo, no negotiation is possible and the regime will fight to the end. Thus a regime might specify that certain policies are negotiable, or that certain types of opposition will be tolerated, but that other policies and procedures are simply inadmissible. Thus a country might insist that its constitution is not negotiable to change by protest. Successful deterrence depends on these boundaries being clear—the state must be sincere in demonstrating that negotiable policies will in fact be flexible and responsive to opposition demands, whereas others will not, if the state hopes to channel opposition into approved channels and thus deter overt conflict. Where such boundaries are unclear, deterrence fails. This may occur either because the state's inflexibility on *all* matters leads the opposition to give up hope of the utility of approved channels, or at the opposite end, because the state's flexibility on *all* matters leads the opposition to hope for radical change if they apply pressure. The former case—inflexibility leading opponents to violent opposition and alliance with rebels—weakened the regimes of Somoza in Nicaragua, Diaz in Mexico, and Marcos in the Philippines. The rise in violence in South Africa beginning in 1984 was triggered by the new constitution which, by excluding blacks, served notice that the regime would be totally inflexible on the issue of black political participation in national politics. The opposite case—the regime tinkering with so many policies and basic principles as to suggest that no hoped-for change is out of bounds—contributed to the fall of the Old Regime in France and in Imperial China.

Third, stable deterrence depends on stable expectations regarding the state's behavior. Deterrence is rarely achieved by promulgation of an abstract agreement; actors are embedded in history, and their expectations regarding future actions are shaped by past experience. Most situations of stable rule are thus the outcome of a long process of conflict and negotiation in which popular groups and elites develop expectations regarding state actions, and have decided that their current situation under the regime is preferable to undertaking the risks of overt opposition. State actions that alter people's expectations regarding state behavior can lead to a reevaluation of the old bargain and lead people to "reopen" the process of negotiation and conflict. Thus in early modern Europe, rebellions occurred most often when changes in the scale or technology of warfare forced governments to change traditional levels or sources of taxation (Tilly, 1975).

Another common cause of rebellions in Europe and Asia was changes in the marketing of grain that increased price volatility or the vulnerability of people to local food shortages (Tilly, 1975; Scott, 1976). In both these cases, the actions of the states or merchants were seen as violating traditional agreements as to how taxes or food supplies would be distributed. Rebellions occurred, not to overthrow the state or destroy markets, but to insist that the state and merchants show greater respect for traditional norms, and that any changes in current practice have some safeguards or compensation for those adversely affected by the transition.

Rebellion can also be triggered when a regime's actions go against traditional expectations of defense of local, regional, or national interests. Thus a state whose foreign or domestic policy leads to loss of territory, denigration of a particular local or regional ethnic group, alignment with traditional ethnic or religious enemies, or betrayal of traditional friends may again upset popular acceptance of the status quo. The Puritan Revolution of 1640 and the Glorious Revolution of 1688 in England both were triggered in part by the King's perceived partiality to Catholics, in both foreign and domestic policy. The South African riots of 1976 were triggered by the regime's announced plans to insist upon Afrikaans as the national language for all South Africans.

In sum, deterrence of violent opposition depends on the regime maintaining sufficiently powerful and well-administered force for effective repression of opponents, keeping opponents isolated while preserving the loyalty of the regime's allies, preserving clear bounds between acceptable and unacceptable actions and policy changes, and preserving stable expectations regarding maintenance of status quo policies and living conditions.

Note that, historically, successful deterrence of rebellion and revolution does not depend simply on alleviation of what modern western observers might decry as "poverty and injustice." Most of the world's population— from Roman slaves to medieval serfs to modern peasants—have endured conditions of severe deprivation, exploitation, and political and economic inequality, with only occasional outbreaks of significant rebellion and only a handful of revolutions. Where rebellions or revolutions have occurred, it is generally because changing conditions—usually in the domains of war or economic competition—have weakened regimes or led to defections by traditional supporters (Goldstone, 1986a,c; Skocpol, 1979; Walton, 1984; Welch, 1980).

The emphasis on regime behavior, and on the action of specific opposition groups, is important. In the 1970s, rebellion and revolution were widely attributed to popular discontent, relative to some expected level of welfare. This "relative deprivation" was held to motivate unrest. Yet even the proponents of this theory (Gurr, 1970) recognized that diffuse popular discontent was insufficient to raise rebellion. It was also necessary that discontent be politicized by organization and leadership, and that the target of discontent—the state—be vulnerable. Opportunities, as well as grievances, are necessary to motivate people to take the risks entailed in rebellion. Thus even popular discontent is unlikely to give rise to rebellious activity if elites and security forces strongly support the government.

I have noted several factors that may lead to the failure of deterrence—new policies that upset the status quo, weakening (or the revelation of weakness) in the regime's repressive capacity, a shift in allies away from the regime or toward its opponents, failure to clearly demarcate acceptable and nonacceptable actions and policies. But once the process of deterrence failure has begun, can it be reversed?

## The Failure of Deterrence

Historical experience shows cases of both possible outcomes of deterrence failure—successful repression followed by renewed deterrence, or a deepening spiral of opposition and decreasingly successful repression resulting eventually in the collapse of the old regime.

Successful repression has occurred where the regime is able to isolate its opponents and crush them by overwhelming force. Restoring order also often required marks of leniency, as long as these were seen as generosity offered from a position of strength. This was the most common outcome of local peasant rebellions in early modern Europe. The regime would bring overwhelming force against the peasant rebels—a trained army sufficient not only to defeat the rebels, but to hunt them down and, if necessary, burn their villages. Yet the regime would generally content itself with merely arresting the ringleaders, who would be blamed for opposing the regime and be publicly and brutally executed. The rank-and-file peasants would be let off, usually with an affirmation that the regime truly did care about their welfare, and with some minor reduction or amnesty of taxes for that year, or an allotment of grain at a fair price. The regime would then, generally successfully, seek to restore the conditions for deterrence (Tilly, 1986; Brewer and Styles, 1980).

Failed deterrence generally becomes a deepening spiral of violence when the regime is unable or unwilling to use crushing force on isolated rebels, either because the rebels have established a broad presence in the society that hinders their being isolated, or because the ability of the regime to marshal and direct its forces is limited by failures of repressive capacity or leadership. Such failures may stem from a government's forces being weakened by war or financial difficulties; or the regime's ability to use its forces may be weakened by irresolute, divided, or inept executive and military leaders. In either case, the response to an opponent's initiation of violent confrontation swings between severe but indiscriminate military actions—death squads and attacks on villages or heavy firing into urban crowds—and weak conciliatory actions—chastising rather than punishing use of force, combined with vague offers of concessions and promise of change.

The swing between severe but indiscriminate actions and weak conciliatory actions undermines what is left of deterrence. For it becomes difficult for the regime, its opponents, and potential allies of either side to determine how far the regime is willing to bend, and how able it is to resist pressure. In the face of this uncertainty, opponents are encouraged to probe by further overt acts, while regime allies are liable to hold back until more certain of the outcome of the struggle. Continued cycles of rebel action, regime wavering, indiscriminate countermeasures, further rebel action, regime concessions, further action, and so forth are likely to lead to further defections among regime allies, as they seek to escape the indiscriminate repression that threatens to engulf them as well as the rebels. Such defections of regime allies then encourage popular opposition, while leading to more wavering or wild countermeasures on the part of the regime. This pattern has occurred in all major revolutions. In France in 1789, when nobles lost confidence in the monarchy and the Court-appointed Assembly of Notables called for a meeting of the Estates General, the crowds of Paris were encouraged to support the Estates. The King lacked the finances and reliable troops to resolve the situation by force, but sought to cow the crowds by troop movements toward Paris. This show of force alarmed and inflamed the crowds, but lacking the nobles' support to use his troops, the King was forced to capitulate. The King's influence then sharply waned, and the Estates General wrested control of national affairs. Similarly in Russia in World War I, in numerous National Liberation movements in the 1950s and 1960s, and recently in the Shah's Iran and Somoza's Nicaragua, the government's swings from severe but indiscriminate actions to weak conciliatory actions and back alienated regime allies and encouraged opponents to push on toward revolution (Dunn, 1972; Furet, 1981; Green, 1984; Walker, 1985a).

## Legitimacy and Concessions

Two questions constantly recur to one poring over the historical record of revolution and its deterrence. First, what is the role of "legitimacy"? This elusive concept suggests that some governments should be more resistant, more capable of deterrence, than others, despite passing crises. Second, we often find that regimes under threat offer numerous concessions and undertake considerable reforms; why are such actions usually ineffective in deterring further opposition?

These two issues are intimately related. Concessions or reforms offered by a legitimate government *are* usually successful in deterring further opposition, but concessions or reforms offered by a government that is already perceived as illegitimate are usually seen as further and convincing proof of its illegitimacy and of weakness. Thus an important factor in the success of reforms is whether they are perceived as generosity from a position of strength or as concessions from a position of illegitmacy and weakness.

Legitimacy marks the difference between authority and power. A state has authority when it can obtain obedience to its actions even from individuals whose private interests are hurt by those actions, because of a belief that such obedience serves some greater good, for example, preservation of custom or law or a religious or ideological goal (Weber, 1947). Service of this greater good "legitimizes" the state's actions. An illegitimate state can obtain obedience, but only by appealing to an individual's private interests through bribery or punishment, that is, by the exercise of power.

In addition to legitimate or illegitimate states, we also speak of legitimate or illegitimate *actions*, by both states and their opponents. Applied to specific acts by a regime or its opponents, the label "legitimate" implies that those acts are in accord with some "ground rules" (Eisenstadt and Curelaru, 1976; Levi, forthcoming) that protect widely valued higher goods—for example, private property, national integrity, personal liberty or security, religious fidelity. An actor who respects those rules thus gains support from members of society because of his commitment to principles that provide a *diffuse benefit*—protection of such higher goods—besides whatever individual rewards or penalties that actor is able to provide to specific allies or opponents. In contrast, a government or opposition that disregards such rules confers a *diffuse disamenity* on subjects or fellow citizens by threatening or withdrawing the protection of such higher goods.

Legitimacy thus is a sanction enhancer: A legitimate government or opposition group, because of the diffuse benefits conferred by its adherence to beneficial "rules," can attract supporters with lesser individual rewards for particular groups than an illegitimate regime. On the other hand, the diffuse disamenities imposed by a regime engaging in illegitimate acts creates a predisposition to seek change in its policies. Such a regime must therefore impose greater penalties on its opponents, and offer greater rewards to its supporters, in order to deter rebellion.[5]

Legitimacy affects deterrence in two ways. First, perceptions of legitimacy affect the nature of conflict between opponents. An actor—whether a regime or a regime opponent—that regards his adversary over some policy issue to nonetheless be acting "legitimately" is likely to take only such actions as will get the adversary to change his policy and not such actions as will destroy the adversary, for that would also destroy the diffuse benefits gained by the adversary's adherence to accepted, beneficial, ground rules. A legitimate government is thus liable to face less severe challenges. An illegitimate government, on the other hand, is likely to be considered worth destroying, for in addition to changing the specific policy in question, the diffuse disamenities can thereby be ended. Conflict between legitimate adversaries is thus liable to be nonzero-sum, with both sides seeking to preserve their diffuse benefits; by contrast, conflict with an adversary deemed illegitimate is liable to become zero-sum, as any gains by the adversary diminish the reach of the valued general principles.

Second, perceptions of legitimacy affect the responses of potential allies to a conflict. An actor that is perceived to be legitimate can draw support from third parties who consider themselves to be gaining diffuse benefits from that actor's adherence to legitimate principles. On the other hand, an illegitimate actor is liable to lose allies as soon as it is unable to provide the special rewards or punishments that maintained those parties' support. Thus if one group in a society rebels against the government, but most third parties consider the government to be legitimate, the rebels are unlikely to gain allies. The regime can then take those steps necessary to restore deterrence—isolation of its adversaries and repression clearly directed against them. Where rebels are considered legitimate, however, and gain third-party support, these necessary steps are difficult; where third-party support is widespread, these steps may be impossible. Thus successful guerilla leaders have learned to accept Mao Zedong's insight that rebels depend on the support of the people as much as fish depend on the water in which they swim (Lewis, 1974; Stacey, 1983; Wolf, 1970).

Historically, perceptions of legitimacy have played a crucial role in transforming political conflicts into rebellions and revolutions. It must be remembered that legitimacy is *not* a substitute for power to reward allies and repress opponents. A regime that has lost the ability to exercise sanctions, such as that of Imperial China in its last decades, will fail, regardless of its proclaimed allegiance to valued ideals. However, legitimacy has a major impact on how *effective* the use of power will be. A regime that has considerable coercive power, but is considered illegitimate, may be unable to use that coercive power effectively—that is, it may be unable to direct its repression against isolated opponents. Moreover, rebellion against an illegitimate government often is directed against that government's very survival, and thus may reach a severity that taxes the regime's normal repressive capacity. Such was generally the case with colonial regimes once a liberation struggle had begun (Chaliand, 1977; Miller and Aya, 1971). Rebels could rarely win an outright victory over an imperial power. However, they could make such victory costly and require a virtual occupation of the entire country. Moreover, by forcing the regime to take such extreme actions, rebels could cause the regime to lose the support of third parties, chiefly the domestic political supporters of the regime. Algeria is the prime example; there the French Army won all the battles, but France lost the war (Dunn, 1972; Wolf, 1970).

In addition, a regime that overreacts to political opponents may lose legitimacy, and thus both lose third-party support and *transform* a policy conflict into a struggle for survival. In many cases—such as Mexico under Diaz, Nicaragua under Somoza, the Philippines under Marcos, and Iran under the Shah—a ruler has feared loss of power so much that political conflicts with opponents over policy issues, such as sharing of power, land reform, and the pace and direction of industrial development, were escalated by extreme measures—martial law, rigging elections, torturing and killing opponents—that were widely considered abrogations of agreed-upon "ground rules." These leaders thus lost support and faced demands for the destruction of their regime rather than merely changes in policy or personnel. Similarly, in the English and French revolutions, the monarchs were initially asked merely for changes in tax policy and for administrative reforms; only when the rulers forfeited their legitimacy by seeking foreign support against their domestic opponents, thus violating important norms, did these rulers lose their crowns.

In short, the ability to use force effectively and restore deterrence depends on perceptions of legitimacy. A legitimate regime commanding moderate forces can usually deter opponents or, if facing a small rebellion, can usually defeat it and restore deterrence. On the other hand, an illegitimate regime with similar forces may be unable to deter opponents. Worse still, if faced with an act of protest, an illegitimate regime—or a regime that responds with measures that lose it legitimacy—is liable to find the crisis escalating as third parties defect. As the crisis deepens, greater force is required to deal with the rebels; yet if such greater force is not effectively deployed, it may create further loss of legitimacy and further defections. The result may be demands by a number of diverse groups for the destruction of the regime. The crisis may then go beyond the ability of the regime's forces to deal with at all, ending in the regime's collapse. Loss of legitimacy is thus part of the spiral of failed deterrence; maintenance of legitimacy is part of success.

Perceptions of legitimacy are difficult to monitor without actually surveying the members of a given society. Moreover, the precise content of legitimacy is subject to constant negotiation and redefinition in all active societies. However, historical patterns suggest that to maintain legitimacy, a government must do most of the following: (1) seek to defend national interests against foreign and internal enemies; (2) use military force in a controlled manner, to protect the population against excessive internal violence and foreign depredation; (3) preserve accepted boundaries between "just" and "unjust" actions by respecting traditional bounds on government authority and by punishing transgressions of law or tradition by other individuals or groups. In some cases, a government may fail to meet these conditions due to a quixotic or incompetent individual leader; when clear rules of succession provide for his or her replacement, a simple coup d'etat may suffice to restore legitimacy. However, in other cases, changing international, financial, or economic conditions may lead to crises that make it impossible for government leaders to meet these conditions, or indeed lead them to take actions that directly oppose them. Thus it was common for leaders of economically backward countries, when faced with threats from more advanced capitalist nations, to embark on policy changes to strengthen their governments that went against traditional practices, and thus provoked opposition (Skocpol, 1979). Where such changes failed to strengthen the government sufficiently to counter the foreign threat, the regime would fail on counts 1 and 3 simultaneously and lose its legitimacy. This pattern occurred in Old Regime France, Tsarist Russia, Tokugawa Japan, and late Imperial China. Alternatively, an authoritarian leader, who has purposely obscured possible lines of succession to entrench his own power and who reacts to opposition by alternating between weak and excessive use of force, may simultaneously fail on counts 2 and 3 and thus lose legitimacy (Goldstone, 1986b). And of course, certain colonial and domination regimes (such as those of former Rhodesia and South Africa) may have questionable legitimacy due to the lack of widely shared principles to which the regime and the population adhere.

An interesting sidelight is that rebellious activity itself may call regime legitimacy into question. Insofar as providing order is one of the functions that legitimate government must perform, a regime that is unable to maintain order in the face of rebellious acts may lose its perceived legitimacy. Thus the inability to deal effectively with the initial outbreak of rebellion may lead to an increasing spiral of rebellion as the regime's ineptness weakens its support. Conversely, the ability of a regime to maintain order may, over time, confer upon it legitimacy. Thus regimes imposed by conquest may gradually, if they maintain their strength and successfully impose order, come to be accepted as legitimate. Yet their foreign nature can lead to a rapid loss of legitimacy if their ability to maintain order breaks down, as happened to the Manchus in twentieth century China.

Where legitimacy is lacking, concessions and reforms are often ineffective in deterrence. This is because illegitimacy itself provides diffuse disamenities, and if the concession or reform is not seen as sufficient to offset such disamenities, it will *not* turn foes into allies. Moreover, if the concession or reform is offered in direct response to opponents' pressure, it will encourage opponents—who will remain opponents as long as the diffuse disamenities of the illegitimate regime continue to outweigh the partial benefits of concession or reform—to continue or escalate their pressure. For such regimes, it is crucial that reforms be offered in a context free of rebel pressure to be effective in deterrence. Moreover, to the extent that reforms appear to be merely window dressing rather than fundamental changes, they are liable to be perceived as attempts by the illegitimate government to cover its illegitimacy, rather than as movement toward greater legitimacy. Such "window-dressing" reforms therefore have little deterrent effect. An example is the current policy in South Africa of announcing that pass laws governing the movement of blacks will be rescinded, whereas the government yet maintains and enforces area laws that prohibit black residence in key areas. The action on the pass laws is not liable to have any effect in quelling regime opposition in this context.

Two more factors deserve mention. First, deterrence may fail against groups that have an apocalyptic mission. That is, groups that do not accept the legitimacy of the current regime, that believe they are destined to play a historical role in opposing it, and that accept any costs they bear as simply tests of their courage and dedication cannot be deterred by the normal calculus of costs and gains. Such groups may welcome martyrdom. But they are rarely large enough to pose a threat to an otherwise stable regime. Thus governments have generally been able to prevent millenarian rebellions from blossoming into revolutions by the measures outlined earlier—isolating the rebels, using crushing force, and preventing regime allies from switching their sympathies to the rebels.

In addition, it must be recognized that violent confrontations at some level are often part of the normal repertoire of political expression. Thus food riots in times of grain shortages, or burnings in effigy and urban demonstrations in times of hardship, are to a degree normal in many politically underdeveloped societies, just as strikes and media criticism are normal political expressions in our society. Accepting such acts allows avoidance of more severe actions; from the point of view of the regime, burning an effigy is preferable to burning manor houses (Tilly, 1986).

Where the line between legitimate protest and rebellious acts is clear, an upsurge in protest is often an alternative, rather than a prelude, to rebellion. Where the state is able to respond positively to acts of legitimate protest, and to isolate and punish those responsible for acts of rebellion, social order is generally maintained. However, where the line between legitimate acts of protest and acts of rebellion is unclear, conflict may escalate and contribute to the pattern of state overreaction and underreaction to opponents' acts. Deterrence of rebellion is thus greatly aided by the existence of acceptable forms of popular political expression (Huntington, 1968).

Where the regime seeks to deter people from engaging in actions that were formerly considered acceptable means of popular expression, such as food riots and mass demonstrations, it is necessary that people be offered some other accepted outlet of political expression, such as party politics. In this case, deterrence involves changes in the repertoire of accepted political expression in the direction of less violent actions and may be considered part of political development, rather than merely state response.

## Rationality and Uncertainty

"Somoza is finished"—EDEN PASTORA, 6/1/79
"I will not resign"—A. SOMOZA DEBAYLE, 6/11/79[6]

I have observed that successful deterrence of rebellion depends on the regime accurately identifying its opponents and their goals and bringing sufficient repressive force to bear to defeat them, while at the same time maintaining adherence to principles of legitimacy that allow it to retain the support of third parties. This is clearly a calculation of some delicacy, requiring both sound information and a careful weighing of actions and their consequences. Yet rebellions often create crisis conditions in which rational decision making and complete information are lacking. As the above pair of quotes indicates, rebels and state leaders may differ widely in their estimates of the rebels' success. Problems of rational action under stress and uncertainty thus complicate deterrence.

Cases of revolution provide evidence that leaders often act irrationally in response to threats—they tend to either over- or underestimate the dangers. This is in part because a leader who admits a serious threat may lose allies; hence there are pressures to ignore or downplay the extent of the danger.

On the other hand, a leader may prefer to magnify threats in order to force regime allies into more active government support. Which strategy is followed depends on the leader's situation and character. A leader who is accustomed to power usually will underestimate the opposition, thus taking inadequate deterrent measures—examples include Louis XVI, the Shah, and Marcos before their fall. The Shah of Iran responded to signs of growing opposition in 1977–1978 with a series of weak and indecisive measures, which Green (1984) believes reflected a self-induced breakdown in the coercive ability of the regime. Green notes that "the Shah resorted to coercion in a reflexive rather than preventive fashion. . . . [E]ven after the imposition of total martial law, [the Shah] never clamped down tightly on the most vocal leaders of the revolution, many of whom, unlike Khomeini, were resident in Iran . . . . [I]t seems that from the very beginning the Shah misread the nature of the opposition to him" (p. 159). On the other hand, a leader who is insecure will likely overreact, lashing out indiscriminately, as did Somoza in Nicaragua and Batista in Cuba; this overreaction leads to further defections of support, further overreactions, and a spiral of escalation. Somoza, in the fall of 1978, subjected his own cities to massive bombing in attempts to drive out his opponents; yet these genocidal tactics simply depleted his resources and drove away his last civilian supporters (Chavarria, 1986). Robert Axelrod has suggested that restoring stable cooperation between adversaries, in the event of a hostile move by one, is best achieved by a response that is neither too forgiving nor too punishing (1984:136–39). It seems that leaders faced with severe threats often have trouble making the right discrimination—they are often quite willing to push too hard or unable to push at all. This is one reason why deterrence breaks down in practice, even if the requisite deterrent force is available.

Shifting from the regime to the opposition, uncertainty regarding the chances for success—or even mere bravado and self-delusion—may lead opponents to overestimate their prospects. The prospects for deterrence then depend on how wide a band of uncertainty can be tolerated. And this, interestingly, seems to depend on the stake of potential opponents in the status quo. For example, let us first consider an oppressed opponent who has little to gain from the status quo of 1, whereas the value of a successful challenge would be 10. If the challenger is already oppressed, he may not have much more to lose, so the penalty for failure may be far less than the potential for gain. Say the opponent evaluates the likely penalty for his action if unsuccessful at $-1$. With this valuation of the alternatives, how high does the challenger have to assess his likelihood of success for the expected value of a challenge to exceed the expected value of the status quo? The answer is that anything over an 18 percent chance of success would lead the challenger to take up arms.[7] Thus to maintain deterrence, the regime must convince the challenger his chances of success are well under 20 percent. That is, the regime must convince challengers that they will almost always lose. This may be difficult for even a powerful regime to do, given the commonplace of overconfidence. So in this case, uncertainty makes a challenge likely.

Now say the challenger is better off, so that the value of the status quo is 5. Successful challenge and penalty valuations remain the same, at 10 and −1. In this case, a challenger must judge his chances of success are better than 45 percent for the expected gain from rebellion to outweigh the expected gain from the status quo. That is, he must think he has at least an even chance of victory, or he is better off as is.

Let us further assume that an opponent is liable to overestimate his chances of success by doubling the objective likelihood of success, and consider a situation in which the objective likelihood of success is 10 percent. For the more oppressed opponents, this is a situation that invites rebellion. Indeed, maintaining deterrence, given the opponent's overconfidence, requires that the regime keep the objective likelihood of success at under 9 percent. Moreover, even if the regime can achieve this, any change in objective conditions that leads to even a slight escalation in the actual likelihood of rebel success can lead to deterrence breakdown. On the other hand, for the opponents who are better off, the regime has considerable latitude. If the objective likelihood of success is actually 10 percent, even the opponent's overconfidence will not lead to overt rebellion; indeed, the objective likelihood of success would have to rise to significantly over 20 percent for deterrence to break down. Thus the regime facing more oppressed opponents rides on a knife edge; the regime with better-off opponents has considerable latitude in which deterrence will remain stable.

Note the difference between the two situations, in which the objective likelihood of successful rebellion, and the valuation of success and the penalty for failure, are in absolute terms the same. Deterrence is more likely to break down where the opponents are worse off; indeed, even if the opponents believed their chances of success were 20 percent in this case, and 40 percent in the better-off case, deterrence would still fail in the former case and remain stable in the latter.

This suggests the enormous power, often overlooked in studies of deterrence, of changes in the status quo. The difference in the status quo affects the relative rewards of success and failure. More important, this difference shifts the impact of uncertainty. In the former case, to achieve deterrence the regime must convince opponents they will almost never win; in the latter the regime must only convince opponents that they will probably not win. By forcing the regime to maintain a far more narrow band of uncertainty, the former case is less stable.

Empirically, the historical evidence seems to validate the suggestions of this simple model. Revolutions are almost never launched by even moderately well-off opponents against a government that seems capable. Rebellions occur when people are being pushed into a deteriorating position—for example, elites who are losing their position or peasants who are losing their livelihood—and/or when the government seems to be so weakened that the chances of success seem overwhelmingly strong (cf. Skocpol, 1979, and Scott, 1976). Deterrence theory, in its simple form, hardly predicts that an opponent who has a 20 percent chance of success is more likely to initiate rebellion than an opponent who has a 40 percent chance of success. But as this example shows, it all depends on where they stand and where they believe they are headed. Any group that feels it may have much to gain and little to lose will be extremely hard to deter, because that requires pushing its perceived chances for success into such a low range that misperception is likely. Hence history reveals numerous brave but unsuccessful rebellions, launched in times of desperation by groups whose position was deteriorating. The calculus of *expected* returns from rebellion versus the status quo shows why one can expect deterrence to fail in such situations. Thus one strategy for successful deterrence is to be strong, but to also offer opponents a significant stake in the status quo. This seems far more stable, given uncertainty, than the alternative strategy of using a regime's strength to maintain an oppressive advantage over opponents.

## Revolution and Deterrence

History shows many instances of successful deterrence of rebellion and revolution. Success involves maintaining legitimacy through positive military and economic performance while avoiding gross violations of accepted norms of justice, maintaining stable expectations regarding regime conduct, the ability to deploy and carefully direct powerful repressive capacities, and maintaining loyalty among regime allies. On the other hand, failure to deter can lead to a spiral of deepening illegitimacy, opposition, violence, and regime collapse. The latter course may be initiated by shifts in international or domestic conditions that weaken the regime or that shift allies from the regime to the rebels. The spiral can also be initiated or deepened by regime policies that are seen as unjust, counter to national interests, or irrational misapplications of force.

Many of these considerations, though drawn from study of regimes and opponents in a domestic political system, appear applicable to confrontations between opponents in an international political system. Though such analogies must be treated with caution and evaluated by those more expert in the field of superpower relations, I hope that some of these conclusions drawn from the study of revolutions may be useful suggestions, or affirmations, of behavior in an international setting.

First, it is important to note that mere strength is not enough to deter regime opponents if they can make gains without outright defeat of the regime. In the international context, this suggests that military strength may deter opponents from outright attack in search of immediate victory (for example, a nuclear first strike or invasion). However, it is not likely to be sufficient to deter actions that seek to influence potential allies or test enemy weaknesses. It should not be surprising that U.S. strategic superiority did not deter the Soviet Union from aggressive actions seeking limited gains in Eastern Europe and Cuba in the 1950s and 1960s, nor is reestablishment of U.S. strategic superiority in the 1990s (even if possible) likely in itself to deter further such actions.

Second, it is worth noting that rebellion often stems not from mere conditions of inferiority or stress, but also from regime actions that suggest that the old status quo will no longer be observed. Thus a policy shift that seems to undermine old agreements—such as new taxes or a new foreign policy—can elicit defensive or aggressive actions from regime opponents anxious to secure their interests in what is now perceived as a changing and fluid situation. Thus unilateral changes in U.S. defense posture that are perceived to upset the status quo (e.g., SDI) may elicit either defensive or more aggressive responses from the Soviets. It is crucial to realize that any status quo is the result of past processes of conflict and negotiation, and that both sides have accumulated a stake in the result. New policies that are seen as departing from the status quo are liable to be viewed *not* as incremental changes, and hence evaluated on their own merits, but as initiatives to a new and less well-defined situation. The result is liable to be a period of heightened tension and uncertainty, which may result in further probing or aggressive moves, until a new status quo is reached that is accepted by both sides.

Third, much of the contest between a regime and its opponents turns on attempts to shift the loyalty of potential allies. Thus the regime seeks to secure the loyalty of elites and key commercial or strategic centers while keeping rural, urban, and regional opponents isolated. In revolutions, regimes lose allies by failure to observe expected traditions of policy and justice, or by inappropriate (either inadequate or excessive and indiscriminate) use of force. Similarly, superpower contests often turn on attempts to secure or shift the loyalty of allied nations. In such contests a superpower also seems most likely to secure its allies' loyalty by maintaining well-established and accepted policies and carefully directing its use of force.

Fourth, deterrence failure need not lead to an ever-deepening spiral of violence and regime collapse. A well-proportioned and well-targeted response to rebellion generally succeeds in averting revolution and restoring deterrence. On the other hand, when rebellion is met with hesitation and wavering between weak and excessive response, then it is likely to escalate into revolution. In superpower relations, where two equal powers face each other, rather than an established regime facing weaker opponents, the notion of isolating and targeting opponents for repression must be handled differently. The notion, however, that well-proportioned responses to a hostile act are most likely to restore deterrence may still apply. Thus one may wish to identify a given hostile act carefully, isolate it from other actions, and adopt a response that is designed to proportionately respond to that particular act. This suggests that the strategy of "flexible response" to an opponent's aggression may be effective in averting a deepening disaster, provided that the response is clear, in proportion to the hostile act, and unhesitating. On the other hand, this finding also suggests that one of the greatest threats of escalation in the event of superpower aggression could come from a wavering response. In particular, a NATO command that responds to Soviet aggression by wavering between use of only conventional forces or a nuclear response invites escalation by either the Soviets or NATO. If NATO conventional forces cannot be confident of meeting the threat of Warsaw Pact conventional forces, then NATO is faced with the choice of either a weak response or escalation to nuclear war. Perhaps fear of such escalation will deter any initial Soviet aggression. However, if such initial deterrence should fail for any reason, the lesson of rebellions and revolutions is that NATO's inability to mount a proportional response makes a spiral of escalation extremely likely.

Fifth, regimes invite opposition and weaken deterrence when they are ambiguous about their domains of flexibility and inflexibility. Superpowers similarly seem more likely to deter opponents from adventurism when both parties clearly understand which are their nonnegotiable, vital principles and which measures are subject to negotiation.

Sixth, one should not underestimate the role of the status quo in deterrence. Under conditions of uncertainty, increasing an opponent's stake in the status quo, provided this can be done without altering the penalties for hostile acts, may be the most stabilizing strategy for deterrence. On the other hand, forcing an opponent into a greatly disadvantageous position may be destabilizing, because this increases the opponent's expected gains from challenging the status quo.

The benefits of legitimacy are much more difficult to obtain in an international context, because it is rarely the case that different countries will have shared norms or value the same general principles. Where legitimacy is lacking, we noted that concessions rarely succeed in deterring further challenges. Thus the general failure of concessions to deter aggression in the international arena—from Chamberlain's failure to deter Hitler to the failure of 1970s detente to deter the Soviet Union from entering Afghanistan—may reflect the lack of a shared sense of legitimate policies. Moreover, deterrence is aided by the existence of legitimate channels for expressing discontent. Where there are no effective alternatives to rebellion for seeking policy change, or where the boundary between legitimate protest and illegitimate rebellion is unclear, use of force by both the regime and its opponents tends to be greater and more risky, with escalation of conflicts and deterrence failure more likely. These findings suggest that the way to avoid greater dependence on force, and greater risks of escalation in case of policy conflicts, is to seek some kind of mutually beneficial "ground rules" for actions in the international arena. Thus an arms control agreement based on adherence to a mutually valued principle—for example, neither side shall have the ability to undertake an effective first strike against an opponent's missiles—is liable to be more successful in deterring further escalation than an agreement based merely on numerical restrictions on specific kinds of weaponry. Of course, international political development that provided a repertoire of effective alternatives to violence for influencing an adversary—for example, an effective world court or joint mediating bodies—would often allow adversaries to avoid more ambiguous, hence risky, actions.[8]

Because international forums, however, have had only a modest impact at best, superpowers are still liable to be the primary judges of the legitimacy of each other's acts. Regimes have lost legitimacy chiefly by weakness or by excessive reaction to opponents, as well as by failure to live up to declared economic or political goals. This finding accentuates the vital importance of measured response. In the superpower context, if a policy change is to elicit a deterring effect, it is crucial that it be seen neither as a concession nor as window dressing. In either of the latter cases, the change is liable to have an accelerating, rather than deterring, effect on further aggression. Avoiding wild swings in policy, eschewing public claims or promises that are unlikely to be realized, and responding to an opponent's acts with a proportionate, measured response seem the best ways to avoid errors of perception that severely undermine deterrence.

Perhaps the single most important finding of this essay is that *strength alone purchases little, if any, security*. Much more important is the ability to accurately target a measured response to aggression, promptly and effectively. A large military capacity, if used indecisively, recklessly, or ineffectively, has never saved a regime from falling by mere threat of its use.

In sum, examination of revolutions and rebellions tells us much about deterrence. This is in part because they involve the occasional complete failure of deterrence, but also because they involve the constant searching for marginal advantage, problems of coalition formation, and attempts to sustain stable relations among groups with opposing goals that typify political conflict in general.

## NOTES

I owe special thanks to Charles Tilly, who started this project and who greatly contributed to the bibliography.

1. There are exceptions, such as recently established states or those suffering from severe defeat in war. For example, the Chinese Nationalists who came to power in 1926 only controlled the cities and were almost immediately under attack from Japan. By the mid-1940s, when the Chinese Communist Party renewed its struggle with the Nationalist government, it is questionable whether the latter's position was clearly stronger than that of the Communists, who at the end of the war controlled a considerable portion of the countryside. Similarly in Russia, whereas the Tsarist regime was strong enough to defeat (but not deter) the Revolution of 1905, by 1917 it was so weakened by World War I that it could no longer defend itself against peasant and worker rebellions.

2. This bare-bones definition of revolution excludes the cultural and social changes that often accompany revolution. I further consider issues of legitimacy later. However, for the immediate purpose of discussing deterrence, it is sufficient to focus on the outcome that the regime wishes to deter—namely the loss of political power to its adversaries.

3. This chapter attempts to synthesize conclusions from a diverse body of literature in political science, sociology, and history. However, the views expressed are the author's own. The bibliography lists the major relevant works. For much more extensive bibliographies, see Goldstone (1982), Gurr (1980), Tilly (1985), and Zimmerman (1983).

4. The problem of aggregating interests to form group interests has received quite a bit of attention in the theoretical literature. In practice, however, group leadership is generally able to articulate and gain support for group goals. Muller

and Opp (1986) have recently demonstrated that individuals engaged in political activity *do* tend to view their actions as pursuit of collective goods and to frame their actions accordingly.

5. There is a tendency in much political analysis to assume that government use of violence is legitimate, but opposition groups' use of violence is illegitimate. This is, in general, *not* true. Violence, like other elements of political action, is subject to "ground rules" that are highly specific to time and place. Thus a regime that responds to political challenges with torture, killing of civilians, or "disappearances" will lose legitimacy where such actions are widely dissapproved of, whereas rebels that capture politicians for ransom, terrorize foreigners, or sabotage government installations may be applauded. On the other hand, rebels who do frequently use torture and kill civilians usually cannot maintain their legitimacy. What matters is not the use of violence per se, but whether the degree of violence and its targets are within generally accepted limits.

6. Quotations are from Booth, 1982, p. 155.

7. In this example, if the opponents have a 19 percent chance of success, their expected value of rebellion is $(.19)(10) + (.81)(-1) = 1.9 - .81 = 1.09$, or 9 percent higher than the value of the status quo.

8. The United States and the Soviet Union currently accept certain "spheres of influence" and policies—such as supporting proxy wars—for influencing adversaries if they step outside of those spheres. Trade sanctions and boycotts of international forums and sports events are also accepted. However, the boundary between legitimate and illegitimate sanctions is unclear, as is the effectiveness of particular sanctions. This situation invites a wide range of sanctioning behavior and escalation as particular measures fail. The results can be seen in unstable U.S. policy, with swings from grain embargoes, Olympic Games boycotts, and arms agreements to their repudiation following a change of administration.

## REFERENCES AND SELECTED BIBLIOGRAPHY

Abrahamian, E., 1980. Structural causes of the Iranian revolution. *MERIP Reports* 87:21–26.

Adas, M., 1981. From avoidance to confrontation: Peasant protests in precolonial and colonial Southeast Asia. *Comparative Studies in Society and History* 23:217–47.

Adelman, J. H., 1985. *Revolutions, Armies, and War.* Boulder, Colo.: Lynne Rienner.

Apter, D., and Sawa, N., 1984. *Against the State: Politics and Social Protest in Japan.* Cambridge, Mass.: Harvard University Press.

Arjomand, S., ed., 1985. *From Nationalism to Revolutionary Islam.* Albany, N.Y.: SUNY Press.

Axelrod, R., 1984. *The Evolution of Cooperation.* New York: Basic Books.

Blok, A., 1974. *The Mafia of a Sicilian Village, 1860–1960.* New York: Harper & Row.
Bond, B., 1983. *War and Society in Europe, 1970–1970.* Leicester: Leicester University Press.
Bonnell, V., 1983. *Roots of Revolution.* Berkeley, Calif.: University of California Press.
Booth, J. A., 1982. *The End and the Beginning: The Nicaraguan Revolution.* Boulder, Colo.: Westview Press.
Bowen, R. W., 1980. *Rebellion and Democracy in Meiji Japan. A Study of Commoners in the Popular Rights Movement.* Berkeley, Calif.: University of California Press.
Botz, G., 1976. *Gewalt in der Politik. Attentate, Zusammenstosse, Putschversuche, Unruhen in Osterreich, 1918 bis 1934.* Munich: Wilhelm Fink.
Boulding, K. E., 1962. *Conflict and Defense: A General Theory.* New York: Harper.
Bresnan, J., ed., 1986. *Crisis in the Phillipines.* Princeton, N.J.: Princeton University Press.
Brewer, J., and Styles, J., eds., 1980. *An Ungovernable People. The English and Their Law in the Seventeenth and Eighteenth Centuries.* New Brunswick, N.J.: Rutgers University Press.
Broeker, G., 1970. *Rural Disorder and Police Reform in Ireland, 1812–1836.*
Brustein, W., 1986. Regional social orders in France and the French Revolution. *Comparative Social Research* 9, forthcoming.
Calhoun, C., 1982. *The Question of Class Struggle.* Chicago: University of Chicago Press.
Cavarria, R. E., 1986. Nicaragua: The Revolutionary Insurrection. In J. Goldstone, ed., *Revolutions.* San Diego and New York: Harcourt Brace Jovanovich.
Chaliand, G., 1977. *Revolution in the Third World: Myths and Prospects.* New York: Viking.
Chapman, B., 1970. *Police State.* London: Pall Mall.
Chorley, K., 1973. *Armies and the Art of Revolution.* Boston: Beacon.
Chesnais, J., 1981. *Histoire de la violence en Occident de 1800 a nos jours.* Paris: Laffont.
Cohen, Y., Brown, B. R., and Organski, A. F. K., 1981. The paradoxical nature of state making: The violent creation of order. *American Political Science Review* 75:901–10.
Cole, J., 1983. Women in Cuba: The revolution within the revolution. In B. Lindsay, ed., *Comparative Perspectives of Third World Women.* New York: Praeger.
Conant, R. W., and Apple Levin, M., eds., 1969. *Problems in Research on Community Violence.* New York: Praeger.
Cronin, J. E., 1979. *Industrial Conflict in Modern Britain.* London: Croom Helm.

Cronin, J. E., and Schneer, J., eds., 1982. *Social Conflict and the Political Order in Modern Britain.* London: Croom Helm.
Dix, R., 1983. The varieties of revolution. *Comparative Politics* 15:281–93.
Dunn, J., 1972. *Modern Revolutions.* Cambridge, Engl.: Cambridge University Press.
Eckstein, S., 1982. The impact of revolution on social welfare in Latin America. *Theory and Society* 11:43–94.
Eisenstadt, S. N., 1978. *Revolution and the Transformation of Societies: A Comparative Study of Civilizations.* New York: Free Press.
Eistenstadt, S. N., and Curelaru, M., 1976. *The Form of Sociology—Paradigms and Crises.* New York: John Wiley and Sons.
Franzosi, R., 1981. La conflittualita in Italia tra ciclo economico e contrattazione collettiva. *Rassegna Italiana di Sociologia* 22:533–75.
Fullbrook, M., 1983. *Piety and Politics.* Cambridge, Engl.: Cambridge University Press.
Furet, F., 1981. *Interpreting the French Revolution.* Cambridge, Engl.: Cambridge University Press.
Gamson, W. A., 1975. *The Strategy of Social Protest.* Homewood, Ill.: Dorsey.
Goldstein, R. J., 1983. *Political Repression in 19th Century Europe.* London: Croom Helm.
Goldstone, J. A., 1982. The comparative and historical study of revolutions. *Annual Review of Sociology* 8:187–207.
———— 1986a. Ed., *Revolutions: Comparative, Theoretical, and Historical Studies.* San Diego and New York: Harcourt Brace Jovanovich.
———— 1986b. Revolutions and superpowers. In J. H. Adelman, ed., *Superpowers and Revolution.* New York: Praeger.
———— 1986c. State breakdown in the English revolution: A new synthesis. *American Journal of Sociology* 92:257–322.
Green, J. P., 1984. Countermobilization as a revolutionary form. *Comparative Politics* 16:153–69.
Gugler, J., 1982. The urban character of contemporary revolutions. *Studies in Comparative International Development* 17:60–73.
Gurr, T. R., 1970. *Why Men Rebel.* Princeton, N.J.: Princeton University Press.
———— 1980. Ed., *Handbook of Political Conflict.* New York: Free Press.
———— 1986. Persisting patterns of repression and rebellion: Foundations for a general theory of political coercion. In M. P. Karns, ed., *Persistent Patterns and Emergent Structures in a Waning Century.* New York: Praeger Special Studies for the International Studies Association.
Gurr, T. R., Grabovsky, P. N., and Hula, R. C., 1977. *The Politics of Crime and Conflict. A Comparative History of Four Cities.* Beverly Hills, Calif.: Sage.
Hair, P. E. H., 1971. Deaths from violence in Britain: A tentative secular survey. *Population Studies* 25:5–24.

Hay, D., et al., 1975. *Albion's Fatal Tree. Crime and Society in Eighteenth-Century England*. New York: Pantheon.
Hoerder, D., 1977. *Crowd Action in a Revolutionary Society: Massachusetts. 1765-1780*. New York: Academic Press.
Hsiao, K., 1960. *Rural China: Imperial Control in the Nineteenth Century*. Seattle, Wash.: University of Washington Press.
Hunt, L., 1984. *Politics, Culture, and Class in the French Revolution*. Berkeley, Calif.: University of California Press.
Huntington, S. P., 1968. *Political Order in Changing Societies*. New Haven, Conn.: Yale University Press.
Isaac, L., and Kelly, W. R., 1981. Racial insurgency, the state, and welfare expansion: Local and national level evidence from the postwar United States. *American Journal of Sociology* 86:1348-86.
Kelley, J., and Klein, H. S., 1980. *Revolution and the Rebirth of Inequality*. Berkeley, Calif.: University of California Press.
Korpi, W., 1974. Conflict and the balance of power. *Acta Sociologica* 17:99-114.
Korpi, W., and Shalev, M., 1980. Strikes, power, and politics in the western nations, 1900-1976. In M. Zeitlin, ed., *Political Power and Social Theory*. Greenwich, Conn.: JAI Press.
Kriesi, H., et al., 1981. *Politische Aktivierung in der Schweiz, 1945-1978*. Diessenhoffen: Verlag Ruegger.
Lane, F. C., 1958. Economic consequences of organized violence. *Journal of Economic History* 18:401-17.
Levi, M., Forthcoming. *Rule and Revenue*. Berkeley, Calif.: University of California Press.
Lewis, J. W., ed., 1974. *Peasant Rebellion and Communist Revolution in Asia*. Stanford, Calif.: Stanford University Press.
Ludtke, A., 1980. Genesis und durchsetzung des 'modernen staates' zur Analyse von Herrschaft und Verwaltulng, *Archiv fur Sozialgeschichte* 20:470-91.
Luterbacher, U., and Ward, M. D., 1985. *Dynamic Models of International Conflict*. Boulder, Colo.: Lynn Rienner.
McNeill, W. H., 1982. *The Pursuit of Power. Technology, Armed Force, and Society Since A.D. 1000*. Chicago: University of Chicago Press.
Migdal, J., 1974. *Peasants, Politics, and Revolution*. Princeton, N.J.: Princeton University Press.
Miller, N., and Aya, R., eds., 1971. *National Liberation: Revolution in the Third World*. New York: Free Press.
Moore, B., Jr., 1966. *Social Origins of Dictatorship and Democracy*. Boston: Beacon.
―――― 1978. *Injustice*. White Plains, N.H.: M.E. Sharpe.
Muller, E. N., 1972. A test of a partial theory of the potential for political violence. *American Political Science Review* 66:928-59.
―――― 1985. Income inequality, regime repressiveness, and political violence. *American Sociological Review* 50:47-61.

Muller, E. N., and Opp, K., 1986. Rational choice and rebellious collective action. *American Political Science Review* 80:471–89.

Munger, F., 1979. Measuring repression of popular protest by English justices of the peace in the industrial revolution. *Historical Methods* 12:76–83.

——— 1981. Suppression of popular gatherings in England, 1800–30. *American Journal of Legal History* 25:111–140.

Oquist, P., 1980. *Violence, Conflict, and Politics in Colombia*. New York: Academic Press.

Paige, J. M., 1975. *Agrarian Revolution: Social Movements and Export Agriculture in the Underdeveloped World*. New York: Free Press.

Parish, W. L., 1981. Egalitarianism in Chinese society. *Problems of Communism* (Jan–Feb):37–53.

Popkin, S., 1979. *The Rational Peasant*. Berkeley, Calif.: University of California Press.

della Porta, D., and Pasquino, G., eds., 1983. *Terrorismo e violenza politica*. Bologna: Il Mulino.

——— 1977. Militia and public order in nineteenth-century America. *American Studies* (April):81–101.

Rudé, G., 1964. *The Crowd in History: A Study of Popular Disturbances in France and England 1730–1848*. New York: Wiley.

Russell, D. E. H., 1974. *Rebellion, Revolution, and Armed Force*. New York: Academic Press.

Salert, B., and Sprague, J., 1980. *The Dynamics of Riots*. Ann Arbor, Mich.: Inter-University Consortium for Political and Social Research.

Schelling, T. C., 1984. *Choice and Consequence. Perspectives of an Errant Economist*. Cambridge, Mass.: Harvard University Press.

Schumaker, P. D., 1978. The scope of political conflict and the effectiveness of constraints in contemporary urban protest. *Sociological Quarterly* 19:168–84.

Scott, J. C., 1976. *The Moral Economy of the Peasant: Rebellion and Subsistence in South East Asia*. New Haven, Conn.: Yale University Press.

Sewell, W. H., Jr., 1980. *Work and Revolution in France: The Language of Labor from the Old Regime to 1848*. Cambridge: Cambridge University Press.

——— 1985. Ideologies and social revolutions: Reflections on the French case. *Journal of Modern History* 57:57–85.

Skocpol, T., 1979. *States and Social Revolutions*. Cambridge: Cambridge University Press.

——— 1982. What makes peasants revolutionary? *Comparative Politics* 14:351–75.

——— 1985. Cultural idioms and political ideologies in the reconstruction of state power: A rejoinder to Sewell. *Journal of Modern History* 57:86–96.

Snyder, D. R., 1978. Collective violence. A research agenda and some strategic considerations. *Journal of Conflict Resolution* 22:499–534.

Snyder, D., and Tilly, C., 1972. Hardship and collective violence in France, 1830–1860. *American Sociological Review* 37:520–32.
Stacey, J., 1983. *Patriarchy and Socialist Revolution in China*. Berkeley, Calif.: University of California Press.
Stinchcombe, A. L., 1965. Stratification among organizations and the sociology of revolution. In J. March, ed., *Handbook of Organizations*. Chicago: Rand McNally.
——— 1975. Social structure and politics. In N. Polsby and F. Greenstein, eds., *Handbook of Political Science*, Vol. 3, Reading, Mass.: Addison-Wesley.
Stohl, M., 1976. *War and Domestic Political Violence. The American Capacity for Repression and Reaction*. Beverly Hills, Calif.: Sage.
Storch, R. D., 1976. The policeman as domestic missionary: Urban discipline and popular culture in northern England, 1850–1880. *Journal of Social History* 9:481–509.
Sugimoto, Y., 1981. *Popular Disturbances in Postwar Japan*. Hong Kong: Asian Research Service.
Tarrow, S., 1983. *Struggling to Reform: Social Movements and Policy Change During Cycles of Protest*. Ithaca, N.Y.: Center for International Studies, Cornell University. Western Societies Program, Occasional Paper No. 15.
Tilly, C., 1973. Does modernization breed revolution? *Comparative Politics* 5:425–47.
——— 1975. Ed., *The Formation of National States in Western Europe*. Princeton, N.J.: Princeton University Press.
——— 1978. *From Mobilization to Revolution*. Reading, Mass.: Addison-Wesley.
——— 1985. Selected readings on political change. Working Paper 19, Center for Studies of Social Change, New School for Social Research.
——— 1986. *The Contentious French*. Cambridge, Mass.: Harvard University Press.
Trimberger, E. K., 1978. *Revolution from Above: Military Bureaucrats and Development in Japan, Turkey, Egypt, and Peru*. New Brunswick, N.J.: Transaction Books.
Traugott, M., 1985. *Armies of the Poor*. Princeton, N.J.: Princeton University Press.
Useem, M., 1975. *Protest Movements in America*. Indianapolis, Ind.: Bobbs-Merrill.
Wallensteen, P., Galtung, J., and Portales, C., eds., 1985. *Global Militarization*. Boulder, Colo.: Westview Press.
Walker, T., 1985a. *Nicaragua: Land of Sandino*, Second Edition. Boulder, Colo.: Westview Press.
——— 1985b. Ed., *Nicaragua: The First Five Years*. New York: Praeger.
Walter, E. V., 1969. *Terror and Resistance: A Study of Political Violence*. New York: Oxford University Press.
Walton, J., 1984. *Reluctant Rebels*. New York: Columbia University Press.

Weber, M., 1947. *The Theory of Social and Economic Organization*, trans. T. Parsons. New York: Free Press.

Welch, C., 1980. *Anatomy of Rebellion*. Albany, N.Y.: SUNY Press.

Whyte, M. K., 1975. Inequality and stratification in China. *China Quarterly*, no. 64:684–711.

Wilson, J., 1977. Social protest and social control. *Social Problems* 24:469–81.

Wolf, E., 1970. *Peasant Wars of the Twentieth Century*. New York: Harper and Row.

Zimmerman, E., 1983. *Political Violence, Crises, and Revolutions*. Cambridge, Mass.: Schenkman.

# 12

# The "Aggressive Male" Syndrome: Its Possible Relevance for International Conflict

## HAROLD H. KELLEY and GREG SCHMIDT

This chapter assumes that decisions relating to nuclear conflict—decisions to make aggressive moves, to threaten retaliation, to escalate the level of attack and counterattack—will be made by individuals and small groups. Furthermore, these persons will often have had personal interaction with their counterparts on the other side of the conflict and will often be in more or less direct communication with them during conflict episodes. These assumptions suggest that scientific knowledge about personal interactions is relevant to anticipating and controlling the course of events during international conflict.

As we have examined the interpersonal literature for its relevance, our attention has been drawn to a body of work that delineates a particular pattern of thinking, feeling, and interpersonal behavior that we will refer to as the "aggressive male syndrome." This pattern is characteristic of a small number of males but can apparently be elicited situationally in very large numbers of males and possibly also females. It is of particular relevance to deterrence theory because one of the syndrome's features is that the person is little inhibited from attack on other persons by the threat of harmful consequences. Indeed, the person may even be stimulated to attack by threats of possible retaliation. To the extent that individuals exhibiting the aggressive male syndrome are able to exert influence on the course of events in an international conflict, the operation of the principles underlying deterrence theory is uncertain. There is some chance that the long-term concrete consequences of nuclear conflict will take a back seat to more immediate emotional reactions and symbolic (e.g., self-esteem-related) consequences.

251

This review first describes a kind of person, the aggressive male, who consistently shows the syndrome. We do *not* present the "aggressive male" as a metaphor for a kind of national state, although he certainly figures in that role in common thought. The present interest is in the aggressive male as a person who dramatically displays a pattern of thought and action that may influence national decision making.

The "aggressive male" figures prominently among the commonly held stereotypes of persons, because of his occasional appearance in our everyday lives and frequent media accounts of his exploits. Accordingly, we must also consider the possibility that "normal" or "rational" actors on one side may conclude that this kind of person is exerting influence on the other side and feel compelled to initiate defensive actions that may then be misinterpreted.

Second, we describe a set of conditions that tend to encourage "normal" people to adopt the aggressive male syndrome, that is, to shift into a state in which they act as if they were "aggressive males." To the extent that these conditions prevail, as they well may during times of crisis, actors not generally disposed to the "aggressive male" pattern may respond to events as if they were so disposed. To the extent these conditions prevail, actors more disposed to the aggressive male pattern may be able to sway their associates to adopt their maladaptive approach to threat and deterrence.

Third, we outline procedures that have been found effective in helping people control their anger and avoid becoming like "aggressive males." These are of potential importance during international crises inasmuch as by following such procedures, the actors on one side (1) may avoid the possibility that they themselves adopt the aggressive male behavior pattern in their decision making and (2), equally important, may be able to assure their counterparts that they have not done so.

Fourth, we outline what is known about the interpersonal experience of boys that disposes them to become "aggressive males." This point reflects our sense that discussions of deterrence theory tend to focus on too narrow a time frame, overlooking the obvious fact that the events at the time of a conflict crisis usually occur in the context of an extended history of interaction between nations and national leaders. Here we shift to an historical perspective on interpersonal episodes of threat and aggression. The developmental history of males disposed to exhibit the "aggressive male" syndrome affords a possibly useful metaphor for patterns of international interaction likely to dispose one or both sides to display analogues of the syndrome. It also affords a perspective from which to analyze a national leader's prior experiences with his opposite numbers, for the purpose of predicting his response to provocations they may subsequently provide.

## The "Aggressive Male" Syndrome

**Table 12.1.** Some Evidence About Male Aggressiveness

1. Boys are more aggressive than girls.
2. That difference depends on the type of aggression but is markedly true for physical aggression.
3. Boys are especially more aggressive toward other boys.
4. There is more physical fighting in pairs of boys than in mixed-sex or female pairs.
5. Boys are more likely than girls to retaliate to physical attack with physical counterattack.
6. Aggressive behavior is the most common behavior problem of boys in school.
7. Wife beating is far more common than husband beating.
8. Homicide by men is far more common than homicide by women, and the victims are more often men.
9. In public opinion polls, capital punishment is endorsed more for men than for women.

SOURCES: Attili (1986), Eme (1979), Feshbach (1970), Gelles (1972), Hokanson and Burgess (1962a, b), Maccoby and Jacklin (1980), Vidmar and Ellsworth (1974), and Wolfgang (1958).

We will briefly consider its implications for avoiding aggressive episodes with a particular counterpart.

Our review draws on laboratory studies of aggression and conflict, child development research, clinical work on the treatment of aggression, sociological evidence about violent adult behavior, and studies of aggression in the schools. The review focuses on *aggression between males* for several reasons: (1) Most of the actors in international relations are men. (2) The relevant research deals mainly with boys, adolescent males, and men. (3) Finally, and probably accounting for that research emphasis, there are many facts indicating that human interpersonal aggression is primarily a phenomenon between males. (Table 12.1 lists a few illustrative findings.)

Although this is primarily the story of the "aggressive male," we also describe a kind of aggression and the immediate and historical conditions under which it occurs. Thus, we provide materials for understanding a person against whom deterrence is less than normally dependable, a psychological state in which, for many persons (perhaps all of us), deterrence is in doubt, and scenarios of interaction to avoid in order to circumvent being in that kind of state or interacting with a person who is. Our review affords a metaphor for the process we fear when we worry about the breakdown of deterrence and the buildup of the conflict spiral. And as this kind of person, or state, or the processes giving rise to that kind of person or state are permitted to play important roles in international processes, it is a model of what we should fear.

## The Aggressive Male

### Who Is He?

The aggressive male is defined by his impact on other people and, therefore, by his social reputation. As a boy he appears in psychological clinics because his parents find him difficult to handle. He is known to his classmates and teachers as being disobedient, starting fights, pushing and shoving other children, and getting what he wants by fighting. He is sent to the school counselor and is identified as having a conduct disorder or antisocial tendencies. In extreme cases, at adolescence he appears in the juvenile courts as a delinquent, and at adulthood he is involved in violent fights resulting in extreme injury or death and is found among the prisoners in correctional institutions. Although such extreme forms of violence occur more frequently in certain social and ethnic groups than in others, male aggressiveness is by no means unique to those social strata (Chapter 16 in Baker and Ball, 1969; Berkowitz, 1962). Much of the evidence cited in our review comes from samples that are quite broad in their class and ethnic composition.

Is aggressiveness as stable a personal disposition as the above implies? Olweus's (1984) review of the literature shows that it is. The results from two dozen longitudinal studies shows that "*there is a substantial degree of stability in aggressive reaction patterns . . .*" (p. 109). When the degree of stability (indexed by the correlation between pre- and postassessments) is plotted against the pre-to-post interval, the line slopes downward from a value of .75 for an interval of one year to a value of .40 for an interval of 20 years. Further, Olweus notes that there is "a substantial degree of cross-situational consistency in the sense that there is a considerable correspondence between aggression data obtained from independent sources or assessments at about the same point in time" (p. 113).

### What Does He Do?

In the family, the aggressive boy behaves in an aversive and demanding manner: screaming, taking things by force, hitting, biting, and so on. In school, he is known for starting and being involved in physical fights. As an adult, he pushes, throws objects at, kicks, hits with hard objects, chokes, and/or uses a knife or gun on his opponent.

Deterrence theory assumes that initial acts of aggression (the ones that are somehow to be deterred) are instrumental, taking advantage of opportunities for gain through strong action. Students of aggression recognize that it is sometimes initiated in this planful way, reflecting "opportunities" and "resources." However, they also identify a kind of aggression that is reactive (to perceived attack or blocking) and impulsive or "irritable." The aggressive male seems primarily to display this latter kind of aggression, triggered by provocation, impulsive and hostile in nature, and directed primarily at injuring the other person.

The aggressive male is not simply "assertive." Some authors (e.g., Hinde, 1985) draw a distinction between aggression and assertiveness. The latter refers to active and strong pursuit of one's legitimate ends but with regard for other persons' rights. In contrast, aggression is defined as behavior that injures another person, that is normatively inappropriate and intentional. The distinction seems to be important in the treatment of aggressive behavior. One component of such treatment is "assertion training," which teaches the aggressive person how to use socially appropriate means to pursue his interests.

## What Is His Reaction to Threats of Retaliation?

### Aggressive Boys

A first clue on this point comes from a laboratory study of boys from several third grade classes, reported by Peterson (1971). The boys were rated as low or high "aggressive" by their peers and then paired off in a learning task that provided one boy an opportunity to deliver irritating noises to the partner. Boys with reputations for low aggressiveness were deterred from aggression (i.e., gave softer noises) when there was a chance of subsequent punishment for it, either because the partner had a reputation for aggressiveness or because the partner would have an opportunity later to retaliate. In contrast, boys with reputations for high aggressiveness gave *louder* noises under conditions of possible punishment, both toward other boys of similar reputation and under conditions of possible retaliation. Peterson writes that his and other studies indicate that "the expectation of punishment [seems] to function as a stimulus for aggressive responding for individuals with a past history of high aggressiveness" (pp. 163–164).

Work by Patterson (1976; Patterson and Cobb, 1971) is quite consistent with Peterson's interpretation. Patterson observed that aggressive boys are little deterred by the threat of punishment from their parents. Specifically, they are twice as likely as normal boys to persist in their aversive behavior after receiving punishment. Based on many studies of aggressive boys and their interaction with their family members, Patterson concludes that their aggression is reactive to other persons' aversive behavior and has been learned through negative reinforcement. This reinforcement is provided when the aggression succeeds in eliminating other persons' annoying actions. Patterson suggests that for the aggressive boy, punishment serves as a cue to "try harder," because he has learned that aggression finally results in other persons (even the parents) ending their deterrent attempts. Perry and Bussey (1984) draw the following conclusion: "One major characteristic of aggressive children, then, is that they have learned to respond to real or anticipated aversive events with strong and persistent aggressive reactions" (p. 217). The conditions under which they learn this are discussed in a later section of this chapter.

With their experience in ridding themselves of annoyance through aggression, aggressive boys in playground groups are likely to get into aggressive interchanges with each other (Patterson, Littman, and Bricker, 1967). Furthermore, with their apparent belief that persistence in coercion finally works, aggressive boys are likely to develop sustained exchanges of aggression. In his comparisons of normal and hyperaggressive 9–11-year-old boys, Raush (1965) found no difference between them in their initial likelihood of reciprocating an unfriendly act (about .80 in both cases). However, the subsequent interaction sequence for the normal boys showed a lower rate of continued unfriendliness than the initial reciprocations would lead one to predict, but the subsequent sequence for the hyperaggressive boys showed a higher-than-predicted rate of continued unfriendliness. In summarizing these results, Raush comments on "the aptitude of these boys for moving rapidly from an atmosphere of friendliness to one of wildly chaotic aggression" and compares this with "the contrasting capacity of normal children to catch themselves up—to reorganize and correct for threats of disruption in group interaction" (p. 497).

Raush also observed that the two types of boys differed sharply in their initial reactions to friendly acts. For normals the rate of reciprocation was .92, but for hyperaggressives, it was only .55. Raush comments that the "disturbed" boys are less able to discriminate between friendly and unfriendly acts. This directs our attention to the cognitive processes that seem to characterize the aggressive male.

Dodge's (1985) recent work on aggressive boys in the early school years shows that their behavior is partly mediated by biases in their attributions of intention. In a standard test situation (Dodge, 1980) a boy is working on a puzzle-assembly task with the possibility of winning a prize. Another boy knocks over his puzzle and the worker then has an opportunity to retaliate. When the intent behind the destruction is clear, either malevolent or benign, all boys, whether aggressive or normal, respond as we would expect, either aggressively or mildly as befits the event. However, when the intent behind the destruction is ambiguous, the aggressive boy thinks it was done on purpose and acts to destroy the offender's puzzle. Dodge and Frame (1982) show that the aggressive boy's bias in attributing intentionality is restricted to interpretations made of aversive behavior directed toward himself (i.e., it is not a general interpretation of negative social behavior). They also show that although the aggressive boy's attribution has some basis in fact (they do experience frequent aggression from others), they are aggressive toward others more often than they are the targets of aggression. The aggressive boy knows his reputation, of course, and he expects hostility from others. In turn, the others expect aggression from him, so they are not surprised when he reacts aggressively to innocent aversive events.

We see that part of the aggressive boy's sense of the social world is that others don't like him and can be expected to attack him when given an opportunity. The aggressive boy's response to the prospect of retaliation from another boy seems to be shaped by the belief: "He's going to be hostile to me when he gets the chance, so I may as well attack him now."

Another perspective on the *intra*personal processes of aggressive boys is provided by their reaction to the suffering of the targets of their attacks. We have seen that their aggression has the goal of ridding themselves of annoyance through injuring the offending person. Consistent with this view are data suggesting that they perceive the suffering of their victims as evidence of the success of their aggression (Perry and Perry, 1974). Moreover, they fail to experience the negative self-reactions to their victims' pain that normal boys do (Perry and Bussey, 1977). Along the same lines, Ekman (summarized in Olweus, 1984) and Olweus (1978) observed that school bullies have little empathy for others and feel little guilt after their attack on a smaller boy. They find it exciting and often feel that "he deserves it." Thus, having injury as his goal in interpersonal attacks, the pain of the aggressive boy's victim serves merely to show the success of his efforts and fails to elicit guilt.

## Aggressive Adult Males

Is the aggressive *boy*'s response to punishment or the threat of punishment with increased aggression also exhibited by aggressive *men*? Two lines of research imply that it is. First, Olweus's review (1984) reports fairly substantial stability of aggression, measured as a general trait, across a period of 20 years. Second, research on adult aggression indicates that the pattern of adult male aggression has many features in common with that exhibited by aggressive boys. Most important are several studies that have reconstructed the interaction process by which adult males get into violent fights. These analyses are particularly relevant to deterrence theory because the fighters fail to pull back from violence *despite their presumed awareness of its possible deadly outcome*.

Berkowitz's researchers (1978) interviewed 65 English men who had been convicted of inflicting injury on another person but not in connection with robbery. Most of the incidents grew out of arguments, quarrels, or a friend's need for assistance. Berkowitz found no evidence that the men were motivated by a desire for approval from onlookers (though other researchers would disagree with this) and only scant evidence that concern about reputation for toughness played a role. He emphasizes that most such aggression is not instrumental in either of those ways. Rather it is "hostile" aggression, oriented mainly toward injuring the other person, characterized by an outburst of rage, carried out without thought of consequences, and finding its immediate and sufficient reward in the injury that is successfully inflicted.

Berkowitz's view is quite close to that of Zillman (1979) and others who emphasize the *affective* components of aggression, specifically, that violent crime and especially homicide is primarily oriented to removing annoyances rather than to attaining various objectives. As we will see later, supportive evidence about the important role of the intrapersonal mechanisms of affect is found in laboratory demonstrations of the efficacy of arousal in enhancing aggression. These "annoyance-riddance" interpretations of aggression are also consistent with Patterson's evidence on the role of negative reinforcement (removal of aversive stimuli) in the development of aggressiveness.

Berkowitz's formulation raises the question of what constitutes the triggering annoyance for such extremely hostile outbursts. He finds the answer to this in the fact that aggressive men are apparently easily angered by threats to their self-esteem: They are highly sensitive to disagreements, criticisms, or boasting that can be taken as insulting, belittling, derogating, or challenging to them personally. From a deterrence perspective, the Berkowitz view of violence emphasizes that the person is unable to control himself. The person does not think much about consequences, either those of approval or reputation, or that he might get hurt (none anticipated losing the fight). The person acts under control of the situation, concerned only with the present.

The notion of "losing control," raised by the studies of both Raush and Berkowitz, is brought into sharp focus by Berdie's account (1947) of "playing the dozens." This term refers to a process of ritual insult that is common (though known by many different names) in groups of young black men in urban ghetto areas. The competition in exchanging ingenious and euphonious insults is highly arousing and can expose a participant to derogation either through his revealed inadequacy in the contest or because the exchange shifts from ritual insults to personal ones. Berdie observed the process as it occurred among black prisoners during World War II. A number of men would join together to torment a vulnerable man (through their increasingly nasty but clever insults) until he began a physical fight with one or more of them. At that point, they regarded the victim as responsible for the fight (he can't "take it") and they went into action in a concerted way that usually left the victim seriously injured. The striking feature of this process is that the victim soon realized what was afoot but was unable to avoid getting caught up in the process despite his awareness of where it was leading.

More explicit information about the "personal feelings" that constitute the intrapersonal mediators of violence is provided by Luckenbill (1977). From analysis of public records and interviews with the participants and observers of 70 instances of criminal homicide, Luckenbill derived the outline of the episode summarized in Table 12.2. In the second stage, the offender (the one who ultimately does the killing) interprets the initial actions of the victim as a challenge to his esteem—as "personally offensive." As the scenario proceeds, the offender takes steps to restore "face" and demonstrate his toughness. The sequence moves on toward its disastrous conclusion as the victim takes up the challenge and accepts the situation as a contest of reputations for courage.

Personal feelings are also involved in sequences leading to assaults on police officers, according to Toch (1969). His analysis is based on interviews both with officers and with men having records of such assaults (referred to here as "offenders"). The following scenario is typical: (1) The officer gives orders, makes demands. (2) The offender shows displeasure with the officer's approach, fails to cooperate, and gives verbal abuse or makes threats. (3) The officer gives additional orders or arrests the offender. (4) The offender shows displeasure with the arrest, makes an effort to avoid it, and becomes violent. The interchange continues until (5) the officer clubs or shoots the offender.

The reactions of these offenders shows a marked similarity to the reaction of aggressive boys: The person responds to a threat from a powerful source with aggression directed against that source. This willingness to attack a person of (objectively) great strength suggests that the offenders have learned to meet threat of retaliation with attack.

A content analysis of the apparent causes of these sequences indicates that the most prominent elements are defense of personal autonomy (touch-

**Table 12.2.** Stages of an Episode of Criminal Homicide

| | |
|---|---|
| STAGE I | • Event is performed by victim (that subsequently is defined by offender as an offense to "face")<br>• Victim's insult, disparagement<br>• Victim's refusal to cooperate or comply with offender<br>• Victim's physical or nonverbal gesture |
| STAGE II | • Offender interprets victim's previous move as personally offensive<br>• Offender learns meaning of victim's move from inquiries made of victim or audience<br>• Offender inputs meaning on basis of victim's prior behavior |
| STAGE III | • Offender makes retaliatory move aimed at restoring face and demonstrating strong character<br>• Offender expresses anger/contempt signifying victim is regarded as unworthy person<br>• Offender issues a verbal or physical challenge to victim |
| STAGE IV | • Victim comes to a "working agreement" with proferred definition of situation as one suited for violence<br>• Victim does not comply, continues performance of offensive activity<br>• Victim physically retaliates against offender<br>• Victim issues counterchallenge |
| STAGE V | • Offender and victim are committed to battle, and do battle; 54 percent are one-sided; otherwise, two-sided. Victim is killed |

SOURCE: Luckenbill (1977).

ing, orders, etc.) and expression of contempt or retaliation. In interviews with 69 violence-prone inmates and parolees, Toch finds that the most frequent themes are "self-image defending" (aggression as retribution against persons seen to cast aspersions on the self-image), "self-image promoting" (violence as a demonstration of worth, toughness, or status), and "reputation defending" (aggressive violence in order to sustain public recognition).

These categories suggest that feelings of being personally attacked or challenged are extremely important in the violence scenario. The movement toward physical violence that characterizes the assault sequence is promoted by intrapersonal events on the offender's side related to evaluations of the self and to affective responses to being touched, given orders, and subjected to restraint. On the other side of the transaction, many observers have commented that police officers are often highly sensitive to the lack of respect shown them (Richardson, 1974).

## Summary

From these various studies of the aggressive male, at various ages and in various settings, we obtain a fairly consistent characterization, the central feature of which is his proclivity to react to punishment or the threat of punishment with counteraggression. In addition, he is emotionally aroused by these events and acts impulsively, with little regard for possible retaliation. Finally, the aggressive male is easily provoked due to his sensitivity to actions on the part of others that can be interpreted as belittling or demeaning and because his expectation of hostility from others leads him to exaggerate the intentionality of others' behavior that affects his interests adversely.

## The State of Susceptibility to Impulsive Aggression

We now shift our focus from a kind of person to a kind of psychological state. This is a state that promotes the kind of angry, impulsive, reactive aggression described above. Our purpose is to show that many of us who would not qualify as "aggressive males" can, under the proper conditions, attain a state in which we too are prone to impulsive aggression: aroused, sensitive to the personally demeaning implications of events, seeing intentionality behind others' negative behavior, oriented to injuring the source of annoyance, and thoughtless of the consequences.

The relevant evidence comes from studies of unselected samples of children, college students, young couples, and so on—samples that presumably include the normal range of predisposition to aggression. In general, these studies reveal the tendencies of ordinary men to increase their aggression in response to the same factors that stimulate the aggressive male. The laboratory studies in this area are especially useful in testing the causal roles that various cognitive and affective processes play in aggression and in revealing the interplay among them. They enable us to move beyond the mere description of the pattern of thoughts, feelings, and behavior of the aggressive person and to draw conclusions about which component processes contribute causally to the pattern and how the various processes work together to promote aggression.

### Provocations to Aggression

As we have seen, interpersonal aggression consists of behavior that harms another person, that is carried out intentionally, and that is inappropriate normatively. The evidence is very clear that the most effective instigation to aggression *is* aggression, that is, an intentional, harmful, counternormative act.

It is our common experience that a physical attack resulting in pain will elicit an aggressive reaction from many men. However, and as we also know from daily life, pain that is delivered accidentally (without intention) or with good intentions results in little aggression. In the laboratory, the role of intention (e.g., knowingly versus unknowingly) has been shown clearly by Nickel (1974), and the role of good versus bad intention (e.g., in the victim's or society's interests versus serving the attacker's personal purposes) by Rule and Nesdale (1976).

The intent behind and appropriateness of another person's behavior usually affect the reaction to it more than the injury it causes. Questionnaire studies show that when there is intent and norm deviation, the action is judged "aggressive" and deserving of sanctions pretty much regardless of the degree of injury (Loepscher et al., 1984). An experiment by Greenwell and Dengerink (1973) is noteworthy for its attempt to distinguish between the pain actually experienced by the victim and that intended by the attacker. Counteraggression closely tracked the latter but was not responsive to the former. It appears that even minor aversive events can elicit aggression if they are attributed to hostile, inappropriate intentions of the provocateur.

The most common method used to elicit aggression in the laboratory is to have one person (a confederate) insult the other one (the subject). This is done on the pretext that the confederate is rendering an evaluation of something the subject has done, and the insult consists of belittling the subject's intelligence, competence, or sophistication (e.g., Hartmann, 1969; Zillman and Bryant, 1974). It appears that in discovering the efficacy of the insult as a provocation to aggression, the experimenters have zeroed in on the same stimulus class to which the aggressive male has been found to be oversensitive.

Under our principle that the main stimulus to aggression is aggression, how does a verbal insult serve to elicit aggression? It is obviously intended to harm the target and is, by definition, unwarranted from the target's perspective. The essence of an insult is its failure to recognize the worth of the target and his deservingness of considerate treatment. In that sense, it attacks his self-esteem. (The negative criticism with which the target agrees would probably not be considered an insult.) In a broader sense, the insult denies the target what he deserves in social exchanges. The "harm," then, is not necessarily immediate or physical but is often in the unfair treatment and lack of respect it promises the target for the future.

It is worth noting here that, as illustrated by the excerpt from Luckenbill in Table 12.2, scenarios of criminal homicide almost always begin with insulting and name-calling verbal exchange before they move to the level of physical violence. And as the "playing the dozens" scenario illustrates, the participants often have no sense of being able to escape from the process before it leads to its terrible conclusion.

If the main instigator to aggression is aggression, where does the process begin? The answer is undoubtedly found in the ambiguity of the three defining criteria for "aggression": harm, intention, and inappropriateness. Interaction moves out of the vaguely bounded realm of the "assertive" but normatively appropriate pursuit of one's interests and into the equally vague category of "aggression" as it passes ill-defined thresholds on those three dimensions. These ambiguities are probably especially great for verbal exchanges, which, with their implied belittlement and devaluative innuendoes, have their importance largely in what they predict for the future of the relationship. Characterization of the "escalation" process must be made in terms of the details of these meanings, the fuzzy boundaries of their categories, and the many kinds of cues by which they are located in their categories.

## Arousal and Emotion

Our common experience tells us that the aggressive person is "aroused" or "stirred up." We see his flushed face, clenched fists, and other signs of muscular tension, and we relate these signs to introspections about our own internal experiences when angry, which include (per Averill, 1982) general tension, restlessness, frowning, flushing or rise in temperature, and shaky, cracking voice. Descriptions of violent interactions almost always include references to the participants' states of arousal.

Experiments clearly show the importance of physiological arousal in aggression. The insulted or blocked person shows increased levels on various physiological measures (Hokanson and Burgess, 1962a,b). Experiments also show that arousal is not a mere epiphenomenon of the aggression process, but rather plays a necessary causal role in it. The most compelling evidence on this point comes from studies of the effects of various types of irrelevant arousal (Zillman, 1983; Konecni, 1975). In the standard research design, the subject is insulted by a confederate and then, under the pretext of having to teach the confederate in a learning task by delivering shocks for his errors, the subject has an opportunity to punish him in varying degrees. Following the provocation but before the teaching session, the subject is aroused by extraneous means, for example, strenuous physical exercise, erotic movies or reading material, violent movies, loud sounds, and pain. The results of many studies show that the arousal produced by such extraneous procedures increases the level of shocks the subjects deliver to the confederate.

Zillman and Bryant have further shown that the person need not be aroused *at the time of aggression* for these two factors to encourage aggression. Rather, as long as provocation occurs immediately before or during arousal, aggression is still facilitated, even when the individual's level of arousal has returned to that of a control group (Zillman and Bryant, 1974), or when a week has elapsed since the provocation and arousal (Bryant and Zillman, 1979). Thus, provocation and arousal can encourage aggression even after arousal has subsided or a considerable amount of time has elapsed since the provocative event.

The effect of arousal is markedly affected by the aroused person's thoughts. In keeping with Schachter's two-factor theory of emotion (Schachter, 1964), the "anger" depends on *both* the physiological state and the accompanying cognitions. Arousal by itself has little effect on aggression. The subject must also be provoked (Zillman, 1983), and the provocation must be (per the criteria of injury, intention, and inappropriateness) one deserving of retaliation. For example, it must be caused by the partner and not by a mechanical failure (Berkowitz, 1981). Furthermore, if the subject realizes that the arousal is due to an extraneous stimulus (e.g., the erotic material), it has no effect (Geen, Rakosky, and Pigg, 1972). So the person must explain the arousal in terms of the provocation and not link it to the extraneous experience.

In procedures similar to that above, extraneous arousal has also been shown to affect *self-reports* of anger (Geen, Rakosky, and Pigg, 1972). More important, it also seems to work the other way, that inducing a person to label himself as "angry" will lead him to deliver stronger shocks to the provoker. (However, the latter seems to work only up to a point. If the person believes he is more angry than is appropriate, he will tend to curtail his aggression [Berkowitz and Turner, 1974].) Individual differences in susceptibility to aggression may be explained, in part, by differential tendencies to label one's own autonomic changes in terms of anger rather than, say, anxiety. This suggestion by Durel and Krantz (1985) is supported by some of their results on the type A behavior pattern.

Why is arousal important in the causality of aggression? The usual answer invokes its functional value in mobilizing the individual to attack enemies, enabling feats of strength and promoting disregard of possible dangers. A nonfunctional answer is provided by Zillman, Bryant, Cantor, and Day (1975): ". . . the cognitively mediated inhibition of retaliatory behavior is impaired at high levels of sympathetic arousal and anger"

(p. 291). Their study shows specifically that arousal interferes with taking account of the mitigating circumstances behind another person's aversive behavior.

## Alcohol and Aggression

We will not review the broad literature on drugs and aggression, but merely remark on a few of those relating to the most widely used drug, alcohol. Alcohol is present in 60 to 65 percent of homicidal interactions (either the victim, offender, or both) and in assaults on police (Wolfgang, 1958; Meyer et al., 1978). Causal interpretations of these data are not possible because all sorts of personal and social factors may contribute both to alcohol use and to the constellation of circumstances that result in violent interaction (e.g., both alcohol and weapons are present in the home). However, laboratory studies show alcohol's clear causal role in aggression. One drink has no effect or even serves to depress aggression. Three drinks substantially increase aggressiveness. However, alcohol in itself is not sufficient to elicit aggression. In much the same way that physiological arousal has little effect without provocation, alcohol enhances aggression only if there is some provocation (Taylor et al., 1979).

The *intra*personal processes involved are not clear. Taylor and Leonard (1983) believe that alcohol has its effects through its known ability to impair complex cognitive processes. More specifically, they suggest that it increases misinterpretation of other persons' behavior and interferes with anticipations of guilt or punishment. There is some intriguing though disputed experimental evidence that people led to believe they have ingested alcohol become more aggressive even though in fact they have drunk only flavored water (Lang et al., 1975). This suggests that some people may use alcohol as an excuse for aggression. Furthermore, knowing about its effects, it is not unlikely that people sometimes deliberately drink in order to prepare themselves for aggressive interactions.

## Attributions and Beliefs

We have already seen that the course of aggression is affected by perceptions of others' intentions and of the meaning of one's arousal. According to Dodge (1985), the aggressive boy is characterized by a tendency to see intentionality behind others' aversive actions where it does not exist. A similar tendency among college students is indicated by Forsterling's evidence (1984) that people who report being angered by the negative events in their lives tend also to believe that other people could control such events.

This tendency is consistent with actor–partner attributional discrepancies that have been found in typical young couples (Orvis, Kelley, and Butler, 1976). When one person (the actor) has harmed or offended the other, the victim explains the event in terms of the actor's personal characteristics (poor judgment, lack of ability, irresponsibility) or negative attitudes toward the victim (lack of concern, selfishness). In contrast, the actor explains the offensive behavior in terms of good intentions or extenuating circumstances and states. Thus, the victim's explanations often imply intentionality whereas the actor's "excuses" often portray unintentional behavior, done because of external circumstances or temporary uncontrollable internal states. It is impossible to know where the truth lies in these disagreements over intentionality and good versus bad intentions. However, the point is that in their interactions in close relationships, run-of-the-mill persons tend to see more bad intentionality behind *others'* aversive actions than behind their *own* similar actions.

This bias is more common in "distressed" relationships (married couples with poor marital adjustment scores and/or seeking counseling) than in normal ones. Members of distressed couples, as compared with nondistressed couples, are more likely to attribute their partner's negative behaviors to internal factors (Jacobson et al., 1985) and to see the partner's behavior as more negative than the partner intended it to be (Gottman et al., 1976).

In the previous sections we saw the important roles that arousal (extraneously produced and possibly below the actor's level of awareness) and provocation play in instigating aggression in "normal" persons. The research on attribution discussed here demonstrates the ease with which negative behaviors are interpreted as intentional and, therefore, provocative, in close relationships that are experiencing active conflict. The obvious implication is that as relationships deteriorate (i.e., as they move along a continuum from friendly to hostile), it becomes easier for persons to view unfavorable intentions and negative attitudes as underlying behaviors that adversely affect them. Thus, under these conditions it may be easier for the average person to slip into the characteristic mind-set of the aggressive male (aroused and sensitive to threats and insults) than he or she realizes.

## Victim's Pain and Suffering

The aggressive male has little empathy for his victims and feels little guilt or pity after attacking them. Experimental research has identified a number of conditions increasing aggressiveness that probably have part or all of their effect through reductions in potential aggressors' responsiveness to the emotional expressions of their victims.

*Diffusion of Responsibility*

Experimental subjects in groups deliver more shock to targets than do subjects acting individually, and the intensity of the shocks delivered by a group increases over time (e.g., Jaffe, Shapiro, and Yinon, 1981). Subjects serving as "advisers" to other subjects induce the latter to set higher shock levels than subjects delivering the shock directly without advice (Gaebelein and Mander, 1978).

*Anonymity*

Anonymity to the victim and to authorities (Prentice-Dunn and Rogers, 1983; Zimbardo, 1970) results in increased shock levels given to fellow subjects.

*Dehumanizing Labels*

Increased shocks are given when victims are given dehumanizing labels. For example, in Bandura, Underwood, and Fromson (1975) the affective label referred to the victims as "an animalistic, rotten bunch."

Under these various conditions, broad samples of subjects can be disinhibited in their aggression, presumably in much the same way as aggressive men are, through dulling their emotional response to their victims and arousing motivation to succeed in eliciting pain.

## Interpersonal Processes

We have seen how the aggressive male gets caught up in the conflict process. He is distrustful of others, expects hostility from them, and manages to gain confirmation of his expectations through his overreaction to minor events. He interprets minor slights or bragging as implying insult, and he reacts in ways that elicit more explicit aspersions. In general, as Raush's study (1965) suggests, the aggressive male has an aptitude for *creating* an aggressive situation to which he responds with aggression.

Experiments with broad samples of subjects have identified circular or spiraling interpersonal processes that have features in common with those generated by the aggressive male. One such process of self-fulfilling prophecy has been documented in the interactions between cooperative and competitive people. From observations of these interactions, Kelley and Stahelski (1970) found that the former often quickly begin to behave in a manner indistinguishable from the latter, that is, the cooperative person begins to act "competitively." The reason is that the cooperative person acts to defend himself against the competitor's exploitation and the behavioral repertoires do not permit clear distinctions between defensive and aggressive actions (Miller and Holmes, 1975). The consequence of the cooperator's rapid behavioral assimilation to the competitor is that the competitor is unaware that his actions are causing it and mistakes the cooperator for a competitive person like himself. Of course, the cooperative person is fully aware of what has transpired and recognizes their different goals in the relationship.

It can be easily seen that as this pattern is repeated in their lives, cooperators and competitors will develop quite different beliefs about people's orientations to social life. A cooperative person will learn that there are both cooperative persons like himself (from his occasional encounters with them) and competitive people (against whom he has to defend himself). However, the competitive person will experience only "competitive" people, some of whom are genuinely so and some of whom, as the research shows, are made to appear so by his own actions toward them. Kelley and Stahelski were able to find considerable evidence consistent with this idea, that cooperative people are aware of individual differences in cooperativeness–competitiveness, but competitive people think the world is almost wholly populated by others like themselves. It seems fairly obvious that competitors' beliefs about other people serve to justify their continued competitiveness and, therefore, are highly resistant to disconfirmation, much as the aggressive boy's belief that others are hostile toward him operates to confirm itself through the interaction process to which it gives rise.

## Summary

Normal nonaggressive people have tendencies, under certain circumstances, to become like the aggressive male. Like aggressive boys, they are inclined to ascribe the aversive behavior of their associates to intentionality and negative attitudes. They are susceptible to provocation, as by personal insults, and given physiological arousal, even from an irrelevant source, their likelihood of aggressive behavior is increased. Given appropriate social settings and derogatory labeling of their potential victims, they seem less inhibited than usual by thoughts of their victims' pain and suffering. Like aggressive males, they are readily caught up in circular interpersonal processes in which their preconceptions about others lead them to act in ways that elicit evidence confirming those preconceptions, this occurring without their insight into the self-fulfilling nature of their beliefs.

## Avoiding the Aggressive Male Syndrome

Here we ask how we ourselves can avoid becoming "aggressive males" in our relationships with others. Relevant to this question are various procedures that have been used to help persons subjected to interpersonal provocations, for example, police officers, control their anger. As noted before, these procedures have two possible implications for international relations: (1) National decision makers may employ them to avoid the possibility that they themselves will act like "aggressive males" in times of crisis. (2) The procedures suggest facts that decision makers may wish to make clear to their counterparts in order to show that they have not lapsed into the "aggressive male" syndrome, but rather can be counted on to control their anger and deal rationally and impersonally with conflict.

The previous section has summarized some of the main conditions promoting the aggressive male syndrome. These conditions imply the procedures effective in preventing its occurrence. The procedures are clearly illustrated by Novaco's methods for helping people deal with severe anger problems (1975, 1977, 1985). These methods have been used successfully both with occupational groups, such as police officers, who are subject to interpersonal provocations and at risk for anger, and with patients having anger problems. Characterized as a cognitive behavioral intervention, Novaco's method deals with arousal, cognitive processes, and social skills. It is a highly eclectic package of procedures, adapted from a number of other clinical researchers with various theoretical perspectives.

First, the trainees are taught to explicitly monitor their states of physiological *arousal* and to recognize the early signs of high activation (fast breathing, strong and fast heartbeat). They are taught to slow down the process and to use deep breathing and muscle relaxation techniques that are known to reduce arousal.

Second, the *cognitive* control aspects of the program emphasize that certain kinds of thoughts are likely to produce anger (per the general notion that our thoughts affect our feelings). Persons are taught to identify the kinds of things they think and say to themselves in provocative situations and are given opportunities to rehearse types of self-statements that better enable them to cope with such situations. Examples are: "Don't assume the worst, and don't jump to conclusions." "Don't take it personally; it could have happened to someone else." "Don't attach undue significance to what the other is doing." "My anger is a signal of what I need to do. Time to talk to myself." "If I find myself getting upset, I'll know what to do."

Talking to oneself in this manner serves to focus the person's attention on his state of arousal and agitation and to deal with the provocation in a realistic way, without erroneous thoughts about why the provocateur is doing what he is. One important purpose of such self-statements is to prevent the provoked person from becoming obsessed with hurting the provocateur and to encourage thought about the potential consequences of losing control. Another purpose is to modify the exaggerated importance the person may attach to particular events. Feeling ineffectual in dealing with the situation is forestalled by self-statements of confidence in one's ability to handle it. Empathy with the other person is also encouraged. Perhaps most importantly, self-statements help the person focus on the problem to be solved and to execute effective problem-solving responses.

Finally, Novaco recommends assertion training, as a means of improving *skills* in handling stressful confrontations and as a set of alternatives to blowing up. The trainees are provided with the skills necessary for them to feel confident that they can handle the situation. For example, they are taught ways of expressing their feelings without offending others. A simple kind of skill training, shown by Sykes and Brent (1975) to be effective for police, is to respond to another person's noncompliance by simply repeating the request. Doing so in a civil manner was found to increase compliance and reduce violent resistance. These authors emphasize that successful police–civilian interactions require that officers exercise leadership and this assumes they can talk effectively and do on-the-spot problem-solving. Without such skills, the officer is prone to fall back on his or her authority and to become aggressive out of frustration with the interpersonal task. More complex skills entail the use of humor, which serves both to reduce the actor's arousal and to take the edge off the confrontation.

In Novaco's tripartite approach (arousal, cognition, skills) it is apparent that cognitive activities hold center stage. They function in relation both to the control of arousal and to the planning and maintenance of effective behavior. Thus the approach focuses on cognitive regulatory processes. What a person thinks and says to himself is assumed to play a crucial role in his efficacy in controlling and redirecting the energies and actions usually played out in aggressive explosions.

## Implications

As applied to national decision makers, Novaco's and similar procedures for avoiding angry, irrational states call our attention to the importance of arousal, thoughts and words, and social skills. Arousal and feelings should be monitored, with concern for arousal caused by extraneous sources (e.g., domestic criticism, the strains on one's patience, the crisis-induced

# The "Aggressive Male" Syndrome

stress) and the possibility of its being unwittingly attributed to anger-justifying provocations. If possible, things should be slowed down, so that arousal may subside.

Decision makers should carefully regulate what they say to themselves and to others, out of regard for its effects on their own feelings and attitudes. Hostile, distancing labels for their opposite numbers are to be avoided, as are labels for one's own feelings that may increase anger. Thoughts about the others' intentions should be carefully scrutinized and checked. Feelings of being personally attacked or belittled should be brought into the open and identified as to their irrelevance to the concrete problem. Thinking should be extended beyond the immediate situation and action, to include the more distant courses of action and their consequences. Goals for resolution of the crisis should be thought about realistically, so one doesn't feel helpless about attaining them. Similarly, the opponent should be thought about in realistic terms—as probably being tractable, as likely to act inadvertantly in ways that are easily interpreted as deliberate, and so on. The opponent's interests and sensitivities should be explicitly considered and actions taken that leave him a graceful exit without loss of face.

The requisite "social" skills are primarily those of communication—making intentions clearly known; avoiding confusing and mixed messages, as through parallel channels; repetition of messages with awareness that their understanding may be impeded by emotional processes on the other side, and so forth. It is important (but difficult to ensure) that the actors not feel helpless in the situation and that they realize that the difficulties inherent in the process impinge upon both sides.

Finally, the preceding suggestions have implications for communication about the conflict process and about how one is handling it. The purpose is to make clear to the other side that one is *not* developing the aggressive male syndrome. For example, communication during a crisis should certainly contain tacit or explicit acknowledgment of the shared risks of errors in perceived intentions. As a further example, it can often be demonstrated that decisions are being made at a deliberate pace, without high emotionality and with attention to the long-range interests of both parties.

## Interaction History of Aggression

We now examine the early interaction experiences of boys who become aggressive males. We will see that aggressive individuals both are shaped by deficits in their interactional environments and, in the long run, unwittingly act to maintain or strengthen those deficits.

We shift here from the compressed time span of the acute conflict crisis to the historical perspective of the broad course of a conflictful relationship. As noted earlier, an aggressive encounter usually occurs in the context of a history of interaction and takes its meaning and draws its dynamics from that context. Any useful analysis of deterrence phenomena must take account of the extended interaction process and its residues that constitute the historical context of a particular challenge and threat episode.

The developmental history of the "aggressive male" is of possible relevance to the international scene in several ways: (1) It provides a metaphor for patterns of international interaction that may suggest useful conceptual parallels for international relations experts. (2) It suggests the terms in which to analyze a national leader's experiences with his counterparts for the purpose of anticipating his response to provocations they may provide. (3) In a highly speculative vein, it may even be suggested that the history of the aggressive male provides a possible analytic framework for psychohistorical studies of national figures, with an eye to estimating their susceptibility to the aggressive male pattern. (4) The interactional experiences disposing a person to the aggressive male pattern may have implications for desirable extended patterns of interaction with one's counterparts. After our review of the developmental literature, we will briefly pursue this last possibility, that it suggests how we might avoid having another person with whom we must interact adopt the aggressive male syndrome.

## The Interactional Antecedents of Male Aggressiveness

The developmental history of any human tendency is obviously a very complex matter. Yet the literature in developmental psychology provides a rather consistent view of those broad features of a boy's early experience that dispose him to be aggressive. In their classic work, Sears, Maccoby, and Levin (1957) found evidence for three major factors: (1) the mother's coldness, (2) her permissiveness toward aggression, and (3) her use of harsh physical punishment. Later work has continued to emphasize these three factors. For example, in Olweus's recent work (1984), he finds evidence for a causal path model in which (1) the mother's negative emotional attitude toward the boy contributes directly to his aggressiveness and also (2) contributes indirectly through her and the father's use of "power assertive" methods of discipline, and (3) her permissiveness toward aggression contributes directly to the boy's aggressiveness. It appears that the aggressive boy comes from a setting in which the mother is cold toward and rejecting of him. She also has a tolerant or lax attitude toward the boy's aggression, but, on the other hand, she and/or the father use strong threats and physical punishment in dealing with him. Olweus also finds some indication that the aggressive boy's "active and hot-headed" temperament contributes to his development, partly through its effect on the mother's permissiveness toward aggression, perhaps because he wears her down.

Olweus notes that, by and large, his work and that of two other sets of investigators (McCord, McCord, and Howard, 1961; Lefkowitz, Eron, Walder, and Huesmann, 1977) are consistent with Sears, Maccoby, and Levin's conclusions regarding mother's coldness, permissiveness toward child's aggression, and use of physical means of discipline. Perry and Bussey (1984) summarize this literature as follows: "Studies of child-rearing correlates of aggressive and antisocial behavior paint a consistent picture. Aggressive children tend to come from homes in which the parents are rejecting, disinterested in their children's development, lacking in warmth and affection, indifferent or permissive toward their children's expression of aggression, and—when they do discipline their children—prefer power assertion, especially physical punishment, over love-oriented discipline and reasoning . . ." (p. 217).

A more detailed picture of the interaction and learning processes that occur under these conditions is provided by Patterson's extensive studies, mentioned earlier (1979, 1985). He has observed preadolescent aggressive boys as they interact at home with parents and siblings and at school with their peers. Patterson's results show that at home (1) the aggressive boy is exposed to low rates of positive consequences (e.g., approval) and high rates of aversive stimulation (scolding, negative commands, disapproval, humiliation, ignoring, etc.) and (2) the boy responds aggressively to these events (yelling, whining, negativism, failing to comply, crying, hitting). Examination of the sequences of such exchanges reveals that the boy's aggressive reaction is often negatively reinforced, that is, strengthened through the subsequent termination of the others' aversive behavior. A typical pattern is an extended coercive interchange in which, to quote Patterson, "the problem child quickly escalated to maximum intensity. He remained at that level until the other person withdrew. Mothers, on the other hand, tended to introduce aversive responses late in the interchange and then quickly to terminate their aversive involvement" (1979, p. 144).

The upshot of this kind of interaction experience is that, as compared with normal boys, the interaction between aggressive boys and other family members is characterized by longer chains of aggressive exchange. As the sequences become more extended, the amplitude of the aggressive behavior increases, with physical attacks becoming more likely. (Most of the hitting occurs in interaction with siblings, so they probably play a key role in training the aggressive boy in physical fighting.) Perhaps the most significant aspect of what the aggressive boy learns is persistence in the face of counteraggression. Patterson lists several studies showing that, as he says, "the coercive child, in contrast to the normal child, tends to *accelerate* ongoing aggression when punished . . . " (1979, p. 137).

From his interactionist perspective, Patterson considers the effect of these sequences on *both* parties to the exchange. He describes the "reinforcement trap" constituted by the process. When the mother "gives in," it increases the likelihood that the child's coercive behavior will occur on future occasions. However, when she gives in, she also experiences negative reinforcement, because the child discontinues its aversive behavior. Thus, the coercive agent (the boy) trains the victim (the mother) in submission, whereas the victim trains the coercer in the use of aggressive actions.

When the process is viewed from the mother's side, Patterson's analysis reveals several important phenomena: (1) She is ineffectual in her discipline, unwittingly training the boy to increase the intensity of his aggression, (2) her disciplinary ineptitude is enhanced by her tendency to desist in aggressive exchanges and let the boy have the last aggressive burst, (3) she lets herself in for a good deal of aggravation from the boy to which she undoubtedly reacts with irritation and anger, and (4) she thereby probably becomes less effective in providing a positive emotional environment for the boy and more susceptible to being caught up in coercive spirals with him.

In general, Patterson's process results are consistent with the correlational studies mentioned before, and, in fact, his work suggests the role that the aggressive boy himself plays in constructing and maintaining the aggression-inducing conditions. As parallels to the three factors of coldness, permissiveness toward aggression, and parental use of coercive discipline, we may draw the following conclusions from Patterson's work: (1) The boy is in a social environment poor in positive consequences but rich in aversive stimulation (e.g., lack of attention, disapproval, negative demands). This environment probably becomes more aversive as it reacts to his learning to use aggression to eliminate annoyances. (2) The boy's aggression is dealt with ineffectually. He is allowed to get aggressive interchanges under way, to increase the intensity of his coercive behaviors, and, sometimes, to have the experience of winning out in the escalating interchange. (3) In general, the other family members use coercive means of interpersonal influence. And in reaction to the boy's growing use of aggression to deal with interpersonal problems, there is likely to be (to quote Patterson) "escalations in the intensity and rate of pain control techniques used by the parents" (1979, p. 142).

Outside the home, the aggressive boy continues to use coercive means of dealing with people. Patterson and Cobb (1971) suggest that aggression in peer and school settings is sustained more for its value in gaining desired rewards than in serving to remove annoyances. Acts of aggression gain attention for the boy and even teachers' scoldings serve to reward his disruptiveness. A social consequence of the continued aggressive pattern is rejection by his peers (Patterson, Dishion, and Bank, 1984), which results in a restriction of his opportunities to learn social skills. In the classroom, the aggressive pattern interferes with studying and classwork and contributes to poor intellectual development. On the last point, Huesmann and Eron (1984) find from a 22-year longitudinal study that aggression at age 8 predicts age 30 intellectual achievement even when the effects of IQ at age 8 are removed.

It is perhaps in these last phenomena that we find the basis for the aggressive male's sensitivity to insult and devaluation. His interaction with the parents, with its disapproval and grudging attention, provides little basis for high self-esteem. He may also develop a sense of himself as a "bad boy," gain some pride from his success as that type of person, and find models for it in TV violence. At school and with his peers, other bases for self-esteem, such as social skills or intellectual accomplishments, are likely to be absent. In short, aggressiveness operates to create and sustain a bad reputation and a self-image in which the positive elements have a very shaky basis.

Following Patterson's example, we have emphasized the interaction processes that give rise to and support the aggressive boy's use of coercion and resistance to deterrence. It must be admitted that this overlooks some of the key individual factors that probably play crucial roles in this developmental history. We mentioned Olweus's evidence that the boy's "active and hot-headed" temperament is a contributing factor. Recent work suggests that boys who are high in activity level provoke their parents into using physical punishment (Perry and Bussey, 1984). Similarly, the irritability (susceptibility to arousal) of both the boy and the mother is probably implicated in the developmental scenario.

## Avoiding Encouraging Others' Aggressiveness

Earlier we noted that the interactional history of the aggressive male may suggest extended patterns of interaction that may encourage national leaders to exhibit the aggressive male syndrome. We will pursue this line of thought only briefly, as we consider the history's implications for the principles one party can follow in order to avoid the development of aggressiveness in his or her counterparts.

As we have seen, the literature on the family history of aggressive boys suggests that the combination of coldness, permissiveness toward aggression, and physical punishment is to be avoided. The desirable relationship, then, is one of "warmth" (where possible, positive interchange, personal recognition, and acknowledgment of legitimate needs), an intolerant attitude toward use of aggression, and, where possible, use of disciplinary means other than physical force.

At the core of these recommendations is the question of effective discipline, and a central problem there concerns the effective use of punishment. It is generally agreed that punishment is effective in deterring aggressive behavior when it is applied quickly, strongly, and consistently. Furthermore, the elimination of the undesirable behavior will be most dependable and enduring when the aggressor is provided with alternative means to achieve his goals (e.g., Carr and Lovaas, 1983). We may note that consistency is both very important (inconsistent punishment is not only ineffective but often yields negative behavior that is very resistant to new punishment schedules or to extinction [Duer and Parke, 1970; Parke and Duer, 1972]), but also involves some very difficult problems (e.g., preventing escape from surveillance; avoiding the appearance of arbitrariness).

The ineffectual discipline of the aggression-training mother violates all of these principles: She is erratic and inconsistent, she is often too mild in her initial response, she doesn't follow through consistently with her demands and insist that they be met, and she only grudgingly provides the positive rewards the boy needs (Patterson, Dishion, and Bank, 1984). She finds her counterpart in the ineffectual classroom teacher who is not "with it," that is, not able to keep track of what the pupils are doing, with the result that she often tunes in to a disruption too late, after it has spread and increased in seriousness, and often scolds an imitator rather than the initiator of the breach (Kounin, 1970).

The preceding comments are too vague to afford any kind of detailed prescription for effective discipline. However, they do point to the necessity of close tracking of the succession of events that constitute the interaction between persons with conflicting interests. In fact, an important feature of the "parenting skills" programs derived from Patterson's and similar research is training parents to observe and record the details of interaction process. For example, they are taught to pinpoint and track the course of tantrums. The essential point here is that subtle details of interaction process have, over time, major cumulative effects. As Patterson writes: "From this perspective, anger and other emotions are the product of a complex process involving subtle interactional patterns that individuals are often not tracking" (1985, p. 97).

Disciplinarians often resort either to ineffectual verbal "nattering" or, at the other extreme, to harsh physical punishment because other means of punishment and behavior shaping are more difficult or less convenient. In the family and school settings, the better alternatives include providing occasions of "time out" (during which, to interrupt a tantrum, the child is physically isolated or otherwise restrained from aggressive action), withholding privileges (and restoring them later as rewards for good behavior), and inattention to and disregard of the aggression (which often requires unusual self-control inasmuch as aggression is "coercive" in eliciting a response). Withholding attention has been shown effective, as a form of "extinction" therapy, in dealing with mild forms of aggression by small children (e.g., Brown and Elliott, 1965; Williams, 1959), but it is not feasible, of course, if the aggressive behavior is objectively intolerable.

It is generally agreed that aggressive behavior is best eliminated by procedures that incorporate training in alternative ways of achieving legitimate goals. This often requires the parents to shift from their usual reinforcement schedules that are impoverished in positive rewards to schedules that include a variety of social and consumable reinforcers. Because such rewards are potentially available from many quarters of the boy's environment, he is likely also to profit from training in the social skills necessary to gain them. It seems that an important part of this training is in assertiveness, that is, in methods of stating his requests in socially acceptable ways and of dealing with others' "demands" in nonhostile ways. A number of studies have shown that assertion training is useful in enabling individuals to bring their aggression under control (Carr and Binkoff, 1981).

The problems of how to avoid encouraging another person to develop an aggressive orientation to your interaction are extremely complex. There is probably no substitute for close analysis of the interaction process with an objective eye to the affective states, attitudes, and attributions it stimulates and promotes. In the area of preventing and dealing with the aggressive male syndrome, there is a great deal more art than science in the procedures experts recommend and use. At the same time, there is an emerging consensus (or so it seems to us) about the proper broad perspective on the problem. This perspective provides an appropriate note on which to end our review.

This perspective is characterized by an apparent antinomy the nature of which is suggested by some of the contrasts mentioned above: warm but not permissive of aggression, providing avenues of positive reward but punishing bad behavior. Further such contrasts are to be found in characterizations of effective treatment programs. For example, in Agee's report (1979) of a successful residential program for destructive adolescents we find these contrasts: a program of concerned control, confrontive but supportive groups, constructively cynical group leaders. The contrast is also implied in the use of assertion training in the treatment of aggression.

It is not too farfetched to find the same apparent antinomy expressed in various procedures that have been shown effective in laboratory research as means of influencing exploitative persons. As an example, consider the tit-for-tat strategy, found empirically to be effective in increasing cooperation in the Prisoners' Dilemma game (Oskamp, 1971) and shown by Axelrod (1984) to be effective in tournaments among competing strategies of interaction. This procedure is characterized by a "positive" side (optimism about the relationship, quick forgiveness) but also by a "negative" side (intolerance of exploitative behavior).

Finally, the general principle is well known to practicing negotiators. It is clearly illustrated by Pruitt's principle (derived from experimental studies of bargaining and confirmed by real negotiators' experience) of being "firm but conciliatory" (Pruitt and Rubin, 1986). We are advised to be firm about our own basic interests but conciliatory toward others through responsiveness to their basic interests. A key feature of being conciliatory is being flexible about how one's interests are to be achieved, in order to have maximum likelihood of reconciling them with others' interests. Thus, Pruitt also describes the policy as one of "firm flexibility"—firm goals but flexible means (Pruitt and Rubin, 1986).

The conflict among the guidelines in these recommendations is, of course, more apparent than real. The contrasting features reflect the complexities—the dilemmas—of relationships that involve both conflicting and common interests (the so-called mixed-motive games). The trick is in applying the complex, double-sided principle to specific situations. The validity of the principle, which can hardly be denied, requires that we avoid simplistic metaphors of our relations with persons in relation to whom we have mixed interests. We must not treat "them" as either our "friends" or our "enemies." It also requires careful analysis, statement, and restatement of both parties' interests and of the gradations from basic, enduring interests to more instrumental and transient ones. Finally, it requires close attention to the ebb and flow of interaction, with a clear-headed view of its implications for one's own interests and an equally clear-headed but empathic understanding of its implications for the other side.

## Concluding Remarks

We conclude our review not with concrete recommendations but with a perspective on the "problem"—the antinomic perspective of "firm but flexible." This perspective will be no news to international theorists and practitioners, though they may find it interesting to see how it appears and is played out in the interpersonal domain. The perspective implies, of course, the partial truth of principles advanced by both "conservatives" ("If we let them get away with it this time, we'll never have credibility with them again") and "liberals" ("We must recognize their legitimate claims and give them opportunities to achieve them"). Reconciling such contrasting ideas is at the core of the art of diplomacy.

That is not to preclude the scientific study and analysis of these matters. Great headway has been made in the field of interpersonal relations in the various detailed investigations of interaction process. However, specific recommendations, say, about effective parental discipline, would require a far better database about interaction sequences and their accompanying thoughts, feelings, and arousal than presently exists (Gerald Patterson's monumental work notwithstanding). In any case, specific recommendations regarding sequences, reinforcement schedules and patterns, and so on derived from interpersonal research will have only limited usefulness at the national level. Two parents have great difficulty in tracking their interaction with a child and being consistent, verbally and behaviorally, in their discipline. The problems of coordination and consistency mount rapidly in complexity in international interactions, as each nation is represented by many different voices and has a frequently changing cast of actors. Furthermore, the differences between the interpersonal and international levels in the repertoires of influence and control are vast. Yet we believe the parallels between international and interpersonal processes are sufficient to warrant further comparison and analysis, with methods and concepts being translated back and forth between the two levels.

This review has been made from an interpersonal and interactionist perspective, which focuses on the relevant sequences of interaction process and the accompanying intrapersonal events. We have painted in broad strokes a picture of the aggressive male syndrome. In doing so, we have had to simplify a great deal and gloss over many details. So our picture is undoubtedly somewhat more vivid than the literature warrants. We must also note what will be obvious, that the research we have reviewed is almost entirely based on studies conducted in the United States.

We do not intend that this paper be taken to imply that the aggressive male syndrome is likely to figure prominently in international interaction. By virtue of his interpersonal style, the classic aggressive male may not be likely to attain positions of authority or high-level influence. Yet, as we have emphasized, many persons have some potential for manifesting the syndrome under the proper conditions, and many more are probably susceptible to imitating the syndrome when they see it expressed under those conditions. Therefore, we find it plausible to believe that distinctive features of the syndrome will be detectable in many crisis situations. For example, in accounts of the Cuban Missile Crisis (Allison, 1971; Kennedy, 1971; Neustadt and May, 1986), there are indications of early alarm and anger (arousal), Kennedy's taking the issue personally and seeing it as a test of his mettle, and impulses to injurious counteraction simply to get rid of the noxious threat. These symptoms subsided with the passing of time and, in fact, there are intimations of measures taken explicitly to counteract the syndrome—for example, by attempting to slow down the process, by shifting time perspective from what to do immediately to the longer view of how any actions would appear to history, and by taking care in the causal interpretation of a critical aversive event (the downing of a U-2 plane over Cuba, which was interpreted as an inadvertant byproduct of organizational routine rather than as a signal in the crisis interaction). The accounts also reveal thoughts on the U.S. side about possible activation of the syndrome on the Soviet side (e.g., images of Khrushchev drinking and becoming agitated) and measures taken to forestall its effect there (to give him time, to avoid provocation to impulsive action, and to provide a resolution that would avoid his humiliation). The interaction process during this particular crisis was certainly not governed by the syndrome we have described here, but its existence as part of the underlying pattern, particularly in the early stages of the incident, seems to us to be clearly evident.

The final interpretation of such episodes must be left to experts. Our purpose has been to draw upon interpersonal research to add to the interpretive tools available for the analysis of international interaction. We have suggested some of the broad kinds of *possible* implications of interpersonal research for international conflict, deterrence, and so forth. Our intention has been to raise possibilities but not to render judgments as to the degree of relevance of this research to the international level. Those judgments must be left to experts in the international relations field.

## NOTE

We gratefully acknowledge the advice of Prof. Gian Vittorio Caprara, Dipartimento di Psicologia, Universita degli Studi di Roma "La Sapienza," and comments on an early draft by Seymour Feshbach, Department of Psychology, UCLA.

## REFERENCES

Agee, V. L., 1979. *Treatment of the Violent, Incorrigible Adolescent*. Lexington, Mass.: D.C. Heath.
Allison, G. T., 1971. *Essence of Decision: Explaining the Cuban Missile Crisis*. Boston: Little, Brown.
Attili, G., 1986. Concomitants and factors influencing children's aggression. *Aggressive Behavior* 11:291–301.
Averill, J. R., 1982. *Anger and Aggression*. New York: Springer-Verlag.
Axelrod, R., 1984. *The Evolution of Cooperation*. New York: Basic Books.
Baker, R. K., and Ball, S. J., 1969. *Mass Media and Violence*, Volume IX. Washington, D.C.: U.S. Government Printing Office.
Bandura, A., Underwood, B., and Fromson, M. E., 1975. Disinhibition of aggression through diffusion of responsibility and dehumanization of victims. *Journal of Research in Personality* 9:253–69.
Berdie, R. F., 1947."Playing the dozens." *Journal of Abnormal and Social Psychology* 42:120–21.
Berkowitz, L., 1962. *Aggression: A Social Psychological Analysis*. New York: McGraw-Hill.
————— 1978. Is criminal violence normative behavior? *Journal of Research in Crime and Delinquency* 15:148–61.
————— 1981. On the difference between internal and external reactions to legitimate and illegitimate frustrations: A demonstration. *Aggressive Behavior* 7:83–96.
Berkowitz, L., and Turner, C., 1974. Perceived anger level, instigating agent, and aggression. In H. S. London and R. E. Nisbett, eds., *Thought and Feeling: Cognitive Alteration of Feeling States*. Chicago: Aldine.
Brown, P., and Elliot, R., 1965. Control of aggression in a nursery school class. *Journal of Experimental Child Psychology* 2:103–7.
Bryant, J., and Zillman, D., 1979. Effect of intensification of annoyance through unrelated residual excitation on substantially delayed hostile behavior. *Journal of Experimental Social Psychology* 15:470–80.
Carr, E. G., and Binkoff, J., 1981. Self-control. In A. P. Goldstein, E. G. Carr, W. S. Davidson II and P. Wehr, eds., *In Response to Aggression*. New York: Pergamon Press.
Carr, E. G., and Lovaas, O. I., 1983. Contigent shock treatment for behavior problems. In S. Axelrod and J. Apsche, eds., *The Effects of Punishment on Human Behavior*. New York: Academic Press.

Dodge, K. A., 1980. Social cognition and children's aggressive behavior. *Child Development* 51:162–70.
——— 1985. Attributional bias in aggressive children. In P. C. Kendall, ed., *Advances in Cognitive-Behavioral Research and Therapy*, Vol. 4. New York: Academic Press.
Dodge, K. A., and Frame, C. L., 1982. Social cognitive biases and deficits in aggressive boys. *Child Development* 53:620–35.
Duer, J. L., and Parke, R. D., 1970. The effects of inconsistent punishment on aggression in children. *Developmental Psychology* 2:403–11.
Durel, L. A., and Krantz, D. S., 1985. The possible effects of beta-adrenergic blocking drugs on behavioral and psychological concomitants of anger. In M. A. Chesney and R. H. Rosenman, eds., *Anger and Hostility in Cardiovascular and Behavioral Disorders*. Washington, D.C.: Hemisphere.
Eme, R. F., 1979. Sex differences in childhood psychopathology: A review. *Psychological Bulletin* 86:574–95.
Feshbach, S., 1970. Aggression. In P. H. Mussen, ed., *Carmichael's Manual of Child Psychology* (rev. ed.). New York: Wiley.
Forsterling, F., 1984. Importance, causal attributions and the emotion of anger. *Zeitschrift fur Psychologie* 192:425–32.
Gaebelein, J. W., and Mander, A., 1978. Consequences for targets of aggression as a function of aggressor and instigator roles: Three experiments. *Personality and Social Psychology Bulletin* 4:465–68.
Geen, R. G., Rakosky, J. J., and Pigg, R., 1972. Awareness of arousal and its relation to aggression. *British Journal of Social and Clinical Psychology* 11:115–21.
Gelles, R. J., 1972. *The Violent Home*. Beverly Hills, Calif.: Sage Publications.
Gottman, J., Notarius, C., Markman, H., Banks, S., and Yoppi, B., 1976. Behavior exchange theory and marital decision making. *Journal of Personality and Social Psychology* 34:14–23.
Greenwell, J., and H. Dengerink, H., 1973. The role of perceived versus actual attack in human physical aggression. *Journal of Personality and Social Psychology* 26:66–71.
Hartmann, D. P., 1969. Influence of symbolically modeled instrumental aggression and pain cues on aggressive behavior. *Journal of Personality and Social Psychology* 11:280–87.
Hinde, R. A., 1985. Categories of behavior and the ontogeny of aggression. *Aggressive Behavior* 11:333–35.
Hokanson, J. E., and Burgess, M., 1962a. The effects of frustration and anxiety on overt aggression. *Journal of Abnormal and Social Psychology* 65:232–37.
——— 1962b. The effects of three types of aggression on vascular processes. *Journal of Abnormal and Social Psychology* 64:446–49.
Huesmann, L. R., and Eron, L. D., 1984. Cognitive processes and the persistence of aggressive behavior. *Aggressive Behavior* 10:243–51.
Jacobson, N. S., McDonald, D. V., Follette, W. C., and Berley, R. A., 1985.

Attributional processes in distressed and nondistressed married couples. *Cognitive Therapy and Research* 9:35–50.
Jaffe, Y., Shapiro, N., and Yinon, Y., 1981. Aggression and its escalation. *Journal of Cross-Cultural Psychology* 12:21–36.
Kelley, H. H., and Stahelski, A. J., 1970. Social interaction basis of cooperators' and competitors' beliefs about others. *Journal of Personality and Social Psychology* 16:66–91.
Kennedy, R. F., 1971. *Thirteen Days: A Memoir of the Cuban Missile Crisis.* New York: Norton.
Konecni, V. J., 1975. The mediation of aggression behavior: Arousal level versus anger and cognitive labeling. *Journal of Personality and Social Psychology* 32:706–12.
Kounin, J. S., 1970. *Discipline and Group Management in the Classroom.* New York: Holt, Rinehart, and Winston.
Lang, A. R., Goeckner, D. J., Adesso, V. J., and Marlatt, G. A., 1975. Effects of alcohol on aggression in male social drinkers. *Journal of Abnormal Psychology* 84:508–18.
Lefkowitz, M. M., Eron, L. D., Walder, L. O., and Huesmann, L. R., 1977. *Growing up to Be Violent.* New York: Pergamon.
Loeschper, G., Mummendey, A., Linneweber, V., and Bornewasser, 1984. The judgment of behavior as aggressive and sanctionable. *European Journal of Social Psychology* 14:391–404.
Luckenbill, D. D., 1977. Criminal homicide as a situated transaction. *Social Problems* 25:176–86.
Maccoby, E. E., and Jacklin, C. N., 1980. Sex differences in aggression: A rejoinder and reprise. *Child Development* 51:964–80.
McCord, W., McCord, J., and Howard, A., 1961. Familial correlates of aggression in nondelinquent male children. *Journal of Abnormal and Social Psychology* 62:79–93.
Meyer, C. K., Magedanz, T., Kieselhorst, D. C., and Chapman, S. G., 1978. *A Social-Psychological Analysis of Police Assailants.* Norman, Okla.: University of Oklahoma, Bureau of Government Research.
Miller, D. T., and Holmes. J. G., 1975. The role of situational restrictiveness and self-fulfilling prophecies: A theoretical and empirical extension of Kelley and Stahelski's Triangle Hypothesis. *Journal of Personality and Social Psychology* 31:661–73.
Neustadt, R. E., and May, E. R., 1986. *Thinking in Time: The Uses of History for Decision-Makers.* New York: The Free Press.
Nickel, T. W., 1974. The attribution of intention as a critical factor in the relation between frustration and aggression. *Journal of Personality* 42:482–92.
Novaco, R. W., 1975. *Anger Control: The Development and Evaluation of an Experimental Treatment.* Lexington, Mass.: Lexington Books.
——— 1977. Stress inoculation: A cognitive therapy for anger and its application to a case of depression. *Journal of Consulting and Clinical Psychology* 45:600–8.

——— 1985. Anger and its therapeutic regulation. In M. A. Chesney and R. H. Rosenman, eds., *Anger and Hostility in Cardiovascular and Behavioral Disorders*. Washington, D.C.: Hemisphere Publishing.

Olweus, D., 1978. *Aggression in the Schools: Bullies and Whipping Boys*. Washington, D.C.: Hemisphere Publishing.

——— 1984. Development of stable aggressive reaction patterns in males. In R. J. Blanchard and D. C. Blanchard, eds., *Advances in the Study of Aggression*, Vol. 1. New York: Academic Press, pp. 103–37.

Orvis, B. R., Kelley, H. H., and Butler, D., 1976. Attributional conflict in young couples. In J. H. Harvey, W. J. Ickes, and R. F. Kidd, eds., *New Directions in Attribution Research*, Vol. 1. Hillsdale, N.J.: Lawrence Erlbaum Associates, pp. 353–86.

Oskamp, S., 1971. Effects of programmed strategies on cooperation in the Prisoner's Dilemma and other mixed-motive games. *Journal of Conflict Resolution* 15:226–59.

Parke, R. D., and Duer, J. L., 1972. Schedule of punishment and inhibition of aggression in children. *Developmental Psychology* 7:266–69.

Patterson, G. R., 1976. The aggressive child: Victim and architect of a coercive system. In L. A. Homerlynck, L. C. Hardy, and E. J. Mash, eds., *Behavior Modification and Families: Theory and Research*, Vol. 1. New York: Brenner/Mozel.

——— 1979. A performance theory for coercive family interaction. In R. B. Cairns, ed., *The Analysis of Social Interactions: Methods, Issues, and Illustrations*. Hillsdale, N.J.: Lawrence Erlbaum Associates.

——— 1985. Microsocial analysis of anger and irritable behavior. In M. A. Chesney and R. H. Rosenman, eds., *Anger and Hostility in Cardiovascular and Behavioral Disorders*. Washington, D.C.: Hemisphere Publishing.

Patterson, G. R., and Cobb, J. A., 1971. A dyadic analysis of "aggressive" behaviors. In J. P. Hill, ed., *Minnesota Symposium on Child Development*, Vol. 5. Minneapolis: University of Minnesota Press, pp. 72–129.

Patterson, G. R., Dishion, T. J., and Bank, L., 1984. Family interaction: A process model of deviancy training. *Aggressive Behavior* 10:253–67.

Patterson, G. R., Littman, R. A., and Bricker, W., 1967. Assertive behavior in children: A step toward a theory of aggression. *Monographs of the Society for Research in Child Development* 32:1–43.

Perry, D. G., and Bussey, K., 1977. Self-reinforcement in high- and low-aggressive boys following acts of aggression. *Child Development* 48:653–57.

——— 1984. *Social Development*. Englewood Cliffs, N.J.: Prentice-Hall.

Perry, D. G., and Perry, L. C., 1974. Denial of suffering in the victim as a stimulus to violence in aggressive boys. *Child Development* 45:55–62.

Petersen, R. A., 1971. Aggression as a function of expected retaliation and aggression of target of aggressor. *Developmental Psychology* 5:161–66.

Prentice-Dunn, S., and Rogers, R. W., 1983. Deindividuation in aggression. In R. G. Geen and E. Donnerstein, eds., *Aggression: Theoretical and Empirical Review*, Vol. 2. New York: Academic Press, pp. 155–72.

Pruitt, D. G., and Rubin, J. Z., 1986. *Social Conflict: Escalation, Stalemate, and Settlement.* New York: Random House.

Rausch, H. L., 1965. Interaction sequences. *Journal of Personality and Social Psychology* 2:487–99.

Richardson, J. F., 1974. *Urban Police in the United States.* Port Washington, N.Y.: Kennikat Press.

Rule, B. G., and Nesdale, A. R., 1976. Moral judgment of aggressive behavior. In R. G. Geen and E. C. O'Neal, eds., *Perspectives on Aggression.* New York: Academic Press.

Schachter, S., 1964. The interaction of cognitive and physiological determinants of emotional state. In L. Berkowitz, ed., *Advances in Experimental Social Psychology*, Vol. 1. New York: Academic Press.

Sears, R. R., Maccoby, E. E., and Levin, H., 1957. *Patterns of Child Rearing.* Evanston, Ill.: Row, Peterson.

Sykes, R. E., and Brent, E. E., 1975. Strategies of "taking charge" in police–civilian interaction. In J. Kinton, ed., *Police Roles in the Seventies: Professionalization in America.* Aurora, Ill.: Social Science and Sociological Resources.

Taylor, S. P., and Leonard, K. E., 1983. Alcohol and human physical aggression. In R. C. Geen and E. I. Donnerstein, eds., *Aggression: Theoretical and Empirical Review*, Vol. 2. New York: Academic Press, pp. 77–101.

Taylor, S. P., Schmutte, G. T., Leonard, K. E., Jr., and Cranston, J. W., 1979. The effects of alcohol and extreme provocation in the use of highly noxious shock. *Motivation and Emotion* 3:73–81.

Toch, H., 1969. *Violent Men: An Inquiry into the Psychology of Violence.* Chicago: Aldine Publishing.

Vidmar, N., and Ellsworth, P., 1974. Public opinion and the death penalty. *Stanford Law Review* 26:1245–70.

Williams, C. D., 1959. The elimination of tantrum behavior by extinction procedures. *Journal of Abnormal and Social Psychology* 59:269.

Wolfgang, M. E., 1958. *Patterns in Criminal Homicide.* Philadelphia: University of Pennsylvania.

Zillman, D., 1979. *Hostility and Aggression.* Hillsdale, N.J.: Lawrence Erlbaum Associates.

——— 1983. Arousal and aggression. In R. G. Geen and E. I. Donnerstein, eds., *Aggression: Theoretical and Empirical Review*, Vol. 1. New York: Academic Press.

Zillman, D., and Bryant, J., 1974. Effect of residual excitation on the emotional response to provocation and delayed aggressive behavior. *Journal of Personality and Social Psychology* 30:782–91.

Zillman, D., Bryant, J., Cantor, J. R., and Day, K. D., 1975. Irrelevance of mitigating circumstances in retaliatory behavior at high levels of excitation. *Journal of Research in Personality* 9:282–93.

Zimbardo, P., 1970. The human choice: Individuation, reason, and order versus deindividuation, impulse, and chaos. In W. J. Arnold and D. Levine, eds., *Nebraska Symposium on Motivation, 1969*. Lincoln, Nebr.: University of Nebraska Press.

# 13

# Aggressive Behavior in Interpersonal and International Relations

## Dean G. Pruitt

This chapter comments on and expands certain points in Kelley and Schmidt's excellent chapter on aggressive behavior (Chapter 12). In the author's view, the ideas presented here are equally applicable to aggression in interpersonal and international relations. This point will be defended in each section of this chapter.

## Antecedents and Functions of Aggression

Kelley and Schmidt indicate that normal aggressive behavior is often generated by a frustration-aggression mechanism. We tend to retaliate when people frustrate us or otherwise harm our interests. Retaliation is especially vigorous if we make the following interpretations about the agents of our frustration: Their behavior was intended rather than accidental; it was due to their greed or their negative attitudes toward us rather than the pressure of external forces; it was illegitimate; it was unfair to us; it belittled us, putting us below their level or casting doubt on our adequacy or strength.

What functions are served by this pattern of responding? It seems to make most sense as part of a *deterrent posture,* aimed at reducing the likelihood that the same or different people will harm our interests in the future. There is no point in trying to deter others from involuntary behavior or behavior that is dictated by strong environmental pressures. Hence, retaliation should be less vigorous in such circumstances. On the other hand, it is important to retaliate against unfair and illegitimate actions, because these set a bad precedent for the future. And it is especially

287

important to punish others for actions that demean our status or make us look weak, because of the need to avoid the appearance of being an easy target.

The point is that the frustration-aggression mechanism, which all humans share, can be viewed as a credibility-building procedure. In addition, the anger or sense of outrage that often accompanies aggression can be seen as having the function of encouraging people to retaliate even though they may get hurt in doing so. Such retaliation is important for avoiding future threats to themselves and others, however painful may be its short-run consequences.

If the frustration-aggression mechanism is part of a deterrent posture, it follows that this mechanism should be especially prominent in environments where people are in constant danger of being exploited and where third-party functions are weak. People are vulnerable and alone in such settings, defending themselves against a hostile world. Hence, they must cultivate an image of toughness and irritability—of readiness to retaliate at a moment's notice. Such settings are sometimes found in thinly populated frontier areas, such as the American West in the nineteenth century. At the other extreme, many sections of inner city America show a similar pattern.

The international system is another example of such an environment, and the frustration-aggression pattern also seems strong in this setting. Statesmen are eternally watchful for actions that harm the interests of their countries and are usually quick to protest such actions or retaliate against the perpetrators. The point is *not* that statesmen become emotional and strike blindly when their countries are challenged; this type of irritability is probably limited to interpersonal relations. Rather, the point is that statesmen, knowing that the international world is something of a jungle, often feel the necessity to retaliate vigorously against harmful actions from other countries, so as to establish a national reputation for toughness. Given this tendency toward national irritability, it is perhaps not surprising that conflict spirals are so easily started and so persistent in the international arena.

## Misinterpretation and Overreaction

Kelley and Schmidt point out that certain conditions encourage us to misinterpret other people's harmful behavior as intentional, aimed at hurting us, and not due to external pressures. Under these conditions, we are also especially likely to misinterpret ambiguous behavior as harmful to our interests, for example, to see threatening intentions in the construction of an airport on Grenada. Such conditions, therefore, encourage aggression and the conflict spirals that often result from aggression.

First and foremost among these conditions is a deteriorated relationship between the parties—distrust and hostile attitudes, a belief that the other is an enemy. As relationships deteriorate, we become increasingly likely to see the other party as posing a threat and to react aggressively toward that party. This appears to be as true in relations between international rivals as it is in a deteriorating marriage. For example, the shooting down of the Korean airliner over the Soviet Union appears to have been a tragic error of misidentification. Yet, impelled by the traditional American view of the Soviets as the enemy, most Americans saw this incident as evidence of a callous disregard for American interests.

In addition to being more prone to retaliate, people in deteriorated relationships are also less prone to engage in constructive problem solving. This is because of a tendency to blame the conflict on the other party and to exonerate ourselves (Sillars, 1981; Syna, 1984). "Let them solve the problem; they're the ones to blame for it."

Other conditions that encourage misinterpretation and overreaction are weak communication with the other party, which makes it difficult for that party to explain its actions; dehumanizing labels; and irritability due to frustration from other sources (Pruitt and Rubin, 1986).

The points just made suggest that ordinary people and statesmen should be especially alert to the danger of overreacting when they are in a deteriorated relationship, when communication is weak, or when they are frustrated for other reasons.

## Strategies for Mixed-Motive Settings

Kelley and Schmidt argue that strategies for controlling other people's aggression "should be characterized by an apparent antinomy," embodying efforts to set limits but to reward the others within these limits. This advice is useful but a bit too narrow. The antinomy they describe characterizes strategies that are reasonable for dealing with *all mixed-motive situations,* not just those in which other people are being aggressive.

One example of the antinomy is the tit-for-tat strategy championed by Axelrod (1984). The other party is to be punished for infractions and rewarded for conciliatory behavior. Research by psychologists shows that this strategy encourages cooperation in mixed-motive settings (Oskamp, 1971). However, a modified tit-for-tat strategy, involving delays in some rewards and punishments, appears to be superior to the conventional strategy in which all rewards and punishments are immediate. In a study by Bixenstine and Gaebelein (1971), the most effective strategy turned out to be one in which the strategist often delayed retaliation until the other party had defected two or three times. In addition, once having retaliated, the strategist often delayed resumption of reward until the other had cooperated two or three times.[1] The delay in retaliation presumably had the virtue of giving the other party a second chance to correct errors of judgment and of making it clearer that it was the other party and not the strategist who had initiated noncooperation. The delay in resumption of reward probably guarded against exploitation of the strategist. There was no way that the other party could gain a unilateral advantage while the strategist was delaying retaliation and then be quickly reinstated so as to set the strategist up for a new period of exploitation.

A major problem with the tit-for-tat strategy is that it is entirely reactive. This is especially problematical when the two parties are not cooperating but see the advantages of mutual cooperation. Under the rules of tit-for-tat, there is no way for either party to test the other's interest in mutual cooperation. What is probably needed under such circumstances is another modification of the tit-for-tat strategy, involving occasional conciliatory initiatives in the form of either cooperative behavior or judicious communication that is designed to explore the other's readiness for cooperation (Pruitt, 1981).

Another example of the antinomy is the firm-but-conciliatory strategy, whose value has been demonstrated in experiments by the author (see Pruitt and Rubin, 1986). People are enjoined to hold firm on their basic interests while at the same time seeking to satisfy the other party's basic interests. This strategy encourages the development of win–win solutions by the strategist. It should also help to convert the other party to problem solving, because it reduces the usefulness of harsh, contentious strategies and gives the other some hope that a win–win solution can be devised.

An illustration of this strategy can be seen in the behavior of President John F. Kennedy in 1961 during the Second Berlin Crisis. The Russians, under Premier Nikita Khrushchev, had been trying to end American occupation of West Berlin by threatening to sign a separate peace treaty with East Germany and buzzing planes in the Berlin Corridor. Recognizing that some concessions had to be made, Kennedy "decided to be firm on essentials but negotiate on nonessentials" (Snyder and Diesing, 1977:566). He announced three fundamental principles that ensured the integrity and continued Western occupation of West Berlin. The firmness of these principles was underscored by a pledge to defend them by force and a concomitant military buildup. Yet Kennedy also indicated flexibility and a concern about Russian sensitivities by calling for negotiations to remove "actual irritants" to the Soviet Union and its allies. This strategy culminated in negotiations that regularized Western rights in Berlin.

While valid in theory, the firm but conciliatory stance is sometimes hard to enact. Twin dangers loom: (1) the conciliatory part of the strategy may be misinterpreted by the other party as a sign of weakness, and (2) the firm part of the strategy may induce escalation by seeming to threaten the other party.

One way of being conciliatory while avoiding the impression of weakness is to stress the other end of the antinomy, remaining visibly firm about one's interests while seeking accommodation. However, this is not always easy. Psychological research suggests several auxiliary tactics available for reinforcing the impression of firmness, including the following:

1. Develop threat capacity and show force, as Kennedy did around the time of his "three principles" speech (Lindskold, 1986).
2. Be consistent in fulfilling one's commitments and threats (Tedeschi, Schlenker, and Bonoma, 1973).
3. Make it clear that one's constituents are quite hawkish and hence that one's conciliatory gestures are controversial at home (Wall, 1977).
4. Employ a "bad cop–good cop" routine, in which a hawkish representative takes a threatening and unyielding initial approach, followed by a dovish representative who takes a conciliatory approach (Pruitt and Rubin, 1986).

The companion danger, that efforts to look firm may backfire and produce escalation, can often be avoided by stressing the other side of the antinomy (i.e., signaling that one is concerned about the other party's interests and is flexible about the shape of the eventual solution). The following tactics, discussed more extensively in Fisher and Ury (1981) and Pruitt and Rubin (1986), should also be considered for this purpose:

1. If threats or force must be used to underline firmness, keep them to the minimum necessary.
2. Employ deterrent threats, in which one tries to prevent the other from taking some action, rather than compellent threats, in which one tries to force some action on the other (Rubin and Lewicki, 1973).
3. Use threats and commitments to defend basic interests rather than particular solutions to the controversy.
4. Make threats and commitments privately, and let the other party concede secretly, so as to avoid embarrassment.

5. Maintain the other's dignity—avoid humiliating the other or demeaning the other's strength or resolve.
6. Reassure the other about the limited nature of one's goals.
7. Be courteous and diplomatic while holding firm.

## Summary

In summary, it can be argued that the frustration-aggression mechanism, with its emphasis on punishing others for willfully harmful behavior that casts doubt on our adequacy, is part of a deterrent posture. It follows that this mechanism should be especially strong in people who must cope with exploitative human environments, such as in American slums and the international arena. People in deteriorated relationships have a penchant for finding new threats from their adversary at every turn and viewing these threats as willful and hostile. Hence it is important in such relationships, whether they be domestic or international, to be especially careful not to overinterpret the adversary's behavior. Kelley and Schmidt's advice to adopt a tit-for-tat or firm-but-conciliatory approach to aggressive others can be broadened to all mixed-motive relationships. Research suggests the advantages of a modified tit-for-tat strategy, in which one delays both retaliation and exoneration and, in periods of extended noncooperation, occasionally probes for a change in heart from the other. Various auxiliary tactics are useful in conjunction with a firm-but-conciliatory strategy to avoid the twin dangers of appearing weak and seeming to threaten the other party.

## NOTE

1. It might be argued, based on research by Axelrod (1984), that no strategy can be superior to the conventional tit-for-tat strategy. The problem with this argument is that Axelrod's tests pitted strategies against each other in computer runs. By contrast, the issue being raised here and in the next paragraph concerns the effectiveness of strategies for inducing cooperation *in human beings*. Bixenstine and Gaebelein's research suggests that the modified tit-for-tat is superior to the standard one for this purpose.

## REFERENCES

Axelrod, R., 1984. *The Evolution of Cooperation.* New York: Basic Books.
Bixenstine, V. E., and Gaebelein, J. W., 1971. Strategies of "real" opponents in

eliciting cooperative choice in a prisoner's dilemma game. *Journal of Conflict Resolution* 15:157–66.
Fisher, R., and Ury, W., 1981. *Getting to YES*. Boston: Houghton Mifflin.
Lindskold, S., 1986. GRIT: Reducing distrust through carefully introduced conciliation. In S. Worchel and W. G. Austin, eds., *Psychology of intergroup relations* (Second Edition, pp. 305–22). Chicago: Nelson-Hall.
Oskamp, S., 1971. Effects of programmed strategies on cooperation in the prisoner's dilemma and other mixed-motive games. *Journal of Conflict Resolution* 10:221–26.
Pruitt, D. G., 1981. *Negotiation Behavior*. New York: Academic.
Pruitt, D. G., and Rubin, J. Z., 1986. *Social Conflict: Escalation, Stalemate, and Settlement*. New York: Random House.
Rubin, J. Z., and Lewicki, R. J., 1973. A three-factor experimental analysis of promises and threats. *Journal of Applied Social Psychology* 3:240–57.
Sillars, A. L., 1981. Attributions and interpersonal conflict resolution. In J. H. Harvey, W. J. Ickes, and R. F. Kidd, eds., *New Directions in Attribution Research*, Vol. 3. Hillsdale, N.J.: Erlbaum, pp. 279–305.
Snyder, G. H., and Diesing, P., 1977. *Conflict Among Nations*. Princeton, N.J.: Princeton University Press.
Syna, H., 1984. Couples in conflict: Conflict resolution strategies, perceptions about sources of conflict and relationship adjustment. Unpublished doctoral dissertation. State University of New York at Buffalo.
Tedeschi, J. T., Schlenker, B. R., and Bonoma, T. V., 1973. *Conflict, Power, and Games*. Chicago: Aldine.
Wall, J. A., Jr., 1977. Inter-group bargaining: Effects of opposing constituent's stands, opposing representative's bargaining, and representative's locus of control. *Journal of Conflict Resolution* 21:459–74.

# 14
# Conclusions

## PAUL C. STERN, ROBERT AXELROD, ROBERT JERVIS, and ROY RADNER

The impetus for this volume was a renewed round of criticism of a view of deterrence that has been highly influential in U.S. foreign policy. Proponents of this view believe that threats, properly made and supported, are both necessary and sufficient for the United States to dissuade adversary states from acting on their desires to change the status quo to their liking. This belief is rooted in two simplifying behavioral assumptions: that states that would challenge the status quo are driven primarily by a quest for gains in international competition and that they pursue this quest as if they were unitary rational decision makers. The critics question both of these assumptions. They argue that national leaders' attempts to alter status quo situations are sometimes influenced by domestic motives, including the need to maintain their power and the desire to maintain their national security, and that when states issue or respond to deterrent threats, they sometimes depart in important ways from standard concepts of rationality. For instance, critics of deterrence claim that challengers sometimes disregard or misinterpret available information that, if heeded, would have convinced them it was not in their interest to initiate a challenge. They argue that when evidence pertinent to a deterrent threat is ignored or misread, deterrent threats can be insufficient to prevent a challenge. The critics also propose that states pursuing deterrent policies sometimes issue threats when no challenge is likely and that such threats sometimes provoke precisely the challenges they were issued to prevent and can therefore be counterproductive.

We convened a workshop in November 1986 to help clarify the issues separating the proponents and critics of deterrence. Participants examined relevant theory and empirical evidence from a wide variety of sources in a search for insights into conditions under which deterrent threats succeed or fail in international crises. Their work, reported in the preceding chapters, provides a basis for more sophisticated evaluation of deterrent strategies.

## The Status of Knowledge About Deterrence

Anyone who has read this volume can no longer retain an innocent belief that deterrence is "obviously" effective—or that it is "obviously" ineffective. We have disturbingly little knowledge to guide our strategic policies, and what little we know is highly uncertain. Every body of knowledge relevant to deterrence requires extrapolation or additional assumptions to be applied to the relationship between nuclear superpowers. Historical evidence from the nuclear era is ambiguous, in part because important facts are unavailable. Generalizations built from studies of the prenuclear era may not hold for deterrence between the United States and the Soviet Union because the possibility of a nuclear response fundamentally alters the context of action. And abstract deductive models cannot, as their own expositors concede and often emphasize, be self-sufficient sources of insight because, in a particular situation, their assumptions may yield results that are "either a good approximation of reality or a caricature" (Schelling, 1960:4). As Robert Wilson notes in Chapter 8, the outcome of a deductive model can depend critically on details of the interaction that are best determined by empirical study of the situation rather than by modeling.

Although knowledge is uncertain, it is significant that widely held beliefs about deterrence have been questioned on the basis of two kinds of historical evidence. In Chapter 2, Richard Ned Lebow reviews one line of criticism, based on detailed analysis of historical cases; Chapters 3 through 5 offer further discussion of the issues Lebow raises. A different line of evidence, from quantitative historical studies, raises similar questions. For instance, it is widely held that military superiority decreases the chances of aggression by an adversary. But as Jack Levy shows in Chapter 6, the available data require at the very least an important refinement of this proposition. They suggest that strategic or long-term military superiority has little relation to the success of deterrence once a challenge has arisen, although local military superiority does increase the likelihood that threats will succeed. The larger point is that a would-be challenger's estimate of the military balance may influence, but does not by itself determine, whether it initiates a challenge.

Such tentative generalizations from history, even those supported by the most extensive studies available, remain of uncertain value. Some writers on deterrence note that for every deterrence failure examined in historical studies there may have been several crises prevented by deterrent threats. This plausible proposition is very difficult to test, however, because it is hard to determine that the absence of a crisis resulted from a deterrent threat. Moreover, debate over whether deterrent threats prevent crises leaves open the crucial question of whether such threats prevent challenges once a crisis arises.

Despite the uncertainties about the meaning of past experience, criticism over three decades (e.g., Deutsch, 1963, 1968; George and Smoke, 1974; Jervis, 1979; Jervis, Lebow, and Stein, 1985) has long since shaken faith in the general validity of classical deterrence theory. For practitioners, it may be dangerous to accept the classical theory in a pure form because by relying too heavily on an elegant model they may ignore particulars that render the model inapplicable. Thoughtful advocates of deterrent policies recognize that the Soviet Union may not seek expansion always and everywhere, that domestic pressures are sometimes influential in decisions to challenge deterrents, and that misinterpretations of critical information sometimes occur. The central disagreements between deterrence advocates and critics, as exemplified in Chapters 2 and 3, concern the frequency, predictability, and influenceability of such exceptions to classical deterrence propositions and, of course, differences in judgment about whether the propositions apply in particular instances. Proponents believe that exceptions to the basic deterrence propositions are infrequent and that deviations from "rationality" on the part of would-be challengers are rare, unpredictable, and uncontrollable except by raising the costs of a potential challenge. Critics believe that exceptions to the deterrence propositions are common, especially during crises, and that deviations from "rationality" can sometimes be anticipated and forestalled by policies of "reassurance" that address the would-be challenger's motives rather than the costs of a challenge. Critics also argue, as already noted, that deterrence policies can be counterproductive under some conditions. Thus, the dispute over deterrence is not so much about the correctness of a theory—the theory is continually being reformulated—as over the answers to a set of conditional questions about deterrence: Under what conditions are states motivated to use threats or force to seek international gains? Under what conditions is foreign policy guided mainly by the international situation rather than by domestic imperatives? Under what conditions is "rational" decision making likely to break down during an international crisis? What can be done to prevent that eventuality in one's own country and in an adversary's?

# Conclusions

As critical as these questions are to international security in the nuclear age, they are far from having definitive answers. The contributors to this volume have explored evidence bearing on such questions. Specifically, we focused on the most general contextual question about deterrence: *Under what conditions do deterrent threats succeed or fail in international crises?* By combining historical data with more indirect evidence from other areas in which somewhat similar processes operate and by drawing on the broad range of behavioral and social science theory, we hoped to uncover new and promising ways of thinking about this question. We hoped to identify new knowledge bearing on the many and often conflicting hypotheses in the literature, or at least to suggest interesting directions for future research.

Our approach was novel. We greatly expanded the usual field of discourse about deterrence by looking not only at evidence from formal analytic models of military threat and response and from historical studies of international militarized conflict, but also at studies of revolution and insurgency, trade wars, oligopolistic competition, and interpersonal conflict. Of course, we did not expect these studies to provide knowledge directly applicable to the superpower rivalry. We hoped, rather, that they might illuminate the issues in new ways by allowing us to look at them from several vantage points at once.

We believe our approach is fruitful in opening some areas for further exploration and in identifying possibilities for cross-fertilization between empirical research and more formal theoretical methods. This chapter explores a few concepts that emerged from our effort that may be enlightening for researchers and practitioners. It examines the importance of whether states agree or disagree about the "legitimacy" of challenges to the status quo and of threats to deter such challenges, and it explores the potential for misperception and misjudgment, the difference between conflicts treated as efforts to enforce cooperation and as struggles for survival, and the effects of a changing balance of power. Finally, it briefly notes some implications of the work in this volume for current issues in deterrence theory: the role of predictable and conciliatory strategies, the concepts of reputation and resolve, the role of domestic factors in international deterrence, and the methodological possibilities of combining empirical and theoretical approaches. We identify a number of hypotheses suggested by the evidence that bear on the questions dividing the proponents and critics of deterrence; in doing so, we suggest variables that are worthy of attention by practitioners, even though knowledge is insufficient to offer practical guidance for any specific situation.

## Legitimacy and Deterrence

Several authors in this volume raise the concept of legitimacy, in one form or another, as an important factor influencing threat-and-response interactions. In some formulations, shared norms are the main focus: Their role is to regulate conflict and forestall challenges. In others, what is important is that different actors may have differing ideas of legitimacy. These differences may explain the breakdown of agreements and the dangerous surprises that occur when one actor does not behave the way an adversary expects. All of the formulations have in common the presumption that actors make judgments about the legitimacy of their own and others' actions and that those judgments affect their behavior.

### Shared Norms

Legitimacy, defined in terms of generally shared norms or standards for the proper behavior of states, is a familiar topic of controversy in the international relations literature. In principle, explicit or implicit shared norms can forestall challenges by setting accepted bounds on international competition; in practice, however, national leaders need to judge where the bounds lie in each situation and whether an adversary is likely to overstep them.

Charles Plott noted at the workshop that shared norms are important in experimental studies of laboratory analogs of international conflict. Players who have the opportunity to talk to each other seem to develop some tacit norms of behavior, and as a result are less likely to make aggressive moves, even when those moves cannot be detected (for a review, see Edney and Harper, 1978). The practical relevance of the laboratory findings is questionable, however, because the effect in the laboratory seems to depend on a broader, cultural norm of equity in interpersonal behavior that game players share (Chamberlin, 1978; Hardin, 1982). Such a norm may not often be shared by national leaders who initially define their relationship as adversarial and who, in any event, are of different cultures.

In international relations, norms, some widely shared and others more or less disputed, are often applied to the use of threats and the initiation of challenges to the status quo. Some norms often cited in support of deterrent strategies are the "rights" to defend one's territory and citizens, to honor commitments to allies, to retaliate against attacks against one's important interests, and to defend against certain means (regarded as illegitimate) for altering a status quo situation. Some norms often cited in support of challenges are the "rights" to incorporate territory populated largely by per-

## Conclusions

sons of the same nationality, to reacquire territory lost by force or "unequal treaty," to assist peoples demanding self-determination or liberation from oppressive regimes, to punish another state appropriately for noncompliance with an agreement, and, for great powers, to establish or maintain nonhostile governments on their borders.

Such norms do not determine policy in any simple way. Norms can conflict with each other. Leaders, even within the same state, may disagree about which norms apply in a particular situation. Moreover, norms are weighed against the material costs and benefits of actions and against the balance of interests between states. Great powers sometimes refrain from claiming what they believe to be their right because of the possibility of escalation; in the nuclear age, the superpowers have avoided situations that might confront their rival with the awful choice of accepting a major setback or initiating the use of force in order to avoid it.[1]

Norms tend to have more force when they are backed by international regimes or institutions that give a potential violator a reasonable expectation that a challenge will entail costs beyond those imposed by the defender (Nye and Keohane, 1977). Institutionalized norms exist in international trade, where the General Agreement on Tariffs and Trade sets fairly explicit limits on legitimate action and makes aggressive actions costly by legitimating particular retaliations (David Yoffie, Chapter 10). The effectiveness of these norms is suggested by Yoffie's observation that trade wars are less common in manufacturing than in agriculture, where GATT norms allow for numerous exceptions and are therefore more ambiguous. The greater predictability of GATT sanctions for industrial trade may increase their effectiveness (see the following). Attempts to create similar international institutions to enforce norms for military and diplomatic conduct have usually been less successful. The most prominent example is the United Nations charter, which expresses such norms and provides for a system of sanctions. The effectiveness of this system has been mixed at best (Haas, 1986). A reasonable hypothesis is that the United Nations is most effective when the nations in conflict are so weak in relation to those attempting to control the conflict.

Some analysts have argued that in the U.S.–Soviet competition, shared norms, made explicit in formal agreements even when not backed by institutions with the ability to impose sanctions, have sometimes successfully constrained the self-interests of the adversaries in political competition. Formal agreements regulate superpower competition in Europe, in the transfer of nuclear technologies to third states, and in the neutralization of Antarctica and the seabed. States can, of course, abrogate or violate such agreements whenever they consider it in their national interest to do so. But there may be costs in addition to those entailed by similar actions in the absence of an agreement: When a state violates explicit norms, its adversaries are likely to conclude that it is unreasonable and will not follow ordinary standards of behavior (Keohane, 1984). They may respond with force, by heightening their defenses, or by declining mutually advantageous arrangements in the future out of mistrust. (The argument that adversary states sometimes have incentives to institute and maintain security regimes has been presented in detail by Stein, 1985b).

In principle, shared norms can also operate effectively within international systems that have neither formal institutions for enforcement nor formal agreements to make the norms explicit. Paul Schroeder (Chapter 4) cites as an example the Russian decision not to invade Turkey in the 1820s. The implicit international norms were apparently strong enough for the Russians to abort a contemplated invasion on the expectation that it would have intangible costs to Russian standing in the community of European states. In that case, norms seem to have effectively deterred a strong nation from exploiting its military advantage. International norms may explain the failure of the United States to threaten the Soviet Union with preventive war when it enjoyed a nuclear monopoly in the 1940s or a vast nuclear superiority in the 1950s, and may also explain the similar restraint the Soviet leaders showed toward China in the 1970s. The leaders of the superior powers may have found it morally repugnant to take personal responsibility for nuclear destruction, as President Eisenhower apparently did in Vietnam in 1954 (Gaddis, 1986:137). Or, they may have been restrained from using nuclear force against a weak adversary by the possible costs to their international reputations. A nuclear state that gains a reputation as immoral can reasonably expect the kind of negative reactions it would receive if it had violated an explicit international agreement.

International norms may also operate through "limited security regimes" within which adversaries observe informal or unwritten rules of behavior. Janice Stein (1985b) identified such a limited security regime that, among other things, specified that Egyptian forces in the Sinai be limited to two divisions and 250 tanks, deployed in the western half of the desert. She argues that this regime, which included both formalized and informal agreements, helped prevent war between Egypt and Israel for 11 years before it was dismantled in 1967. Similarly, Alexander George (1983:376–378) has argued that the unwritten agreement that ended the Cuban Missile Crisis has continued to be the reference point for U.S. and Soviet behavior in Cuba and to regulate superpower competition in that area.

The shared fear of nuclear conflict gives the United States and the Soviet Union a strong incentive to devise limited security regimes, at least for preventing accidental nuclear war. Numerous formal agreements regarding

# Conclusions

the Hotline, incidents at sea, and so forth have been negotiated to put such limited regimes in place, and unwritten norms for crisis management seem to be generally observed by both superpowers (George, 1984). Despite the importance of such shared norms, however, they cover only a small part of the range of possible conflicts between the superpowers.

## Differing Ideas of Legitimacy

Differing notions of the legitimacy of various foreign policy actions can affect the ways national leaders interpret each other's threats or demands and therefore the ways they respond to them. Even a claim of legitimacy for certain actions by a state that seems spurious from its adversary's perspective can be important for the adversary to take into account because it can provide strong cultural, psychological, or political motives for the state making the claim to strive for particular interests.

Ideas of legitimacy can be important when nations differ about which norms apply in a particular situation. Paul Schroeder's (Chapter 4) concept of failed bargains suggests that a crisis can arise when one state judges that another has violated shared standards of behavior by breaking a stated or tacit agreement, whereas the leaders of the other state, citing different norms, believe they are acting legitimately. In Schroeder's reading of the Fashoda crisis of 1898, the French were surprised when the British broke tacit rules of the European balance of power system by threatening war over a non-European dispute. The British, presumably, thought their threat of force to defend their interests was perfectly legitimate. Similarly, Britain and Argentina in 1982 applied different norms to their relations in the Falklands/Malvinas (Lebow, Chapter 2). For Argentina, the Malvinas were a colonial anachronism, legitimately removed from the international scene; for Britain, however, the Falklands contained a loyal British population legitimately to be defended from foreign attack. Although this was not a failed bargain in Schroeder's terms, it is plausible that the fundamental difference over which norm was applicable contributed both to British laxness about its deterrent and to Argentine willingness to challenge it.

A similar instance in superpower relations is the demise of the U.S.–Soviet detente of the 1970s, which some observers trace to different understandings of the detente agreements and of which actions were legitimate within their framework. According to some analysts, each superpower chose to interpret the agreements as providing legitimacy tailored to its international goals. The United States saw detente as applying constraints on Soviet behavior in a broad range of issue areas, including involvement in "wars of national liberation." The Soviet Union saw detente as restricted to issue areas that had the most to offer it, such as trade and strategic arms control, and as not applying to some of the areas most important to the United States, such as the war in Vietnam. These differing views of what constituted the norms of action contributed to the collapse of detente (Breslauer, 1983:326–27).

As Jack Goldstone pointed out in Chapter 11, conflicting judgments of legitimacy can be important even when the adversaries share a common cultural background. Support for revolutionary movements increases when regimes violate existing social norms: Peoples revolt against sudden tax increases, even where taxes were already exorbitant; and where traditional modes of expressing discontent, even symbolic ones, are suppressed, revolts become more likely. In short, people who do not revolt in the face of extreme inequality become more likely to revolt when the dominant regime takes actions widely judged to be unfair (Scott, 1976). That is, deterring revolt becomes far more difficult when the regime's legitimacy is undermined.

Of course, judgments of legitimacy are often manipulated. Norms are invented or twisted to serve as justification for one's action or as a basis for condemning an adversary's behavior. Revolutionary leaders develop rhetoric to emphasize the legitimacy of their demands and question the legitimacy of dominant regimes, and in international affairs, state leaders often use legitimacy claims to justify policies, mobilize popular support, and win over public opinion in other nations. But even claims made for political purposes may have substantive effect on a conflict. Leaders can become constrained to action by notions of justice and injustice widely held in their countries, even when they were themselves responsible for promoting those notions to gain support. Efforts to manipulate notions of legitimacy to gain public support may have been the trap that ensnared the Argentine junta in the Falklands/Malvinas war of 1982 (Lebow, 1985) and the force that impelled Nasser to attack Israel in 1967 and 1969 (Stein, 1985a).

For such reasons, it is wise for leaders to be aware of their adversaries' perceptions of legitimacy. These perceptions may be predictive of an adversary's challenges and its behavior in the face of challenges or threats. For instance, it may be more difficult to deter or reverse the actions of an adversary that sees its challenge to a status quo situation as perfectly legitimate. It may be possible, however, to forestall a challenge by acting to ameliorate what the adversary perceives as injustices. A Soviet decision to ease the emigration of Jews might forestall punitive policy decisions in the United States. In short, regardless of whether states share notions of legitimacy in international behavior, judgments about legitimacy are important because they influence that behavior.

## Hypotheses About Legitimacy and Deterrence

Legitimacy as perceived by the parties to an international conflict may affect the conditions under which they initiate challenges, misinterpret each others' defensive actions as provocations, and interpret an adversary's concessions either as resolutions of the conflict or as signs of weakness. Thus, judgments about the legitimacy of threats or challenges may be a key variable determining whether deterrent threats produce restraint or escalation. Decision makers may find it useful to consider perceptions of legitimacy when they prepare to make threats or challenges or to respond to them.

The following specific hypotheses about legitimacy are suggested by the contributions to this volume:

1. A challenge that is perceived by the defender as reflecting a legitimate claim is more likely to be met with concession than one that is perceived to violate norms of international competition. This is because such a challenge leads the adversary to expect that a concession will not produce more challenges. An instance may be the British reaction to German behavior in the decade prior to 1914 (Lebow, 1981). This hypothesis has also been suggested by Snyder and Diesing (1977) and by Cohen (1978, 1979).[2]

2. A concession that is readily interpretable as adherence to a shared norm is less likely to be interpreted as a sign of weakness and therefore to lead to further challenges than one made without a shared norm to govern it (see Snyder and Diesing, 1977).[3] Britain's concessions at Munich in 1938 may illustrate this point. The British thought, in part, that their concession was based on the norm of self-determination, a norm that Hitler stressed and that the British thought he believed in. However, Hitler did not seem to understand that the British response depended on the issue of self-determination, so he took the concessions as a sign of weakness and expected until the very last that the British would back down from future challenges as well.

3. A threat is less likely to be challenged when it defends a generally recognized legitimate interest; a challenge is less likely to meet an aggressive counterresponse when it is aimed at securing such an interest. The logic behind this pair of hypotheses is that backing away from a threat or challenge does less damage to a national leader's domestic position if the leader and his countrymen see the threat or challenge as legitimate. Similarly, it does less damage to a state's reputation when the threat or challenge is seen as legitimate abroad. After World War II, colonial powers often used the norm of self-determination to avoid a choice between war and loss of face when challenged by insurgencies in their colonies.

4. A threat or challenge that violates an adversary's sense of justice is more likely to lead to escalation than one that is neutral with respect to the adversary's sense of legitimacy. An instance may be the U.S. response to the 1950 invasion of South Korea.

5. When a challenger sees its challenge as the legitimate exercise of a right or the implementation of an agreement, the challenge is not easily deterred, and a response to such a challenge is likely to be met with escalation. The challenger will be pressured by norms within the state and by their translation into domestic political pressure to push on to win, as may have happened in Argentina in 1982.

6. When an adversary contemplates a challenge to a state's interests because it senses an injustice, it may be possible to prevent the challenge by policies that alleviate the sense of injustice but still protect the interests at stake.

7. A state threatened with dishonor according to internally held standards may choose to challenge an adequate deterrent and initiate a losing war because it prefers an honorable defeat to a dishonorable one. Lebow (1981) argues that Spain provoked the United States to war in 1898 partly to avoid the humiliation of an expected loss of Cuba to local revolutionaries.

These hypotheses can be investigated further by case analyses. Many of them can also be incorporated into formal models of threat–response interactions that include the decision-making processes of national leaders. Such formal models could explore relationships that involve different combinations of adversaries' judgments about the legitimacy of their own and their opponents' actions by representing a national leader's judgments of legitimacy as subjective probability judgments of an adversary's responses to different policy alternatives. For instance, leaders will expect adversaries to be restrained in response to legitimate claims. Thus, theoretical as well as empirical researchers can employ ideas of legitimacy, and especially differing concepts of legitimacy between states, to study the dynamics of international threats and responses. We believe such an accommodation between historical and formal methods would be healthy for research on deterrence. We also believe that attrition to an adversary's notion of legitimacy is a useful component of prudent policymaking in international conflicts.

## Misperception and Misjudgment

A major theme in debates about deterrence has been that of systematic biases in decision makers' perceptions and judgments. Deterrent strategies presume perceptiveness among national leaders, so any limitations or systematic biases in their information processing, whether caused by their emotional reactions, their cognitive limitations, or the limitations of those who provide them with information could threaten the success of these strategies. In particular, many critics of classical deterrence theory claim that national leaders often misjudge expected outcomes from issuing threats or challenging them. These critics, drawing on literature in psychology and organizational behavior, point to limitations on information processing imposed by people's inability to assimilate huge amounts of information; to biases introduced by some of the "shortcuts" or heuristics people use to compensate for cognitive limitations; to biases introduced when organizations with parochial aims are called upon to provide information in the service of national goals; to problems of individual stress and group decision making in crisis; and to biases introduced when leaders' desires to achieve certain goals lead them to distort available evidence to make those goals seem more attainable. These points have been raised in numerous accounts of international conflict (e.g., Allison, 1971; Halperin, 1974; Holsti, 1989; Janis, 1982), and their implications for deterrence have been explicated by George and Smoke (1974), Snyder and Diesing (1977), Jervis (1979), Lebow (1981), and Jervis, Lebow, and Stein (1985). Many of the points are summarized by Lebow in Chapter 2.

One potential source of misperception, concerning judgments of intention, deserves more elaboration here. In assessing threats to national security, leaders in the nuclear age, as in previous eras, must consider not only an adversary's capabilities but its motives and intentions. Increases in the French nuclear arsenal, for instance, do not greatly upset the West Germans because they do not interpret those actions as hostile.

The social-psychological literature shows that a judgment that another's action is hostile depends on a recognition that it violates some norm of social action combined with an attribution that the norm-violating behavior was intended (Heider, 1958). Moreover, judgments of others' intentions are systematically different from judgments of one's own, with people often seeing others' behavior as determined by stable traits while seeing their own as determined by situational constraints (Monson and Snyder, 1977; Nisbett and Ross, 1980). That tendency can make judgments of an adversary's behavior impervious to evidence that it is responding to situational forces. For instance, in laboratory studies of simulated conflict situations, people with competitive orientations see their opponents as motivated competitively regardless of their actions (Kelley and Stahelski, 1970). The international analog is a situation in which national leaders misperceive foreign actions that threaten their interests as resulting from an intent to threaten when they may in fact have been responses to political conditions unrelated to the nation whose leaders perceive the threat. In such a situation, the leaders who initiated the action do not perceive themselves as threatening, so are likely to misunderstand the responses of adversaries who see them that way. The literature on international conflict includes references to the kinds of misperceptions that would occur if states acted like individuals making social attributions (Jervis, 1976; Jervis, Lebow, and Stein, 1985:14–18).

In Chapter 13, Dean Pruitt specifies interpersonal conditions that make such misperceptions more likely. People attribute malevolence more often in relationships that have already deteriorated, when one side has pinned "dehumanizing" labels on the other, and under conditions of high arousal, especially recent frustration. Analogy suggests the hypothesis that deterrent threats are likely to lead to a misperception of hostile intent when the relationships between states or their leaders have these characteristics or when the recipient of the threat has recently been frustrated in foreign policy. In Chapter 12, Harold Kelley and Greg Schmidt show how interactions that an individual perceives as a threat to his self-esteem can impair perception and derail "rational" calculations of self-interest, leading beyond misperception to an aggressive response pattern that does not take into account the expected value to the aggressor—a possible analogue for some challenges to deterrence that occur despite obvious military inferiority.

One need not go far to find international situations that recall some of these interpersonal processes. Pruitt (Chapter 13) cites as a prime example of attribution bias the U.S. reaction to the Soviet destruction of Korean Air Lines Flight 007 in 1983. Despite evidence that the Soviets mistook the plane for a U.S. reconnaissance flight whose path had crossed that of the Korean plane, many U.S. public officials and journalists saw the incident as reflecting characteristic Soviet contempt for law, decency, and innocent human life (Hersch, 1986). The Soviet view was, of course, quite different. The Soviets justified their actions in terms of their right to defend their borders, but they might also credit situational factors, such as the presence of U.S. reconnaissance flights in the area and the sensitivity of military tests being conducted at that place and time, as influencing the decision. It is plausible that the U.S. inference of Soviet malevolence was made more likely by a deteriorated relationship (the breakdown of detente and Soviet defense buildups), the use of dehumanizing labels (President Reagan's rhetoric about the Soviet Union as "the evil empire"), and recent frustrations (Soviet advances in Afghanistan and Central America and U.S. humiliations in Iran and Lebanon). Certainly, the U.S. reaction was much different when Israel destroyed a Libyan airliner in 1973, an event described in some U.S. press accounts as "tragic" rather than malevolent (English and Halperin, 1987:64–67). It is also interesting to note that U.S. and Soviet leaders justified their positions by reference to different norms of international behavior: the right of free civilian air travel (U.S. statements) and the right of self-defense (Soviet statements).

The syndrome of misattribution of malevolent intent may help explain what J. L. Snyder (1985) calls the "perceptual security dilemma," the situation in which one state's efforts to increase its own security are interpreted by another as plans to attack, even though the changed military situation may not objectively put the second state into increased danger. As Snyder suggests, the judgment of malevolence that is central to that dilemma can result from the fundamental attribution error. The psychological literature summarized by Kelley and Schmidt and by Pruitt goes farther by suggesting some hypotheses about the conditions under which individuals perceive malevolence and under which, consequently, perceptual security dilemmas are most likely to occur. Scholars could explore those hypotheses by reexamining historical security dilemmas.

For example, Lebow (Chapter 2) discusses the Cuban Missile Crisis of 1962 in terms of attribution error. In his account, the Soviet action was in large part a situationally determined response to a security threat, yet in the United States at the time, the introduction of missiles into Cuba was perceived as an unprovoked malevolent act. It seems plausible to link the U.S. judgment to the deteriorated state of U.S.–Soviet relations and to recent frustrations in Berlin and the Bay of Pigs. And there are reports that President Kennedy initially responded to the Soviet action as a threat to his or the nation's self-esteem (Allison, 1971:193–94, 230–31).

Such psychological dynamics can, as Kelley and Schmidt show in Chapter 12, lead beyond misperception to the escalation of conflict. In interpersonal relations, there is a tendency for individuals who see their self-esteem as threatened to act emotionally rather than rationally, disregarding expected utility and acting to punish adversaries without considering the cost to themselves. This interaction pattern may be relevant to international conflict in at least three ways. First, national leaders may act as if they were engaged in interpersonal conflict and escalate irrationally. The rhetoric of national leaders suggests that like Louis XIV (*L'état c'est moi*), they sometimes take national threats or challenges personally. One instance was the German Kaiser's reaction to events during the July crisis of 1914 (Lebow, 1981:140–47). Often, however, this tendency is only temporary or is restrained by advisers who keep cooler heads (George, 1986).

Second, national leaders use metaphors of threats to personal self-esteem to evoke nationalistic fervor in support of confrontive policies. For instance, in the U.S.–Libya confrontation in the Gulf of Sidra in 1986, Colonel Qadhafi in effect dared the U.S. Navy to cross a "line of death" in the Gulf, and U.S. officials, invoking schoolyard language about bullies, gained considerable public support for military action.

Third, national leaders may use emotional responses strategically in response to minor threats in order to create a reputation for aggressive responses and thereby deter more serious threats. This strategem is an example of what is sometimes called the rationality of irrationality (see Schelling, 1960: Chapter 8). The net effect of such interaction dynamics is to make it difficult to control conflicts that pose threats to self-esteem on one side or the other.

As already noted, the literature on interpersonal relations (Chapters 12 and 13) specifies some conditions under which the affective quality of a relationship is conducive to misperceptions that tend to intensify conflict. The analogies to international relations have also been noted. It remains for researchers to see whether those conditions or the personalized reactions they often produce tend to be present when national leaders deviate from "rational" decision-making processes during international crises. There is already some evidence that in U.S. policymaking, higher-quality crisis decision making is strongly associated with more favorable outcomes both in terms of U.S. interests and decreased tension (Janis, 1986). The concepts developed in Chapters 12 and 13 identify contextual factors that may provoke affective reactions and thus predispose to deviations from optimal decision-making process.[4]

Another possible source of misperception might be a stable tendency of some actors to see ambiguous situations as threatening and of others to see the same situations as benign. In particular, national leaders may see in ambiguous events "evidence" that confirms their prior beliefs about their adversaries' hostile or benign intent. Following familiar psychological processes, they may believe ambiguous evidence that supports those presumptions and discount disconfirming evidence (Ross and Anderson, 1982). This sort of bias has been mentioned in the literature on international conflict (Holsti, 1967; Jervis, 1976: Chapter 4; Lebow, 1981:153–69), and may be critical to deterrence relationships. It may be especially important in U.S.–Soviet deterrence relationships because both U.S. policy analysis and classical deterrence theory have long assumed hostility, or at least expansionism, as the basis of Soviet international behavior. It is plausible that this psychological tendency both reflected and reinforced the tendency among U.S. leaders to interpret ambiguous Soviet foreign policy actions as challenges. If so, U.S. leaders may have become prone to perceive challenges in a range of situations and therefore to err on the side of overattributing aggressive motives.[5] Of course, the same psychological processes that can predispose analysts to excessive suspiciousness can also promote a false sense of security when an adversary is seen as peaceful or when its past nonaggressive behavior is taken as the most important indicator of present intent.

The contributions to this volume raise two broad hypotheses about the causes and consequences of systematic misperception and misjudgment in international conflict:

1. National leaderships facing threats are less likely to evaluate their options rationally: (1) when relations with the adversary are poor or deteriorating, (2) when the threat bears on matters of personal or national self-esteem, and (3) when the leadership has experienced recent frustration of its international ambitions or is otherwise in a state of high arousal or tension. Deficits in rational decision process may include failure to consider carefully the possible costs of the chosen option (Kelley and Schmidt, Chapter 12) or other failures identified by Janis (1986), which include failure to consider and evaluate the full range of alternatives, poor information search, failure to reconsider previously rejected alternatives, and failure to work out detailed implementation, monitoring, and contingency plans.

2. To the extent the above conditions of internal arousal are present, states are more likely to respond to threats with escalation. In particular, states that have been weakened in their international positions are likely to respond aggressively to threats.

To the degree that these hypotheses are correct, it is particularly important that under conditions that jeopardize careful decision making, national leaderships have in place institutions and procedures to guard against precipitous action on their own part and that they obtain and utilize sources of countervailing information and advice prior to making decisions (George, 1980, and Janis, 1982, have developed sets of suggestions). It would also seem prudent for policymakers to be sensitive to the possibility that decision makers on the other side may be suffering adverse effects of arousal and tension and to try under those conditions to avoid unnecessary challenges. Such restraint may be difficult in periods of deteriorating bilateral relationships, but it is more practicable when an adversary's recent foreign policy frustrations came at the hands of a third party. These policy suggestions are important but also controversial—they are easily misconstrued as criticisms of the competence of key policymakers. There is a need, therefore, for further study of the psychological propositions about decision making that underlie them.

## Types of Conflict

The contributions to this volume suggest that international conflicts can vary greatly in their nature and that in different types of conflict different strategies are effective for the participants. Deterrent threats, in particular, may be more relevant and more effective in some types of conflicts than others. Although it is not yet clear how many useful distinctions can be made between types of conflict, it seems worthwhile to note that conflicts vary according to the extent of commonality of interests. At one extreme are conflicts in which shared interests predominate, which we call conflicts to enforce cooperation. At the other are conflicts in which interests are directly opposed, that is, conflicts that approximate a zero-sum situation, which we call struggles for survival.

## Conflicts to Enforce Cooperation

One type of conflict can occur within an international regime from which the potential adversaries receive ongoing positive benefits. Its aim is to enforce the rules of that regime. In such regimes, states are in continual interaction governed by explicit or implicit shared norms of conduct. Norms decrease the costs of action in an international regime because they add predictability to participants' behavior; thus, actors stand to gain by enforcing cooperation, even on minor points (Keohane, 1984:Chapters 6, 7). Although the benefits of international regimes constitute an incentive to avoid conflicts, once conflicts arise, they have the potential to degenerate into spirals of increasing tension in which each side may overestimate the hostility of others.

The prototypical conflict is one in which one actor punishes another for violation of the norms of a regime: Economic conflicts provide the most frequent examples. In international trade, because of the strong incentives to avoid trade wars, it is unusual that prolonged trade wars occur (see Chapters 9 and 10); when they do occur, they are often fought to enforce conformity to a notion of fair trade practices. In oligopolistic competition, conflicts to enforce cooperation can occur when a firm judges that another has breached a collusive arrangement (see Chapter 8). Political conflicts to enforce cooperation may occur between allies or close trading partners.

Analysts suggest that participants in such conflicts can most effectively maintain cooperation by using predictable strategies (Axelrod, 1984) and by making threats that are limited to the act being deterred rather than coupled to separate issues (Yoffie, Chapter 10). Threats are likely to work in conflicts to enforce cooperation in part because both sides, although wanting to cheat, gain major advantages from continued cooperation. Of course, either side may inadvertently overreach itself; in using threats to gain maximum unilateral advantage it may bluff and end up in undesired conflict. Nevertheless, the fact that both sides have strong incentives to continue cooperation usually prevents unrestrained conflict or even the threat of military force in international economic competition.

## Struggles for Survival

In contrast, violent outcomes are frequent when conflicts are rooted in a fundamental opposition of interests. At the extreme, such conflicts may become struggles for survival: Conflict tends to continue until one side or the other is destroyed or completely vanquished and the other side emerges as victorious. Theoretically, if each side correctly estimates the other's strengths and plans, such struggles need not occur because the weaker side would attempt to appease the stronger with substantial, even sweeping, concessions. But because national leaders do not always have correct information and do not always draw appropriate conclusions from the information they have, long and bloody conflicts can occur between unequal forces. The obvious international example is a war fought for unconditional surrender; great power conflicts over political hegemony can also have this character.

In acute conflicts of this kind, it theoretically benefits participants to withhold information about their resources and intentions and to surprise the adversary by attacking with full force and when least expected (Axelrod, 1979). Much of U.S. and presumably Soviet military strategy is designed to guard against just such behavior by the adversary; thus, both states act in this respect as if the other sees the relationship as a struggle for survival.

However, the advent of nuclear weapons has altered the desirability of warfare as a solution to acute conflicts of interests. Although relations between nuclear superpowers such as the United States and the Soviet Union may be driven by strongly opposed interests, conflict between them is not a zero-sum situation because in an all-out struggle, neither side could realistically expect to come out a winner.

The analogues of military struggles for survival that are discussed in this volume are all conflicts in which an interaction that involved some mutual benefits becomes transformed into a struggle for survival. These include revolutions in which the dominant regime has lost its legitimacy (Goldstone, Chapter 11) and certain price and trade wars (Chapters 8, 9, and 10). Apparently, many conflicts can take on characteristics of conflicts to enforce cooperation or struggles for survival depending on the actions of the participants and their interpretations of each other's motives. The United States and the Soviet Union, like competing business firms, are in an ambiguous position regarding the nature of their conflicts. Although they are engaged in ongoing and often fierce competition, they have a shared interest in avoiding warfare that could devastate both sides. In this sense, the central problem of the U.S.–Soviet competition is to keep the various component conflicts, most of which have mixed-motive aspects, from being interpreted as nothing more than battles in a general struggle for survival. To the extent that they can be treated more as conflicts to enforce cooperation, U.S.–Soviet conflicts may be kept limited, predictable, and capable of resolution. If success at resolving some conflicts makes other conflicts more tractable, the result would be to make the world much safer. Thus, the study of how states become subject to internal revolution and of how international regimes degenerate into trade wars may have insights to offer for preventing a struggle for survival between the United States and the Soviet Union.

## Hypotheses About Transformation of Types of Conflict

Little research has been done on how mixed-motive conflicts between states become transformed into struggles for survival, but four hypotheses readily suggest themselves for study:

1. If the mutual benefits of continued interaction are increased, conflicts are more likely to be perceived and treated as efforts to enforce cooperation. This suggests that each explicit political agreement and each increase in interdependence in trade or technology will reduce the likelihood of all-out conflict in that issue area and may also alter the way the participants treat conflicts in other areas. The limited evidence on this set of propositions is not conclusive (Gasiorowski, 1986), and further study would have obvious importance.

2. Increasing mutual awareness of the necessity and benefits of cooperation will make it less likely that a conflict will be treated as a struggle for survival. This proposition suggests that benefits might be gained by convincing citizens and policymakers of the nonzero-sum aspects of U.S.–Soviet competition. Although it may seem obvious that nonzero-sum thinking will yield nonzero-sum policies, it is not. It is hard to know whether decades of efforts by scientists to tell the world of the physical, climatic, ecological, and medical effects of nuclear war have significantly

altered security policy in the United States or the Soviet Union. At least three empirical questions need answers: Do such educational efforts change the policy attitudes of their lay or expert audiences? Does heightened awareness of the horrors of nuclear war or the possible gains from cooperation lead policymakers to act differently? And does increased public awareness of the threat of nuclear war or the benefits of cooperation operate through the force of public opinion to bring about more cooperative security policies? There has been little careful investigation of these questions; there is some evidence, however, that strategic policy in the United States is influenced to some degree by public opinion (Russett, 1989).

3. Struggles for survival sometimes begin when adversaries do not share a common view of the extent to which their interests converge. What may look to one party like a mixed-motive conflict may seem to the other as a struggle for survival. For instance, the 1941 embargo against oil for Japan seemed to Westerners a controlled response, aimed at producing moderation in Japanese policy in the Far East. The Japanese, however, saw it as a strangle hold on their economy and responded with a surprise attack, to which the United States in turn responded with all-out war (Lebow, Chapter 2). The implication is that it is important to pay attention to the adversary's definition of a conflict situation.

4. Employing strategies that are effective in struggles for survival may help precipitate all-out conflict. National regimes have precipitated revolutions in this way; a recent example may be Ferdinand Marcos's use of intimidation, assassination, and election fixing to prolong his rule in the Philippines, thus provoking the successful coalition of his opponents into "people power."[6] The Japanese attack on Pearl Harbor may be an example: Despite the extreme character of the attack, the Japanese apparently believed the Americans might respond with only limited warfare.

## The Effect of a Changing Balance of Power

Some writers on deterrence claim that the expectation of adverse changes in the balance of power may encourage national leaders to consider initiating war before the adversary becomes too strong; such perceptions may determine whether deterrents succeed or fail (Organski and Kugler, 1980; Levy, 1987). Specifically, these writers argue that when one actor believes war is likely eventually and judges that its chances of success will diminish in the future, it may challenge a deterrent and initiate a war even if it believes its chances of winning to be small. This sort of decision can follow directly from a rational calculation of expected value. Such considerations figure prominently in one explanation offered for the Japanese attack on Pearl Harbor: The oil embargo confronted Japanese leaders with the grave prospect that the longer they waited, the worse their chances for success would become in a war. Because they considered a war to be preferable to accepting U.S. demands that Japan give up its imperial ambitions, they attacked the United States even though they realized their inferior position (Lebow, Chapter 2).

The hypothesis about expectations regarding the future balance of power comes from observations of small numbers of particular historical cases. It was therefore interesting to note some parallels in other areas of study. John Conybeare notes in Chapter 9 that although all-out trade wars are uncommon, some of those on record were initiated by weaker trade partners who believed that their power was declining further and that intensified competition in the present might forestall that decline.

Another historical analogue exists in the study of empires. Historians have long speculated that declining empires are more dangerous than expanding ones. In terms of deterrence theory, this hypothesis is a special case of the one described above, in that a declining power is one that expects its chances of winning a war to be less in the future than in the present. Thus, historical evidence on the behavior of declining powers such as Austria before World War I generally supports the hypothesis that such powers are prone to involvement in war (Schroeder, Chapter 4).

The issue of expected changes in the balance of power has potentially significant implications for U.S.–Soviet relations. Some strategists have proposed a U.S. strategy of advancing national goals by policies aimed at bankrupting the Soviet economy or driving wedges between national groups within the Soviet Union. In this view, a weakened Soviet Union would be less dangerous to the United States. The above paragraphs suggest a counterargument, that decline might tempt the Soviets to challenge U.S. interests, an eventuality that could have disastrous consequences because of the availability of nuclear weapons. Evidence is far from sufficient to resolve the issue, but the controversy underlines the importance of understanding policymakers' sensitivity to expected changes in relative strength. The issue might potentially be explored by analyzing historical records about the beliefs of national leaders who initiated challenges despite military inferiority, by quantitative studies that include trends in national resources as well as the current state of such resources, and by formal models that build in expected future payoffs as a variable.

## Implications for Current Issues in Deterrence

### The Role of Predictable and Conciliatory Strategies

The themes of consistency and predictability recur in this volume in a variety of contexts and with different apparent implications for the use of threats. At the interpersonal level, Kelley and Schmidt's review (Chapter 12) suggests that the aggressive response syndrome is best avoided by a firm but conciliatory strategy involving a number of specific tactics that Dean Pruitt identifies in Chapter 13. Jack Goldstone's review of the literature on revolutions (Chapter 11) reaches a similar conclusion: Deterring revolution seems to be most effective when force is used consistently, whereas erratic applications of force leave openings for insurgent movements. Goldstone's implicit caution to regimes is that threats of force that are not quickly and reliably carried through to action act as incitements to violence. John Conybeare (Chapter 9) suggests that although trade wars are usually short, they can become long when participants cannot maintain a consistent strategy. He cites the Anglo–Dutch trade wars of the seventeenth century as a case in point.

Jack Levy (Chapter 6) reports some evidence from the quantitative international relations literature consistent with the interpretation that deterrence is more likely to work when the deterrer uses a firm-but-fair reciprocal strategy than when it uses a bullying or a broadly conciliatory one. These data seem consistent with the analysis of the iterated Prisoners' Dilemma game that shows the relative long-term advantage of strategies like tit-for-tat that are reciprocal and that, because they are predictable in rewarding cooperation and in punishing defection, may be considered "firm-but-fair" (Axelrod, 1984).

This review suggests that except in "struggles for survival," some version of consistency or predictability in response both to threats and cooperative overtures is a useful strategy in international competition, both for the individual participants and from the standpoint of achieving equilibria that no participant is tempted to upset. However, the discussions in this volume do not clearly reveal the mechanisms or processes that make such a strategy effective. In the deterrence of nuclear war and in other international competitions with partial convergence of interests, it is critical to specify what tactics an actor should and should not make predictable and to specify the types of actions that merit a conciliatory response. Game theory shows that the situation is complex. In noncooperative situations, mixed strategies that involve both deterministic and randomized responses may be required to sustain a stable solution (see Chapter 8; see also discussions of threats "that leave something to chance," e.g., Schelling, 1960). Game-theoretic approaches seem particularly suited for exploring further the matters of predictable and conciliatory strategies.

## Reputation

Reputation is often cited as important to deterrence in that a potential challenger will take into account the adversary's reputation for defending its interests when evaluating the chances that a challenge will be resisted. Some of the contributors to this volume have noted advances in conceptualizing or measuring reputation that might make the concept easier to investigate.

Jack Levy, for example, notes in Chapter 6 that quantitative studies can distinguish between the ways a nation has responded to a particular challenger and the ways it has responded to all challengers. The work of Huth and Russett (1984, 1988) suggests that the detailed and specific history of interactions with a particular challenger may be a better predictor of the outcome of a future crisis than a shallower history of responses to all challengers. This sort of research begins to clarify what determines a state's effective reputation in the eyes of challengers.

Until recently, game-theoretic analysis had not made much systematic effort to model reputational effects, but interest in the problem is increasing (Wilson, 1985), and the contributors have noted some ways to address it. One is to treat reputation as the adversary's subjective probability that a player is using a particular strategy. Thus, in a Prisoners' Dilemma game, if one player believes there is a probability, even a small one, that the opponent will respond to that player's moves, it pays to be conciliatory or to reciprocate cooperative responses; the usefulness of that approach increases when interactions are expected to continue for a long time (Wilson, Chapter 8; Axelrod, 1984). Another approach is to treat reputation in terms of short-term gains foregone in the expectation of greater future gains (O'Neill, Chapter 7).

## Resolve

Resolve is sometimes difficult to distinguish from the concepts of interest and commitment. It might be defined, however, as the willingness to incur costs to defend one's position.[7] In Chapter 7, Barry O'Neill reports on a formal model that uses such a definition and reaches the surprising conclusion that the purpose of arms races is to show resolve by "publicly dis-

## Conclusions

play[ing] the infliction of hardship on oneself by throwing money away." Similar arguments have been made by some observers of the U.S.–Soviet arms competition, who draw the analogy to a tribal potlatch in which two chiefs demonstrate their wealth and importance by disposing of valuables while getting nothing in return. In this view, the superpowers spend billions on weapons systems not to protect their retaliatory capacity but to demonstrate to their adversaries and possibly also to themselves that they are willing to make large sacrifices to maintain their national interests and their great power status (Jervis, 1987). These arguments suggest that a formal model like O'Neill's may have some relevance for real-world situations.

This volume suggests some ways researchers could assess the importance of resolve. Although measurement of resolve is difficult (Maoz, 1983, is one of the few to attempt it systematically), a possible indicator is suggested by David Yoffie's finding (Chapter 11) that threats of trade sanctions are more effective when there is a domestic consensus supporting the sanctions. Measures of domestic public opinion may be indicators of the costs of not defending commitments, at least in democratically responsive states, and may therefore be a useful proxy for resolve.

The preceding discussion of legitimacy suggests other ways to quantify resolve. We hypothesized that states would be more resolute in pressing challenges when they saw their aims as legitimate, and that defenders would be less likely to make concessions when they had the same view of their own aims. These hypotheses can be explored for particular cases through the historical record, in quantitative studies that measure resolve in terms of national leaders' statements about legitimacy, or in models that incorporate adversaries' subjective probabilities for each others' responses.

## Domestic Factors and International Deterrence

The work of Lebow (1981; Chapter 2) and others has pointed to domestic forces as influential in states' choices to challenge other states' interests. The general claim that foreign policies largely reflect domestic pressures and dynamics is a long-standing one in the study of international politics (e.g., Rosecrance, 1963). Indeed, some of the most important treatments of the origins of World War I take this position (Fischer, 1967, 1974), and similar arguments have been applied to the Soviet Union (Pipes, 1984). The arguments, supported by historical cases, emphasize national leaders' focusing of their attention on domestic problems to which foreign policy actions may offer solutions, rather than outward toward the external environment, as emphasized in classical deterrence theory. Some historical evidence suggests that changes in domestic conditions can induce national leaders who would otherwise refrain from challenging another state's interests to initiate a challenge—even, on occasion, one from which their own state stands to lose internationally. The key question for scholars and decision makers alike is: What conditions, if any, can bring about such actions?

The most common answer in the literature is that a threat to domestic support for a government can push its leaders into ill-considered foreign adventures (for a review of evidence on the "scapegoat hypothesis," see Levy, 1989). The contributions to this volume suggest two other conditions that might have the same effect. The concept of legitimacy suggests the hypothesis that national leaders can become constrained to act in the international arena by notions of justice and injustice widely held in their countries, even notions they themselves have promoted for political purposes (Russett, 1989, reviews evidence on the effectiveness of foreign policy actions for increasing domestic support for regimes). As noted earlier, this process has been implicated in two wars in the Middle East and in the Falklands/Malvinas War of 1982.

Knowledge about the dynamics of interpersonal and intergroup conflict suggests other factors that might create domestic pressure to challenge an international status quo (Kelley and Schmidt, Chapter 12; Pruitt, Chapter 13). Deteriorated relationships and interactions that threaten self-esteem predispose actors to behave emotionally, in ways that may not coincide with their best interests. Two analogous propositions might be tested as hypotheses about international relationships: that when international relations are deteriorating or when international conditions raise doubts about a nation's "self-image," national leaders experience increasing domestic pressure in the form of public opinion in favor of aggressive responses, even poorly considered ones.

The above hypotheses suggest conditions under which domestic pressures are conducive to failures to "rationality" in decision making and to consequent deterrence failures. The scapegoat hypothesis can be examined in quantitative studies that track the initiation of and response to international challenges as a function of support for the government in power and indicators of domestic economic or political difficulties (Levy, 1989, has reviewed the limited literature); the other hypotheses tie international challenges to domestic public opinion about international relations and the changing rhetoric of political debate. More specifically, these new hypotheses imply that when there is increasing support in public opinion and mass media for the idea that a state's international claims are its legitimate right and when an international conflict is increasingly discussed in the emotional language of self-esteem, there is an increased likelihood of failures of "rationality" in the foreign policy decision process and failures of deterrence. If such relationships can be confirmed, they would have implications Lebow has outlined elsewhere (Lebow, 1981). They would imply that governments are most likely to initiate challenges and to respond aggressively to external challenges when there is strong domestic support for their international positions couched in language of justice or national self-esteem. They would further imply that it is riskier to deter governments or to challenge their interests at those times.

## Combining Empirical and Theoretical Approaches

As several contributors persuasively argue, theoretical analysis of deterrence is by itself often misleading or indeterminate in the absence of inputs from experience. In Chapter 8, Robert Wilson shows how game-theoretical analyses of oligopolistic competition can yield almost any result depending on assumptions about behavior and decision processes in firms, and suggests that the correct assumptions must be found empirically. In a similar vein, Barry O'Neill, in Chapter 7, argues that some deterrence games have no equilibria without knowledge about how players infer opponents' goals from their behavior. And John Conybeare, in Chapter 9, notes that although the economic theory of trade wars predicts that they will not occur, some still do; he and David Yoffie (Chapter 10) use historical evidence to suggest hypotheses about the conditions under which deterrence will fail and trade wars will break out.

The import of these arguments is that theorists of deterrence need to build on empirically supported propositions about how actors choose: about the nature of bounded rationality, the nature of private information, the genesis of one player's expectations about the other's behavior (the other's "reputation"), and other behavioral and information-processing variables. Purely theoretical analyses have limited value because their behavioral assumptions, particularly the assumption of rational action, are only conditionally true; inductive researchers can provide critical data to support or reshape such assumptions or to specify conditions under which they do or do not apply. Martin Shubik, in discussion during the meeting, offered a clear statement of the respective roles of game theory and empirical studies of deterrence processes: "Game theory factors reality . . . mathematical approaches deliberately take the social psychology out of the situation to see what is left." While it is important and instructive to do this, for policy purposes both the rational analysis and the "social psychology" are needed. Empirical studies are necessary to understand what decision makers are doing when they deviate from existing models of rational behavior.

As we and the contributors have noted, game theorists and other modelers are beginning to build models based on empirically supported principles of decision making. Empirical social science can sometimes assist the modeling enterprise by finding measures for such variables so they may be specified in a particular model, making the models more useful as representations of reality and as clarifications of concepts developed in ordinary language. It can also be helpful by continuing to identify potentially important variables whose implications can be explored by formal analysts as well as by empirical scientists.

## Summary

The contributions to this volume demonstrate that even though there is no direct experience bearing on the question of when nuclear deterrents are likely to fail, the question can be illuminated by a range of empirical knowledge. We have discovered parallel findings in several different fields that have certain formal similarities to nuclear deterrence. These findings provide some empirical basis for confidence that particular factors are worthy of special attention by researchers and decision makers in the context of superpower conflict. Moreover, concepts from single fields can sometimes provide useful perspectives.

For researchers, the disparate perspectives represented here suggest some specific ways to expand on and enrich the standard rational-actor paradigm of classical deterrence theory. These contributions point to ways to investigate systematically the roles of attributions of legitimacy, cognitive limitations and biases, domestic political motives, perceived and actual commonality of interests, changing balances of power, predictable and conciliatory strategies, and a defender's reputation and resolve in the creation of deterrent threats and in states' responses to them. In several instances, the research direction involves increased collaboration between formal theorists and inductively oriented scholars.

For policy analysts and political leaders, this volume suggests a number of factors to consider, along with those emphasized by classical deterrence theory, in evaluating policy alternatives. We briefly restate three points in the form of signposts for decision makers:

1. Consider the situation from the adversary's point of view. In particular, take into account the legitimacy of claims from the adversary's per-

spective, the adversary's domestic political problems that might provide a temptation to challenge another state's interests, and the adversary's likely concern that any resolution of a conflict be honorable.

2. Be especially cautious about potentially provocative actions when bilateral relations have deteriorated, when your nation or the adversary has suffered recent foreign policy setbacks, or when leaders on either side feel strong pressures to act to preserve national "self-esteem." These conditions may predispose leaders to disregard or misinterpret critical information and to escalate conflicts, even when it may not be in their interest to do so.

3. Reconsider the widely held strategic idea that it is advantageous to attempt to weaken possible adversaries economically and in other ways short of war. Although measures to weaken the economies or undermine the political structures of other countries may give one's state an advantage in international competition, they may also motivate the leaders of those other countries to challenge one's interests, even in spite of an unfavorable balance of military forces.

Present knowledge is insufficient to offer specific guidance on when to alter policy in accordance with these warnings. Enough knowledge exists, however, to justify the careful consideration of them by policymakers. We hope that more detailed future investigations of the phenomenon of deterrence will help national leaders to avoid dangerous international conflicts and to find constructive and creative solutions when such conflicts do arise.

## NOTES

We thank William Estes, Alexander George, Jack Goldstone, Jo Husbands, Richard Ned Lebow, Jack Levy, and Herbert Simon for helpful comments on earlier drafts.

1. We thank Alexander George for calling these points to our attention.
2. Defenders' perceptions are multiply determined, of course; a national leader who sees an adversary as implacably expansionist may believe that all concessions, even to legitimate claims, will encourage further challenges.
3. Jack Goldstone makes a related point in Chapter 11. He argues that concessions offered by a government that is perceived as legitimate will often be successful, whereas they will be taken as signs of weakness, as would be expected from classical deterrence theory, if the government is seen as illegitimate.
4. These hypotheses pertain to "irrationality" in decision processes rather than in the policies that result from leaders' decisions. As George Quester notes in Chapter 3, and as others have long remarked (e.g., Schelling, 1960), apparently

irrational policies may have strategic value in international competition. But it is important to distinguish between apparently irrational acts pursued for strategic gain and the unpredictability of responses that can result from suboptimal decision processes.

5. Because of the price of error, it is often prudent to act as if an adversary's intent is less benign that it appears. Nevertheless, decision makers are probably better served by an unbiased assessment of an adversary that leaves a margin for error than by an assessment clouded by unstated preconceptions about the adversary.

6. The authors thank Jack Goldstone for this example.

7. This formulation should not be construed as static. What a national leader is "willing to pay" as judged under normal conditions may or may not match the choices actually made in a crisis. That fact is what tempts states to test each other's resolve.

## REFERENCES

Axelrod, R., 1979. The rational timing of surprise. *World Politics* 31:228–46.
——— 1984. *The Evolution of Cooperation.* New York: Basic Books.
Allison, G. T., 1971. *Essence of Decision.* Boston: Little, Brown.
Breslauer, G. W., 1983. Why detente failed: An interpretation. In A. L. George, *Managing U.S.–Soviet Rivalry: Problems of Crisis Prevention.* Boulder, Colo.: Westview, pp. 319–40.
Chamberlin, J., 1978. The logic of collective action: Some experimental results. *Behavioral Science* 23(6):441–45.
Cohen, R., 1978. Threat perceptions in international crisis. *Political Science Quarterly* 93(1):93–107.
——— 1979. *Threat Perception in International Crisis.* Madison, Wisc.: University of Wisconsin Press.
Deutsch, K. W., 1963. *The Nerves of Government: Models of Political Communication and Control.* Glencoe, Ill.: The Free Press.
——— 1968. *The Analysis of International Relations.* Englewood Cliffs, N.J.: Prentice-Hall.
Edney, J., and Harper, C. S., 1978. The commons dilemma: A review. *Environmental Management* 2:491–507.
English, R. D., and Halperin, J. J., 1987. *The Other Side: How Soviets and Americans Perceive Each Other.* New Brunswick, N.J.: Transaction Books.
Fischer, F., 1967. *Germany's Aims in the First World War.* New York: Norton.
——— 1974. *World Power or Decline.* New York: Norton.
Gaddis, J. L., 1986. The long peace: Elements of stability in the postwar international system. *International Security* 10(4):99–142.

Gasiorowski, M. J., 1986. Economic interdependence and international conflict: Some cross-national evidence. *International Studies Quarterly* 30(1):23–38.

George, A. L., 1980. *Presidential Decision-Making in Foreign Policy: The Effective Use of Information and Advice.* Boulder, Colo.: Westview.

——— 1983. *Managing U.S.–Soviet Rivalry: Problems of Crisis Prevention.* Bounder, Colo.: Westview.

——— 1984. Crisis management: The interaction of political and military considerations. *Survival* 26(5):223–34, September-October.

——— 1986. The impact of crisis-induced stress on decision making. In F. Solomon and R. Q. Marson, eds., *The Medical Implications of Nuclear War.* Washington: National Academy Press, pp. 529–52.

George, A. L., and Smoke, R., 1974. *Deterrence in American Foreign Policy: Theory and Practice.* New York: Columbia University Press.

Haas, E., 1986. Why we still need the UN: The collective management of international conflict, 1945–1984. *Policy Papers in International Affairs,* No. 26. Berkeley, Calif.: Institute of International Studies.

Halperin, M. H., with Clapp, P. and Kanter, A., 1974. *Bureaucratic Politics and Foreign Policy.* Washington, D.C.: Brookings Institution.

Hardin, R., 1982. *Collective Action.* Baltimore: Johns Hopkins University Press.

Heider, F., 1958. *The Psychology of Interpersonal Relations.* New York: Wiley.

Hersh, S. M., 1986. *The Target Is Destroyed: What Really Happened to Flight 007 and What America Knew About It.* New York: Random House.

Holsti, O., 1967. Cognitive dynamics and images of the enemy: Dulles and Russia. In D. Finlay, O. Holsti, and R. Fagen, eds., *Enemies in Politics.* Chicago: Rand-McNally.

——— 1989. Crisis decision making. In P. E. Tetlock, J. L. Husbands, R. Jervis, P. C. Stern, and C. Tilly, eds., *Behavior, Society, and Nuclear War,* Vol. 1. New York: Oxford.

Huth, P., and Russett, B., 1984. What makes deterrence work? Cases from 1900 to 1980. *World Politics* 36(4):496–526.

——— 1988. After deterrence fails: Escalation to war? In M. Wallace, ed., *Accidental Nuclear War: A Growing Risk?* London: Butterworth.

Janis, I. L., 1982. *Groupthink: Psychological Studies of Policy Decisions and Fiascoes.* Boston: Houghton-Mifflin.

——— 1986. Problems of international crisis management in the nuclear age. *Journal of Social Issues.* 42(2):201–20.

Jervis, R., 1976. *Perception and Misperception in International Politics.* Princeton, N.J.: Princeton University Press.

——— 1979. Deterrence theory revisited. *World Politics* 31(2):289–324.

——— 1987. The symbolic nature of nuclear politics. Paper issued by the Department of Political Science, University of Illinois at Urbana-Champaign.

Jervis, R., Lebow, R. N., and Stein, J., 1985. *Psychology and Deterrence.* Baltimore: Johns Hopkins University Press.

Kelley, H. H., and Stahelski, A. J., 1970. The inference of intentions from moves in the prisoner's dilemma game. *Journal of Experimental Social Psychology* 6:401–19.

Keohane, R., 1984. *After Hegemony.* Princeton, N.J.: Princeton University Press.

Lebow, R. N., 1981. *Between Peace and War: The Nature of International Crisis.* Baltimore: Johns Hopkins University Press.

———— 1985. Miscalculation in the South Atlantic: The origins of the Falklands war. In R. Jervis, R. N. Lebow, and J. G. Stein, *Psychology and Deterrence.* Baltimore: Johns Hopkins University Press.

Levy, J., 1987. Declining power and the preventive motivation for war. *World Politics* 40(October):82-107.

———— 1989. The causes of war: A review of theories and evidence. In P. E. Tetlock, J. L. Husbands, R. Jervis, P. C. Stern, and C. Tilly, eds., *Behavior, Society, and Nuclear War,* Vol. 1. New York: Oxford.

Maoz, Z., 1983. Resolve, capabilities, and the outcomes of intrastate disputes 1816–1976. *Journal of Conflict Resolution* 27(2):195–229.

Monson, T. C., and Snyder, M., 1977. Actors, observers, and the attribution process: Toward a reconceptualization. *Journal of Experimental Social Psychology* 13:89–111.

Nisbett, R. E., and Ross, L., 1980. *Human Interference: Strategies and Shortcomings of Social Judgment.* Englewood Cliffs, N.J.: Prentice-Hall.

Nye, J., and Keohane, R., 1977. *Power and Interdependence.* New York: Little, Brown.

Organski, A. F. K., and Kugler, J., 1980. *The War Ledger.* Chicago: University of Chicago Press.

Pipes, R., 1984. *Survival is not enough: Soviet realities and America's future.* New York: Simon and Schuster.

Rosecrance, R., 1963. *Action and Reaction in World Politics.* Boston: Little, Brown.

Ross, L., and Anderson, C. A., 1982. Shortcomings in the attribution process: On the origins and maintenance of erroneous social assessments. In D. Kahneman, P. Slovic, and A. Tversky, eds. *Judgment and Uncertainty: Heuristics and Biases.* New York: Cambridge University Press.

Russett, B., 1989. The democratic governance of nuclear weapons. In P. E. Tetlock, J. L. Husbands, R. Jervis, P. C. Stern, and C. Tilly, eds., *Behavior, Society, and Nuclear War,* Vol. 1. New York: Oxford.

Schelling, T. C., 1960. *The Strategy of Conflict.* Cambridge, Mass.: Harvard University Press.

Scott, J. C., 1976. *The Moral Economy of the Peasant: Rebellion and Subsistence in Southeast Asia.* New Haven, Conn.: Yale University Press.

Snyder, G. H., and Diesing, P., 1977. *Conflict Among Nations: Bargaining, Decision Making, and System Structure in International Crises.* Princeton, N.J.: Princeton University Press.

Snyder, J. L., 1985. Perceptions of the security dilemma in 1914. In R. Jervis,

R. N. Lebow, and J. G. Stein, *Psychology and Deterrence*. Baltimore: Johns Hopkins University Press, pp. 153–79.

Stein, J. G., 1985a. Calculation, miscalculation, and conventional deterrence. I: The view from Cairo. In R. Jervis, R. N. Lebow, and J. G. Stein, *Psychology and Deterrence*. Baltimore: Johns Hopkins University Press, pp. 34–59.

——— 1985b. Detection and defection: Security "regimes" and the management of international conflict. *International Journal* 40(4):599–627.

Wilson, R., 1985. Reputations in games and markets. In G. F. Feiwel, ed., *Game-Theoretic Models of Bargaining*. Cambridge: Cambridge University Press.

# Contributors

**Robert Alexrod** is Arthur Bromage Professor of Political Science and Public Policy at the University of Michigan. His research interests include international politics, mathematical modeling, evolutionary biology, and artificial intelligence. He has authored or edited five books, including *The Evolution of Cooperation* (Basic Books, 1984). He is a member of the National Academy of Sciences and the winner of a MacArthur Prize Fellowship. He received his B.A. from the University of Chicago in mathematics and a Ph.D. in political science from Yale University.

**John A. C. Conybeare** is a professor of political science at the University of Iowa. His teaching and research are in international relations, with emphasis on political economy and public choice issues. His most recent work has been on international trade conflict and has been published as *Trade Wars* (Columbia University Press, 1987). He received his B.A. in economics and political science from the Australian National University and A.M. and Ph.D. degrees in government from Harvard University.

**Michael G. Fry** is a professor of the history of international relations at the University of Southern California and a scholar-in-residence at the Washington Program of the Annenberg Schools of Communication. His current research is on political legitimation and decision making, historical influences on policy formulation, and the foreign policy of the Lloyd George government, 1916–1922. His most recent book is *Dispatches from Damascus, Gilbert MacKereth and British Policy in the Levant, 1933–1939* (1986). He received his B.S. in economics and Ph.D. in international history from the University of London.

**Jack A. Goldstone** is an associate professor of sociology and political science at Northwestern University. His research interests are on the study of revolutions and political crises. His works include *Revolutions: Theoretical, Comparative, and Historical Studies* (Harcourt Brace Jovanovich, 1986) and *Origins of State Crises: Political Breakdown in* *the Early Modern World*, forthcoming from the University of California Press. He received his Ph.D. in sociology from Harvard University.

**Robert Jervis** is a professor of political science and member of the Institute of War and Peace Studies at Columbia University. He is currently working on problems of psychology, decision making, and cooperation. Among his publications are *Perception and Misperception in International Politics* (Princeton University Press, 1976) and *Psychology and Deterrence* (with Richard Ned Lebow and Janice Stein; Johns Hopkins University Press, 1985). He received his Ph.D. in political science from the University of California at Berkeley.

**Harold Kelley** is a professor of psychology at the University of California, Los Angeles. He has previously been on the faculties of the University of Michigan, Yale University, and the University of Minnesota. His research and theoretical interests are in interpersonal relations and in the development of the theory of interdependence. His publications include *Attribution in Social Interaction* (General Learning Press, 1971) and *Interpersonal Relations: A Theory of Interdependence* (with John W. Thibaut; Wiley, 1978). Kelley received his Ph.D. in group psychology from the Massachusetts Institute of Technology.

**Richard Ned Lebow** is a professor of government and director of the Peace Studies Program at Cornell University. Before that, he was a professor of strategy at the National War College and a scholar-in-residence at the Central Intelligence Agency. His publications include *Psychology and Deterrence* (with Robert Jervis and Janice Stein; Johns Hopkins University Press, 1985) and *Between Peace and War: The Nature of International Crisis* (Johns Hopkins University Press, 1981). Together with Janice Gross Stein of the University of Toronto, he is currently finishing a book on superpower crisis prevention and management.

**Jack S. Levy** is an associate professor of political science at the University of Minnesota. His research focuses on the question of the causes of war from several different theoretical and methodological perspectives. He is the author of *War in the Modern Great Power System, 1495–1975* (University Press of Kentucky, 1983) and has contributed articles to numerous scholarly journals. Levy received a B.S. in physics from Harvey Mudd College and M.A. and Ph.D. degrees in political science from the University of Wisconsin, Madison.

**Barry O'Neill** is an associate professor of industrial engineering at Northwestern University. His research interests include applied game theory and the escalation of war. His publications include "A Problem of Rights Arbitration from the Talmud," in *Mathematical Social Sciences* (1982), and "A Nonmetric Test of the Minimax Theory of Two-Person Zero-Sum Games," in *Proceedings of the National Academy of Sciences* (April, 1987). He holds B.A. and Ph.D. degrees in mathematics from the University of Michigan.

**Dean B. Pruitt** is a professor of psychology at State University of New York at Buffalo. He specializes in the psychology of social conflict and does laboratory and field research on negotiation and mediation. He is the author of *Theory and Research on the Causes of*

*War* (Prentice-Hall, 1969) and *Social Conflict: Escalation, Stalemate, and Settlement* (Random House, 1986). He received a Ph.D. from Yale University and did postdoctoral work in psychology at the University of Michigan and in international relations at Northwestern University.

**George H. Quester** is chairman of the Department of Government and Politics at the University of Maryland, where he teaches and does research in the fields of international politics, American foreign policy, and defense policy and arms control. He has taught previously at Harvard, Cornell, U.C.L.A., and the National War College. He has an undergraduate degree from Columbia and completed his Ph.D. in political science at Harvard.

**Roy Radner** is a distinguished member of the technical staff at AT&T/Bell Laboratories and is a research professor at New York University. His research interests include theories of decentralization and incentives, theories of sequential games with uncertainty, economics of long-distance telecommunications, and strategic and economic aspects of national security. His publications include *Economic Theory of Teams* (with J. Marschak; Yale University Press, 1972) and "A Model of Defense-Protected Build-Down" in A. M. Weinberg and J. N. Barkenbus, eds., *Strategic Defenses and Arms Control* (The Washington Institute, 1987). He received his Ph.B., B.S., and M.S. in mathematics and Ph.D. in mathematical statistics from the University of Chicago.

**Greg Schmidt** is completing his doctoral dissertation at the University of California, Los Angeles, in psychology and holds a B.A. from the University of Denver in psychology and German. His research interests center on utilizing concepts from interdependence theory and attribution theory to examine close relationships.

**Paul W. Schroeder** is a professor of history at the University of Illinois at Urbana-Champaign, specializing in European international politics from the eighteenth to the twentieth centuries. He is the author of three books and many articles in this field and is currently writing a general history of the European states system from 1789 to 1848. He holds an M.A. in history from Texas Christian University and a Ph.D. in history from the University of Texas at Austin.

**Paul C. Stern** is study director of the Committee on Contributions of Behavioral and Social Science to the Prevention of Nuclear War and staff officer of the Committee on Risk Perception and Communication at the National Research Council. His current research is on the formation of social attitudes about environmental policy. His publications include *Evaluating Social Science Research* (Oxford, 1979) and *Energy Use: The Human Dimension* (with Elliot Aronson; Freeman, 1984). Stern received a B.A. from Amherst College and M.A. and Ph.D. degrees in psychology from Clark University.

**Robert Wilson** is a professor at the Stanford Business School. His research is on applications of game theory to topics in economics. His current work is on models of bilateral bargaining. He holds an A.B. in mathematics from Harvard College and M.B.A. and D.B.A. degrees from Harvard Business School.

**David B. Yoffie** is an associate professor at the Harvard Business School in the business, government, and competition area. He previously taught in the political science department at Stanford University. His present research focuses on theories of industrial organization and their application to the political economy of international trade. He received his bachelor's degree from Brandeis University and his master's and doctorate degrees from Stanford University, where he specialized in international political economy.

# Index

Adversary's viewpoint, 320–21
Affect. *See* Emotion
Agadir crisis, 70
Aggressive behavior, 287–92. *See also*
    Aggressive male syndrome
  antecedents of, 287–88
  in deteriorated relationships, 289, 292
  functions of, 287–88
  misinterpretation and, 288–89
  in mixed-motive settings, 289–92
  overreaction and, 288–89
  as retaliation, 287–88
  signaling concern and, 291–92
  strategies for mixed-motive settings, 289–92
  symptoms vs. causes of, 31
  weakness and firmness and, 291
Aggressive male syndrome, 251–80
  adult aggressive males, 257–60
  aggressiveness as stable personal disposition, 254
  alcohol and, 265
  arousal and emotion in, 263–65
  assertion training and, 270, 277, 278
  assertiveness vs. aggression, 255
  attribution of intentions and, 256–57, 262, 265–66
  avoiding, 269–71

  avoiding encouraging, 275–79
  behavior of aggressive male, 254–55
  beliefs and, 265–66
  boys, aggressive, 255–57
  criminal homicide, stages in, 259, 260, 262–63
  definition of aggressive male, 254
  dehumanizing labels in, 267
  developmental history of, 271–75
  discipline and, 276–77
  in distressed relationships, 266
  evidence about, 253
  family history of, 271–75
  firm but flexible policy and, 278, 279
  friendly acts, reactions to, 256
  impulsive aggression in, susceptibility to, 261–68
  insults as provocation in, 259, 262–63, 275
  intentions, attribution of. *See* attribution of intentions, *above*
  interaction history of, 271–79
  interpersonal processes in, 267–68
  losing control in, 258, 263
  mothers in, 272–74, 276
  national decision makers and, 270–71
  Novaco's anger control method, 269–70
  playing the dozens in, 258, 263

Aggressive male syndrome (*continued*)
  provocations to aggression, 261–63
  psychological susceptibility to aggression in, 261–68
  punishment and, 255–61, 276–77
    ineffectual disciplinarians, 276–77
    reaction to threat of, 255–61
  victim's pain in, 266–67
Air warfare, 52–53
Alcohol and male aggression, 265
Algeria, 233
Alliances/Allies. *See also* Deterrence, extended
  rebellions and revolutions and shift in loyalty of, 240–41
  since 1945, 91–92
Ambiguous situations as threatening, 308–9
Anger control method, 269–70
Anglo-Dutch relations, 193, 315
  trade wars, 315
  wars of seventeenth century, 193
Anglo-French relations, 68, 69, 71, 73, 78–80, 192
  crises, 68, 69, 71, 73
    of 1803, 68, 71
    of 1840, 69, 73
    of 1845–1846, 73
    of 1876–1898, 69, 78–80
  trade war, 192
Anglo-Russian crisis of 1800–1801, 68
Antisubmarine-warfare, 141
Appeasement, 21, 90, 91
Arms races, 22, 88, 206–7
  restraining, threats and, 22
  trade conflicts and, 206–7
Arms systems, two tier, 92
Arousal and male aggression, 263–65
Assertion training, 270, 277, 278
Assertiveness vs. aggression, 255
Attributions of intentions, in male aggression, 256–57, 262, 265–66
Austro-French crisis of 1798–1799, 68, 74
Austro-Prussian crises, 68, 69, 71–72, 73
  of 1793–1795, 68, 72
  of 1809, 71
  of 1866, 69, 71–72, 73

Austro-Russian crises, 67, 69, 70, 71, 74, 75, 77–78
  Bosnian crisis of 1908–1909, 67, 70, 71, 74, 77–78
  of 1877–1878, 69, 75
  of 1884–1886, 69, 75
  of 1908–1909, 70, 71, 77–78

Balance of power
  in bipolar, nuclear world, 95
  changing, 313–14
Bargaining/bargaining behavior. *See also* Failed bargain crisis
  behavior, 115, 116
  in international trade conflicts, 197–99
  in oligopolistic competition, 181
Bay of Pigs, 110
Behavioral assumptions, 294
Berlin Blockade, 110
Berlin Crisis, 110, 137
Berlin Crisis, Second, 290–91
Bermuda II agreement, 197
Bias, 40, 256–57
  in attribution of intentions, 256–57
  motivated, 40
Bilateral agreements, failed bargain crises and, 73–74
Bipolar world. *See* Superpowers
Bismarck, 71, 74
Blackmail, 177–78
Blockade, 53, 54, 110
Bolstering, 39–40
Bosnian crisis, 67, 70, 71, 74, 77–78
Brinkmanship, 32, 67

Capability, 7, 19, 100–2, 113, 117–20
  objective vs. perception of, 101–2
  perception of relative, 102
  quantitative studies of role of, 100–1, 120
  selection bias problem, 117–20
  superiority of strength, 43, 240, 295
  threats and, 19
Capability model, resolve model vs., 102, 103
Capability-threat model, 102–3

# Index

Catholic Bishops of U.S., 85
Causal relationships, counterfactual hypotheses and, 110
Chain Store Paradox, 141
Chicken game, 21, 55, 56, 137, 141, 163, 207
Chicken War, U.S.–EEC, 193, 202, 203, 206
China, 40, 227, 234, 235, 300
   Imperial, 234
   –India conflict, 40
   Manchu, 235
Civil War (U.S.), 31
Classical deterrence theory, 5–8
   assumptions of, 10
   critics of, 5–8, 26, 296, 305
   historical evidence and, 6–8, 10
   opportunity and, 28
   propositions of, 5–6
   threats in, 18
Coase conjecture, 178
Cobden–Chevalier Treaty of 1860, 192
Cognitive factors. *See also* Psychological critique of deterrence
   conjectures about others' responses, 203–4
   in trade wars, 203–6
Colonial powers after WWII, 303
Commitment, 7, 19, 176–77
   cooperation and, 176–77
   threats and, 19
Commitment theory, 18
Communication, 7–8, 41, 178–80
   in games with private information, 178–80
   threats and, 19
Compellence, 103–4, 105, 110, 212
   deterrence vs., 110, 212
   success of, definition of, 105
Compellent power, definition of, 144
Competition, oligopolistic. *See* Oligopolistic competition, deterrence in; Superpowers
Concessions, 21, 242
   in rebellions and revolutions, 242
   threats and, 21
Conciliatory strategies, 315–16
Conflict of interest, 144, 311–12

Conflict situation, threats and, 21
Conflict-spiral theorists, 7
Consistency, 315–16
Contestability of markets, 177–78
Controlled pressure or strategic response, threats and, 20
Conventional deterrence, 60–62
Conventional weapons, 92
Cooperation, 170, 185–86, 310–11
   conflicts to enforce, 310–11
   deviations from, policing, 170
   Prisoners' Dilemma and, 185–86. *See also* Prisoners' Dilemma
Cooperators and competitors, beliefs of, 268
Correlates of War studies, 102–5
Costs, 6, 19–20, 41
   of challenge to status quo, 6
   of status quo, 19–20
   threats and, 19–20
Counterfactual hypotheses, 110
Counterforce attack, 53
Countervalue attack, 53
Credibility, 109, 146, 158, 216–17
   definition of, 158
   game theory of, 146
   of threat, 109
   in trade deterrence, 216–17
Crimean War, 69, 73, 76–77
Criminal homicide, stages in, 259, 260, 262–63
Crises. *See also* Trade conflicts; specific countries
   instability in, Stag Hunt game and, 143–44
   international. *See* International crises
Crisis-bargaining behavior, 117
Cuba, 227, 237. *See also* Cuban Missile Crisis
Cuban Missile Crisis, 10, 41–46, 137, 280, 300, 307

Deadlock game, 193, 201, 202
Decision making in trade deterrence, centralized vs. decentralized, 218–19
Decoupling deterrence threats, 22, 217–18

Deep pocket hypothesis, 182–83
Defensive avoidance, 39–40
Dehumanizing labels, 267, 306
  male aggression and, 267
Demonstration effect, 158, 183
Detente, 95, 301–2
Deteriorated relationships, 266, 289, 292, 306, 318, 321
  domestic pressure in, 318
  male aggression in, 266
  misinterpretation and overreaction in, 289, 292, 306
Deterrence
  abstract deductive models of, 295
  as American idea, 52–54
  assessment of, 61–62
  backfire of, 35–37
  behavioral assumptions in, 5–10, 294
  combining empirical and theoretical approaches to, 319–20
  compellence vs., 110, 212
  as context-dependent, 9
  definition of, 100, 157–58
  empirical analysis of, 26
  evidence about, 8–12
  extended, 63, 108–9, 111, 112–17
    failure of: escalation to war, 114–17
    ties between protégé–pawn, 108–9, 111, 113, 114, 116, 117
  general vs. immediate, 99–100
  generalizations from history, 295–96
  military strength/superiority in, 43, 240, 295
  nuclear arsenals and, 3
  political critique. *See* Political critique of deterrence
  problems in applying, 41–46
  propositions about, 5–10, 19–22
  psychological critique of. *See* Psychological critique of deterrence
  in rebellions and revolutions, 22, 239–43. *See also* Rebellions and revolutions
  status of knowledge about, 295–97
Deterrence by denial, 53, 63, 117
Deterrence by punishment, 53, 54, 117
Deterrence failure, 52–63
  definition of, 115–16
  deterrence as American idea, 52–54

  of extended deterrence, 114–17
  historical evidence on, 29–30
  nuclear vs. conventional, 60–62
  predicted by deterrence theory, 63
  in oligopolistic competition, 163
  operationally defined, 112
  rationality in, 55–58
  in rebellions and revolutions, 224, 229–30
  social science of, 58–60
  universe of relevant cases, 41
  war as, 54, 60
Deterrence instability, 145–46
Deterrence matrix, 28
Deterrence strategy, 25–26
  deterrence theory vs., 25
Deterrence success, 61–62
  causal inference to, 120
  definition of, 105, 108, 109–10, 112, 115–16
  minimum conditions for, 100
  in rebellions and revolutions, 222, 226–29
  test of, 61–62
Deterrence theory
  behavioral assumptions, 5–10
  criticisms, 46–48
  deterrence failure predicted by, 63
  deterrence strategy vs., 25
  as influence theory, 9
  international system and, 76
  new variables, 48
  opportunity in, 26–27
  propositions of, 5–10
  rationality in, 6–8, 25
  universe of relevant cases, 41
  utility in, 31
  weighing variables in, 48
Deterrent posture, 287–88
Deterrent power, definition of, 144
Deterrent threats. *See* Threats, deterrent
Diplomatic alternative, threats and, 21
Diplomatic historians, 86
Diplomatic strategies, 115, 116
Distressed relationships. *See* Deteriorated relationships
Doctrine of flexible response, 6
Dollar auction game, 142–43
Domestic factors, 317–19

# Index

Domestic problems, 21–22, 47, 216–17, 321
  solving, 21–22
  trade deterrence and, 216–17

Economic theory of deterrence. *See* Oligopolistic competition, deterrence in
Eden Treaty of 1786, 192
Egypt–Israel relations, 32–34, 35, 37, 300, 302
Emotion, 263–65, 308. *See also* Frustration-aggression mechanism; Self-esteem
  deterrence and, 308
  male aggression and, 263–65
Empirical evidence on deterrence, 17–22, 26
  on deterrent threats, 17–22
  historical evidence. *See* Historical evidence
  quantitative evidence. *See* Quantitative studies of deterrence
England. *See also* entries beginning Anglo-
  Argentina and, 301, 302, 304, 318
  English Revolution, 222–23, 224, 233
  Falklands/Malvinas War, 301, 302, 304, 318
  Hanseatic League, trade conflicts with, 193, 202, 203
  at Munich in 1938, 303
English Revolution, 222–23, 224, 233
Entrants to markets, 160, 161–62
Evidence. *See also* Empirical evidence; Historical evidence; Quantitative studies of deterrence
  evaluating indirect, 10–12
  sources of, 8–12
Expectational equilibria, of dynamic expansion games, 175
Expectations, 175–76, 227–28
  expected outcomes, misjudgment of, 305
  of retaliation, cooperative outcomes sustained by, 175–76
  of state's behavior, 227–28
Expected utility model, 109
  extended, immediate deterrence cases in, 112–14

Japan in WWII and, 111–12
  power politics model vs., 104–5
  utility of peace of attacker, 113
Extended deterrence, 63, 108–9, 111, 112–17
  failure of: escalation to war, 114–17
  ties between protégé–pawn, 108–9, 111, 113, 114, 116, 117

Face-work, threats and, 22
Failed bargain crises, 66–80
  1789–1914, 68–70
  bilateral or trilateral agreements and, 73–74
  definition of, 67
  international system and, 74–80
  kinds of, 71–72
  powers not party to, 74–75
  reaction of other powers in, 74–75
  reasons for failure, 70
  threats and, 72–73
  usefulness of concept, 70–72
Failure of deterrence. *See* Deterrence failures
Fait accompli, threats and, 20
Falklands/Malvinas War, 301, 302, 304, 318
Families of aggressive males, 272–74
Fashoda Crisis in 1898, 69, 78–80, 301
Finnish resistance in 1940, 31
Firm-but-conciliatory strategy, 278, 290–92
Firm-but-fair strategies, 315
Firm-but-flexible policy, 278, 279
Flexible response, 6, 241
  doctrine of, 6
  in rebellions and revolutions, as strategy in, 241
Folk theorem, 175, 185
Force
  deployment of, in rebellions and revolutions, 226
  military strength/superiority, 43, 240, 295. *See also* Capability
Foreign policies, 317–19
France. *See also* entries beginning Franco-
  Algeria and, 233

*Index*

France (*continued*)
  French Revolution, 222, 224, 230, 233
  Old Regime, 227, 234
Franco-German crisis of 1911, 70
Franco-Italian tariff war of 1886–1898, 193, 201, 204
Franco-Prussian war of 1806, 68
Franco-Russian crisis of 1810, 68–69
Franco-Swiss tariff wars of 1892–1895, 193, 204
French Revolution, 222, 224, 230, 233
Frustration–aggression mechanism, 287–89, 292

Game theory, 134–51, 315–16
  bounded rationality in, 150–51
  Called Bluff or Bully, 198
  Chain Store Paradox, 141
  Chicken game, 55, 56, 137, 141, 163, 207
  compellent power in, 144
  conflict of interest and, 144
  credibility in, 146
  crisis instability and Stag Hunt game, 143–44
  Deadlock game, 193, 201, 202
  definition of, 134–35
  definition of basic terms by, 146
  deterrent power in, 144
  Dollar Auction game, 142–43
  equilibrium-selection criterion, 167, 169, 170
  of escalatory war, 142
  folk theorem, 175, 185
  games in extensive form, 151
  George Smiley game, 179–80
  high-game theory, 135
  illustrative models, 173–86
  of incomplete information, 150
  information in, 150, 174–86
  irrational behavior in, 172
  low-game theory, 135
  multiple equilibria, 167–68
  non-zero-sum games, 141
  of oligopolistic competition, 165–69
  optimal strategies, 145, 167
  Prisoners' Dilemma, 141, 143, 167, 170, 171, 176, 185–86, 192, 201, 205, 207, 208, 278, 315, 316
  proto-game theory, 135, 140, 141
  purposes of models, 136–49
    baseline prediction, 142–43
    to collect situations with same structure, 136–38
    dynamics of strategic interactions, 145–49
    facts and fallacies, 141–42
    measures for variables, 143–45
    organize analysis of single situation, 138–41
  rationality defined in, 142–43, 166
  reputation, 316
  resolve, 147–49
  self-damage in, 147–48
  stability–instability in, 145–46
  Stag Hunt game, 141, 143
  strategic balance in, 145
  subgame-perfect equilibrium, 167
  subgame strategy, 168
  tit-for-tat strategy, 185–86, 278, 289–90, 292, 315
  trends/history of, 149–51
  two-by-two games, 136–37
  for U.S.–Soviet Union nuclear war, 138–40
GATT. *See* General Agreement on Tariffs and Trade
General Agreement on Tariffs and Trade (GATT), 192–93, 206, 207, 212, 213, 217, 218, 299
George Smiley game, 179–80
Germany, 87, 200, 303, 307
Glorious Revolution of 1688, 228
Grenada, U.S. invasion of, 289
Guerilla warfare, 226, 232
Gulf of Sidra, 308

High Seas Fleet, German, 87
High-game theory, 135
Historical evidence
  on bipolar world, 91–96
    nuclear world and, 95
  classical deterrence theory and, 6–8

## Index

on communication and perceptiveness, 7–8
on declining powers, 314
on deterrence failures, 29–30
diplomatic historians, 86
on failed bargain crises, 66–80. *See also* Failed bargain crises
generalizations from, 295–96
indirect, evaluating, 10–12
theoretical considerations, 85–87
on trade wars, 192–94
universe of relevant deterrence cases, 41
on World War I, 87–88
on World War II, 88–91
Hitler, 303
Homicide, stages in criminal, 259, 260, 262–63
Honor, 304
Humiliation, 292
Huth studies, 107, 112–17, 118, 119, 120

Inattention, threats and, 20
India, 28, 40, 55
 –China conflict with, 40
 –Pakistan War, 28, 55
Industrial base, 102
Influence theory, deterrence theory as subset of, 9
Information
 asymmetries in, 164
 complete, games with, 174–77
 incomplete, games with, 150
 limits on processing of, 305
 in oligopolistic competition, 164, 166–67, 171–73
 private, 178–86
 uncertainty, 145–46
Initiation theory, 18, 103, 104, 105
Initiator, interests and resolve of, 121
Insult and male aggression, 259, 262–63, 275
Intentions, attributions of, 256–57, 262, 265–66, 288–89, 305–7
 aggressive male attributions of, 256–57, 262, 265–66
 misinterpretation of, 288–89
 misperception of, 304–9

Interest
 conflict of, 144, 311–12
 fundamental, 311–12
 game theory and, 144
 of initiator, 121
 threats and, 19
International bargaining. *See* Bargaining
International conflicts, 310–13
 transformation of, 312–13
 types of, 310–13
International crises. *See also* Failed bargain crises; specific countries
 categories of, 67
 historical evidence on, 6–8
 superpower crises, 10. *See also* Cuban Missile Crisis
International system, 74–80, 93–94
 definition of, 75–76
 deterrence theory and, 76
 failed bargain crises and, 74–80
 since 1945, 93–94
International trade conflicts. *See* Trade conflicts
Iran, 23, 29, 227, 230, 237
 –Iraq War, 28, 29
 Revolution, 227, 230
Irish Easter Rising, 31
Israel, 28, 32–34, 35, 37, 300, 302, 307
 –Egypt relations, 32–34, 35, 37, 300, 302
 –Lebanon occupation and war, 28
 Libyan airliner and, 307
Issue linkage, trade deterrence, 217–18

Japan
 Tokugawa, 234
 in WWII, 34–35, 37–38, 53–54, 111–12, 113, 313, 314
Jewish revolts against Romans, 31
July crisis of 1914, 307

Karsten, Howell, and Allen study, 105–7, 119
Korean airliner, 89, 306
Korean War, 40

Lebanon–Israel war, 28
Legitimacy, 230–36, 242, 298–304, 317
  definition of, 298–301
  differing ideas of, 301–2
  hypotheses about, 303–4
  to maintain, 234
  in rebellions and revolutions, 230–36, 242
  resolve and, 317
Libyan airliner, 307
Limit pricing, 180–81
Limited probe, threats and, 20–21
Limited security, 300
Losing control, 258, 263
Low-game theory, 135

MAD (mutually assured deterrence), 88
Market competition, deterrence in. *See* Oligopolistic competition, deterrence in
Maximum tactics, 205
Mexico, 227, 233
Middle East wars, 137, 318. *See also* Iran; Israel
Militarized Interstate Dispute (MID) project, 102
Military capabilities. *See* Capability
Misjudgment, 37–38, 47, 305, 309, 321
  attribution of intention. *See* Attributions of intentions
  hypotheses on, 309
Misperception. *See* Misjudgment
Most Favored Nation (MFN) norms, 201
Mothers of aggressive males, 272–74, 276
Motivated bias, 40
Motivation, 27–29, 46, 105, 160, 228–29, 289–92
  of aggressor, 105
  of challenger, 27–29
  of firms, 160
  mixed-motive settings, 289–92
  opportunity vs. vulnerability in, 41, 46
  in rebellions and revolutions, 228–29
Munich (1938), 303
Mutually assured deterrence (MAD), 88

NATO, 62, 63, 241
  deterrence, test of, success of, 62

Naval operations, 53, 54, 141
Need, 7, 20, 27. *See also* Conflict of interest
  perceived, 7, 20
  theory of, 27
Nicaragua, 227, 227, 230, 233, 237
Nicholas I, 74
Nonnuclear deterrence, 11–12, 13
Non-zero-sum games, 14
Normative theory, 85
Norms, 298–301, 303, 305
  behavior violating, 305
  of self-determination, 303
  shared, 298–301
North's 1914 Project, 101–2
Novaco's anger control method, 269–70
Nuclear deterrence, 3–22
  conventional vs., 60–62
  evidence on, 6–12
    historical, 6–8
    sources of, 8–12
  nonnuclear deterrence and, 11–12, 13
  threat and response dynamic and, 3
  trade war deterrence and, 206–8, 211–12
Nuclear weapons, 92–93, 147

Oligopolistic competition, 157–86
  bargaining in, 181
  Coase conjecture, 178
  communication and signaling in, 178–80
  conclusions about, 169–72
  contestability of markets in, 177–78
  cooperation in, 175–77, 185–86
    and commitment, 176–77
    and expectation of retaliation, 175–76
    and Prisoners' Dilemma, 185–86
  correlated strategies in, 173
  deep pocket hypothesis in, 182–83
  demonstration effect in, 158, 183
  deterrence failure in, 163
  disequilibrium wars in, 164
  dynamic expansion games in, 175
  entrants in, 160, 161–62
    costs to enter, 161–62
    definition of, 160

# Index

equilibrium wars in, 164
equilibrium-selection criterion in, 167, 169, 170
game theory analysis of, 165–69
  games with complete information, 174–78
  games with private information, 178–86
  illustrative models, 173–86
information in, 164, 166–67, 171–86
  games with complete, 174–78
  games with private, 178–86
limit pricing in, 180–81
literature on, 160–61
means of deterrence in, 162
motivation of firms in, 160
policing deviations from cooperative behavior in, 170
predation in, 182–85
price wars in, 182–85
signaling in, 162–63
strategic substitutes and complements in, 174–75
theoretical models for, 161
war in, 163–65
wars of attrition in, 181–82
Opportunity, 6–7, 26–27, 28, 41, 46
  aggression as driven by, 28
  vulnerability vs., 41, 46
Optimal outcomes, in rebellions and revolutions, 225
Optimal strategies, 167
Optimal tariffs, 192–95
Optimal threat, 145
Overreaction, 288–89

Pakistan–India War, 28, 55
Peace, expected utility of, to attacker, 113
Peace of Campo Formio, 74
Peace-through-strength hypothesis, 100–1
Pearl Harbor. *See* Japan in WWII
Perceived necessity/need, 7, 20
Perceptiveness, 7–8. *See also* Misjudgment
Perceptual security dilemma, 307
Period of danger theory, 87
Philippines, 227, 233, 313
Playing the dozens, 258, 263
Policymakers, 32, 39–40, 320–21

defensive avoidance pattern of, 39–40
inner-directed, 32
signposts for, 320–21
Polish-Saxon crisis of 1814–1815, 69
Political critique of deterrence, 25–48
  deterrence theory vs. deterrence strategy, 25
  historical evidence and, 29–31
  political failings, 31–35
Political factors, domestic, 21–22, 216–17
  political goals, trade wars and, 202–3
  solving domestic problems, 21–22
  trade deterrence, 216–17
Portugal and Goa, 55
Potlatch, 317
Power politics model, 100–1, 104–5
  expected utility model vs. 104–5
Predation, 182–85
Predictability, 315–16
Price wars, 182–85
Prisoners' Dilemma, 21, 141, 143, 167, 170, 171, 176, 185–86, 192, 201, 205, 207, 208, 278, 315, 316
  finitely repeated, 185–86
  infinitely repeated, 186
  threats and, 21
Proto-game theory, 135, 140, 141
Psychological critique of deterrence, 25–48
  backfire of deterrence in, 35–37
  bolstering in, 39–40
  challenger's insensitivity to warnings in, 39–40
  deterrence theory vs. deterrence strategy, 25–26
  flawed assessments in, 37–38
  historical evidence and, 29–31
  inner-directed policymakers in, 32
  motivated bias in, 40
  motivation in. *See* Motivation
  primacy of self in, 46
  spread the alternatives in, 39
  wishful thinking in, 20, 27, 37
Punishment. *See also* Retaliation
  aggressive males and, 255–61, 276–77
Puritan Revolution of 1640, 228

Quantitative studies of deterrence, 99–122
  capabilities, 100–1, 117–20

Quantitative studies of deterrence (*continued*)
  role of, 100–1
  selection bias problem, 117–20
  conflicting results, 116
  Correlates of War studies, 102–5
  extended deterrence, 107–17
  general vs. immediate deterrence, 99–100
  Huth studies, 107, 112–17, 118, 119, 120
  Karsten, Howell, and Allen study, 105–7, 119
  North 1914 studies, 101–2
  Russett studies, 107–17, 118, 119, 120
Quemoy, blockade of, 110

Rationality/Rational choice
  antirational perspective, 60
  applicability of models of, 59–60
  bounded rationality, 59, 150–51
  broader formulation of, 26
  failure in, 318–19
  game theory definition of, 142–43, 150–51, 166
  of irrationality, 308
  limits to, 8
  overstating, 57–58
  in rebellions and revolutions, 224–25, 236–39
  in social science, 59–60
  understating, 55–57
Reassurance, threats and, 21–22
Rebellions and revolutions, 222–43
  allies, shift of loyalty of, 240–41
  ambiguity of nonnegotiable principles in, 241
  antiguerrilla campaigns in, 226
  apocalyptic mission, groups with, 235
  assumptions of theory of, 225
  concessions in, 230–36, 242
  deteriorating position in, groups in, 239
  deterrence and, 239–43
    deterrence failure, 224, 229–30
    deterrence success, 222, 223, 226–29
  diffuse benefits in, 231
  diffuse disamenity in, 231
  English Revolution, 222–23, 224
  expectations of state's behavior in, 227–28
  flexible response strategy in, 241
  force in, deployment of, 226, 240, 243
  French Revolution, 222, 224
  groups of individuals acting in, 224
  legitimacy and, 230–36, 242, 302
  legitimate protest vs., 235–36
  motivation in, 228–29
  as normal political expression, 235–36
  optimal outcomes in, 225
  rational choice in, 224–25
  rationality and uncertainty in, 236–39
  relative deprivation in, 228–29
  repression of, successful, 229–30
  South Africa, 223, 226, 227, 228
  spiral of violence and regime collapse in, 241
  status quo and, 240, 241–42
  terminology, 222–23
  theories of, 223–25
  window-dressing reforms, 235
Reciprocity, stabilizing effects of, 121
Reputation, 19, 116, 121, 185, 288, 316
  of defender, 116, 121, 288
  threats and, 19
Resolve, 147–49, 316–17
  definition of, 316
  demonstrating, game theory approach to, 147–49
Resolve model, capability model vs., 102, 103
Response theory, 18
Retaliation, 175–76, 255–61, 276–77, 287–88
  aggressive behavior as, 287–88
  aggressive male reaction to threat of, 255–61, 276–77
  expectation of, cooperative outcomes sustained by, 175–76
Revolutions. *See* Rebellions and revolutions
Rhodesia, 234
Risk aversion, 20, 204–5
Risk theory, 87
Roman Empire, Jewish revolts in, 31
Russett studies, 107–17, 118, 119, 120
Russia. *See also* Soviet Union

# Index

341

Germany tariff war of 1893–1894 with, 200
−Japan War of 1904, 70
Russian Revolution, 230
Tsarist, 234
−Turkey relations, 300
  crisis of 1821–1823, 69, 75, 76
  war of 1807, 68
  war of 1828, 69
Russian Revolution, 230

Scapegoat hypothesis, 318
Second Moroccan crisis, 70
Security dilemma, 7, 35–36, 85
Selection bias problem, capabilities and, 117–20
Self-damage, 147–48
Self-determination, norm of, 303
Self-esteem, offenses to, 260, 262–63, 275, 289, 292, 318, 321
Signaling, 162–63, 178–80, 291–92
  of concern, 291–92
  in oligopolistic competition, 162–63
Singer's Correlates of War project, 102–5
Smoot–Hawley tariff, 194, 205
Snyder's stability–instability paradox, 146
Social science disciplines, and deterrence, 58–60, 90.
  historically sensitive, 90
South Africa, 223, 226, 227, 228, 234, 235
South Korea, 63, 304
Soviet Union
  China and, 300
  Stalin, 61, 62
  −U.S. relations
    bipolar world of, 91–96
    competition in, 11
    Cuban Missile Crisis, 10, 41–45, 137, 280, 300, 307
    detente, 95, 301–302
    deterrence and, 9–12
    game theory for war between, 138–40
    nuclear weapons as new parameter, 92–93
Spanish-American War of 1898, 304
Spanish Marriages in 1845–1846, 73

Stability–instability paradox, 146
Stag Hunt game, 141, 143
Stalin, 61, 62
State, theory of nature of, 85
Statesmanship, strategy vs., 92
Status quo, 6, 19–20, 240–42
  costs of, 19–20
  costs of challenge to, 6
  in rebellions and revolutions, 240, 241–42
Strategic balance, game theory and, 145
Strategic complements, 174–75
Strategic industry policy, 195–99
Strategic substitutes and complements, 174–75
Strategic trade policy literature, 212
Strategy
  optimal, 167
  statesmanship vs., 92
  tit-for-tat, 185–86, 278, 289–90, 292, 315
Suez Canal crisis, 37
Superpowers, 9–12, 91–96
  bipolar world of, 91–96
  crisis, 10
  Cuban Missile Crisis, 10, 41–46, 137, 280, 300, 307
  detente in, 95, 301–2
  dimensions of competition between, 11
  nuclear weapons as new parameter, 92–93
Survival, struggles for, 311–12
Systems theory, 85

Tariffs, 192–95, 206, 207, 212, 213, 217, 218
  General Aggreement on Tariffs and Trade, 192–93, 206, 207, 212, 213, 217, 218
  optimal, 192–95
Thirty Years' War, 193
Threats, deterrent, 17–22, 72–73, 105–7, 109, 145, 199–206
  conflict situation and, 21
  credibility of, 109
  definition of, 105
  empirical propositions about, 17–22

Threats, deterrent (*continued*)
  failed bargain crises and, 72–73
  optimal, 145
  reassurance and, 21–22
  side receiving, 19–21
  side using, 19
  threatener's perceptions, 106
  in trade conflicts, 199–206
  utility of, 118
Tit-for-tat strategy, 185–86, 278, 289–90, 292, 315
Trade conflicts, 191–208
  in agriculture trade, 217–18
  arms races and, 206–7
  asymmetries of size in, 193–95
  Called Bluff or Bully in, 198
  centralized vs. decentralized decision making in, 218–19
  Chicken game in, 207
  cognitive factors, 203–6
  compellence vs. deterrence, 212
  conjectures about others' responses in, 203–4
  credibility in, 216–17
  Deadlock game in, 193, 201, 202
  decoupling linked issues in, 217–18
  domestic politics in, 216–17
  domestic regulations as disguised trade barriers in, 205–6
  General Agreement on Tariffs and Trade (GATT), 192–93, 206, 207, 212, 213, 217, 218
  historical cases, 192–94, 211–19
  hypotheses about, 216–18
  international bargaining in, 197–99
  international norms and, 218
  issue linkage in, 217–18
  large countries in, 192–93
  in manufactures trade, 219
  maximin tactics in, 205
  Most Favored Nation (MFN) norms, 201
  normative nature of theory and, 212
  nuclear war and, 206–8, 211–12
  number of actors in, 201–2
  optimal tariffs in, 192–95
  political goals and, 202–3
  power to mediate in, 207
  Prisoners' Dilemma in, 192, 197, 201, 205, 207, 208
  relative equality of power in, 207
  risk aversion in, 204–5
  size as threat variable in, 199–206
  strategic industry policy in, 195–99
  strategic trade policy literature, 212
  textile case of 1969–71, 213–14
  threat variables, 199–208
  time and threat, 200–1
  Tragedy of the Commons and, 201, 202
  transactions costs in, 203–4
  U.S.–EEC, 193, 202, 203, 206
  U.S.–Japan semiconductor agreement, 214–16
Tragedy of the Commons, 201, 202
Transaction costs, 203–4
Treaty of Amiens of 1802, 68, 71
Trilateral agreements, failed bargain crises and, 73–74
Triple Alliance, 203, 205
Two-by-two games, 136–37

Uncertainty, 145–46, 236–39
  in game theory, 145–46
  in rebellions and revolutions, 236–39
United States
  –EEC trade conflicts, 193, 202, 203, 206
  –Japan semiconductor agreement, 214–16
  –Japan textile negotiations of 1969–71, 213–14
  –Libya confrontation, 308
  –Soviet relations
    bipolar world of, 91–96
    Cuban Missile Crisis, 10, 41–45, 137, 280, 300, 307
    detente, 95, 301–2
    deterrence and, 9–12
    dimensions of competition in, 11
    nuclear weapons as new parameter, 92–93
    war, game theory for, 138–40
Utility in deterrence theory, 31

Venice–Genoa trade wars of thirteenth century, 193
Versailles Treaty, 89, 93

# Index

Vietnam/Vietnam War, 141, 302
Vulnerability, opportunity vs., 41, 46

War, 5, 93, 103, 104, 105, 114–17, 163–65, 181–82. *See also* Rebellions and revolutions
   of attrition, 163–64, 181–82
   causes of, 5
   deterrence failure: escalation to, 114–17
   initiators of, 103, 104, 105
   as legitimate instrument of change, 93
   in oligopolistic competition, 163–65

War initiators, 103, 104, 105
War of attrition, 163–64, 181–82
Window-dressing reforms, 235
Wishful thinking, 20, 27, 37, 38
World War I, 36–37, 38, 40, 87–88, 93, 317
   origins of, 38, 87–88, 317
   security dilemma and, 36–37
   wishful thinking in, 38
World War II, 31, 88–91
   Finns in, 31
   Japan in. *See* Japan in WWII
   origins of, 88–91